D0906147

Dear Larry,

Hope you enjoy
the book...

Best Wishes,

Mark Moore

SAVING
THE
GAME

SAVING THE GAME

Pro Hockey's Quest to Raise Its Game
from Crisis to New Heights

MARK MOORE

McCLELLAND & STEWART

Library and Archives Canada Cataloguing in Publication

Moore, Mark, 1977–
Saving the game : an inside look at pro hockey's struggle to
survive / Mark Moore.

ISBN 13: 978-0-7710-6434-0
ISBN 10: 0-7710-6434-9

1. Hockey. 2. National Hockey League. I. Title.

GV 847.M66 2006   796.962'64   C2005-907324-1

We acknowledge the financial support of the Government of Canada through the Book Publishing Industry Development Program and that of the Government of Ontario through the Ontario Media Development Corporation's Ontario Book Initiative. We further acknowledge the support of the Canada Council for the Arts and the Ontario Arts Council for our publishing program.

Typeset in Janson by M&S, Toronto
Printed and bound in Canada

This book is printed on acid-free paper that is 100% recycled, ancient-forest friendly (100% post-consumer recycled).

McClelland & Stewart Ltd.
75 Sherbourne Street
Toronto, Ontario
M5A 2P9
www.mcclelland.com

1   2   3   4   5   10   09   08   07   06

CONTENTS

FOREWORD

The world of hockey in 1972 was one that every fan understood. There was the love of the game, there was skill and sacrifice, there was triumph and disappointment, there was a spirit of competition. Since then, a lot has changed in the sport. Some of those changes have been positive. There have been advances in methods of fitness training, skill development, and injury treatment. The sport has grown in different places, and new countries have emerged as rivals on the stage of international hockey, in forums like the Olympic Games. At the same time, a number of challenges have also emerged, both on and off the ice, that affect everything from how the game is played, to the values transmitted by our sport, to the importance of those values to society, to hockey's prosperity in the days to come.

Our game was in rough shape not long ago. Coming off a season in which fans, commentators, and even players voiced growing discontent with the style of play, while TV audiences continued to decline (I too watched less and less of the professional game, bored by what it had become), the situation only got worse. A labour dispute between players and owners cost us all the entire 2004-5 NHL season. With the tug-of-war between the NHL and NHL Players' Association happening daily, each side telling self-serving stories to the media, the game and its fans were caught in the middle. Now that the lockout is over, the games are on, and all involved are resigned to finally making things better, Mark Moore reminds us that it is time for the game itself to be given first priority.

From the moment I started reading *Saving the Game*, it was evident that this book is different from most hockey books out there. Like any good book, it is quite simply an engaging read. But it also tackles many of the issues of our sport comprehensively and with an uncommon depth of insight. It takes the challenges and changes in our game and addresses them with courage and a constructive approach. Do I *always* agree with him; certainly not, but the perspective of this former player is clearly something rare and special that sets this book apart. Even among player perspectives, the book is unique – it is written not out of the self-interest so often heard today from people in the hockey industry, but from the perspective of the game itself, and for the good of everyone touched by it.

It is a book filled with many great ideas that are clearly the product of long thought and deep consideration; Mark has brought up issues I had never even considered throughout a life in the game. He is concerned with giving the hockey fan a voice in the game, something that has been lacking in the past, yet is essential to protecting the sport and improving its future. He also focuses on the necessity of players, leagues, and fans working collectively to guide the sport into the future, and that's where this book's greatest significance will be. *Saving the Game* unmistakably calls for attention and discussion by people around and within the game. It should spawn debate in arenas, on TV, and in boardrooms – and through debate we can hope to elevate the game.

As an avid reader, I am selective about the books I choose. As someone who has spent a life in hockey and in the public eye, I am even more selective about what I endorse. But this is a project I am glad to stand for: I applaud Mark for a great book, and I highly recommend it to the reader. I have really enjoyed reading *Saving the Game* and I hope you do too.

Paul Henderson
Toronto, Canada
December 2005

INTRODUCTION

I first met Mark Moore in December 1999, while doing a story for the *Globe and Mail* in my role as a member of the *Globe*'s sports department. At the time he was a senior defenceman at Harvard, and the oldest of three brothers all playing on the same team. Steve was a rugged, high-scoring junior forward and Dominic was a highly touted rookie with quick feet and soft hands. The angle for the feature was initially quite simple: three brothers from what seemed an ordinary Ontario family all playing hockey for Harvard. Amazing. But in the course of doing the piece, the background became even more remarkable. Their mother had suffered a near fatal brain tumour when Mark was just twelve, and the recovery was long and difficult. Faced with adversity, Mark responded by only increasing his focus on his two main occupations – school and hockey. His example of hard work, dedication, and perseverance set the tone for his brothers, and their passion for hockey carried over into the rest of their lives, leading to incredible results.

That focus and devotion to hockey was no accident. The game of hockey in our country is indeed best described as a passion: a collective ritual that brings together a wide and diverse land by way of a common pursuit. The game, at its best, is played with passion, one almost unmatched in any other sport.

And courage. Climbing over the boards means competing in a confined place, on a slippery surface, against big bodies moving fast. You go as hard as you can, take a brief rest, and go hard again. It's fast, and unrelenting, and Canadians love it.

But lost in the passion – lost in any passion, quite often – can be the importance of reflection. The game is played and followed with our hearts, and requires a deep commitment. Missing sometimes is perspective, or sober second thought.

For Mark Moore, the passion for hockey took him on a journey from shinny on Ontario ponds as a kid, to the sport's leading high school – Toronto St. Mike's – to the prestigious Crimson of Harvard University. He was drafted by the National Hockey League's Pittsburgh Penguins, signed a contract with them, and embarked on a career in professional hockey. On his journey he saw the game in all its forms – from small-town children's leagues, to junior and college in the big city, to NHL training camps, to stops at different places in the minor leagues. He even had a taste of international hockey at training camp for the Canadian National Team, and in Europe studying under a renowned coach from Russia. There have been both highs and lows. He's had the pleasure of skating with his hero, Mario Lemieux, of reaching the American Hockey League's Calder Cup Final, and of seeing his youngest brother, Dominic, thrive as a rising star with the New York Rangers. He's also seen his own career being bogged down by injuries and eventually halted by post-concussion syndrome in just his third season. He also saw his brother Steve become embroiled in one of the most notorious moments in the sport's history: Vancouver Canucks forward Todd Bertuzzi's on-ice attack on Steve, then enjoying a promising rookie season with the Colorado Avalanche. Anyone with a bank of experiences like those I've mentioned would be worth listening to for their reflections on the game.

But there is another side to Mark that makes this contribution doubly compelling: He may just be the smartest hockey player ever to lace on skates. If he'd never touched a hockey stick he would still have fit in just fine at Harvard. Mark scored a near-perfect 1590 out of 1600 on the U.S. college board's feared Scholastic Aptitude Test (SAT). With a knack for analysis and problem-solving, he graduated from Harvard's Department of Mathematics, an intense program that only hands out around thirty degrees per year. His office exploits often leave even brothers Steve and Dominic shaking their heads. While at Harvard, Mark fractured the wrist on his writing hand, putting him in danger of falling months behind at school. Mark soon found he could write with his other hand, as long as he wrote everything backwards, which he did with his professors' blessing. The teaching fellows deciphered and graded his assignments with the aid of a mirror.

Since the Harvard days, I have continued to follow the progress of the Moores behind the scenes and sometimes in print, as Steve and Dominic went on to success in the NHL, and Mark has battled and still battles against the post-concussion syndrome that halted his career. Once again, I find Mark responding to adversity in constructive and amazing ways. In *Saving the Game*, Mark takes the sport he has lived and loved so dearly and reflects its strengths and flaws in the mirror, for all to assess. He brings a mathematical rigour to the pursuit of understanding and the search for solutions, yet one driven by a deep-seated and unquestionable devotion and passion for the game, bolstered by triumphs and tested by disappointments.

The book itself is divided into four sections (First Period, Second Period, Third Period, and Overtime) that each effectively explore important aspects of the game. Topics covered range from factors behind the NHL's lockout and the impact of its new collective bargaining agreement, to grasping nuances of recent rule changes and other proposals, to the need to strengthen the health and safety of those trying to weave magic on the ice. *Saving the Game* is the story of the incomparable sport of hockey, its greatest challenges, the collective efforts that have begun to address them, and a number of innovative ideas to help hockey reach new and greater heights.

From the time I first met Mark Moore while he was playing for Harvard, I quickly realized he was not your average hockey player. From the first page of *Saving the Game* I am sure you will quickly find it is not your average hockey book.

Michael Grange
Globe and Mail
Sports Department

WARM-UP

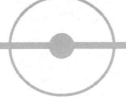

CHAPTER 1

THE STORY BEHIND
THE BOOK

Saving the Game explores the most burning issues of professional hockey. It is not a condemnation of the sport; in fact, I believe (and this book will argue) that hockey is the greatest sport in the world. Yet not long ago the game was in a place where many observers would have said that such a claim was so untenable as to be absurd. Since that time, some important positive steps have been taken, and appreciated by passionate followers of the sport. But ultimately, even those who nurtured the improvements know that challenges remain, and more work's to be done to raise the game, in all aspects, to where everyone devoted to it wants it to be. "It's a process," NHL VP and chief of hockey operations Colin Campbell said. "It's still a work in progress," said the lead player on the reform committee, Detroit's Brendan Shanahan. This isn't a book about how to rebound from the lockout, or adding a little excitement to the game for 2005–06 – by the time the book comes out, my assumption is that those issues will have successfully been resolved. This is a book about the most important issues in the sport at a deeper level, and over a longer term. It's a book about raising the game to heights that those who believe in it, believe it can climb.

How this book came to be written is a simple story to tell but, in certain parts, impossible for any words to adequately describe.

From the time I was old enough to skate, my life had been spent in the game of hockey. As with many people involved with the sport, some of the issues now or recently pre-eminent are not new to me but had existed in a vague form in the back of my mind for a while. A little more than two years ago, in September 2003, they had been forced to the forefront by what was the most difficult phone call I had ever had to make. Having spent my life in the game, having dreamed and worked for twenty years to try to make it in the National Hockey League, having "paid my dues" and persisted through three frustrating years as a pro waiting for a real opportunity, I finally had one – from the team I had always idolized and dreamt of playing for as a kid. It was a chance to start with their top farm team, and try to earn a promotion up. Instead, on that day in September, I had to tell the Montreal Canadiens I couldn't accept their offer. I was 26 years old, I had missed the last three-quarters of the previous season with a concussion, and I knew that this opportunity was in all probability my last, best chance. They asked me if I was sure. With my body trembling, my mind filled with disappointment and frustration, and my voice breaking, I said that I was. I didn't have a choice – my concussion had dragged into the dreaded post-concussion syndrome, where after each period of feeling better came renewed periods of feeling worse again, and no predictable end in sight. The doctors wouldn't clear me to play, and the reality that was so hard to accept was that I couldn't anyway.

Over the next few weeks, a lot of things ran through my head as I watched from the sidelines as training camps began, and then the season, and for the first time in twenty-three years – since I was 3 years old – I was not playing hockey. I thought about why I couldn't play when I wanted to so badly, about my injury and how it occurred, about other players in similar situations, about timing and opportunity, and a hundred other things . . . thoughts about my career, about the sport, about the industry. At the end of those few weeks, sometime in October, I decided to write down some of the thoughts churning in my mind. Less than an hour later, I had a list of issues in hockey that was nine pages long. Most of these had existed in public debate for a while already; yet seeing a list of them all together on paper, I was shocked by the scope and magnitude of the problems. They encompassed virtually every aspect of hockey, penetrated the deepest levels, and included multiple items of major significance. That exercise was a revelatory experience; it signalled that the game was in serious trouble, far beyond the day-to-day problems of every sport or every aspect of society. I intended, when I felt well enough, to try to organize these thoughts into a useful form.

As time went on, watching my first ever hockey season as a spectator rather than as a player gave me a new perspective on the game and some of these issues. Whether sitting with fans in the stands at live games, or listening to commentators on TV, or reading what the journalists were saying in the newspapers about "the issues in hockey," I could see hockey as people outside the industry saw it. At the same time, my experience of hockey from "the inside" as a long and recent participant was still fresh in my mind, enabling me to compare the two perspectives, and combine outside observation with inside understanding into a broad and balanced point of view. Over those months, the thoughts coalesced into the outline of a book. I talked to friends who had recently retired and others who were playing at the time about writing this book when I was able, and publishing it under the title "On Thin Ice."

But on March 8, 2004, the ice was shattered. That night, I sat down in front of the TV to watch a hockey game. My brother Steve, a rookie forward with the high-flying Colorado Avalanche, was facing off against the Vancouver Canucks at GM Place in Vancouver. However, this wasn't a hockey game I could enjoy; instead, I had to watch in apprehension. Certain Canucks had been promising revenge against Steve for three weeks since he had inadvertently injured one of their players with a check in a prior game that was ruled, reviewed, and confirmed clean. I had heard, along with the rest of the public – repeated over and over on radio stations, television, and newspapers across Canada and the United States – the outrageous threats: "There's definitely a bounty on his head," the Canucks' Brad May had said; "No way that punk will be in their lineup in March [when they would come to Vancouver]," threatened the 245-pound Todd Bertuzzi.

That night was to be the last meeting of the season between the two teams, and I was nervous as I sat watching the TV. Meanwhile, several other members of Steve's family who reside in British Columbia were watching at the arena in Vancouver, including Steve's cousin Mikey, a youngster carrying a Canucks pennant. Late in the first period, Steve scored a goal that set an NHL record for the fastest four goals by one team in NHL history. However, with the score between the teams quickly becoming lopsided, I was too tense to celebrate. "Situations will present themselves," Bertuzzi had told the media earlier; retaliation would "absolutely" be had. A little more than eight minutes into the third period, I saw Bertuzzi skate over and up behind Steve. The play went all the way down the ice and back, and there was Steve again, with Bertuzzi still strangely right behind him, following him. *What was he going to do?* The telecast panned away, following the puck, while I worried what might be about to happen. "Steve, watch out!" I exclaimed futilely from 2,700 miles away. The camera came back; Steve was lying face down on the ice, motionless, in a pool of blood. The commentators fell silent; trainers and medical personnel surrounded him; there was no movement or response. *Was he paralyzed? Was he dead?* The horrific scene continued for what seemed like an eternity, interrupted by a commercial for the National Hockey League, during which I ran to phone relatives at the game.

Then – caught by a camera that had followed them – the television replay showed what had happened to Steve. I saw in terrifying slow motion the disturbing images that have now been permanently etched into the minds of millions of hockey fans. I was in complete and utter disbelief. The images collided with and shattered my ideas of what was possible in hockey and in life. The ground gave way beneath me. Of the family at the arena, my uncle Jim, a doctor, went down to ice level; others were stuck in the stands, devastated. Mikey, bawling, tore his Canucks pennant to shreds. Paramedics ran out onto the ice; Steve, still immobile, was lifted onto a stretcher and wheeled off the ice. Then he was taken by ambulance to the hospital. Back at home, I anxiously awaited word by the phone. Then it came: Steve was alive, but his neck was broken. He also had a serious concussion and other injuries. Further tests were needed to determine whether the neck injury would threaten his life or mobility. In anxious agony, I waited and prayed. It was an agony that only gradually and partly subsided. The ensuing days, full of fear and despair, were just the beginning of an ordeal still ongoing in many forms.

In the meantime, the public reaction toward the incident was immediate and overwhelming. Several Vancouver fans phoned the police from GM Place to demand Bertuzzi be arrested. The following day, the film of the incident was played over and over, literally around the world, to stunned outrage. Headlines screamed of a dark day in hockey history. Intense criticism stormed around the Canucks, the league, and the sport itself. There had been plenty of talk around troubling issues in hockey for some time, but now it was no longer a question whether hockey had major problems, but what all they included, what to do about them, and in some circles, whether anyone should further bother about a sport in which something so contemptible could occur. The unfathomable assault – coming with widespread public disaffection with the quality of play already there in the background, and a potential lockout looming overhead – plunged the game into the cold water of crisis. A widespread conviction of the need for major reform in hockey erupted, unprecedented in intensity and reach in the history of the game or, to my knowledge, of any major sport.

But throughout all this passionate discussion, a fully accurate and deep understanding of both the etiology of problems and the larger issues – of the living breathing nature of them as they exist in the game, and how they feed into each other in corrupting it – seemed to remain agonizingly elusive. Acclaimed responses, consensus solutions to the problems were certainly still nowhere to be found.

For quite some time, our family was preoccupied with Steve's health, and with the aftereffects of what happened. When I finally got around several weeks later to thinking about the sport on whose ice the incident occurred and rejoining the now subsequently enormous attention, consideration, and controversy around its issues, it was clear that even deeper questions and more intense scrutiny were warranted than I had applied so far. This process that began with shattered ice ended with a crystallization in my mind. Ideas I had prior were focused, given intense personal importance, and a sense of urgency beyond the necessity they already had. Others were forever altered. My perspective had changed.

Just months later, what was for many the third and final strike came against a game gone wrong: the cancellation of the 2004–05 season over a financial dispute between the league and the Players' Association. Shut-out fans were angry with those involved, and disillusioned with the game itself. Polls said many were turning away, once and for all. But in my case, it had a different effect: it reinforced me in joining those others who hoped that the absence was more sabbatical than mere suspension, and that ultimately from all the pain, something larger, more valuable, and lasting could be gained.

As the league resumed for 2005–06, a beginning to this was indeed on offer through some changes made to try to win back fans – and savoured by them it was – abetted by a healthy marketing blitz, and alongside pure relief at the game's return. Yet only the extremely naive, or someone not being honest, would say there isn't still a lot of work to do.

To many long-time but late-suffering passionate supporters like myself, professional hockey is like a legendary animal of wondrous and wide-ranging appeal that in recent years was hunted, endangered, and driven into a kind of captivity. But yet we remembered what this game was like in nature, we saw what its essence tells us it can be, if nurtured and freed. To us, that quest is not only something important but something sacred. As much as the game was engulfed in crisis, and beset by problems, as popular as predictions of the game's demise had been, I believed in the game implicitly, and still do. I am sustained by a vision of the game: unleashed from all of its chains, soaring above the world of sports, and the world of entertainment. It is not a vision born of flight of fancy or hallucinogenic drugs, it is born of first-hand experience and memory of great moments in the sport, of an intimate knowledge of its inherent potential, and ideas about how to set it free. I firmly believe that there are courses of action that will do more than bring the game back from the brink, but bring it new glory, unprecedented prosperity, while protecting the integrity of the game. Now more than ever, supporters of the game thirst for them.

In response to that common objective, what emerged is the present work, which hopes to help contribute in a meaningful and positive way to that undertaking – enjoining the common quest for answers and understanding behind them. This book is a roadmap of my vision.

Therefore, if it isn't already, let me now make clear that this book is not about the Bertuzzi incident, or our family's nightmare experiencing it: I have not been entrusted by the family to act as a spokesperson on that matter, and this book does not purpose to do so. Nor is this book a story of my own injury, career, or life in the game, which in themselves are certainly of little interest or consequence. Nevertheless, in writing about the game, these experiences are significant to and cannot and should not be deleted from my frame of view, nor from realities of what has happened, and happened in the game. This is a book personally informed, but generally directed. Also, let me say that this is not an exhaustive account of every issue in every form, level, age, place, and aspect of hockey in the world. As one current player and future Hall-of-Famer told me during my search for answers, "that would be an encyclopedia." Instead, this book is principally about the professional game in North America, its kingpin the NHL, and its most major and most pressing issues, plus whatever other matters the pursuit of those bring in tow.

In contemplating these, my objective isn't to criticize the game or to vilify anyone – more than enough of that has been done elsewhere, and ultimately it usually accomplishes nothing except to ostracize reform from reality, polarize incongruent points of view, and paralyze constructive action. It is always easier to destroy than to build, to assail than to understand, but nobody gains from it, much less the game. On the other hand, I am not trying to defend or exonerate the game either. Where there are real problems – and here there unquestionably are – attitudes of denial and defensiveness serve nothing other than to hasten and deepen deterioration, continually invite more criticism, and *guarantee* the worst possible result. There is a third option: and that is to openly and honestly appraise, seek to thoroughly understand, praise progress where it has occurred, and strive to correct deficiencies where they remain. We can be sick and tired of *criticism* without ignoring issues and abandoning the search for answers. Following this third way leads us on a journey inside the game, into its issues, exposing their causes, explaining their inner workings, getting to the heart of things, and seeing what answers we find – answers for raising our game. In the process, we face certain issues gripping all professional sports, and sports' role in society, and hope that our model for hockey matters to the reckoning and raising of those games (and perhaps some other institutions) too.

From the point of view of this book, these are my only goals. If I had any axe to grind, it has been buried: I no longer have any vested stake in the game to espouse. And I have no "sour grapes" toward the game about my career either – injuries unfortunately happen, and they happened to happen to me. Likewise, if one supposes I am writing in the interests of my brothers, they will quickly see that's not what this is about. And not something they asked or may have necessarily wanted me to do. I am striving and attempting to write solely in the interests of the game – what's right, what's good for the sport, for everyone involved, without intended partiality or prejudice. If such a point of view sounds strange, maybe it's because, sadly, it isn't taken enough. Many of the suggestions in this book I expect people will like, or come to like. Somewhere, there may be a suggestion they don't. As they say, "you can please some of the people some of the time, but you can't please all of the people all of the time," I hope that even then, people will still respect the hard work, hard experiences, and dedication behind this, and the spirit it was written in of trying to serve the game. Indeed, during the lockout, there was frequent mention of "the good of the game." Coming off it, with old challenges still needing work beyond positive steps taken, and new challenges added on top, the game truly needs that attitude – on the part of as many as possible – to meet its goals in the mid- to long-term. It needs us to evaluate things not from where we stand in relation to the game, but stepping inside the shoes of the game itself.

And I also hope that even though of course each person comes to the game armed with their own strong conceptions and opinions, that in reading this book they will find room to temporarily put them on hold, read with an open mind, consider the arguments, and then decide anew. This book – read in these ways – will challenge people to question some long-held assumptions, just as uninvited experiences in the game forced me to do the same.

I hope this journey sounds engaging. I can promise this is no dull academic treatise, not another tiresome philosophical musing about issues but without answers, but rather a to-the-point quest for solutions, built for application. The end is not curiosity, but conviction. Along the way, I hope there are some interesting glimpses into the world of professional hockey and sports, and some ideas from them that are relevant outside – the two unique and surviving treasures of a former player. I have tried to write this book for the long-time fan or player, for the casual observer, and for everyone in between – for anyone who cares or wonders about hockey. And I hope you enjoy it.

But ultimately, in the eyes of the author, the success of this book will not be judged by whether some admire it, or how many copies it sells, or the accuracy of its findings, but how it is reacted to; in other words – on the ice. Ideas are but seeds in the mind; to bear fruit they require limbs. I hope that the people with the power to decide the future of the game do what needs to be done. And that their objective is the most possible, not the least necessary; after all, the game has more to potentially gain than to lose from where it stands on the scale of its ability. I hope that players use the courage they display on the ice to stand up off the ice for what is right, in spite of various potential pressures at times. I hope that as many people as possible respond by thinking of what they can do, rather than purely wondering what someone else will do. And better yet, that they not just ask but act. Hockey is a great sport, a special sport, that could and should be the greatest game of all. This book is written in service of that game and all who love it, in the hope that it is of some benefit to the common goal, a most worthwhile goal, of raising our game.

Hockey has long been much more than a sport to Canadians. Paul Henderson's famous goal in the 1972 Summit Series captivated an entire nation. (*Canadian Press TRSTR*)

CHAPTER 2

APPRAISING OUR GAME

THE GAME

The game of hockey, in its essence, is not just any sport; I think it truly is the greatest sport in the world, by far.

Think of the great games you've played: the spirited midwinter pickup game on the local frozen lake, the intense playoff against your arch-rivals that stretched into double overtime, the day everything seemed to flow beautifully, the old wooden arena transforming into a cathedral of the sport. Think of the great games you've seen: the time your son or daughter came out of the dressing room after the game with a sparkling smile from ear to ear; the first time your father took you to a professional game and you left in awe at the speed and ability of the pros. Relive the great thrillers you remember on TV: Messier and the Rangers defeating Bure and the Canucks in Game 7 of the 1994 Final; the epic battle between the Habs and Bruins that turned on Don Cherry's extra man; the amazing grace of the 3-3 match between the Canadiens and the Soviet Red Army on New Year's Eve 1975. The feeling you got in those games was so engaging, so captivating, so truly exciting. *A midwinter night's dream.*

Or think of the great periods in the game's glorious past: the era of Hull's 'Hawks, Lafleur's Habs, Orr's Bruins, Gretzky's Oilers, or Lemieux's Penguins. Remember that special team you played for as a kid, that storybook season, that tournament where your child surprised even you. *What a remarkable sport.*

Think of the great *plays* you've experienced: the time your favourite moves worked perfectly, the defenceman fell down and the goalie went sprawling the wrong way and you coolly deposited the puck in the empty net. Or the time your check rifled a shot labelled for the top corner and your goalie saved you, snatching the puck out of thin air. Or the time your daughter chased an opponent down on the backcheck, dove, and knocked the puck away. Recall moments like these that were amazing, exhilarating, out of this world. Picture the astonishing plays you've seen from the pros that you can rerun as a highlights reel through your mind: Bobby Orr scoring and soaring through the air; Glenn Anderson going end to end to deflate the Flyers in the final game; Dominik Hasek's astounding flipover save, Mario Lemieux turning Hall-of-Famer Ray Bourque inside out and roofing it over Andy Moog and saying afterwards, "I always wanted to do that." *What a game!*

Compare hockey at its best through memories like these to the best any other sport has to offer and you realize there is no comparison. For sports participants, it has all the elements you could desire: speed, skill, smarts, physicality, flow, teamwork, direct competition, natural rules, emotion, desire, hard work, and much more. It doesn't just have them, it has them *to the max.* Hockey is the fastest sport both physically and mentally, requires the most skill, is the most aggressive, demands the most complex teamwork, relies on the most instincts, and thrives on the most emotion of any game in the world.

Hockey has a lot going for it as a spectator sport as well. The intense action that makes it fun to play makes it great to watch. Local teams create loyalties and impel us to root for "the good guys" versus "the bad guys." A progressive "regular season" gives fans something to follow daily and digest, and a suspenseful playdown tournament is dessert. Further, more than any of the other major sports in North

America, hockey is played worldwide at an elite level, which makes possible great international tournaments like the Winter Olympics (where it is the only major team sport) as well as the World Cup. At these events, patriotic feeling is aroused alongside the natural intensity of the game, making for dramatic contests and a tremendous opportunity to alight spectator passion. With all these flavours of popular appeal, topped with distinctive uniforms and served *on ice*, hockey has all the advantages an entertainment business could ask for in a competitive marketplace. And with so many games, plus several major tournaments, the ability to capitalize on it is there in spades.

The essence of hockey, with its matchless combination of speed, grace, desire, and élan, offers incredible prospects for success. Hockey should be the world's greatest sport, and a leading form of entertainment.

From a personal standpoint, certainly my brothers, Steve and Dominic, and I long ago decided hockey was a game without equal. You might assume that, with all three of his sons in pro hockey, our father pushed us in the game. In fact, although both of our parents encouraged us to play hockey as well as other sports, my dad never even played organized hockey. He played competitive football and basketball and was most into tennis. My mother, before a brain tumour and a stroke tragically left her half-paralyzed, raced in triathlons. As kids, we played almost every sport out there and, like a lot of kids, took them pretty seriously. But when the time came that my brothers and I had to choose between sports, we all chose hockey. There just wasn't anything that could come close to matching the fun and fulfillment of playing hockey. I don't just mean any other sport, I mean *anything*. Our grandparents had backgrounds in music, painting, engineering, and business, and we had the capacity and diverse influences to have gone down a lot of different roads. Speaking for myself, I never found anything so fulfilling as hockey, this activity that requires all of your physical, mental, and emotional powers: your concentration and quick thinking, your creativity and inspiration, your sheer speed, strength, and endurance, your hustle and desire. It is especially fulfilling in these moments where you put it all together under pressure and intense competition. And it's all for fun. It's like being a cartoon or movie-action hero, only for real, with a live audience, and without a script.

Now that I can no longer play, I'm searching harder than ever for something that compares. I still haven't found it. I doubt that any exists.

The same thing was true when it came to watching the game. I was one of those kids who never much liked to sit around and watch anything. I had to be running around, reading, doing something. But hockey was the exception – to sit down on a Saturday night and watch the great NHLers play on *Hockey Night in Canada* was always a thrill. The Leafs would fly up and down the ice, playing their hearts out and usually losing in those years, but who cared? And there was also the added treat of the occasional Habs game on "the French channel" featuring my original hero, Guy Lafleur. My fondest TV memory is sitting on the edge of my seat and then leaping out of it when my "next" hero, Mario Lemieux, took a drop pass from Wayne Gretzky and put it in the top corner to win the Canada Cup '87. Nearly twenty years later, whenever I hear a replay of play-by-play announcer Dan Kelly's voice saying, "He scores! Mario Lemieux! With 1:26 remaining!" it still sends shivers down my spine.

These cherished stories of playing hockey outside in the winter until fingers froze and curling up on the couch by the fire to watch *Hockey Night in Canada* are not just mine and my brothers' (or yours or your sisters'), they belong to an entire country. And not just one generation of Canadians, but their parents' generation, and their parents' before them. And in recent years, Canadians have come to realize through international tournaments and the "European Invasion" of the NHL that there are people in other countries with similar feelings and fond memories about the game. In the United States, they still talk about the play of Hobey Baker, the "golden boy" of early American hockey, who drew huge crowds in New England and New York before the First World War, and was one of the great athletes of his time. He so loved the game that one version of his legend has it that he killed himself because at war's end, he could no longer play. The NCAA (National Collegiate Athletic Association) player-of-the-year award is named after him.

Several decades later saw the "Miracle on Ice," voted the greatest moment in American sports history. An underdog American team defeated the mighty Soviet squad to win the Olympic hockey gold at Lake Placid in 1980. "It was the greatest sporting event I ever saw. The hype that was built up around it was unbelievable. You had these college kids playing against the best team in the world. I think their triumph really opened eyes," said former NHLer and current coach Tony Granato. More recently, America has produced a slew of players of world-class individual ability, including the outspoken Jeremy Roenick, who likes a lot of sports but pronounced hockey "the best damn sport on Earth." Hockey remains the only sport in the United States that has been widely supported in places where it isn't really played. And the level of dedication it has inspired in some areas is downright surprising. U.S. presidential contender (2004) and current senator John Kerry wrote in his book *A Call to Service: My Vision for a Better America*, "I'm so addicted to ice hockey that I still fantasize about starting a professional over-50 senior league."

Elsewhere, in places like Russia, Sweden, Finland, the Czech Republic, and Slovakia, hockey is one of the favourite pastimes. In many other parts of Europe, it has a following as well. According to *Tropic of Hockey* author Dave Bidini, you can even find a few passionate fans of the game playing hockey in places like India, Hong Kong, Mongolia, and the Ivory Coast. Devotees the world over see in hockey an amazing and special game, what should be the world's premier sport and an exceptional brand of entertainment.

All of this gives a sense of professional hockey's great potential: on the ice, in the thrills and fulfillment it can offer players; in the stands and wherever fans gather to enjoy watching on television; and at the bank, for the financial dividends that can flow through the sport down to team owners and league personnel and partners. But if these are the possibilities, the realities have been something short of this. And what the game has been in a golden age or can aspire to at its height remains some distance out of reach.

In fact, very recently, the situation was quite dire. On the ice, there was widespread criticism about the entertainment quality of the contemporary game: "A stifling, mind-numbing, clog-the-neutral-zone trap . . . has killed the entertainment value in what can be an extremely exciting sports spectacle," said Vancouver reporter Elliott Pap. A "sad . . . watered-down product hardly worth viewing," wrote *Edmonton Sun* sports editor Mario Annicchiarico. Goals-per-game were in continuous decline, down nearly three per game since the mid-1980s. The star of that decade, Wayne Gretzky, said, "We've lost our creativity. Guys like Jean Beliveau, who grew up skating on the pond, and guys like Bobby Orr, who grew up skating on lakes . . . the imagination they had . . . Everything is so structured now. I think we've lost the imagination." Bright lights, glitz and glamour, fancy new stadiums and uniforms couldn't hide forever what was happening on the ice. "The National Hockey League is ruining the game of hockey," wrote the editors of Canada's leading national newspaper, the *Globe and Mail*, in a three-part series titled *Saving Canada's Game*. Voicing the concerns of fans everywhere, *The Hockey News* despaired of their sport being carried "forward into an increasingly dull and dreary future."

At the same time, injuries were surging. Concussion rates reached the staggering level of 10 per cent of the workforce per year, several stars were missing from action at any given time, felled by everything from battered joints to frightening eye injuries to ruptured spleens. The sport's image suffered assault from incidents of extreme on-ice violence, and at progressively worse levels from when Dino Ciccarelli was jailed for striking Luke Richardson in 1988, to the McSorley slashing incident in 2000, to Bertuzzi's attack on Steve in 2004. Simultaneously, regular violence endangered players' safety like never before. On and off the ice, rink rage was indeed all the rage – with players, coaches, and officials at each others' throats (literally, in the case of a heavily publicized incident at a youth game in Ontario). The professional game's next generation of officials was jeopardized as ten thousand amateur officials in Canada (one-third of the total) quit each year, according to Larry Scanlan's recent book, *Grace Under Fire*.

Off the ice, the picture was no better. Across the league, a third of franchises' attendance was down in the last full season. Spotty crowds were spotted in several places – not just in frontier markets like Carolina or Nashville, but in traditional hockey homes like Pittsburgh and Chicago. In the American market, where twenty-four of the NHL's thirty teams reside, there was especial trouble: regular-season TV ratings declined 21 per cent on ESPN and ESPN2 since 1999–2000, and playoff ratings went down 39 per cent since 2000 to 0.69 (just 592,000 homes) on ESPN, and 19 per cent to 0.37 (314,000 homes) on ESPN2. Those put hockey behind auto racing, arena football, and women's basketball. Another report put the ratings behind poker, pro bowling, and even dog shows. Broadcasters ABC and ESPN did not renew deals with the league, even at reduced prices, and as a result the league now has deals with NBC for zero dollars in rights fees (any profits made after the network recoups its costs would be shared, but lately networks have been losing money on hockey) and the OLN (Outdoor Life Network). In Canada, prime-time World Cup audiences were down 23 per cent in 2004 compared to 1996. The tournament finale drew less than the CFL's Grey Cup game. Teams were losing money (more than $200 million annually, combined, according to the league); some went bankrupt, others were reportedly on the verge. A labour dispute with players over salaries was unable to be resolved quickly, and calling the situation "unsustainable," the league shut down operations, putting an exclamation mark on its troubles.

The NHL's entire 2004–05 season was lost to this "lockout." The season's revenues went with it, and the game's position was hurt with fans and corporate partners for when it resumed. In mid-lockout, 37 per cent of Canadian self-described NHL fans said they didn't miss the game, according to a Decima poll, and only 28 per cent of all Canadians said they missed the game. A COMPAS poll found interest down 30 per cent. In the United States, a Zogby-ESPN poll found

56 per cent of Americans were not even aware there was a lockout; only 6 per cent had "great interest" in watching when hockey returned, 83 per cent had little or no interest. The *USA Today*'s Jeff Zillgitt summed up the situation: "Management and players have alienated casual fans and devastated hardcore fans. Alienation and devastation have turned into indifference. Few things are worse than someone who doesn't care." Hall-of-Fame goaltender and Canadian Cabinet minister Ken Dryden worried, "I think that there are a number of fans in [Canada] who have sensed over the last number of months that actually maybe [following hockey] was more habit than it was passion. I think for the great majority it's still a passion, but others have discovered that maybe it was something else. And so, as much as this can be problematic in the U.S. and that's where it's usually talked about, I think it's also a problem in this country." Even by the league's own projections, the post-lockout economic picture didn't look rosy.

In virtually every major area, and by virtually any reasonable measure, the signs of sickness were evident: "NATIONAL ADDICTION NEEDS PROFESSIONAL HELP," read a headline in Canada's largest newspaper. "NHL SKATING ON THIN ICE," read one in America's largest paper. Pro hockey was a game in crisis. And everyone was suffering: "At the end of the day, we're all losing," Wayne Gretzky said. "The players are losing, the fans are certainly losing, and the owners are losing. Nobody is winning here." Even the squabbling sides in the contentious lockout seemed to at least agree on that score: "There seemed to be an understanding across the table of where we are, and that we have to work together to dig ourselves out of the hole we dug ourselves," NHL vice-president Bill Daly said.

When the lockout finally ended in July 2005, with a new salary-cap-laden labour deal, that digging out indeed began. Unprecedented player movement saw for perhaps the first time small-market teams like Edmonton, Pittsburgh, and Nashville acquire big-ticket players like Chris Pronger, Sergei Gonchar, and Paul Kariya respectively. A package of fan-friendly rule changes was promised to try to woo back fans and provide a bit more excitement in the game. And two saviours were heralded – the "return" of an old one through Wayne Gretzky's decision to take over as coach in Phoenix, and the inauguration of a new one as first overall draft pick Sidney Crosby turned pro in Pittsburgh. Combined with fans' basic refreshment of the game's return and a well-orchestrated marketing campaign that trumpeted an all-new NHL, a considerable buzz was generated for the game leading up to the 2005–06 season. Throughout the pre-season, the game has looked better on the ice, and the positive steps have been gratefully received by most players as well as media watching. There is a new air of openness and receptivity on the part of the game, and a corresponding new air of hopefulness and positivity on the part of fans. And contrary to some expert predictions, I expect a strong initial rebound for the game.

But at the same time, the war is far from over. The bounce back from the lockout is just one battle, the first battle. Whether that captured ground is held will require much more than a "fresh start" because the earlier negative momentum was not gained by accident. Ultimately, the fate of the game will depend on the status of its "fundamentals": the quality of the game, the accessibility of the game, the feelings of its following, and the depth of its support across society. And beyond the prosperity of the industry, issues remain. On the ice, the changes made and the progress evident in the early results are just the first steps needed to return the game to how it is meant to be played. Off the ice, there is much to do to repair and improve the relationships that nurture the game. The progressive steps taken need to be followed further; the positive momentum sustained by continued action.

The grave danger only so recently departed, in truth, is not far away. Washington Capitals owner Ted Leonsis not long ago called it a "fundamentally broken" industry: "ratings are down, the love of the product is down, attendance is down, and yet, prices for ads and tickets go up," he summarized. Over a longer term, much of that may still be true – the fundamentals need work. And the road isn't going to get easier. Despite a probable warm reception for the game's initial return, the lockout may yet have an impact in the mid- to long run, compounding challenges. It has already hurt TV deals, which will affect both revenues and visibility into the future. As well, as Dryden said, even the most passionate fans have learned they can live without the game; the compulsion to watch will have to come from the game now, not from fans themselves. Even Gary Bettman conceded, "I think there will be a tremendous amount of damage. . . . The revenues will obviously decline . . . that is simply a reality of where we find ourselves."

Aside from the lockout, other outside trends are active. Modern culture is increasingly intolerant of violence, modern media has an increasingly bright spotlight to shine on incidents, and modern technology spreads stories in seconds. Newsreel violence has huge potential to distort perception of the game. Olympic producer Ralph Mellanby, a former head of *Hockey Night in Canada* for twenty years, whose son Scott plays in the NHL, explained from where he lives in Atlanta: "Down here, hockey is on a par with pro wrestling and roller derby. Stuff like that."

In Canada, *Maclean's* magazine noted that boys' hockey registration has been stagnant despite a rising population, and more boys are going into other sports, while more girls are playing hockey. Violence, it would seem, is inducing parents to keep their sons out of hockey. For participants and fans, a cosmopolitan age has brought scores of new alternative sports and activities to people's doorsteps; and a digital age offers thousands of entertainment options – from video games to DVDs – while encouraging a culture of instant, constant sensory gratification. Against this competition, the game will have to be more than okay or pretty good, it will have to be *as incredible as possible*. And last but not least, changing demographics pose another challenge. High costs of ice, equipment, and insurance are making the game inaccessible to lower-income classes, even as the upper classes are not necessarily those most deeply enamoured with the game, and have access to more alternatives.

In the United States, the broadcasting move to OLN, which reaches fewer homes, is a move more toward the periphery of the TV market at a time when, with entertainment sources fragmenting, time is running out on making a mass breakthrough. In Canada, extremely high immigration is beginning cultural shifts. Soccer has replaced hockey as the sport with the most participation. And the vast majority of immigrants come from countries unfamiliar with hockey, so the sport has to quickly win their interest before their incumbent interests potentially shift the market-balance and hockey loses its dominating hold on the Canadian population. Some believe that in the mid- to long-term, the NHL's survival may be at stake, through all these issues. Others worry whether hockey will remain a sport of beauty, respect, importance, and prosperity. In April 2005, in an editorial in the Lawrence, Massachusetts, *Eagle-Tribune*, one of the game's true heroes, Bobby Orr, summed up that danger in a single word: "Our sport is in danger of becoming *irrelevant.**"

On the other hand, a very different future is possible too. Spreading information and entertainments means more competition, but hockey itself can ride that wave to new opportunities in untapped markets. While an era of unprecedented media attention and business sophistication brings dangers, it also brings new possibilities, if the game can recapture the on-ice brilliance it has manifest at times in the past. The phenomenal success that football – a sport similar to hockey in many ways – has enjoyed in public following and economic riches (as a roughly $6 billion-a-year industry, and climbing) shows what is possible. The emergence of the formerly regional sport of Nascar racing into national sports-market prominence shows a breakthrough can be made. And hockey has far more grounds of spectator appeal than car racing, more than five times as many games as football, and a warmed throne atop the Winter Olympic launchpad. The sport faces demographic challenges, but also has demographic advantages and characteristics of unparalleled potential attraction to both sporting participants and entertainment consumers. The storied, beloved history of the game shows what profound positive feelings the game can elicit, what meaning the game can achieve; in today's and tomorrow's world, the sky is the limit for what the game can enjoy

---

* Italics added by author.

if it can build on the progress that has recently been made, gain more support and more momentum for what further needs to be done, and use them to break through and realize hockey's incredible potential.

The challenge is to make sure the latter future is grasped, not the other. And this requires taking on the larger issues, at deeper levels, and thoroughly tending to fundamentals.

THE QUEST

But who cares whether hockey fades quietly into the night or roars back and perhaps someday realizes its potential? For me, that answer is clear, in that I've spent my life in the game, and have a profound passion and conviction for it as a sport. For millions of Canadians, hockey has a similar kind of importance. Hockey in Canada is a source of heroes and celebrities, a grounds for international rivalry, and a focus for macho and military-type expression. It serves Canadians as a major measure of success, a defining element of culture, and a central fixture of the national history and heritage. Far more than just the national sport, hockey is something at the core of Canada's national pride, national identity, and collective psyche. It represents to Canadians what in the United States is embodied in perhaps twenty separate things, and what soccer is in other usually underdeveloped and thereby underdiversified countries: a frequently fanatical pursuit, practically a matter of life and death. Indeed, it is probably the most important cultural property the country has ever had. Is there another developed country in the world with such equity in, so much riding on a single sport?

"From the Dawson City team that travelled 6,400 kilometres to play the Ottawa Silver Seven in 1905 (only to lose 23-2), to the Montreal riot when Maurice Richard was suspended in 1955 and forced to miss the playoffs, to Paul Henderson's enduring fame for scoring the winning goal in the 1972 Summit Series, the game has attained the status of national myth. Foster Hewitt knew whereof he spoke when he opened his broadcasts with 'Hello, Canada.'"

So the *Globe and Mail* stated in its editorial series *Saving Canada's Game*. Indeed, not long ago, more than 57,000 fans braced temperatures approaching -20°C to watch an outdoor hockey game held at Edmonton's Commonwealth Stadium. "The sport that is the national obsession," is how Peter Mansbridge summarized it, on CBC *National News*. For right or wrong, it simply is that hockey (at least up till now) has possessed quasi-religious importance in Canada. Given such material, pyscho-social, emotional, and spiritual investment in hockey, how can it be anything other than critical to Canada to see the game saved and supportively stewarded into the future?

Hockey is not only important to Canada, but also to the game's millions of participants and hardcore followers in American cities such as Minneapolis, Boston, Buffalo, and Detroit, for example, and in European countries like Russia, Sweden, Finland, and the Czech Republic. Or, for that matter, to its passionate partisans elsewhere and anywhere: a sometimes surprising panoply of people from famous celebrities such as Neil Young, Denis Leary, Goldie Hawn, and Bjorn Borg to those unknown souls playing hockey in the foothills of the Himalayas or along the Ivory Coast.

The quest to save hockey is important to a somewhat different set of people, for a completely different set of reasons as well, for in many respects, hockey's current struggle embodies the plight of all the major sports. On an increasing basis, professional sports are facing similar issues: fractious labour relationships, erosion of rules, the challenge of adapting to changing circumstances, the growing influence of business and "showbusiness" values, and rising fan alienation. But for various reasons, some sensical, some coincidental, hockey is in many respects on the front line – the lead soldier in sports' struggle to come to grips with their future in society. Carrying that flag may not have been voluntary, but it is real. And in a copycat world, these other sports see more than a glimpse of their fight in hockey's fight, more than a glimpse of their future in hockey's future. For their assurance they would like to see hockey succeed; for their benefit, they would like to observe how.

Beyond particular professional leagues or bodies, the issues at stake in this struggle go to the heart of the importance of sports in general. Sports foster values of striving, learning, growing, and developing, and impart other important life lessons that are not always found in the classroom. They encourage self-realization, and give us a vehicle for self-expression. Sports nurture physical fitness and its relation to mental health against the background of a modern-world way of life that is increasingly negligent of these things. Sports offer young people a healthy preoccupation and pastime amidst a sea of unhealthy alternatives. They provide (or are supposed to) a wholesome, positive form of entertainment. Sports serve as a potential unifying force among people, rallying them around a city or country, while affording a friendly form of competition and partisan rivalry against others. Sports are so important to society, we must see them succeed. Yet their changing nature in a changing world leaves them an uncertain future.

Lately, hockey has been in the lab, under the proverbial microscope. For the good of itself and its ardent supporters, for the good of society for whom its challenge embodies so much, this sport must be supported in its quest.

TOWARD UNDERSTANDING

Recently, there has been unprecedented agreement that the game is facing serious challenges. "Where is this game going?" Bobby Orr asked in his editorial in the *Eagle-Tribune*. "The game has never needed more caring, more focus and more guidance. . . . There is no more time to waste," he wrote. Active player Brendan Shanahan convened a panel in December 2004 on what could be done that led to some of the positive changes so far, explaining, "For me, [the lockout has] been a real wakeup call. I have a lot of pride in my sport and most people haven't even noticed we're not playing." Former Stanley Cup–winning coach Jacques Demers said, "The game is not being played the way it should be." Ottawa Senators GM John

Muckler said, "There has to be a change. There's no question about it. . . . Something has to be done." Voicing popular sentiments, legendary fan favourite Guy Lafleur said, "The game isn't the same any more and everybody is panicking. What the hell is going on? It's not the same. It's a boring game. It's this, it's that. People come to me and say your days were the best. . . ." Lafleur's opinion was that the NHL would never return the game to how it should be, until people make it: "Why don't the people get together and make the change? If the NHL doesn't do anything, ask the people to do the change," he advised. In fact, the NHL has recognized some of the issues and took steps prior to the start of the season. But there is still plenty to do, and plenty left for the people to suggest.

But before suggestions must come understanding. What are the real issues, the burning problems? Even as that question is just the beginning, the answer is where consensus already starts to break down. Many casual observers have in recent years had the vague notion that "something is rotten in the state of hockey" but don't pretend to really know what. More serious fans often have specific ideas about what ails the game, but are limited by lack of experience of things on the inside. Assumptions cover for things they can't know, but something gets lost in the substitution, and that can lead to misconceptions. Meanwhile, people on the inside are often so much in the middle of things that the larger perspective that sees those in context, and the dispassionate perspective that appraises them objectively, are obscured from their point of view. Quite often we see disagreement, sometimes fierce disagreement, even within the game, on many of its issues. The lockout probably helped people gain perspective from a step back, but has also hurt by deepening divisions. So opinions remain discordant, and the picture remains muddled. But we need that picture clear, to set the focus for everything that needs to be done after. If we get lost here, the end objective – raising our game – becomes virtually hopeless.

This is where this book hopes to help. I don't claim any special intelligence or perception – particularly not after a major head injury! – but I've lived through the issues in the game first-hand as a player, studied them and talked to many others in and out of the game about them, and thought about them as long and hard as anyone might care to do. My life, short as it has been perhaps, has been almost entirely spent in competitive hockey. The game, the way it works, how it has changed, its problems – I have experienced all from many different angles, including playing in Canada as a youngster growing up, then in the United States in college and pro, and playing in small towns like Sarnia, Ontario (where I began), and big cities like Boston. I've been the smallest player on the ice, fearing for my life as a teenager going into rough towns, and later the biggest player on the ice, getting a penalty practically every time I sneezed. I've played in both the provincial junior and NCAA college ranks, and lined up at both forward and defence at every level right through to pro. I've experienced the game in its epicentre of Toronto and in its remote outposts such as Georgia and Carolina. I've faced off with and against NHL all-stars and recreational players who could hardly skate, and with every kind of player in between. Also important, I believe, is that the time I played is the time in question with regards to this book: the span of my career from the Quebec peewee tournament to my last professional game in 2002–03 is roughly the period through which the game's main problems emerged in significance. As a former player who no longer has a vested interest in the sport, I can be objective without being as far removed perhaps from today's game (and also having at least one brother still playing) as someone who last played twenty-five years ago, before most of the current problems reached the fore. Let no one mistake me for a Hall-of-Famer or yet even a major-league veteran, but when we are talking about problems in the game, I've had more than my share of experience with them, to be sure. More importantly, this work isn't just my ideas. I have talked to Hall-of-Famers, and many many other players, and countless other people in and out of the game, about their views, over the course of my career and after. Players from everywhere in the world, from every background, of every type and level shared their perspectives with me. Then with all their views (and my own experience) still fresh in my mind, I suddenly found myself injured, sitting in the stands, spending more time with off-ice staff and fans than with players. I got to see and hear things from their vantage point. Hearing from others only increased after what happened to my brother Steve. Everyone I meet brings up the game and its issues, tells me what they think, and asks me what I think. Thus partly by choice and partly by unchosen circumstance have I been in close touch with diverse groups, from people who know nothing about the game to people who know nothing but the game. And throughout all this time, I thought about the issues often and at length. Some of them were in my mind long before March 8, 2004, long before the previous September. They'd been somewhere in the back of my mind since I was in my mid-teens. Occasionally they'd go to the front, like the time I sat alone in the Crimson Sports Grille (now called the Red Line, ironically enough) in Harvard Square and shed a few tears on the bar-top as Mario Lemieux waved to the fans and first skated off into retirement, frustrated by rising, rampant interference tactics hampering his and others' ability to use their amazing skill.

I tried to analyze things, to make sense of them, to find answers, the right answers. I still do; overdo, some would say. That's probably the only remaining relic of my education in math – a field where your job is to find those answers or bust. With math problems, usually you get a feeling when you've got it right, some kind of intuition, but sometimes it takes a mistake, or an accident, or the pressure of a ticking clock to force you to think about things in the right way before they become clear. I believe the same is true in life, and that is what has happened to me in hockey. I prepared for twenty years for a career in professional hockey, only to have it overcast and then ended by injuries, before it could even get off the ground. Then in a year I spent coming to grips with that, I saw my brother Steve, who had followed in hockey, become the victim of something so awful and beyond anything I'd ever seen in the game it seemed inconceivable. Then the lockout came, and I saw what happened to the fans, as well as how the fans were feeling about those of us associated with the game and about the game itself. I've done my long hard thinking. I've studied, researched, listened, heard. And by a slow, gradual, often involuntary, sometimes osmotic process, things crystallized in my mind, at least that's what my intuition tells me. But you can decide for yourself as you read on, judging each message not on my word but on the strength of its argument.

This book is a comprehensive and intensive look at the issues that people who care about the game care about, a journey in search of the answers we all want. I believe it is the first book to do this. The premise is that the "crisis" in hockey was perhaps exaggerated at times but was neither imaginary nor yet fully over. Steps have been taken, progress has been made, but serious issues remain to be dealt with in many aspects of the sport: from the fun and excitement it should offer, to its administering of competition, to the physical health it should promote, to its workings as a business and relationship with society. And they impact everyone touched by the game. If the game can thrive, everyone associated with it can benefit: players, managers, executives, and fans. But if the game struggles, all of us suffer, as we've seen. In my view, there are four main areas that the game must focus on to recapture past glory and realize the positive side of its potential:

1: The thrill of the sport. Over recent years, the professional game deteriorated in the eyes of many. Speed, skill, offence, flow, and open-ice hits dwindled under the prevailing style of play, replaced by a lot of "trapping" and "obstruction," a gruelling, grinding, goaltending-dominated game. Many long-time fans found it unfamiliar and painfully static, while new spectators whose attention was captured by the allure of a new "major sports team" in town didn't see enough to get hooked on the game they encountered. Players didn't enjoy this style either. New rules for 2005–06 should help, and through the pre-season the game is clearly better; but there is still a marked deficit between it and the thrilling game we saw in the '80s (recently refreshed in our memories due to the old games being replayed on TV during the lockout). Some of the new rules are a promising start and look to have yielded an improvement that is appreciated, but the changes that have occurred since the game's heyday are more profound, and there is more work to do to maximize the game's excitement. A great game is the key to retrieving old glory and achieving new breakthroughs – and answers are available to unleash the full genius of the game, to the benefit of all involved.

2: The conduct of the competition. The way games are decided, the character of the game players "play," the way the game is officiated are all important aspects of the competition in hockey. Each has been gradually distorted over the last fifteen years, as conditions changed, and teams pushed on the rules, and the rules couldn't or didn't push back. Ultimately, that means negative feelings that take away from enjoyment. 2005–06's rule changes should help in some regards, but there is further to go to strengthen the way competition is conducted in the sport. A game that gives everyone a good feeling about the way it is conducted, win or lose, is a sport with a strong foundation for the future and for dealing with other issues that will always come up. And it is within reach, with a few key recognitions and reforms.

3: Health and safety. Security is an important prerequisite to playing sports; fitness is an important intended result. Contact sports have always carried a risk of injury, but with the number of serious injuries, especially concussions, occurring recently, the toll of injuries is running high. At the same time, violence has clearly been a problem for the game – both through the fouls that are somewhat regular, and through some extreme incidents that have happened. A season off may have provided some time to cool down, but a lot more is needed to make hockey a sport that is safer to play, and that people (including parents) perceive to be more safe to play. Some smart steps can improve health and safety in the game, so that the game can attract wider followings rather than narrower, as time goes on.

4: The financial side. The much-chronicled recent financial woes and throes of the sport reached a low point in the 2004–05 lockout, when teams sat idle, players lost incomes, and fans were driven away. A new salary cap should help control costs, but, on the flip side, revenues are a big question. Inside hockey, the "Holy Trinity" of sport, business, and public is threatened by internal conflict and external developments (not unique to hockey, but no less dangerous at that). A strong rebound from the lockout is needed and should be achieved, but a larger-scale, longer-term plan is required to preserve the relationships at the heart of the game, and grow the game in the future. Exposing and refocusing on fundamentals while delegating what are distractions for the business elsewhere should pay off for players, owners, management, and the public. And some novel but sound ideas should help create the breakthrough that has agonizingly eluded the game for so long.

FROM UNDERSTANDING TO ACTION

Sorting out the game's issues into intelligible portions and important priorities is, as mentioned, just the first step in the trek from Egypt to the promised land. The next step is to achieve deeper understanding of the underlying roots and essential details of the main problems we have identified – and this has proved even more elusive. From there, the search is for solutions – ones that will address all the facts we've found, ones that can be tried, will work fast, and will last. So far, many of these have not yet been uncovered. With the never-simple matter of turning intentions into reality still remaining, not surprisingly in view of all this, the challenge is largely ahead.

Part of the difficulty has been that the situation is indeed genuinely complicated, with several simultaneous factors each compounding the effect of others and confounding understanding and resolution of the others. At the same time, the nature of making changes is breaking new ground unfamiliar and untested. It is highly abstract theoretical territory, and there are plenty of pitfalls and no job, no training that provides a roadmap telling you where to go. This causes confusion and contributes to the disagreement that we have seen, which further locks up the wheels of motion. And when things do get going, it produces the familiar one-step-forward, one-step-back that arises from uncertainty and results in inconsistency – inconsistency that angers everyone and invites a backlash that so often sends things crashing back to square one. Hopefully, this book can help with some of that.

However, another reason for inaction in the past has been an inboard resistance to change within the game. For example, take the issue of the style of play. Those who watched the game over the last fifteen years or so saw the style transform from a fast-paced, fluid, freewheeling, end-to-end game epitomized by Wayne Gretzky's electrifying Edmonton Oilers into a static, disjointed game with few chances, little excitement, and rare goals, perfected by Martin Brodeur's suffocating-defence New Jersey Devils. "Stupid, simple hockey" that "hurts our crowds" is what the Devils' John Madden, who was a poster boy for it, called it. But while this style caught on and gained hold, action to stop or reverse it remained stalled. Some minor "tweaks" were toyed with. "Sometimes, we fool ourselves, and put in rules that aren't effective," Toronto Maple Leafs coach Pat Quinn admitted to reporter Jim Kernaghan of the *London Free Press*. "We, of all the [major sports] seem to do it every year. We look at it and look at it and look at it. . . ." We tweak and we tinker. "And to tinker . . . as is constantly being discussed – will do little to solve the big-picture problems with the NHL game," said *Toronto Sun* sage Steve Simmons.

As time went by, only one substantial solution was tried: eliminating the player interference that had spread and hamstrung skill. Not surprisingly, it involved no change to the rules short of a new name for interference: obstruction. More importantly, although the plan was promised several times, most recently in 2002–03, it was never really successfully and permanently implemented. Meanwhile, goalie equipment was allowed to grow to the point where it rendered should-be goals into saves, and even should-be great saves into routine ones. An immediate rule change to stop and reverse this clearly could've helped stem it before it got to the point it did.

Perhaps most important of all, bigger rink sizes could have been mandated (as are used in U.S. college and international hockey), when twenty-four teams built new arenas over the period since 1990. This would have given offensive players more room to work with and helped open up the game, but it didn't happen.

All of these solutions were put forth and argued for by many observers at the time; some were favoured by notable experts on the game, but in the end, they were not carried out. Clearly, part of that was a resistance – a resistance to altering the game, the rules, or even the extent to which the existing rules were enforced. And that resistance, added to the difficulties inherent in making any change, always carried the day. The style problem reached the point where, in 2003, the Stanley Cup champion Devils had trouble filling their own building in the early rounds of the playoffs, Stars netminder Marty Turco had the lowest goals-against average since 1947, and as *The Hockey News'* Ryan Hickman put it: "Catcalls from fans and media that the playoffs were less than exciting were backed up by low TV ratings." The next year, scoring and ratings went down again, emblemized by a Stanley Cup Final that upheld the rule "first goal wins" through all seven games. A similar thing happened over recent years with the majority of the main issues now challenging the game. Financial trouble, injuries, and violence all emerged as problems – the need for action became apparent, criticism emerged, and discussions were had – yet effective response lagged, until crisis arrived. It took a lost season, all of its fallout and associated fears, for the game to finally be spurred to those significant actions it has now taken.

RESISTANCE TO CHANGE

What was behind it? Some people blamed it on the "suits": the commissioner and other non-hockey-background executives, who they believed to be resisting change for "business reasons." Some believed, for example, the NHL's business experts deliberately left the game bottled up because they thought it was good for business. "Commissioner Gary Bettman speaks of his 30-team league humming toward parity. Of course, there'll be parity," the *London Free Press*'s Kernaghan wrote. "Stars are impeded from showing their full talent, as Wayne Gretzky, Mario Lemieux and others have said time and again. . . . That's the trouble. A lot of people running the game know what will happen [if they open the game up]."

Others blamed inaction on a preoccupation with legalities, or pure ignorance. "This league is run by lawyers who have no concept of the game's priorities. They break land-speed records rushing to the courthouse to protect their copyright if someone displays an unauthorized image of a Stanley Cup. . . . But they don't have the guts or the gumption to do a single thing to prevent the ruination of what was once a spectacular game," accused *Toronto Sun* columnist and *Hockey Night in Canada* Hot Stove panellist Al Strachan. Newspapers called for the firing of Gary Bettman. Player Brett Hull said, "For the ten years that he's been in the game, the game has gone to pot. I know you can't just blame him, but he's also the commissioner and so you have to point the finger at him"; many other disgruntled players and fans have blamed him as well.

Personally, I don't believe it's fair to have put all the blame on the commissioner and other front-office executives. Surely they have the best interests of the game at heart. Where there had been a resistance to change among the "suits," it may have been because they hadn't grown up immersed in the game, and may not have felt that with several complex and overlapping problems that they understood it thoroughly enough to chart the course of change. And with a hundred-year tradition, thousands of players, millions of fans, and billions of dollars at stake, in a field often said to be reluctant to embrace those who haven't played the game, it was no place for guess-moves. There may have been a resistance there, but it's at least understandable that they may have wanted to proceed with some caution and deference, not as a bull in a china shop.

Others blamed hockey-side experts: general managers who sat on the board of governors, "hockey operations" executives with the league, and others. Many critics believed they had the authority and position to change the game but refused: "the undercurrent of denial and stubbornness is incredible," wrote the *Pittsburgh Post-Gazette*'s Shelly Anderson. "These cement heads at the NHL don't get it," said Ralph Mellanby. Some accused them of an attitude of "let's do the least necessary" instead of "the most possible"; others said they lacked respect for outsiders' points of view: "Every so often, they get together with a few equally insular general managers and pronounce the league in excellent shape. . . . The league's stance – as represented by the general managers and the executive level – is the usual one: The game is great and we don't want to make any substantive changes," decried Strachan after the 2003 playoffs.

Again, I personally don't believe this is totally fair. Many GMs and hockey-side executives are among the sport's soundest judges, and all of them share a level of experience and passion for the game that are beyond question. For those among them who may not have supported change, it was probably the result of absorption in something so much for so long that naturally one takes the way things are for granted, and spends less time wondering whether there is another, better way. This is why even the most successful companies combine to spend billions annually on outside consulting. In my own case, that experience was forced upon me by injury: being outside the game, for the first time since I was five, allowed me to step back and see new things, or rather see old things from new angles. Also, playing and managing hockey, like many occupations, did not train a person for dealing in abstracts or theoretical concepts, but rather to master things the way they are – a very different skill. That's why great players haven't especially often seemed to make great coaches. And it's why governments lean on academic professors moreso than industry leaders as policy advisers in reforming laws. So where people may have perceived a lack of initiative for change on the part of expert hockey officials, it is neither unexpected nor outrageous that they wouldn't run afield of or beyond their own experience.

Others alternatively blamed certain hockey "expert commentators" or public figures associated with the game who may not have had direct executive power but held influence over large numbers of people involved. They were faulted for either overdefensiveness or overcriticality that each obstructed the mustering of an accurate and objective view of the game and its needs. The power of some of them was such that *The Hockey News* devoted an editorial to defending the change movement against denunciations as a "threat to the integrity of the game," and proponents of change as weak, ignorant, or unfaithful. "Don Cherry exemplifies the hostility to change," opined the *Globe and Mail* in its own look at hockey. "In his bullying, hectoring, plain-spoken way, he expresses a fear among Canadians that the game no longer belongs to them." Others have accused his co-host, Ron Maclean, of being an example of apologists who too often would obscure the game's problems with nostalgia, so that little real progress could be made. And still others, including many players, blamed what they perceived as the overblown, cartoonish, or constant attacks by some critics as distracting from the most important issues, and from the search for solutions, and alienating those that must make them. While there is no question that defensive reactionism, whitewashed celebration, or unconstructive condemnation were not what the game needed, it nevertheless does not make sense to heap all the blame for slow progress on these commentators. They have a job to do – which is to voice opinions about the game: can we fault them for voicing their own? Other times, in the interests of "balanced reporting," media organizations sometimes find commentators who can fulfill different "roles" or offer different "spins" on an issue. Some of the judgments would be right, some would be wrong, typically varying by the situation moreso than the person. Just like anyone else, commentators and columnists can speak, and we can listen, but what matters was for everyone involved to make their own judgment (as the commentators do) and choose their own position based on what they've seen and in their own mind decided. That's how to ensure the right popular attitudes and direction for the game.

Another group sometimes identified as a problem was the pro players, or their association. They were accused of an inflexibility that thwarted progress. "There's nothing wrong with hockey," ESPN quoted NHLPA president and Vancouver Canuck Trevor Linden less than a week after the Bertuzzi incident. A few months later, many observers condemned Linden's NHLPA for filing a labour grievance to block on-ice changes that NHL vice-president and director of hockey operations Colin Campbell had gone to great lengths to sponsor in the interests of improving the game. "It's frustrating," an annoyed Campbell confided at the time. "I thought it was for the players that we were trying to improve the game." A lot of the public and media have seemed to think that the players may be good at hockey, but aren't the most intelligent or most open-minded people around. I've certainly run up against that belief enough times myself. And all this was before polls during the lockout showed strong fan antipathy toward players in that dispute. Others blamed the union itself: "To me [former head Bob] Goodenow has shown no interest in helping build the game and helping sell the game. He's done nothing but take from the game . . . when he had that power, he ruined it," Flyers GM Bobby Clarke alleged shortly after the season was cancelled.

Once again, in my view, singling out players or their association would be unfair. First of all, recent polls have shown a majority of players do support change, many, radical change. In a survey published midway through the 2003–04 season in *The Hockey News*, an enormous 93 per cent of players recommended changes to the game. That number surely grew even higher since. But if, on any particular issue that is important to the game, a significant number of them had resisted, it may have been for some of the reasons mentioned earlier. Players have a huge vested interest in the game. As much as some view that as a reason to disqualify opinions, it's as much a reason to respect them. The players have spent a life in the game, love the game, and make a career in the game. Changes don't affect anyone as much as them. That's a good reason for caution, and I've been in that boat. Another problem is, hundreds of players meant dozens of different opinions about what should be done; it was hard to agree on anything. Not only that, but it wasn't up to them. They didn't make the rules (although with the new Competition Committee that includes some players, they do have a say in them now). As for the Players' Association, they couldn't take sides on a contentious issue without alienating some of their own members. And with little say, they had little incentive to take such leading positions. It just doesn't make sense to heap all the blame at the feet of the players or their association either.

The fact is, all of these groups share responsibility for the game and its direction, perhaps some more than others, but none of them all. And all of these groups would have to overcome any resistance to do their part in what the interests of the game may call for: going forward. As far as individuals, my objective is not to judge people or the past, but rather just advocate for the future of the game. And so I am not going to cast blame or condemn people because I believe it's counterproductive to the goal of getting everyone to get behind what needs to be done. Clearly, in the past, a resistance to change was an obstacle to that – a kind of trump card: if there isn't a will, there won't be a way. And it froze the game like a deer in the headlights when it needed to use all its speed and agility to react. That resistance to change is by no means peculiar to hockey. It's human nature. Change means leaving the familiar for the unknown, which is scary, so we try to control by resisting. Even the most proper changes incite us to react with fierce resistance: to take an extreme example to illustrate the point, not all that long ago a war was fought on this continent over the abolition of slavery! But at the same time, change is inevitable. From birth to death, it is the only constant: roles, circumstances, and preoccupations change; old memories fade, while new ones are made. Outside of us, seasons, governments, eras transform – even the universe itself is expanding. Those changes that happen gradually, imperceptibly, automatically don't strike us, and pass without inducing a reaction. But the changes someone proposes up front or imposes from up top do, and in the strongest way. Against them collides our desire to control by resisting – the immovable object against the unstoppable force. But it is flawed; the notion that we can keep things a certain way permanently is impossible, as absurd as trying to stop the hands of a clock to gain time. Instead, by resisting the changes we can control, while other ones proceed on their own, we guarantee that change happens in chaotic and undesirable ways.

A BIT OF BACKGROUND

Some of those ways can be understood, if you will pardon the brief digression, by analogy to two basic science concepts underlying the world we live in:

The first one is the law of entropy, also known as the second law of thermodynamics. It is a fundamental law of science, based on probability, and governs all things in the universe. Officially, it stipulates that "For any isolated system, the overwhelming probable course of events takes the system over time to a state of increasing disorder (or 'entropy')." In plain terms, this means that things naturally deteriorate on their own, unless work from outside is done to stop and reverse this. Organization tends to break down into chaos. Likewise, in human organizations, we construct rules to preserve order, and supply energy continually to uphold them. And when something breaks down, we have to add more energy from outside to repair it, and try to preserve it for a while, anew. What we want to save, we have to take care of in this way. The more we let something spontaneously change for the worse, the more we need to actively do to restore it.

The second scientific concept that can help us understand change in hockey is evolution. Evolution states that living things evolve over generations. As conditions change, we need to change with them. And in competition for limited resources, we need to change to stay ahead (*survival of the fittest* is the phrase we all know). One of my Harvard professors, Stephen J. Gould, made a reputation as co-author of a widely accepted theory of evolution called punctuated equilibrium: it states that much of evolution is not gradual, but rather features long periods where things stay the same, "punctuated" by brief periods of massive-change-in-crisis. Likewise, human organizations need to adapt to changing conditions, need to evolve to stay ahead of the competition, and the more critical the circumstances, the greater and more urgent the change must be.

Twenty-five years ago, Chrysler Motors was a company on the verge of collapse. A program of extraordinary change – replacing executives, selling and acquiring new divisions, securing government help, and unveiling radical new vehicles like the K Car and the minivan – saved the company and turned boss Lee Iacocca into an American legend. Another American legend, pop music star Madonna, has repeatedly "reinvented herself" to stay successful – and shared that secret in using it as the name of a recent tour. Others have not evolved enough fast enough, joining the dinosaurs, the dodo bird, and the discotheque. In the case of organizations, if the Roman Empire – undisputed ruler of Earth for a thousand years (and surviving for two thousand, if you include the Eastern half) – can fall, what organization can *possibly* think itself immune to that which follows decline? The law of evolution, in a nutshell, is adapt or go extinct.

The underlying situation in hockey is well understood using as a paradigm these two principles. The style of play and entertainment value, confirmed by TV ratings, attendance, and reviews, fit a pattern of decline. More and more infractions (hooking and holding, crosschecking, goaltender interference) disordered play. An erosion of discipline has been manifest in dirty play and violent incidents. And the financial picture's deterioration took the form of bankruptcies and losses, and disintegrating relationships between players, management, and fans. As far as parallels to evolution, threats have developed: there have been changes in the size, speed, and skill of players, and in equipment and tactics – huge changes in the physical conditions and mechanics of the game. Hockey has also seen equally huge simultaneous alterations in the money, pressure, media attention, and "political" importance of the game – a huge change in the "mental" character and intensity of the game. Together, it's an effectively different sport than it used to be, or than it is at non-professional levels. All this in a world boasting an increasing proliferation of other alternatives and sophisticated operations competing for devotees and entertainment dollars, which hockey has to compete with to survive. Virtually all the issues can be understood with reference to these principles: a game that had deteriorated due to natural forces, a game out of sync with new conditions. And since these processes don't reverse themselves, the game is being challenged to adapt to deal with all this.

"Games evolve," Calgary Flames star Jarome Iginla, arguably the game's marquee player (certainly in Canada) said in telling *The Hockey News* he is in favour of radical changes, "and I think it's time for us to try to take some bold steps forward. Fans have indicated for the past 10 or so years they have been less than happy with the product. Even as a player, I think hockey is a great game; I love the intensity and the skill, but I think there could be some improvements and hopefully we could get back to playing a little bit more thrilling hockey. . . . I think everybody in the game has to be involved."

HEEDING THE CALL

In his editorial, Bobby Orr called for the same thing: "It is clear that the priority of every person involved with pro hockey needs to be a mutually healthy league with a vision for moving our game forward." Anyone who has been to the Hockey Hall of Fame has probably stood in the life-sized replica dressing room of his arch-rival Montreal Canadiens, where the bronze faces of the greats from the team's storied past stare down from the wall, emblazoned with the words from Colonel John McRae's famous poem, *In Flanders Fields*: "to you from failing hands we throw the torch, be yours to hold it high." The game of hockey was cradled with great care in the hands of our forebears, held aloft until hands failed, and then handed down so that the torch would remain always high.

From generation to generation was the torch passed, and now it is in our hands. To let its flame flicker or let it fall, or hold it high and raise it higher, is our choice, a choice to be made not with words but with actions.

To those for whom it means so much and who love the game as much as I do, this duty as "keepers of the flame" is almost sacred. For others, it is still important: the nature and meaning of the sport for the future are at stake, the experience of players and fans today and tomorrow are at stake, the financial fortunes of those invested in the industry are at stake. All of us share a common goal: to safeguard and raise the game.

In that campaign, there are certain parts to be played. Needed above all is the support and commitment of NHL top executives, the board of governors, general managers, and special committee members who rule the NHL. What the NHL will do, or not do, they will decide. Behind them must be professional players and their associations, supporting the right moves for the sport, and for everyone touched by it. Physically and mentally, it has been difficult for me to write this book. In putting forward a progressive program of action, Brendan Shanahan and Colin Campbell sacrificed their time and undertook personal risks as well. So did the many others who assisted and supported them, put forth other proposals that may not have ended up being adopted, or have made various other kinds of efforts recently or in the past. Hopefully others will make sacrifices to do what seems right to them for the sake of the sport. Star players – who have the least to fear and the most influence – could particularly help by standing up for the right thing, like Iginla, even if not always the most popular thing. Players' associations can't just consider their members' financial interests, but other kinds of interests, and other players: past and future players. All these things will provide leadership from the professional ranks. That, we have to have. The NHL in particular sets the standard for everything in hockey: from rules, to style, to attitudes, to equipment.

But there needs to be support beyond as well. Commentators can especially mind the mental influence they have, much as players are required to as behaviour role-models. Every other group involved with the game, from minor pro leagues, to minor hockey leagues, to European leagues, to international associations, to equipment manufacturers, to news media have an influence – in one way or another. Government and governing bodies, on behalf of everyone in the sport, and everyone in the public, do too. And if fans, members, and voters speak, those that want their support will listen. All of this will put a weight behind positive movements that will help push them through. Ultimately, sports are for the people; raising our game is for the people.

For each person involved, the challenge is the one I began to take up when I had to put down my skates: Look long and hard at the game, where it's been, where it is, where it's going. Is the current state the right one, the best one? Look long and hard at your role in the game, at the game's role in you. What does the game mean to you? What does the game need from you?

PAST, PRESENT, AND FUTURE

In some way, it may not be easy. But hockey players (and the fans that see them give their sweat and blood for a chance at a sip from a silver cup) know as much as anyone that few worthwhile things are easy. As players, we could never have set skate on ice, never survived being benched by a coach, never coped with the age at which begins bodychecking, never left home for junior or college, never have dealt with being traded, without accepting that challenge. Everyone from the businessmen serving in management positions to the fans sitting in arenas have faced challenges in life that have forced us to change for the better. And the game itself, particularly in its early years, and perhaps more than any other sport, has shown an ability to survive and thrive on change.

In fact, the first "recognized" hockey game of record, in 1875 in Montreal, featured nine players aside. In 1911–12, the NHA became the first league to play the six-on-six game still used today, eliminating the rover position, to change the game from the seven-man hockey that dominated the previous thirty-five years. When the NHL began, goalies were prohibited from going down to make a save, until that was changed by President Frank Calder in 1917–18.

In the '20s, a scoring problem developed, as defences stacked up to prevent goals. Lots of things were tried, including banning more than two defenders from remaining in the defensive zone when the puck left, whistles and faceoffs if the team leading was judged to be ragging the puck, and a legislated shrinking of goalie pads – twice. It didn't work. And the problem continued to worsen, culminating in the Canadiens' George Hainsworth recording 22 shutouts and a 0.92 GAA in 44 games in 1928–29. In all, there were 120 shutouts in 220 games that season. The next year, a *revolutionary* change was introduced – the forward pass – which had not been allowed in hockey before. It more than doubled the number of goals. The Boston Bruins' Ralph "Cooney" Weiland (who later coached at Harvard) obliterated the previous scoring record held by "The Stratford Streak," Howie Morenz. And nobody complained, the game just grew more popular.

As time went on, boards were added, natural ice gave way to artificial ice, the game was changed from two periods to three, Zambonis were invented, and in 1949–50 with the coming of television, the ice was first painted white. Blue lines had been added in 1918–19. In 1943–44, the era of the modern game began with the creation of the red line, which added offence and sped up the game, and led referee and former all-star player King Clancy to proclaim, "I'd say it was the biggest change hockey ever made, and perhaps the best." At first, hockey had no substitutions; rosters have changed several times since, to 12 players (1925–26), then 15 (1929–30), then 16 (1953–54), and now 18 (1954–55). The rules regarding penalties have changed almost constantly over the century-plus history of the game. In 1976–77, spurred by the violent antics of the Philadelphia Flyers, better known as the Broad Street Bullies, the NHL instituted an instigator penalty consisting of a five-minute major and game misconduct for instigating a fight, a rule clarified in 1992–93. It took thirty years and the loss of several teams for the NHL to get down to the "Original Six" in 1942, and then after twenty-five years, they doubled the league's size overnight, added another two teams in 1970–71, two more in 1974–75, and four more in 1979–80. Goalies did not wear masks until Jacques Plante was cut by an Andy Bathgate shot in 1959–60 and decided he would give it a try. Stan Mikita and Bobby Hull brought in the curved stick and slapshots in the '60s. Patrick Roy and company brought in the butterfly goaltending technique in the late '80s. "The single dominant feature of this century has been change," Ken Dryden wrote in his history of the game in the compendium *Total Hockey*.

Other sports have made changes too. Baseball dropped the mound from fifteen to ten inches in 1969 to adjust the pitching-batting balance. Lately, smaller diamonds have been built, to increase the number of home runs. Football goalposts were moved back from the goal line and placed on one stanchion in 1966. More recently, they instituted video replay and the "coach's challenge," as well as two-point conversions that had only been in the NCAA previously. These changes in football garnered generally positive reviews, and without losing the integrity of a game that is certainly big on tradition. "If you look at other sports – basketball comes to mind with the three-point line – and look how good that has been for that sport," Jarome Iginla said. Indeed, the introduction of the three-point line, added in 1979–80, helped spread out the game and diminish the giants-inside style in which Wilt Chamberlain was able to score a hundred points in a game. Along with the ban on zone defences, these changes were critical to saving basketball from sporting oblivion and allowing it to emerge into the limelight it has enjoyed since.

Hockey is a game with a lot going for it, and a lot of resourcefulness when it needs it. Over the last several years, it has become clear the game has reached another point in its life where this is being called upon. For the game to have survived in the past, this has been inevitable. For the game to endure and thrive in the future, it is necessary. But it can also be exciting. The physical world's most famous symbolization of that is a caterpillar – at a certain point, a caterpillar forms new cells called "imaginal" cells so different from its old cells that its own immune system tries to destroy them. But it can't keep pace with the creation of new imaginal cells, and when a critical mass of them is reached, the caterpillar melts into a kind of primordial soup, enclaved inside a chrysalis, out of which the caterpillar emerges as a dazzling, flying, amazing animal-flower called a butterfly. One or the other of that sense of compulsion from behind or of excitement ahead has always been for me the motivation that made the most difficult adaptations much more manageable. They transform an obstacle into a challenge.

Recently, and now, more and more people with the game in their hearts are feeling the same way. "I love hockey. It's a great game. But at the same time, I realize it needs to change," said former NHL forward and current commentator Andy Brickley after participating in Brendan Shanahan's panel. The *Toronto Star*'s Damien Cox wrote: "Interestingly, there does seem to be a consensus these days both inside and outside the NHL that changes are needed to improve the appeal and excitement of the game, a consensus that wasn't there even six months ago. At the recent world junior championships, it was striking to experience how open NHL general managers and scouts were to the most extreme rule change ideas." A TV program was in the works, titled *Changes on Ice*, putting microphones on four former NHLers: NHL VP Mike Murphy, St. Louis Blues coach Mike Kitchen, commentator Greg Millen, and junior hockey coach Greg Gilbert, as they watched an American Hockey League game and mulled over potential rule changes. Harry Sinden of the Boston Bruins, age seventy-two, officially proposed eliminating the red line and expanding the neutral zone, a novel idea that he and GM Mike O'Connell tested with the Bruins' minor-league franchise in Providence, and demonstrated for the NHL brass in spring 2005. "It's a bit avant garde," Sinden said, "but I'm going for it." "Maybe that's what this game needs to make it better . . . a radical change," said John Muckler, who has been around so long he once coached John Brophy, the former Leafs coach who was himself more than seventy years old when he coached me a few years ago. At age seventy-one, Scotty Bowman, the all-time winningest coach and regarded as one of the game's most beautiful minds, took it a step further and sponsored his own list of radical changes, including the addition of two new lines at the top of the circles, four-on-four in the last five minutes of a game, and three-on-three in overtime. Perhaps the game's most famous other brain, Ken Dryden told a hockey symposium in New Brunswick that hockey needs a "complete, thorough, ambitious and fundamental review of all aspects of the game and we need it now." When so many of the longest-serving patriarchs and brightest minds of the game are leading the push for major change, it says something, something hard to ignore. How can someone like me hide resistance behind the name "traditionalist" when the men who built that tradition, and thrived in it since before I was born, are themselves for radical reform? "It's tough to make some of the changes that have been proposed, but we have to be bold," said Jarome Iginla.

So far, some significant changes have been made. This of course started with a new CBA – ending the 301-day "cold war" that threatened the sport and establishing a more stable financial footing for the game, reducing the financial discrepancies between teams, and moving to create a "Groundbreaking Owner-Player Partnership" for the future. Just bringing the game back brought enormous relief to fans (as well as those in the industry)! And additional excitement was added through the return of Gretzky as a coach, eighteen-year-old phenom Sidney Crosby's entrance into the league, and a new press and marketing push headlined by the ad campaign "my NHL." Among the off-ice changes, novel player movement that saw small-market teams land big-ticket players excited fans in those cities. On the ice, there was finally to be a response to long-time pressure for change. Meetings were held to consider potential rule changes to increase excitement, selected people were invited to give input; scrimmages were held with amateur players using radical rule differences, and intriguing pictures of novel "bow"-shaped nets surfaced. Out of this, "a package of rule-changes that accentuates offense and maximizes the excitement and entertainment of NHL hockey" was selected for 2005–06. The changes adopted included reducing goalie pads by an inch (and other parts totalling "11%"), and increasing the end zones by four feet at the expense of the neutral zone. The "tag-up" offside rule would be put back in. The two-line pass would be eliminated, as it is in U.S. amateur, NCAA, and international hockey. Shootouts would decide tie games, as pro hockey's minor leagues, the AHL (AAA) and ECHL (AA), have done. A strict crackdown on hooking, holding, and interference was promised. And a few other items. Through the 2005–06 pre-season, those changes have made it from on paper to on the ice, and the game looks to be better for them.

This program of change should help contribute to a strong initial rebound for the game, and create some interesting sidebars as the new changes and other alternatives are debated around the game. And some of these changes should produce truly historic achievements if they can be sustained. But there are more tests left ahead. "It's hard to predict the Canadian viewing public's habits, but I would guess that early on, the ratings will be pretty significant," said TSN hockey analyst Bob McKenzie. "Whether that holds . . . a lot of it will have to do with the product. If . . . the games are exciting . . . I think there's a chance for them to stay high. If after a month, it's the same old, same old, I think we'll lose some people." In the mid- to long run, in a few months or a few years, when what the Canadian Press called the "honeymoon period" is over, the "longer-term impact of the [lost season] is unclear," it said. Hockey fans had learned how to live without the game. "If [after all that's happened] they don't make it better for the fans and more affordable and a more exciting game, then shame on everybody," Jeremy Roenick said. "No, it won't be a shame," Kevin Roberts of the *South Jersey Courier Post* said, "It will be worse. It will be a case study in how to kill off a good thing." That may be an overstatement, but with the internal challenges, and all the external trends mentioned earlier, sports professor Andrew Zimbalist of Smith College said, "hockey is going to have a long, uphill struggle."

For preserving the positive momentum of the return, and ultimately raising our game to its potential, a number of issues remain within the game. Beyond a potential cooling-off period during the lockout layoff, key on-ice objectives of reducing injuries and violence remain to be addressed. Within the conduct of competition, a number of important but less-obvious items remain as well. As far as the excitement level in the game, a gap remains between our improved game and the exhilarating game of the '80s we dream of having back, the game that is possible, that can fuel the breakthrough to wider audiences the sport has craved for years. Off the ice, fundamental relationships within the sport will need to be nurtured over the years to come. A great start has been made, but more needs to be done. World-class marketing and positive press are a great complement to, but no substitute for maintaining that momentum by continuing to change and build solid strong fundamentals in the on-and-off ice domains of the sport. That is the challenge at hand.

The good news is, among the changes, and perhaps most important among them, was a new openness and commitment to improving the game. As well as – symbolized by new improvement committees that included players – a level of co-operation toward it unprecedented in recent memory. Underscoring that point was the league's new marketing slogan replacing the old one, "Game On," not with "Game Back On" but "It's a Whole New Game."

WHICH CHANGES?

But what changes should be made? "Basketball has its three-point play that rewards teams for taking risks on offence. Why don't we have that? . . . It's as simple as asking 'is it a viable alternative and will it enhance the game,'" Colin Campbell told reporters. "What will be the 'forward pass' of our future?" Ken Dryden asked. We've got to get it right. Making the wrong change delays getting the right one, and sometimes makes things worse. Making the wrong change can cause frustration and anger for those people caught in the middle, and can result in a backlash and a loss of support when we finally get it right. The seamless glass installed in the '90s to aid spectator sightlines is a good example. The hardness and inflexibility of the new glass was accused by many of contributing to player concussions, including ones suffered by all-stars Michel Goulet, whose career was ended, and Mike Modano. And so the seamless glass had to be taken back out. For any or all of these reasons, we have to get the changes right.

There are certainly no shortage of answers and opinions abounding out there. Journalists have plenty – argued in columns, listed in periodicals, and debated on TV. Players, managers, and "expert" commentators hold a variety of opinions too. Journalists sometimes accuse hockey people of letting the truth be blinded by vested interests or muted by fear of reprisals. Players sometimes accuse the media of expressing their opinions too freely and too often without having enough of a stake in the outcome to do so responsibly. One hockey "expert" will disagree with another hockey "expert," one media member with other colleagues. And then there are diehard fans with their own beliefs and estimations, developed from downloading those "expert" opinions and adding in their own experience and judgment. And beyond them is the great ocean of the public, whose relative wisdom and opinions run the full gamut of possibilities.

And many of the more oft-repeated "solutions" are actually not the solutions some might believe them to be. Let me use an example that was a popular suggestion and that has in fact been adopted by the NHL for the 2005–06 season: "eliminating the red line." Some, including some "experts," touted this as the optimal way to open up a boring, bottled-up, defence-oriented game. The change was to eliminate the rule that barred a team from making a "two-line" pass from behind their own blue line to beyond the centre red line, in which case the play would be blown dead with a whistle. The thought among supporters of this change was that eliminating this rule would spread the players out more, especially in the crowded neutral zone, and allow players to carry the puck through or make exciting long passes that instantly shift a team from defence at one end to offence at the other. Look at the Olympics, and U.S. college hockey, proponents said, they don't have the red line, and the game is more exciting. But although they may have seen more exciting games in those places at times, and in the NHL this season, the absence of the red line couldn't have been the reason.

The proof is not far away: there are U.S. college teams whose players are at similar skill levels to pros, and that play the same defensive style of hockey – with no red line – and it still works. And they do it with smaller-sized players and on a bigger-sized rink, and in some cases it has worked even better than in the pros! I've seen this first-hand from having played college. In 2003–04, the NCAA circuits my school plays in, where several teams play that style, had goals-per-game of 5.34 (ECAC) and 5.36 (Hockey East). That's not far off the NHL's 5.14 that year – and it was with only *some* of the college teams playing that style. Cornell, the New Jersey Devils of the NCAA, has had GAAs of 1.26, 1.90, 1.34, 1.73, and 2.18 going back the last five seasons. "People talk about the red line. I watched it for years scouting in [U.S.] college and it doesn't do what people say it does," St. Louis Blues GM Larry Pleau said.

The same thing was evident during the lockout year (2004–05) in Europe. NHL players played with no red line on even bigger international-sized rinks, and the story didn't change. The goals-per-game were 5.37 in Finland, 5.66 in Sweden, 5.36 in the Czech Republic, and in the Russian Superleague – arguably the best – just 4.65! "It's a bad call," winger Slava Kozlov said playing in his hometown of Voskresensk. "Every team plays the trap. You have four or five guys waiting at the blue line. They should bring back the red line. The game is too slow." Leafs coach Pat Quinn, watching the games from Europe, agreed: "We're not going to open up the ice as a lot of people think by taking out the red line. You're worried about the trap and defensive systems . . . and they're worse than we are."

How could that be? Well, a team can still block off the neutral zone with players, the only difference is that instead of playing the "neutral zone trap" from the top of the faceoff circles back to the red line, they play it from the blue line back to the other blue line (using the offside call instead of the two-line pass). Turnovers occur slightly farther back, so that not only is Team A still unable to get through, but Team B is now farther away from generating offence on the counterattack. As a result, it causes even more of the game to be played in the neutral zone and farther away from the offensive net. Also, it is almost impossible to mount an aggressive forecheck. Your opponent can now float their forwards at the far blue line waiting for a pass without having to worry about being called for two-line pass. So you have to keep your defencemen back out of the forecheck to prevent a breakaway against. If you send forwards on the forecheck, all the opposition defence have to do is shoot it by them without even thinking, and they're out of their zone. This kills the efficacy of any offensive forecheck, which means if teams want to win, they are induced to sit back in the neutral zone trap.

Sure, some college games are more exciting than pro, but that's because not as many college teams play these defensive systems. It's a different culture, with less importance on winning and more on fun and development, sustained by "tenured" coaches that don't get fired, and a captive audience that is always there, win or lose. Also, players play these systems less diligently at the college level because they need to find a way to stand out for pro scouts watching, not fit imperceptibly into a seamless defensive machine. The 2002 Olympics were exciting because of the supercharged patriotic atmosphere, the attacking style the teams simply *chose* to use, and the extra room to make plays on the bigger Olympic rink size. It wasn't because there was no red line. "Go back to the [1998] Olympics and watch the Czechs play the Russians in the gold medal game," Larry Pleau suggested to those dubious, referring to the 1-0 win by the Czechs in a game that featured some of the best offensive talents on Earth. "You talk about less chances and no scoring, go back and watch that game." In the 2005 pre-season, NHL teams appear unused to the change, so the better game on display is essentially what we'd see if the red-line removal hadn't been part of the package of changes. However, as the season goes on, more teams will figure out how to play with it, and some of the modest gains in the sport may, if anything, diminish. We need a different answer for how to make the game more exciting.

For all of us, the objective is the same: improving the game's situation as much as possible as fast as possible, in ways that are practical, lasting, and faithful to the integrity of the game. Searching for solutions is the present task. But sorting through the maze of confused and conflicting observations, opinions, interests, and ideas to try to find the right ones can get really muddy. And in the end, the right solutions can't be counted on because of who thinks of them, or who espouses them, or how popular they are, or how painless they are, although all these things can to some degree be factors. The only reliable method is to clarify priorities, get clues by analyzing past and present experience, and draw observations. Then apply logic to the observations, and from thought-experiments draw conclusions. And then we test them on the ice. Ultimately we will know the right solutions are the right solutions because they work (although unfortunately no book can implement that). The challenge of finding them, the desire to test them – in the hope of enjoining and building upon the work begun of raising our game and leading it to realize its potential – that's what this book is about.

FIRST PERIOD

THE THRILLS OF THE GAME

"We could go up and down, lose 6-4 and you'll have a good time and I'll be out of a job in a year. My job is to win. If you want offence and excitement, go watch basketball."

— Minnesota Wild coach Jacques Lemaire

"The game sucks. I wouldn't pay to come watch. The whole style of the game is terrible. There's no flow to any game at all."

— Veteran all-star winger Brett Hull

"'Tis the sport to have the enginer hoist with his own petard."

— Shakespeare, *Hamlet*

PROLOGUE

Imagine a team of guys skating on a sheet of ice inside a wooden cage, flying and dancing around at full speed, while simultaneously handling a puck with great skill and shooting it at high speeds. Imagine them doing this while having to avoid opposing players coming at them, who are allowed to run into them with full force. And if they get by them, they come face to face with a masked goalie guarding a net. It almost sounds unbelievable, too exciting to be true, but that's hockey in pure form, an athlete's dream come true, an entertainment watcher's too. Fast, flowing, frantic, nonstop, full-out action from end to end. The suspense of being at any moment a split second away from a goal, a dazzling move, a tremendous body-check, or an amazing save. Such a wide wealth of thrills involved: from mad rushes, tic-tac-toe passing plays, satisfying hits, diving defensive plays, to blazing shots and eye-popping stops. Put it all together and you have a game that can be literally captivating. As both player and spectator, I can remember great games where the action was so continuous you actually needed something to calm you down afterwards! In a sense, take any other sport, and change it to make it more exciting, and you end up with hockey. For example, take soccer, freeze the field to make it faster, give the players sticks to free up their feet to fly, shrink the nets so the goalies always have a chance, and you have hockey: at its best, the perfection of sport.

But somehow, in recent years, to many people, professional hockey became boring. The picture described above started to seem like a fantasy that couldn't have been real (that is, until one watched older games replayed on TV during the lockout). The excitement the game was born with found its way in chains. Part of the effect of those chains was parity: close games, tight standings. Some may have thought that would be a good tradeoff and cultivate more fans. It didn't work out that way – beyond the novelty or the glow of winning, new fans were not hooked by the game itself; and old fans were turned off by the stifled style. We had to sell the sport itself. That was also consistent with what we knew of other sports: The NFL had plenty of blowouts but full stadiums and a multibillion-dollar-a-year TV deal. Baseball was built on the backs of dynasties, basketball on the wings of superstars like Michael Jordan, superstars that in hockey were held back from shining.

As hockey emerged from its lockout, a consensus was clear: restoring the thrills to the game was a key part of restoring and raising our game.

Bobby Orr takes off on one of his spectacular end-to-end rushes, in an era when defenders had less size and speed, leaving puck carriers more space and time. (*London Life-Portnoy/Hockey Hall of Fame*)

CHAPTER 3

UNLOCKING ALL OF THE GAME'S EXCITEMENT

TRAPPED IN THE TRENCHES

In recent years, hockey's style of play changed. The exciting elements of the game that we treasured in bygone eras – through an Orr rushing from end to end, a Lafleur making a mad dash, a Gretzky pulling up and making an incredible pass, a Lemieux turning hapless defenders inside out – disappeared. A suffocating style set in, took hold of the game, and choked these pleasures out. What was left was a game of restricted movement and flow of play, few scoring chances, and few goals. "Listen to anyone, the NHL has never been worse," Sun Media's Mike Ulmer wrote in the throes of it. "It is colourless. It is boring. Goal-scoring totals are as svelte as supermodels."

Whatever your taste in excitement – breakaways, end-to-end rushes, dekes and moves, spectacular saves, or open-ice hits – all of it became few and far between. In their place was a ton of outlet passes, neutral zone turnovers and regroups, dump-ins and dump-outs, mucking along the boards, and scrambles in the slot – not real exciting stuff. In all, there seemed to be little pace, little space, few (clean) hits, and not enough action.

Fans didn't like what they were seeing. Forced off the ice by injury, I was able to slip into the skin of a fan and see what they saw. In three hours of seated attention, there were few excitements. When they occurred, the effect on the crowd was visible, audible, palpable; and that only made it sadly clear how rare the thrills were. In the old days, I remembered going to Maple Leaf Gardens when we were lucky enough to get tickets, and those exciting moments seemed to happen every shift. In the new game, partisan rooting and suspense regarding the outcome still could be compelling, and the game was never as boring as some said (it still had a lot more action than baseball or golf, for example), but it was certainly not what hockey used to be or could be. What was, when I was a kid watching the pros on TV, essentially a contest of who could best take the other by storm had been transformed into essentially trench warfare on ice, with the painted lines as the trenches, and the players the barbed wire.

On the ice, players weren't delighted with the change either. They played the style they were playing because it worked, because coaches expected them to, and because that was their job. How many times did players say "I know it's boring hockey, but we have to play it"? Joe Nieuwendyk said last season: "[They] play a high-risk, high-reward game. It might be exciting for the fans, but we don't want to get into that. I'd much rather have a 5-2 win and tighten up defensively." During Calgary's playoff run, top-line centre Craig Conroy said, "We want to be able to win every game 1-0. That's our team philosophy. That's our game, and that's the way you win in the playoffs. We have to play a defensive game." The competition and pressure to perform would always be intense, engaging, addictive in a way, but hockey's style of play itself was no longer exhilarating, but static and wearing. "It's a wonderful game with wonderful players, and it's turned into a snail's pace out there. . . ." Brett Hull said. "It's not a lot of fun . . . As much as it's a game, it's not a lot of fun to play any more."

Objective facts confirmed subjective observations: In what many believe was the most exciting decade of hockey, the 1980s, goals-per-game averaged more than 7 every year, 7.63 for the decade. That crept down to 6.19 in the 1990s, basically in steady decline, and in the new millennium it has dropped farther, down to a puny 5.3. Over the five seasons from 1981–82 to 1985–86, the Edmonton Oilers by themselves averaged 5.29 GPG, more than the game average of both teams *combined* in the NHL in 2003–04 (5.14). The Oilers' average of 5.58 in 1983–84 is more than both teams combined averaged from 1996–97 to 2003–04. In the last full season, the highest-scoring team in the league was Ottawa with 262 goals. That would have made them the lowest-scoring team in the league in 1985–86. The league's leading scorer, Tampa's Martin St. Louis, finished last season with 94 points, second place was 87. Compare that to Gretzky's 215 points in 1985–86.

Meanwhile, only twelve players in the whole league managed the standard of a point-per-game, and the three winners of the Rocket Richard Trophy for most goals fell far short of the benchmark of 50 goals, coming in at 41. No one scored 60 goals in a season since Mario Lemieux and Jaromir Jagr did in 1995–96; Gretzky once scored 92. Last year, Flames netminder Miika Kiprusoff led the league with a goals-against-average of just 1.69, three goalies were below 2, and the league average was 2.41, which might have won you the Vezina for best goalie in Billy Smith's day. Toronto's Ed Belfour had 10 shutouts in just 59 games, eerily reminiscent of George Hainsworth's signatory shutout feat eighty years ago. Then the playoffs began, and it got worse: the goals-per-game went down to 4.42. If you factor in all the overtime periods, the figure is even lower, translating roughly to a comparable 4.24. The goals-against-average league-wide in the playoffs was down to 2.02, which might have got you considered for the Vezina in the season that had just ended! In the Cup Final, expected by some to be a high-scoring affair, the goals went down even farther, to a microscopic 3.86 per game (just two for the winning team!), and an average of just 24.4 shots per team per game. Throughout the playoffs, a sad new rule took shape: first goal wins. The team that scored the first goal won seventy of the eighty-nine post-season games. That's a nearly 80 per cent success rate, and astonishingly it covered all seven games of the Cup Final.

Then came the World Cup, boasting the world's best players. But some of the key stats only got worse again. The team that scored first was an incredible 17-1-1 in the tournament, a 90 per cent success rate. Goals-per-game in the tournament were just 5.47, and only 4.64 in the games played in North America! Canada's Martin Brodeur finished the tournament with a mind-boggling 1.00 GAA and a .961 save percentage (which means he saved more than 96 per cent of all shots on him!). Objective statistics on scoring chances, odd man rushes, and other similar gauges of excitement aren't available, but would show similar patterns of decline. Not surprisingly, TV ratings went down with them. In Canada, the audience for the final game was about two-thirds smaller than it had been two years before for the Olympics. It was lower than the number that watched the same year's Canadian Football League Grey Cup. In the United States, ratings for the tournament were an anemic 0.4 (just 349,000 households), among the lowest in sports.

C.S.I.: HOCKEY

So how did a game that was fire on ice fall into a pit of mud? There are a lot of theories and hypotheses about why the game became that way, held by various people outside the game, and while I can understand how these might seem right from those vantage points; some of them are contradicted by the facts. One of the most popular misconceptions was that the game became boring because expansion diluted the talent pool and the league was filled with a bunch of pluggers. In reality, the skill level of players in the league has only become better with time. *Sports Illustrated*'s Michael Farber noted, "The general skill level of players has improved considerably since the so-called Golden Age of the 1950s." Al Strachan explained further: "In recent years, the talent pool has grown at a level far greater than that of previous years – and far greater than the rate of expansion. Europeans are taking to the game more than ever . . . It might not be easy to see it on a year-to-year basis, but if you think of the game 10 years ago and compare it to today's, you'll find that the players are much bigger, yet they're faster, stronger, and in far better condition. If you think the talent is diluted, name a player who doesn't skate well. Name a player who doesn't have a good shot. Or can't pass. Even the enforcers can do all those things. If they can't, they don't stay in the NHL. The talent level is simply too high." He's right. The old pros have said so too, time and time again, everyone from Orr to Gretzky. Step on the ice with these "pluggers" and you'll quickly understand. There have been more people playing, more countries playing, and better skill development methods than in generations before. There are tons of hidden stars nobody knew were there in recent years, because the style of play restrained them from shining. The more we can open up the style of play, the more that mistaken belief will happily be discarded. That, I can guarantee. Also, the fact one could see (as I did during the lockout) junior games – for example – featuring players with obviously less developed skills, yet games that were often more exciting, shows that skill deficiency simply could not have been the reason.

Nor was the problem what some others believed, conversely: that the players in the modern NHL are so skilled, that defensive players had no weaknesses for offensive players to exploit, so that an overabundance of skill turned the sport into a static game of waiting for mistakes. Proof that couldn't have been correct was available by recalling examples like the Canada Cup '87 or more recently the 2002 Olympics, where you had the world's very best players against the very best and the games were super-exciting. Uninspiring pro hockey wasn't a product of the calibre of the players.

Was it a question of the passion of players? Were the modern game's "millionaire" players lazy or disinterested? Most certainly not! In recent years, more players have worked harder than ever to keep those big salaries they earn. The business of being a pro athlete has gotten a lot more serious since the days when stories were told of the legendary partying of Babe Ruth, and even over recent decades. Players have had to take the term *professional* to new levels: strict diets, health supplements, nutritional consultants, personal trainers, and intensive off-season training with off-ice workouts two or three times a day, and few breaks, are just some examples. NHL players know there are hundreds of aspiring replacements in numerous leagues just below them, waiting for them to slip, to be lacklustre, for any opening to take those million-dollar jobs. There is more pressure than ever from the Big Business operation above them to perform. On the ice, the competition among teams has been more evenly matched and the races tighter than ever. Anybody who thinks players were disinterested should step on the ice during a playoff game (for which the players do not even receive salaries): they would be in for a rude awakening!

Was inflated goalie equipment behind it? It didn't help, but the issue was more than just "low scoring," it was "boring." If the game remained the same, but a few more shots went in, people would still not have been satisfied; whereas, if there were dynamic moves and frequent chances, but goalies making great saves, the game witnessed would have been far more exciting. So the principal issue, in terms of excitement, is not goals, but the character of play. It's the amount of chances generated, *and how*, as people like Colin Campbell and Martin Brodeur have pointed out, rather than the percentage of shots that a goalie misses.

In that case, some people might argue, it must have been the coaches' fault – for ruining hockey by demanding a dull, predictable, mistake-avoiding style their personality must have preferred or their desire for control required. But the problem with that is, that style was working. That's why it spread across the league and beyond in the first place. Coaches were just doing what worked, which it was their job to do. If it didn't work, they would have had to abandon it, or else then we could blame them. But since it was working, we can't ultimately fault the coaches.

So what was the real reason behind it? The overwhelming cause of the transformation of the style of play in recent years has been a triple combo of: bigger faster players, plus defensive schemes, plus obstruction-harassment, which equals no room to do anything. These three things work together with a negative synergy the same way poor diet, lack of exercise, and high stress compound each other in contributing to hardening of the arteries and heart disease. Players are much bigger and faster and more mobile than ever before. For example, in 1952, the average NHL player was 5'10¾" and 175 pounds. In 2003, the average player was 6'1" and 204 pounds. A few years ago, I was at a sports banquet at my old high school, St. Michael's in Toronto. One of the students' parents at my table near the back asked who some of the people up front were that people were shaking hands with. "And who's the shorter fellow?" they asked. "Actually, if you were to go up there, you'll see he's not that short," I said. "That's Senator Frank Mahovlich." The parent who had grown up idolizing Mahovlich and his mates could not get over the sight of the Big M standing next to current NHL defencemen John Jakopin (6'5" 240 lbs.) and Andy Sutton (6'6" 235 lbs.) Players have indeed gotten very big now, and they continue to get bigger. They have grown an average of two inches and sixteen pounds in the last twenty-seven years. In my career, at one point, I played forward on a line where all three players were close to six-foot-four and weighed more than seven hundred pounds combined – without equipment. It was almost comical to see the problems it caused the opposition. And as Leafs legend Doug Gilmour and others have pointed out, perhaps more significantly, player equipment (not just goalie equipment) has proportionally grown far more than even the players have.

In addition to size, speed has increased. Modern NHLers skate up to thirty miles per hour, perhaps two-thirds faster than in Rocket Richard's era. Further, as Ken Dryden has emphasized, shift lengths have progressively dropped from about two minutes apiece in the 1950s to a little over one minute in the 1980s, to an average of about forty seconds today. This means players are travelling full out to human capacity at all times.

Combine the growth of players' size and speed with defensive team systems like the "neutral zone trap," which was broken in by the New Jersey Devils in 1994 and is now played by every team in the league at times, and another partnered system for the defensive zone. Working together, they make sure everyone and everything is covered and cut off. Now mix in the hooking and holding ("obstruction"), and crosschecking and slashing ("harassment"), which exploded in the late '80s to early '90s and thereafter spread across the league. Obstruction-harassment stifles and neutralizes skill and in recent years took away what little chance remained of offensive players finding openings or beating people one-on-one to create chances or excitement. "Obstruction is something new in hockey," Dryden wrote, deriding its effects on the game in an editorial for the *Globe and Mail* in spring 2004. All in all, Mario Lemieux said, "it's totally different," referring to the modern game versus when he came into the NHL in 1984. "The athletes are a lot bigger and stronger and faster. And the coaching is better. The goaltenders are way better than before. The pace of the game alone is very quick. The average height of a player is probably six-two or six-three now compared to about five-ten. The ice surface stayed the same, but the players got bigger." The result is crowded ice: you try to move, but there are people everywhere. There's not enough room or opportunity on the ice to make exciting plays. The game got caught in a "squeeze" composed of three things: the size and speed, the defensive systems, and the obstruction-harassment. This "squeeze" is not the "neutral zone trap," but includes "the trap" as one of the defensive systems employed within it. The point of the "squeeze" is, when you don't have the puck, to force the opposition who have it into the least dangerous areas, then gradually "take away time and space" until they can do nothing further, and they turn it over. And it's worked.

The result has been an overwhelming advantage to the defence, neutralizing offence, chances, and excitement. Played this way, hockey becomes a game of positioning and mistakes (much like a defensive football game) rather than skill and moxie, like it should. To one watching a game from a bird's-eye view, it may seem questionable that there is no space – it may seem like there is lots of open ice down there. But most open ice is irrelevant to the play. For the players on the ice, only certain space is "in play" at any given time. It's like the movie *The Truman Show*, where there's sunny skies all around, but a little rain cloud follows overhead of Jim Carrey's character wherever he goes: If you imagine being the puckcarrier down on the ice and how the play would look from there – or with those helmet-camera shots on TV, you can actually see – space is a lot tighter.

At the end of the chapter is a diagram of what an offensive player is up against in the neutral-zone trap (it's hard to depict the other parts of the "squeeze" – size and speed, and obstruction – with Xs and Os!). As a player tries to carry the puck up ice, he is funnelled to the boards then checked, producing a turnover (see Trapped, page 98). If he had a slight opening, it would be closed by the obstruction. Teams wait for a mistake to get an odd-man rush on transition and capitalize on the mistake, or they soft-dump the puck by the other team's trap, try to fight to regain control of it along the boards in the zone, and then run a pick to spring someone free or throw it at the net and crash the net. Voila, the hockey complained about as boring. In the zone, the defensive team system, we can call "the vice" – where the play is pushed to the corner, the puckcarrier's support options closed in on, and then the screws simply tightened (aided by latching onto the puckcarrier with obstruction-harassment), until the puck pops out, and the defence sends it out of the zone, ending the scoring threat.

In the past, able to be revisited through old games replayed on "classic" sports channels or during the recent stoppage, NHL hockey was not like this. But things changed, and changed enormously.

This is not to say that "the squeeze" was the sole and exclusive cause of a lack of excitement in pro hockey in recent years. There have been other minor causes. For one, improvements in the quality of NHL coaching mean that almost all teams now employ the best available strategies of the day, which lately were the defensive ones mentioned.

Many players have complained, too, about poor ice quality, especially in certain places where arenas overbooked for other shows hurt ice maintenance, or at certain times such as the playoffs when the hot outdoor temperatures can wreak havoc on ice-making. Like

Tampa in June, for example. "It was awful. It's not an excuse because both teams have to deal with it. But it's definitely a factor in the game," Lightning defenceman Dan Boyle said after the first game of the 2004 Cup Final. According to ESPN's E.J. Hradek, "Most people asked, in both dressing rooms, felt the same." Flames coach Darryl Sutter said, "As the period goes on, it's really tough. . . . We couldn't do anything with the puck. You have to deal with it, but you wish it was better."

There are also too many games, given how gruelling pro hockey is today with the physicality of the game and all the travel. And that makes for some unavoidably tired, lifeless games. In 2003, disappointed fans in Toronto watched their team get blown out in Game 7 after a hard-and-close-fought series with the Flyers. Exhaustion was the obvious culprit. NHL teams today play eighty-two games in a season. Compare that to college, where there are about thirty-five, or European pro hockey, where the various leagues have around fifty. Further, the strain induces coaches to adapt a style that is sustainable over a long haul, especially in the playoffs, and that means, yes, "the squeeze."

But in spite of these other factors, by far and away the over-whelming issue with respect to excitement is the "squeeze"-trifecta of big mobile players, defensive schemes, and obstruction-harassment clogging the ice surface so that the game's finer elements are choked out. This is what has been responsible for dramatically altering the game of hockey from its roots and exciting potential, and "ruining it," as people say, by creating a situation where offensive initiative is penalized and static defence is rewarded. Understanding how these three elements work together to stifle excitement is key to the quest for the game to break free.

UNCHAINING THE GAME

What can be done about the issue of the style? The squeeze has been strangling the sport like a constrictor. And since the style of play is something so fundamental to a sport, not surprisingly, a lot of hockey's other issues are tied into this as well. Solving it quickly and thoroughly is essential for the game.

At this point, thankfully, opposition to action has dwindled, and the time for waiting for clear to become clearer, or for hoping and tinkering have passed. The NHL has committed itself to a program of improving the excitement in the game, and announced changes aimed at doing just that, beginning with the 2005–06 season. Perhaps more importantly, it seems a large majority of players (as confirmed by polls), managers, and executives – as well as the fans, media, and former players who have been calling for it for years – are now behind the initiative. The sport has taken promising and important steps.

Beyond this, the question remains what the solutions themselves are. During the meetings and debate over what steps to take, an incredible number of suggestions have been put forth, thrown around, and considered. Some are bigger changes than others, some are more radical than others, some are more popular than others, but the most important thing is what they will do.

Let's first start with the changes actually adopted and implemented for 2005–06:

- Calling the illegal obstruction-harassment: This is by far the biggest and most far-ranging item in the package promised by the NHL. And it involves no change to the rules of the game, just better enforcement of the existing rules – ensuring it is faithful to the basic and historical nature of the game that long-time hockey fans believe in. If the NHL can successfully remove all this hooking, holding, interference, slashing, and cross-checking from the game – allowing players to try to make skilled plays without being impeded – the game should definitely be more exciting.

- Shrinking goalie pads and equipment: This is another good step, as reductions have indeed been needed for equipment that grew far beyond protective needs. It should provide some added goals, and added excitement through more plays (such as a player shooting from off the wing) qualifying as scoring chances. But even scoring chances themselves are only one part of the game, and the reductions announced are not huge, so alone, this is just one small piece of the puzzle.

- Eliminating the red line (the two-line pass call): This was, for many people, a "radical" change – something that had never been part of the NHL game. And the NHL surprised many critics by having the courage to make such a radical change. That should be lauded, and no one should lose sight of that. As far as this particular rule itself, however, I don't think it is the answer some may have thought. It provides more space depthwise in the neutral zone, but none laterally, which is the bigger issue as far as clogging the ice to stop rushes. There might be a few "home run" passes for breakaways, especially early in the season before defencemen adjust, but in the long run, as I explained in detail in the last chapter, it may prove somewhat detrimental by eventually discouraging teams from forechecking, and *forcing* them to sit back in the defensive trap more than before. Proof of that comes from leagues where no red line has always been the standard: I experienced it playing college hockey in the United States; and to those who watched European pro league games on TV during the lockout, it was evident there (with NHL players, and despite a bigger rink). "You do see that," Ken Hitchcock said. "There's no forecheck."

- Moving the blue lines out from the end boards four more feet: Increasing the offensive zones by four feet should boost powerplays; the very best teams' percentage may go from 20-25 per cent to 25–30 per cent. And especially if more penalties are called in the obstruction crackdown, this should produce more goals. More goals is good. But do people want a lot more powerplay goals? I don't know . . . I imagine about half will and half won't.

- Moving the nets back two feet: In theory, this puts the puck in front of the net more in the offensive zone, but conversely leaves less space behind the net to make a play, so there could be more turnovers on the end boards and play there, or with no red line, defencemen just dumping the puck out to the far blue line to avoid this. That would mean less sustained puck flow, fine breakouts, and speed-rushes, which in my view are part of what's exciting. But in reality, two feet are not going to have much impact positive or negative.

- Return of the tag-up rule: It was eliminated a few years ago as part of an earlier stage of the same effort to try to add skill and excitement to the game. The thought then was to stop players from immediately dumping the puck in and playing a boring dump-and-chase game. Now we are restoring the rule. It never mattered to me one way or the other, but ultimately, whichever is preferred, going in circles can't be going forward.

- Restricting the area in which goalies may play the puck: In most cases, goalies will still be able to play the puck – and that's only fair, because playing the puck is a skill, and an important link between goalies and the rest of the sport they are part of. But there are certain cases where a defencemen going back for the puck is caught in a "sitting duck" situation and can get clobbered and injured; traditionally, goalies have played the puck in these cases. Now if that happens on a "soft dump" in the corner, they won't be able to. And I don't see how these restrictions are really going to add any significant excitement to the game anyway.

- No line changes for a team that ices the puck: This will also create a few more goals over the season as tired defensive players have to stay on for the defensive zone faceoff after icing the puck. But it's not going to produce a huge number of goals. And what we're really after isn't more goals off faceoffs, but more exciting end-to-end action minute by minute.

- Shootout in the event of a tie: Personally, I like shootouts. I've always found them fun to participate in and to watch. On the other hand, I have personally suffered the unthinkable – yes, played for a team (in the minors) whose playoff spot came down to a shootout on the last game of the season – and lost. One alternative would be to hold shootouts before or after games simply as an exhibition or for some separately counted competition (perhaps something like the Molson Cup standings for a game's Three Stars), rather than as a tiebreaker. That way, if shootouts are exciting, you have them *every* game instead of just in tie games, and you could have every player shoot rather than just three (and have them shoot without their helmets so the fans can identify with them more). Otherwise, I have mixed feelings, and in most polls I've seen, fans are split about 50/50 on the idea of shootouts. In that case, I guess tie goes to the shootout!

On the whole, the idea of a "package" of rule changes is that hopefully there's some strength in numbers; but on the other hand, we don't want to sacrifice quality for quantity. There are some good rule changes in here, by far the most significant being the obstruction clampdown. What's good about that one is it directly addresses one of the three components of the squeeze, which has been strangling the game. In the 2005 pre-season, the results have indeed looked good: there have been more skilled plays, more lead changes, and more scoring. Through the pre-season, there have been an average of 17 powerplays per game versus 11 in the 2003–04 regular season, and 6.2 goals-per-game versus 5.2 in the 2003–04 regular season. That's evidence the crackdown is happening, and it's working. The game is more exciting, and fans and media have been pleased with the change. There have been some complaints from players and coaches about the penalties being called, and the consistency of the calls, but overall the reviews from people in the game have also been positive – another good sign. "For the most part, we have noticed a difference in the game," Colin Campbell said. "The real test will come when the games are for real and points are at stake." Indeed, previous intended clampdowns started out strong, only to tail off as the season wore on, games carried higher stakes, and calls were more significant. Will a more resolute campaign this time stay the course, carry it through, and sustain it permanently? Many remain skeptical. But I am optimistic that this time it will. And that's because the lockout seems to have helped everyone recognize the importance and urgency of restoring excitement to the game, and enduring whatever is necessary to see it through. I am worried about subsequent seasons, though, as teams and players will always be pushing on the rules, and will the enforcement still have the focused and determined energy to resist that they have now? The jury is out; we will see.

In the meantime, considering the effect of the whole package of changes, it is unlikely the game will continue to be as much better as the season goes on as it has been through the pre-season and may be at the beginning. Some of the exciting unpredictability that comes from teams not knowing how to play with all these new rules at this early stage will fade as they gradually get the hang of them. Powerplays will drop as players learn to stop taking penalties, and goals-per-game presumably with them. Goalies will get used to their new equipment. Teams will likely hang back more, without the red line. That brings us to the biggest problem – that teams can and do still play the squeeze with these changes. Without obstruction-harassment, it's harder, and perhaps not as ironclad, but it's still effective. Several years ago, I thought eliminating all the obstruction was *the* answer to liberating the game. But notwithstanding the failed attempts in the past, players have continued to grow in size and speed, and coaching has continued to improve since the time when I believed this crackdown was the answer; and at this point, it's clear that even without restraining, teams can still clog the ice with big fast players playing legal defensive systems. For example, a lot of people mistakenly assumed the 2004 Cup finalist Calgary Flames were a clutch-and-grab team, but while they were a stifling defensive team, they actually were below-average offenders at obstruction. This is partly why they were able to stay out of the penalty box better than their opposition, and use that to help win games. The Flames did it with size (especially on defence), speed (especially at forward), and positioning in the system, with a comparatively little amount of obstruction-harassment. And players are only getting bigger and faster, and coaching only better. The campaign against the "O-H" is necessary for several reasons, as we will discuss in the next section; and the game will always be more exciting without it, and players and fans grateful for it. But even in this pre-season – there are, for the first time in a while, lots of elements of the game we want, but still lots we don't. For example, there is more of an offensive-zone puck control game now, but there still isn't the up-and-down, on-the-edge exhilarating game we had in the '80s, and could have now – or even better with the superior training and skill development methods, and players from all over the world of today's NHL. So ultimately we are left with this: in the long run, a sustained clampdown may or may not be realizable (in isolation); and given the trends and circumstances, I don't think it's enough. If people are pleased with the results of the clampdown, that's all the more reason to continue searching for more excitement, continue along the path of opening the game up more.

What can help us do this? What about some of the other things considered by the NHL, or suggested in other fora. Let's look at some of these suggestions, as well:

• Increasing the size of nets: This would have the same effect as shrinking goalie equipment, which was chosen instead. And indeed the goalie equipment reduction is better, because without it, equipment would just be enlarged further to cover slightly bigger nets. If the nets were expanded more than that, it could distort the game, as the nets become out of proportion with the rink. And certainly for goalies, it would fundamentally alter their game, to a game like soccer, where in some cases the netminder *literally* has no chance. "Artificially" adding goals like this would not be ideal.

• Increasing the width of lines: From what I've seen in the AHL where they tried this out (and AHL fans seemed to agree), it yielded no significant benefit.

- No limit on stick curves: Only so much of a curve is beneficial, and more than that is worse. In fact, quite a few players don't even use the maximum curves allowed now. So I don't see how increasing the permissible curve would really help.

- Scotty Bowman's idea of a "stretch line" across the top of the circles: If this idea has been accurately reported, it allows the offensive player to make a pass from beyond this stretch line as though he were already over the blue line. In essence then, what it does is allow the player to easily pass his team's "blue line," taking the two-line pass rule out of play. As such, it is equivalent to removing the red line, whereby there is no two-line pass rule at all. The one difference is the Bowman proposal has an advantage in that it doesn't allow teams to immediately dump the puck to the far blue line from behind their own net, which kills forechecking and almost forces teams to play the trap where there is no red line. It's creative and ingenious, but ultimately it's indeed only a "stretch." That's because while it doesn't *force* teams to play the trap, it nevertheless still *allows* them to, exactly as they can and do with success in leagues where there is no red line: by sitting farther back, and using the back half of the neutral zone (i.e., the icing line and the offside line).

- Moving both blue lines to the top of the circles (the Bruins' idea) or eliminating the blue lines altogether (i.e., no more offside): Indeed, if you're trying to enlarge the depth of the neutral zone, the blue lines are the lines you need to move or remove. The problem is, doing so would ultimately make for a more stationary game with less skating, the ultimate game of dump-down and dump-back. Players would end up stationed at either end of the rink, and you would have a sport something like ping-pong. Several sports, including soccer, water polo, and hockey, felt this was unattractive and tried to avoid this in creating their offside rules. It's an interesting and original idea, but certainly it would make for a sport far from what we know as hockey.

- Eliminating icing: This would be similar to eliminating offside.

- Three points for a win: This idea fails to understand that teams aren't playing defensively in order *literally* not to lose, they're playing defensive hockey as a means to win. Defensive hockey is what wins. Adding to the number of points for a win changes nothing. In addition, I don't like it because there is something not only untraditional but inequitable about unbalancing wins and losses. Three-point wins means a team that loses half of four games has more points (6) than a team that goes undefeated with a win and three ties (5 points). We need to address the style question directly and on the ice.

- No backward passing or no backward skating: Now that's just *weird* . . . (I guarantee no defenceman suggested this one!)

The list could go on – there are an endless number of potential ideas, but just tossing out suggestions is like throwing a net into the water and hoping you come out with a fish. The way this book was written starts with the problem or objective, tries to understand how things work, and seeks to identify that which addresses it. In this case, the target is the squeeze. Taking a closer look at the squeeze, what is it possible to do? We can't legislate a shrinking of players, and we wouldn't want to lessen their speed. Calling a penalty for playing a defensive system like the trap (something along the lines of the illegal [zone] defence rule in basketball) is not practical in hockey, where there are too many different situations and too many variations on the defensive systems to create a clear, fair, and effective rule. In fact, things like that were tried in hockey back in the 1920s when the game had the same kind of low-scoring problem – they were tried in several imaginative variations. None of them worked, and the problem just continued getting worse. One clear and simple idea, the allowing of the forward pass, was what eventually broke the game free from its chains. But in recent years, new ones formed. Of the trio of components behind the squeeze, obstruction-harassment is the only one you can work on alone. But as we saw, even without it, the squeeze can still stand on its other two legs and keep a hold on the game.

But what if we look at their combined effect – which is to clog the ice? Indeed, the bottom line is, there is no room on the ice any more. Can we find an antidote to address that fact? Maybe. There are two ways to improve traffic – build more roads or take some cars off the road. So what if we take one of the two referees and one of the linesmen off the ice (or someone may suggest to take both linesmen off and replace them with some kind of laser line-calls, or off-ice officials)? Well, firstly, I don't recommend this, and secondly, it wouldn't help anyway. These officials are not in the play, so we would not create any space around the puck, we would create space in the opposite empty corner where nothing is happening anyway. As explained earlier, there is plenty of empty ice already, but it is irrelevant to the play at any given time. Meanwhile, removing officials would just invite more obstruction-harassment. So in the end, it would be counterproductive.

What about increasing the ice size? Going to a wider-sized rink would help (The NHL's surface is 85 feet wide, college is typically 90, and international is a 100), but altering rinks doesn't seem to be possible from a practical standpoint. So has said NHL commissioner Gary Bettman on several occasions. Supposing they could be enlarged, how much would it help? Well, if surfaces were widened only a little, say to college dimensions, it wouldn't change much. Alternatively, if they were widened more (to international dimensions), then this is no panacea, as those who have complained about the European game have observed. That's because wide surfaces increase the amount of ice farther away from the net and from scoring chances, and turn hockey into a more localized, more stationary game – detracting from excitement. On balance, bigger rinks would still be a benefit, by creating more space. But the trade-off would get worse with time as players continue to get bigger to fill a marginally wider rink, and meanwhile we would still be stuck with a higher proportion of ice (and play) farther from the nets. So it's not a great option in theory, and in reality, it's been called no option at all: most teams have only recently built new arenas using the existing eighty-five-foot specifications, and according to the commissioner, they can't realistically be changed. The style issue can't wait for the next generation of new arenas, so we must take these realities into account.

After a great deal of thought and evolution of my ideas over the course of my time in hockey, it is now clear to me that the best solution to free all the game's excitement up, and indeed the only practicable way out of the squeeze, is to switch to four-on-four. I arrived at this conclusion from two opposite starting points. On one hand, I started with the excitement issue and heard various ideas on how to solve it, like everyone else. Personally, I started with more "conservative" opinions, watched some of them fail, saw others' flaws and limitations, came to understand what was happening and the way things were going, and over the course of several years arrived at four-on-four as the only option, the last resort that would not drastically change the character of the game, while still solving the problem. On the other hand, I saw teams play four-on-four, and played it myself in game situations, and really enjoyed its dynamism and excitement and unpredictability compared to the rest of the game, so that over time it seemed more and more to me like a great solution to play it all the time. How simple and practical to implement it was as a solution, compared to other ideas proposed, was also compelling. And increasingly, I realized what a host of remarkable side benefits (as I will explain) four-on-four would have on hockey's other pressing problems including injuries, competition, and violence. Here was a one-item stand-alone solution that would unquestionably open up the clogged ice surface, restore an incredible excitement level to the game, and even help other problems – all while being something both familiar and faithful to the essence of the game, and fantastically easy to implement. When what seems the only solution is such an outstanding solution, what more could one ask for?

Of course, some will feel the game must be played with five aside, that this is fundamental to the game's integrity, and that it must be preserved at any cost. However, there is in fact little evidence to support such sentiments. The ultimate and most ironic proof is that the number of players has changed several times already. The first "recognized" hockey game of record featured nine players aside. Then seven-man hockey evolved and dominated for thirty-five years. Only then was the "novel" six-aside game (including goalies) invented to try to improve the game, eliminating the rover, and leaving the five skaters we have today. Presumably opponents of the change said the same things about five-on-five then that opponents of four-on-four would say now: that the game was supposed to be six-on-six, that five-on-five was a distortion, a radical change, that there wouldn't be enough players on the ice, that nobody would like it, and the game would be ruined. It didn't work out that way. The "renegade" league that invented it, the NHA (today's NHL) is the one pro hockey league from the time that survived. And I certainly haven't seen anything written in the literature of years after, or heard any old-timers who were alive for the change as kids clamouring in years past "if only we would go back to six-on-six!" Things change, people accept them, get used to them, and those changes then become entrenched, and become something that inherently "can't" be changed. The long view sees through such claims transparently.

The fact is, growing up, on a rink here, on a street there, we have all played hockey three-on-three, four-on-four, six-on-six, ten-on-ten. We knew what to call it, we knew what to do. It was never really any different, other than how often we touched the puck and how much room there was once we got it. Several amateur recreational leagues (including kids programs) have recently elected to play hockey four-on-four, to enhance enjoyment.

Further, four-on-four has long been part of formal and official hockey – going back more than eighty years to when teams took a man off for penalties – in cases where both teams had simultaneous penalties. And it has been the form of play of NHL regular season overtime since 1999, to overwhelmingly rave reviews and few complaints. Four-on-four is hockey, as much as the rest of the game; it isn't a shootout, it isn't a distortion, it's hardcore hockey – moreso even than powerplays – just one less player aside. It is a natural and commonly existing form of the game.

I understand and respect that a lot of people would be opposed to it. But to purists like me, making the switch to four-on-four is highly preferable to other strange and scarier proposals. And ultimately once we get our head around it, there's no need for it to be a big deal: there really is nothing special about the number five. What is sacred and worth preserving isn't a number, it's the nature and essence of the game. Four-on-four does this. It doesn't distort one component in relation to others, unlike many of the other rule changes that have been considered. The truth we overlook is how the wonderful nature and essence of the game – fast, free-flowing, highly skilled, physical, unpredictable end-to-end action and excitement – has already been changed through bigger players, technology, and coaching into something very different. Four-on-four would only change it back, recapture the essence and basic style that have been lost, return hockey to how it was meant to be played, how it *used* to be played. We should look at it as returning hockey to how it was in its heydays, in the '50s to '80s: players are bigger and faster, so compensate with one less player.

To put it another way, if we were to fixate on numbers, what is important to the integrity of the game isn't a cardinal number of players, but the *ratio* between the space players cover and the size of the surface, because this is what determines the style, nature, and excitement level of the game. A hundred years ago, they found this ratio that created a game both wonderful and unique. For a long time, that ratio called for six skaters, but as the game changed, preserving that critical ratio meant the number of skaters had to change to five. But now players are bigger and faster and cover more ground: so the ratio has become skewed again. Going to four-on-four would in effect restore the ideal ratio. We should preserve the ratio and abandon the number, not preserve the number and abandon the ratio (along with the nature and excitement of the game).

Another way to see it is that, in fact, in a very direct way, the defensive schemes' reliance on overloading the puckcarrier with more than one checker is an implicit admission that there are too many players on the ice, because teams have an extra that they can afford to send on the puck. And so four-on-four should be seen not as a violation of the integrity of the game, but as its restorer; not as a change to the essence of the game, but as its liberator.

"A lot of people are impressed by the openness of four-on-four overtimes and also wouldn't mind seeing an experiment in regulation time. . . . Everyone knows a rink surface established a century ago for smaller players is too crowded for the giants of today," Jim Kernaghan wrote in the *London Free Press*. Indeed, whenever I hear fans or read news columnists raving about an NHL game from the night before – even in the obstructionless 2005 pre-season – it is invariably a game that went into overtime, where the last thing they saw that left such a wonderful lasting impression in their minds was the wildly exciting four-on-four extra period. Not that it's just fans or media. Not long ago, I remember hearing Scotty Bowman say on *Hockey Night in Canada* that he was excited by what he saw from four-on-four, and thought we should try more of it. Recently, he has taken it a step further by officially proposing four-on-four in the last five minutes of regulation, then three-on-three in overtime. That way, it would prove more clearly to doubters that four-on-four, not the no-lose situation of overtime, is most of what makes the overtimes so exciting. Bowman also probably had practical considerations in mind: a gradualized introduction was in fact exactly how the forward pass came in – by zone at first, and with regulations, and ultimately in 1929 across the board, because it was so effective and popular.

Whenever today's games are four-on-four, the action is end to end, and creativity is freed from system straitjackets. The speed of the game picks up, and crowd interest follows; even the fan who doesn't understand the game can sense something has happened – the game has opened up, a chance, a goal could occur in a few seconds. The crowd tension is palpable. It is like when one team is pouring it on, and the crowd rises in anticipation. Only with four-on-four it's both teams, one after the other, constant and continuously, and unpredictably, in succession. Players get going, and fans are amazed at their speed. There is room for skilled moves and exciting one-on-ones. There are opportunities for big open-ice hits, which light up crowds. Chances at one end are immediately followed by chances at the other. And goals, yes, no shortage of goals! Sitting in the stands with fans since being injured, I've noticed it's as if they hold their breath for the entire overtime, and exhale only when it's over.

An entire game four-on-four would be unbelievably exciting; people would watch from the edge of their seats. Games would be awesome. Hockey this exciting isn't a utopian dream: some of us can remember games being like this in the past when the game captured Canada's heart. That excitement has now been crowded out, and only partly let back in with the changes in 2005, but with four-on-four, it can be fully recovered so that in the future hockey can breakthrough in the United States, capture the sporting world's heart, and the sky's the limit. If anything, the NHL would have to worry about *too much excitement* with four-on-four, and might need to sell sedatives at the concession stands! That's a problem most sports and entertainment businesses would like to have!

The reasons why this would work are simple. With four-on-four, there simply is too much room on the ice for the squeeze to be effective, even with big fast players, even with ingenious coaches and their defensive schemes, even with obstruction-harassment. Teams are therefore forced into playing offence and generating their own chances, because they will be surrendering chances whether they like it or not. Four is simply not enough players to clog the ice and trap the puckcarrier, just as if you don't have enough bricks to build a wall, you need a different strategy of defence, likely one that places some of the onus on offence. Four players is not enough to spare an extra and leave somebody open. Four is not enough to collapse around your net and still pressure the puck, taking away time and space for making a play. One mistake leads to a scoring chance, and there is enough room for them to be exposed. One great play leads to a scoring chance, and there is enough room for them to happen.

In a more general sense, it puts more onus on players' complete abilities and less on team systems, fixing a balance that has been out of whack recently. Player and fan alike will love the return of individual creativity to the game. Spectators will better identify with player personalities for their own appreciation and for the benefit of the game. Four-on-four creates room for good things to happen, but doesn't create *too* much room, the way three-on-three would. Four-on-four restores what may formerly have been a perfect balance at five-on-five between offence and defence, between individual and team play, between skill and positioning – before things changed. As former Hartford Whalers coach and TSN expert hockey analyst Pierre McGuire wrote in *Total Hockey* about the introduction of four-on-four overtimes: "Some teams tried to play defensively at first, but that didn't really work because attacking players had too much time and space. That's the beauty of four-on-four: the better players can really utilize their skills. It really gives the game an element of excitement in this era of dominant defensive hockey. Four-on-four also adds an element of athleticism to the game. . . . If you ask the players, I would guess that 90 per cent of them love four-on-four because it gives them a chance to go out and really play, to let their hair down, so to speak. The only way to try playing four-on-four safely is a puck-control game, to deny the other team the puck. But that is also the way to win at four-on-four." Coaches have tried to systemize four-on-four and can't. It's a game that is free-flowing, creative, and exciting – everything hockey should be. The proof is in the play, which we have all experienced or seen, and many would like to see more.

As a solution, four-on-four would reinforce itself in certain ways. By restoring the premium on speed and skilled play, it would ensure that top players continue to play as long as they can. Ironically, four-on-four would also facilitate eliminating obstruction-harassment. With more room, players will be going faster and be harder to obstruct. With fewer players on the ice, it will be easier for referees to see fouls, and because the fouls will more clearly detract from scoring chances, the referees will unhesitatingly make the calls. And the O-H will be less effective to use, because coaches will know it is going to be called more, and because the offensive player still has enough room to make the play despite it. As its advantages diminish, it will be used less. With four-on-four, the obstruction clampdown could probably be achieved at half the strain and twice the results.

In addition, switching to four-on-four would have a variety of side benefits:

- It would reward teams for skilled play, hard work, hustle, and desire, rather than prizing system execution, overcoaching, and other aspects that have dominated in recent years. This would make the players (and fans) happy as the team that seems naturally to "deserve" to win shall.

- It will reduce injuries in general, and dramatically cut down the number of concussions. Collisions are the essential cause of most of them, but with more room on the ice and less static play along the boards, there will be a few more open-ice hits, but far less collisions in total. More room per player means more time to see things coming and more space to get out of the way, and thus fewer collisions and better ability to brace for the ones that remain.

- Four-on-four would encourage all players to have some competence at all aspects of the game. Forwards will have to be able to defend, defenders will have to be able to generate offence. I think this is truer to the spirit of hockey than the overspecialization of recent years.

- Four-on-four would favour a blend of attributes, not just size, which would allow talented players of all shapes and sizes to thrive again.

- A game so exciting it was compelling would draw viewers and cause revenues to skyrocket at a time when they need some rocket fuel to put the lockout behind them and make a new breakthrough. A revamped hockey could fulfill the public's thirst for new, better, and more spectacular entertainments.

What would be the drawbacks? What's amazing about four-on-four is there really aren't any substantial drawbacks. People will say the game is supposed to be five-on-five, but that isn't a drawback, it's an opinion – an opinion challenged by history in which that wasn't always the case, and by present conditions.

Some might worry it will end physical play, an integral part of hockey, but this is completely wrong. I like physical hockey, but not dirty hockey, and in fact, with four-on-four there will be more great pure open-ice bodychecks, more interesting one-on-one physical battles, but less stationary grinding in the corners, stickwork, bumping, and clutching. It will be more of the kind of physical play people like and want and less of the kind they don't want. It will be tough but legal physical play, and I think both players and fans will appreciate it.

Critics will say the players will get too tired, but this makes no sense. Teams could keep the same number of players, but rearrange them into six forward pairs and three defence pairs, or five and four for example. There would be more skating, but less upper-body pushing and physical grinding between heavy bodies, which always wore me out more than all the skating in the world. From my experience, I don't think there's any chance of it being a problem. But if it was, then give teams a few more timeouts, and longer pauses for TV timeouts (which might yield more revenues). In exchange for a more exciting game minute by minute, that is a deal any fan would take in a second.

Some may worry that star players will get on the ice less, making the game less exciting. First of all, I don't believe they would need to be on the ice less, given the above. Secondly, they would be far more free to do a lot more when they are out there, and I think they would eagerly embrace that. Most importantly, there are numerous exceptionally talented players who have been there but whose talents were obscured and hidden in a game that gave them no room to shine. With four-on-four, they would come out. There is nothing remotely resembling a shortage of skilled players. Further, four-on-four would make the game more exciting and amazing at every moment, whether the very top "stars" are on the ice or not. And as Pierre Mcguire said, the vast majority of star players would appreciate four-on-four.

People will say it will place too much of a premium on skating. However, lately there has been too much of a premium on size and not enough on skating with the puck. Size will always be an advantage, just as it was for Gordie Howe on the much less crowded rink of his day, and it would continue to be with four-on-four. This is particularly true because there would be more one-on-one battles, where size is a big advantage. Four-on-four will still prize size, but other things as well. It will put size back in balance with other formerly important attributes of the game from the '80s or before.

Some may predict that teams will just tie up players without the puck so that games become overrun by "shadowing," or become a monotonous one-on-one show. In fact, with more room, it will be harder to tie up people, and if a team guards all of the opposing players too closely and the puckcarrier beats his check (which he'll have more room to do), he'll have an open road to the net. If teams were literally interfering with players including before they even get the puck (which they already do in the playoffs, by the way), then as previously discussed, it will be easier on a less crowded rink for referees to see and call such interference. In the four-on-four portions of the game that are already there and have been for years, such strategies have not succeeded in locking up the action.

But won't four-on-four reduce parity and widen scores, and thus make games less compelling? I don't believe this is correct. Even if scoring margins are wider, in a wide-open game, a team is never out of it. In recent years, a team gets a one-goal lead and the game, by the recent stats, is typically over. With the obstruction clamp-down, this looks to be less true, and fans are enjoying it. Opening the game up with four-on-four would create even more lead changes, more comebacks, more exciting scoring chances and goals, and more entertaining play regardless of the score. When hockey was "on the brink of stardom" at the time Gretzky's Los Angeles Kings made it to the Final and the following year when the New York Rangers won the Cup, hockey was a more wide-open game with much less parity. Since then, parity has increased, and the game has declined. By some predictions, hockey has gone from "the next big thing" to "the next dead thing." We must sell the sport, not the score – just like the NFL and every other successful sport does. Let's focus on making the action compelling, not the score. Otherwise, why play the games, or why play them fairly? We could just make them "virtual," or orchestrate them like pro wrestling! Parity is something that takes care of itself, and it will, because the game has always been one that depends on an entire team, not just the strongest links, but the weakest, and those in between, and how they all work together. So there should be more parity than one might think, maybe even the same as now. Hockey has always been a game, even in the wide-open '80s or the era of any dynasty, that on any given night, the outcome was uncertain – and that's what's essential to sports, not true parity. In fact, some significant parties in the sports market such as major league baseball and ESPN with its approach to selling hockey have clearly preferred dynasties to parity as a foundation on which to market their sports. No matter how you cut it, it's no issue. Go to four-on-four, and don't worry about the score.

But what will we call the positions? If these are our only prob-lems, it's time to count ourselves lucky! Right and left forward; centre goes the way of the rover.

But won't the players just get bigger and fill the rink again? And then we'll have to go to three-on-three? If you understand the math-ematics, you will agree there is little chance of this. A player-per-side is a significant change in the amount of space, that's why this will work in the first place. It will also decrease the premium on player size so there isn't the huge inboard pressure for it to increase that exists now. Some will say that coaches will just adjust and find another way to systemize the game, and close it back down again. But the truth is with enough space, hockey is a game that depends more on individual and collective playing talent than on coaches' systems. That resistance to systemization is what makes hockey so beautiful compared to so many other sports. It took nearly a hundred years of the game for coaches to have the conditions necessary to bottle up hockey. By going to four-on-four, the genie is out of the bottle. No matter how ingenious coaches are, putting that genie back in the bottle is going to be impossible. At least for another hundred years!

Will it work "too well"? Some may complain there will be too much scoring: it will rewrite the record books, and the old records will become meaningless. This is another way of saying the game will be too exciting! People probably thought those same things in the '80s when Gretzky & Co. rewrote the offensive record books thanks to new skills and technologies, better training, and more games. It wasn't a problem, it was simply the most exciting hockey in NHL history. Such concerns could have been raised when Cooney Weiland and others rewrote the record book after the introduction of the forward pass, or Bobby Hull and compatriots with the slapshot and the curved stick. But never were these a problem, and seldom were they complained about. Instead, they were lauded. They were exciting, and they enhanced the game. Lately, the record books have been rewritten in the other direction, by goalies and defensive exploits, again thanks to changed conditions in the game. Conditions are always changing – if you want to separate eras in record books, go ahead – but it makes no sense to leave a game languishing and even risking financial peril because one fears making it exciting will eclipse old figures in a book! Baseball certainly learned this using the home-run record-smashing chase to finally climb out of the shadowy fallout of its work stoppage.

I also don't think four-on-four will be as high-scoring as some people think. Overtime right now is a no-lose scenario, so that is not an accurate measure of goals. It will improve scoring, not to lacrosse-like levels but hopefully back to where hockey scores were in the 1980s, or to what most would say is about the right amount. What it would be is a lot more chances, a few more goals, and plenty of close calls and great saves. What about powerplays? Will they be too significant? There are plenty of options to deal with such issues, including both subtracting players from penalized teams as we do now, or instead giving the opposition an extra player. So we could go five-on-four, then with another penalty five-on-three. Or four-on-three then five-on-three. If it's five-on-four first, the issue is moot because it's the same as the present. If it's four-on-three, maybe that deters penalties better and helps clean up the game. Either way, it is a choice: the status quo, or maybe something better.

"It's too radical." The way the game is played has already radically changed in a short period (about fifteen years) due to all the things cited in this chapter. It radically changed from a fast, free-flowing game into a slow trenchlike game, from a game of talent and creativity to a game of systems and execution, from a game of hard work and desire to a game of coaching and technical adherence. These are all radical changes. But because they happened gradually and on their own, we underappreciate just how radical they were. When things have changed like this, they require a recalibration in response. Four-on-four changes the game back to what it was, to what it is supposed to be, to what we want it to be. It is radical only in comparison to the already radically distorted and substandard style of recent years.

Others agree: Not just some of the game's greatest thinkers, like Scotty Bowman and Ken Dryden, who also advocated it. Not just some of the star players I have heard or talked to whose games it would most liberate. Not just expert commentators and columnists like Pierre Mcguire. But even people you might not expect, people that have made a career out of protecting what they perceive as the integrity of the game. This ought to tell us something. "Of all the solutions I've heard, this is the best one," Don Cherry said. "You wouldn't have to worry about obstruction or trapping." And when

I was talking to Doug Gilmour, who said he was a "traditionalist," at first he was resistant, but later when we were discussing the lockout, he brought up four-on-four on his own as maybe an ideal way for the game to rebound from it. Lamenting how hockey was behind poker and dog shows in TV ratings, and in danger of losing legions from live audiences, he said, "You know what, maybe we do need to go to four-on-four . . . come out with tons of excitement and speed and flow in the game, and really get the players and fans into it." I suggest, and many others who have thought about it agree, that what is truly radical is to leave the game in a state less than what's possible, less enjoyable to fans and players, and potentially endangering franchises or the economic prosperity of the game.

As the supporting words of industry-veterans like Cherry imply, many of the other solutions proposed are at least as radical as four-and-four, while otherwise measuring up a lot worse. They may seem smaller, at first blush, but by distorting one component of the game in relation to others, or injecting new things that have never been part of the game in any form, many of these would change the game more radically than simply playing the same game, but with one less player on an overcrowded surface, as we already sometimes do. It is also riskier to put in things that have never been tried than it is to expand the use of something like four-on-four that has long been part of the game and accepted and appreciated as such.

The only other potential alternative remotely faithful to the integrity of the game, in my mind, is a combination of increasing the size of the ice, completely eliminating the obstruction-harassment (as we hopefully have begun to do), and further reducing the size of goalie equipment (substantially). It would require all three to really improve the game in the way that is hoped. Two, as discussed earlier, wouldn't do it. And even with all three, we would have an inferior solution. The game would be opened up, but not as much. Play would be more localized like in soccer. And we would only buy some time while players grow to fill a slightly wider rink, and the squeeze becomes effective again. Most significantly, such a plan already has three strikes against it: obstruction clampdowns have tailed off before and will be tough to maintain in isolation over the long haul, goalie equipment clampdowns have been similarly ineffectual or insufficient, and bigger rinks have been deemed impossible.

The result is, you come to the realization, as I did, that four-on-four is the only option left. Thus, it is not only a faithful and effective solution, but the only viable solution to get the game itself back to how it was, and make any substantial breakthrough with new or casual audiences. The "NHL has to go to four-on-four," expert commentator Steve Simmons wrote in the *Toronto Sun*. It is "inevitable" within twenty-five years, Ken Dryden said a few years ago. We can either do it now, when it can help the most, or do it later. Why suffer longer, take risks, why delay the inevitable? Especially when what four-on-four promises is so remarkably attractive on every front. That's the beauty of it: we come to it reluctantly, but are then taken by it overwhelmingly. It preserves the integrity of the game, solves any boredom issue with a bang, creates a game so exciting it's compelling, and brings along a whole bunch of unsolicited side benefits: from facilitating the removal of interference, to cutting down on injuries, to enabling teams to reduce payroll without decreasing salaries, to improving ratings and revenues. If the game is to reachieve its past glory or reach its potential, it simply needs to go to four-on-four.

At the same time, there are further improvements that are not necessary but can help supplementarily, such as:

- Trying to improve ice quality: Steps have been taken, including the NHL's hiring of ice expert Dan Craig to assist teams, but those measures could be strengthened. The league can work more with franchises on the one hand and set tougher standards on the other. Standards that carry real ramifications for failures, captured by random inspections or upon complaint. If a team is in breach, they are fined, lose a home game the following season, or suffer some other material penalty.

- Cutting down the length of the season: As many players have suggested, the season is too long and has too many games given the modern game's physical demands. Players these days train all summer and come to camp in shape already; most spots at tryouts are foregone conclusions. If we cut the length of camps and the exhibition schedule, and start the season earlier, and play a few less regular season games, even a little more rest goes a long way to better hockey. This might improve people's perception of the game too, as hockey currently extends into summer, the climax coming when the last thing people are into is games on ice.

A question of timing remains. Should four-on-four be phased in, as occurred with the forward pass, and as Scotty Bowman and Red Wings executive Jimmy Devellano seem to be pushing toward with their proposal? Or would it makes sense, as Doug Gilmour thought, to move to it as soon as possible after the lockout, and use it to put to bed long-time complaints and disillusionment, and break through with casual fans or new fans with a thrilling splash? That's a question I can't answer. I would say "as fast as practically possible," for sure. If that means phasing it in through extended overtimes, and then by period or even five-minute segments of periods at a time, to conquer by degrees the opposition and inertia the idea is bound to have, so be it. Other strategies of gradual implementation could include pre-season games, exhibition games in the midst of the regular season, or setting an advance date of implementation (like say a year) and giving notice (the way cities have recently done with bans on smoking in restaurants and bars), before ushering it in. Then hopefully players, officials, and spectators would have sufficient time to adapt. The longer we wait, the more to lose, the less to gain.

But beyond this, making the change would make the game truly awesome again. The crowded rink that crowds out creativity and excitement would get less crammed, providing some much needed breathing room for the thrills to return. The suffocating style of play would fall away once and for all, and oxygen would automatically flow in through the spirit and skill of the players, restoring the health of the game. Antagonists that predicted hockey's demise would be in for a rude awakening, which would be especially satisfying to hockey enthusiasts. If we are afraid of making mistakes, let us make the mistake of too much excitement, not too little. If we are going to suffocate watching hockey, let it not be from lack of air, but from holding our breath in awe.

TRAPPED

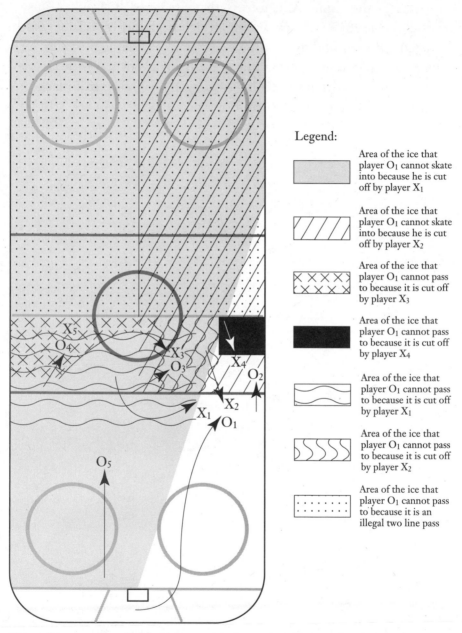

Legend:

Area of the ice that player O_1 cannot skate into because he is cut off by player X_1

Area of the ice that player O_1 cannot skate into because he is cut off by player X_2

Area of the ice that player O_1 cannot pass to because it is cut off by player X_3

Area of the ice that player O_1 cannot pass to because it is cut off by player X_4

Area of the ice that player O_1 cannot pass to because it is cut off by player X_1

Area of the ice that player O_1 cannot pass to because it is cut off by player X_2

Area of the ice that player O_1 cannot pass to because it is an illegal two line pass

Player O_1 comes from behind his net with the puck and tries to head up ice. But the rink is effectively cut off by the other team.

Note: If the red line is eliminated the configuration is similar, except that the trapping team uses their own blue line (the offside call) instead of the red line (two-line pass) to enforce the trap.

EPILOGUE

From a great game whose style had declined to one many said was boring, hockey has started to rebound. The potential was there, the game had been there in the past, it remained there in flashes, and now the commitment was there to open it up again. "I think if we can . . . really give back the game to some of our great players then it's going to be really, really exciting," Mario Lemieux said in support of recent talk of rule changes. With the changes implemented by the NHL for 2005–06, we should see more of the incredible abilities the world's most highly skilled athletes have spent a lifetime building: darting around at high speeds on thin blades on a slippery surface, dangling a puck from a stick like on a string, dodging opponents, dashing in on goalies, trying to deke or drive the puck by them into the net.

But as the game tries to strengthen its popularity, and indeed to make a breakthrough with the wider American public, more is possible. And for those ecstatic with the positive play bursting out with removal of the restraining obstruction, more can be done to free up the excitement in the game.

Removing one skater from the ice aside to play four-on-four is the key to creating too much time and space for the clogging defensive style of "the squeeze" to restrict the sport's natural and inherent speed, skill, creativity, and initiative. A little space in the serpent's coils is the difference between suffocation and escape. Without the squeeze, we would see a game that matches our fondest memories, our highest hopes for enhancing the excitement level in the game. It would arise spontaneously from players finding freedom to manoeuvre and play, much as the benefits from the tight penalty call policy should do by removing actual physical restraining. As a result, the game would be filled with end-to-end rushes, swings of momentum, uninterrupted action – like the great "barnburners" of the past.

For players, this would be an exhilarating game, the triumph of hustle, desire, and inspiration in flight – the kind of game I played as a kid, where winning or losing, shift by shift, you couldn't stop smiling. For fans, it would be the kind of game we recall watching from the edge of our seat, holding our breath for twenty minutes at a time. It would be that electrifying dynamism that in short flashes has made the game of recent years a tantalizing but enigmatic character to new or casual acquaintances – only for the whole game. It would be a vindication of those who believe in hockey.

It's a big change, one that for that reason is hard to accept. It is comparable to the NHL's decision in '28–'29 to introduce the forward pass, which then broke open a suffocated game. It is comparable to the NHL's decision in '43–'44 to add a red line to create a more thrilling game, which lifted the game to new heights of popularity, and old King Clancy called "the biggest change hockey ever made and perhaps the best." Four-on-four is also a big change, but it is also one that, as Ken Dryden said, is "inevitable" in recalibrating for what has become an overcrowded ice, and one that should be immensely positive like the forward pass and red line.

As you watch games this season, keep an eye out for the times when the game is four-on-four, and ask yourself whether four-on-four isn't still the most thrilling part of what should be a new and improved game. And whether you wouldn't mind seeing more of that; whether the game might find it a breakthrough with audiences and in revenues.

SECOND PERIOD

THE CONDUCT OF
THE COMPETITION

"It's the strangest playoff series I've ever played in. On the ice, when we were shaking hands with the Ducks, a couple of their guys told me 'We have no business being here. We didn't deserve to win.' They saw it. They felt it. They didn't feel they deserved to win. What could I say? That I agree with them? We were all in shock. . . . For someone who knows the game and truly watched the series, the guys didn't quit, the guys didn't play soft, the guys didn't play easy. It was just baffling. We deserved so much better."

– Detroit Red Wing Brendan Shanahan

"This is horrible. Joe Sakic, Peter Forsberg, and I have talked about it and come to the conclusion that this does not make any sense . . . we talked about how sorry we feel about the guys coming into this league. You cannot enjoy this any more. . . . Hockey has, in mine and many others' minds, taken a negative direction. . . . All sense of creativity in the game is gone. It is very sad. Everybody is the same. Everybody should play the same way. And then you add all this hooking, obstruction . . . I know I don't want to be a part of this for many years. The NHL should take a big responsibility. It seems like it doesn't interest them at all. They talk about different things every year, but . . . nothing happens."

– All-star forward Teemu Selanne

"[The referee] says he doesn't see it. What the hell is he looking at? How does he not see it? How does he not see blood dripping all over my face and on my jersey? Absolutely terrible. Wake up, NHL. Wake up. I'm bleeding like a stuck pig. It's ridiculous. Have the referees responsible for their actions too."

– Forward Jeremy Roenick

PROLOGUE

Perhaps even more fundamental to a sport than its level of excitement is the nature of the competition within it. There are several aspects to the conduct of competition – the team aspect, individual aspects, officiating, and to some degree certain off-ice issues. These are as important to the enjoyment of those involved with the game, and therefore to its ultimate prosperity, as excitement is.

But in recent years, changes in hockey distorted the competition of the game, often in fractured or non-obvious ways, so that it was most evident in that something had insidiously ate away at the positive feelings of the game – diminished satisfaction and positive sentiments from the experience of playing or watching.

As something so fundamental to a sport, to the feelings of those involved around it, and thus ultimately to its future support and following, the conduct of the sport's competition is another major issue – the second major issue – that needs to be addressed in raising our game.

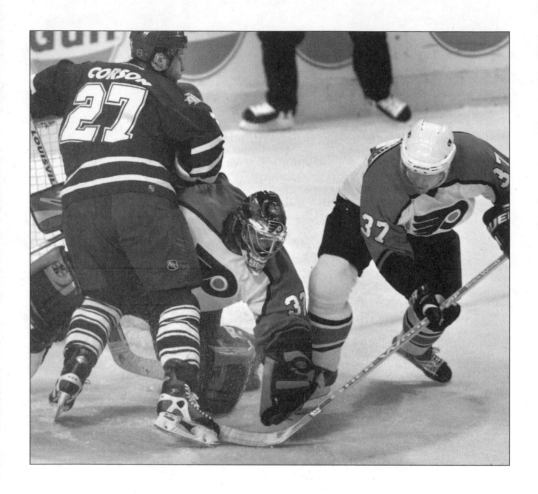

Crash the net. Goaltender interference is one of a few factors that acquired a new importance to the outcome of games. (*AP Photo/Rusty Kennedy*)

CHAPTER 4

REANOINTING THE SOUL OF THE GAME

WHAT HOCKEY'S ALL ABOUT

What sports do is administer competitions to determine outcomes (i.e., wins and losses). For each sport, the competition is different: Each sport begins with a vision, with certain elements in it to be the grounds of competition. Take golf, for example. Envisioned was a game of striking a ball into a distant hole, and its elements would be distance, accuracy, and consistency. Upon this foundation, of course, was built an elaborate set of rules such as the number of clubs you can use, and what to do if you hit your ball in a "hazard"; and the contest would be measured by who could get their ball in the hole in the least number of strokes. But going back to the original vision, if golf's competition is on the right grounds (which I believe it is), then the person who best masters the elements (distance, accuracy, consistency) in a given competition will generally end up taking the least shots and win. From the rushing, free-flowing game on ice that was the vision for hockey, the elements would have been carrying the play, generating more scoring chances than you allow your opponent, and doing a better job of trying to capitalize on them – which we have historically acknowledged as the proper grounds of competition by using the popular term "outplaying them" to describe these in combination. If you outplayed the opposition, you should win, and if the game was being played on the right grounds, you generally would.

For most of its history, hockey was indeed played on its right grounds. The team that outplayed the other would usually win. *Usually* because there are always flukes and exceptions – cases where extraordinary luck or goaltending might make up a difference. There's nothing we can or should do about that. Such "aberrations" are part of what makes sport interesting. But by and large, in hockey the side that played with the greatest skill, hard work, and desire would prevail.

But over recent years, the professional game changed. And it came to be that the team that outplayed the other – carrying the play, controlling the puck, generating more chances, exhibiting them with skill – would lose as often as win. And even when they won, they might barely win, despite outplaying the other team badly, or win by force of luck or, more commonly, win thanks to other factors that had little to do with those fundamental elements of the game. For me, this was something I didn't notice as distinctly when I was playing, because in the middle of the competition, you have no time to think, just to play; you know the score, and that's the only thing to focus on. But meanwhile, over the last several years, this pattern in outcomes became progressively more true.

For some people, the issue broke the surface when they witnessed the unheralded Anaheim Mighty Ducks sweep the defending Cup Champion first-place Detroit Red Wings in four straight games in the first round of 2003, despite – in the eyes of most observers – Detroit outshooting, outworking, outhitting, outchancing, and outplaying the Ducks in each game. "It was a very frustrating series for us. . . . We beat them everywhere but on the scoreboard," Wings defenceman Mathieu Schneider summarized. A few days later, people witnessed another example when the juggernaut Colorado Avalanche succumbed to the expansion Minnesota Wild.

For me, the issue became overwhelmingly clear watching the Avalanche game in and game out (as my brother Steve was playing for them) over the course of the following 2003–04 season, my first season on the sidelines after being injured. Here was a Colorado team that already had a star-studded lineup, and then added Paul Kariya and Teemu Selanne in the off-season, giving them perhaps ten future Hall-of-Famers on the roster. They also had an unsurpassed work ethic, bolstered by mile-high conditioning. Before the season, expert analysts almost universally expected the Avalanche to blow teams out all season and roll to the Cup. It didn't work out that way at all; there was hardly a single game that wasn't agonizingly close, and more often the great skating of Kariya and the pinpoint shot of Milan Hejduk weren't what made the difference, but grinding winger Steve Konowalchuk creating havoc in the opposing goal crease and a puck dribbling in at a key time, or goaltender David Aebischer stopping everything at his end. Ultimately, their season came to an end at the hands of the San Jose Sharks, a team considered to be in a rebuilding year, which pre-season analysts said had fewer solid NHL-calibre forwards than the Avalanche had stars. It was déjà vu for what had happened the year before against Minnesota.

Now I love upsets as much as anyone, if an underdog rises to an occasion and a favourite chokes, and that does happen; but in all three examples, and countless less obvious cases, what happened was more than that. The underdogs played great, but the favourites didn't choke – their great players played as hard as they could, but it wasn't enough. Hockey's traditional winning formula – to try harder and harder, to bear down more and more – couldn't turn the tide. Team talent, effort, and desire – all the "right" things – were no longer what it was about. Other things made the difference.

Across the board of pro hockey in recent years, a new pattern took shape: outplaying the opposition in the intended and conventional sense no longer dictated outcomes. Instead, ulterior factors were deciding games. The grounds of competition were no longer those charted in the blueprint of the game, but others.

Although this distortion happened gradually and without as much recognition as some of the other issues in the game, there is no question it was a big part of why there was so much frustration within and outside the game in recent years. For players, coaches, and managers, having your team dominate the opposition yet lose could be exasperating. In the pressured environment of the modern game, that's no trifle. At playoff time, it could be downright crushing: "It's like a nightmare," Schneider described. And any player would tell you, as Shanahan claimed some Ducks did, that it was not made up for by winning in cases where you knew in your heart your side was outplayed. The joy of victory in those cases would admit a somewhat unfulfilled feeling. For fans too, the satisfaction of seeing their team win when they were outplayed was outweighed by the bitterness of seeing them lose when they dominated and seemed to overwhelmingly deserve to win but didn't. It just wasn't natural. On the whole, statistically it might come out even, but emotionally for the sport as a whole, it was lose-lose, just different sides on the wrong end at different times, contributing to what was turning fans off the game.

STOLEN KEYS

So what was behind this puzzling turn of events? It wasn't "just the way things were," because they never used to be that way. Something changed. It wasn't that increased parity meant nobody really outplayed anybody any more, because frequently we saw one team observably outplay another but still lose. It wasn't luck, because luck is blind and evens out, yet some teams won consistently and others lost consistently. And luck could not explain how determining outcomes could have changed over time. There had to be something in the modern game today that nullified the importance of outplaying and neutralized the benefits of team skill, hard work, and desire. In doing so, it paved the way for other factors to assume control over who won – elements we never imagined or intended or wanted to be so important.

So what was it that was neutralizing the right things, and what were these other factors that instead came to matter most in deciding games? A familiar villain – the same "squeeze" that choked out excitement in the last chapter – is what pried the power out of outplaying and stole the thunder of skill, hustle, and desire. This is no coincidence, for surely the inventors of hockey intended to have the factors that should govern outcomes be things tied to excitement.

But how does the squeeze neutralize the effect of outplaying? In trying to outplay their opponents, a team tries to chase them down when they have the puck, win battles, and win races for loose pucks to obtain possession. Once they have the puck, they try to maintain possession and manoeuvre into scoring position through skilful skating and passing plays, and then employ deft shots or dekes to score.

But against the squeeze, the latter type of offensive game would get caught up in a spiderweb of defensive players and sticks, and the more a team would try to push through it, the more counter-productive it would become – through mistakes producing chances the other way, or simply getting worn out (which explains why so often when a team finally tied the score, they often fell behind again after). This is what players meant when you would hear them say during losing streaks, "We're working hard, but we're not working smart." Instead, when there were no openings, it was better to give the other team the puck, almost like a grenade, and let them blow themselves up with a mistake or wear themselves out trying to play through it. "It's like watching a game of long baseline tennis, lobbing the ball back and forth, waiting for a mistake," former Bruin Terry O'Reilly said. The side playing the squeeze at a given time did not expend a ton of energy or desire chasing the play, or an abundance of skill either. A comparatively passive scheme, it prized instead positioning, size, and disciplined adherence to the system. Trying to outplay, to outhustle, to *outwant* one's opponent were no longer the strategies. (Please see graph on decreased scoring, page 125.) Like trench warfare, the strategy was to stay in position, and let your opponent's initiative and exertion be his downfall.

There were still a few exceptions where skill came into play – on the powerplay, or when there was a breakdown in the defences and a team got a chance – but these were the exception not the rule. The notion that hockey was a game of more skill, more hustle, more heart was no more than a romantic relic of a bygone age in professional hockey – an age that faded away as the squeeze gained hold over the last fifteen years.

Turning now to the question of what elements of the game acquired a new critical influence on winning, we begin with the following components of the squeeze that obviously soared in importance as factors.

- Obstruction-harassment: Over the years, the amount of obstruction-harassment dramatically increased to where in recent years there were countless hooks, holds, crosschecks, slashes, and other infractions a game. Even the notoriously rough Philadelphia Flyers of the '70s were nothing compared to the mid-to-late-'80s Flyers, who were nothing compared to the Flyers another fifteen years hence – in terms of purely the total number of rulebook infractions taking place. The reason was the enormous rise in O-H. Yet as the number of infractions dramatically increased, the number of penalties handed out stayed about the same. The thinking must have been that there is a certain number of penalties called per-game that is "the right amount" (either inherently right, or right in terms of finding a balance between penalizing illegal play and avoiding disrupting the flow and basic structure of the game and "letting teams play").

  But if we look at the fraction of fouls occurring called, we get a very different perspective: so if in the 1950s, there were 20 infractions a game and in recent seasons there were 200 (or about three per shift), and just 5 penalties called aside both times, then the number of penalties remained the same but the fraction of fouls called went from 5/20 to 5/200. This means illegal play went up 1,000 per cent! By not changing the number of calls while the number of infractions enormously did change, the game was radically altered. What an awful penalty for bad math! The overwhelming majority of infractions occurring were obstruction-harassment. Examples include: a player hooked trying to rush the puck, blocked trying to forecheck, impeded trying to get open for a pass, crosschecked trying to control the puck in the zone, held in front of the net, hacked on the hands as he tries to shoot, or being "picked" by an offensive player as he tries to play legitimate defence low in his own zone.

Imagine how an incredible superstar like Martin St. Louis would feel trying to fight through this constantly – with all the things he could do with his skill unimpeded, and how further difficult it was to fight through it with his small body. For Mario Lemieux, it was a major reason he cited for why he first retired. "When a guy like Mario Lemieux leaves the game and tells you why he's leaving and you don't address it, that's stupid," Brett Hull said at the time. A while later, Hull decried after a game: "Who won the rodeo tonight? It's embarrassing. I wouldn't pay money to watch that. And they wonder why attendance in the league is down."

The point is, as things like stickhandling, passing, and shooting decreased in importance, hooking, holding, and crosschecking as a team rose. Teams that learned to do this the best – from the Blackhawks in the early '90s to the expansion Panthers of the mid-'90s, to the Dallas Stars another five years after that – were successful. Teams that didn't typically weren't. So there was a huge rise in obstruction-harassment, and in its importance in determining games. And these were not appropriate factors, they were in fact illegal plays!

• Coaching: It used to be that occasionally a great coaching move could make a difference at a key time (think Jacques Demers's illegal stick call on L.A.'s Marty McSorley in the final in 1993), but by and large, the game was determined by the talent and effort of the players. Again, things changed. Coaching improved enormously, and its importance along with that. "When we played, the players had control of the game," Marcel Dionne, the NHL's fifth-ranked all-time leading scorer recently commented. "Today, the coaches have control."

A great coach armed with effective defensive systems, the big fast players he needed to play them, and a knack for instilling discipline could take a team of comparatively unheralded players and shut down a virtual all-star lineup – thoroughly and consistently. That's what Ron Wilson of San Jose did, and Mike Babcock of Anaheim did to Detroit in 2003. A coach could get a one-goal lead and sit on it all game. A coach could take a team that had struggled for years and quickly turn them into a champion team (see 2004's finalists, Tampa and Calgary). The coach became the most important guy on a team. Hockey had become like football, but hockey is not supposed to be like this. "I went to a football game and a hockey game broke out," legendary junior hockey coach Brian Kilrea of the Ottawa '67s said recently, putting a sad modern spin on Rodney Dangerfield's old joke about it breaking out at a boxing match. The relative importance of coaching rose tremendously.

• Size and speed: Size and speed used to be components of skill and ability (think of big Gordie Howe and speedy Mike Gartner, for instance) but only components. But size and speed rose in importance over and above and independent of total ability. Sometimes teams preferred to have big fast skaters who could be plugged into the system than more highly skilled players with little place to use their skills and a counterproductive tendency to try. Sportswriter Bruce Dowbiggin wrote that a scout on the draft floor recently told him no team was even considering a defenceman under six-foot-one. "Size and speed, size and speed, size and speed . . . that's everything today," Bobby Orr said so emphatically it stuck in my mind when I met him while I was at Harvard, as though while Orr accepted it, he was still amazed by it. Indeed for it to be "everything," or *so* predominant, is strange and unnatural in hockey.

In addition to these elements from the squeeze, other factors grew in importance as the traditional keys to winning declined:

- Goaltending: Goaltending has always been important in hockey, and it should be, alongside the rest of players and the rest of play. But recently the goaltender's importance dramatically increased thanks to major improvements in technique and training, the adoption of bigger equipment, and the implementation of team defensive schemes that limited the number of chances and heightened the significance of one missed save. Goaltending went from an important factor and occasionally the deciding factor to an often dominating factor. According to TSN's long-time respected hockey commentator Dave Hodge, goaltending used to be important, but it became everything. He noted the oft-heard mantra "If he can see it, he will stop it," as something new, something that could never have been said about Terry Sawchuk or Glenn Hall or the greatest goalies of any past era. Reflecting this increased importance, goalies won three of the last eight Hart Trophies for league MVP, after none in the previous thirty-five years since 1962. A team could get a one-goal lead and, without further scoring, help the goaltender take that the rest of the way. Every year lately, a team perceived to have few of the traditional elements of success has seemed to ride a hot goalie deep into the post-season. Goaltending acquired a new dominance over games.

- Goaltender interference: As chances dwindled and goaltending improved, it became harder and harder to beat a goalie fair and square. As a result, the use of goaltender interference as a tactic soared. Going to the net grew from screens, deflections, and rebounds to a more literal idea of "crashing the net" and getting in the way of the goalie trying to make a save. If it worked and wasn't called, it made a huge difference: a goal instead of a shot, which was especially significant with games tight and goals few. Goalie interference, the converse of the goaltending that

improved so much, was another thing that gained major importance in today's game.

- Diving: In a sense, diving is the flip side of the obstruction-
  harassment. When a team did it comprehensively and effectively,
  it could throw off the other team's use of hooking, holding, and
  crosschecking, as they would get too many penalties. With play
  bottled up at even strength, drawing powerplays gave teams a big
  advantage, almost like lottery tickets with a 20 per cent chance
  of a game-winner. "I have had referees say, 'You don't want to
  get a reputation like Darcy Tucker or Theo Fleury,'" said forward
  Mike Comrie a few years back. But why wouldn't he? Those guys
  drew a powerplay or two per game for their teams, which was a
  huge asset to their side. Diving was another element that rose in
  importance in determining the modern game.

- Special teams: It used to be that teams felt that if they outplayed
  the opposition at even strength, they would typically overcome
  any special teams deficit and still win. But with so few goals and
  chances at even strength, the relative importance of special teams
  rose immensely. Teams rightly sensed a critical opportunity to
  score on the powerplay where there was no squeeze and they
  had a man advantage. Most teams had powerplay specialists like
  Nashville defenceman Marek Zidlicky, third-best on his team in
  scoring (and fourth among defencemen in the league), but
  second-worst in plus-minus. A better-known example might be
  Phil Housley at the end of his career. Teams hired assistant
  coaches to specialize on special teams, as in football. Special
  teams were another key factor in deciding games in recent years.

- Fluke plays and mistakes: These have always played a role in
  games and occasionally been the deciding factor. (Edmonton
  defenceman Steve Smith's goal on his own net in the 1986 playoffs against the Flames comes to mind.) It's not that these odd

plays have happened more often of late, actually they've probably happened considerably less often. But the tight modern game amplified the significance of any unusual plays or silly mistakes that occurred – as if a musician were to sound a wrong note during a long monotone drone versus in the middle of a chaotic orchestral flourish. It's the same wrong note, but it's going to sound a lot worse. Think of all the times in recent years that extreme exceptions decided the day. Off the top of my head: Colorado's Patrick Roy lifting his glove off the ice to show off a great save against Detroit but forgetting the puck, which Steve Yzerman poked in, the turning point of that series and of Detroit's march to its last Cup; Montreal's Alexei Kovalev dropping his stick against Boston after being slashed in 2004, costing the game and nearly that series; the puck flipped over Dan Boyle's shoulder in the 2004 Final and took a funny bounce to give Calgary a game-winning goal. Clearly, the significance of these anomalous plays is no longer trivial or only occasionally important. In the low constant hum of the game in recent years, these dissonant notes stood out like piercing performance-ruining shrieks.

Together, the foregoing factors increased their sway as the traditional ones fell. And replacing skill, exertion, and desire were three new keys to victory – what could be called the officiating balance, the goaltending balance, and the peripherals balance.

The "officiating balance" refers to what a team could get away with to their benefit vis-à-vis the rules compared to their opponent. So teams would use as much illegal obstruction-harassment (and other types of infractions) as they could to gain an advantage in the play of the game, and at the same time try to draw opponents into penalties through things like diving, or inciting opponents into retaliatory fouls. Whoever did a better job of this of course had an advantage. But in the tight modern game, every call was magnified in importance, so that made it a huge advantage. A couple years ago, on a call-in sports show, I heard an elderly gentleman say that he had been a hockey fan since the 1930s, and that he couldn't stand the modern game because it was a contest of "the best cheater wins." He was talking about clutching and grabbing, and trying to suck players into dropping their gloves (to get an unsportsmanlike conduct penalty). Obviously, that characterization was an exaggeration, but it did capture how the new importance of this officiating balance is one thing that has disillusioned many about the game in recent years.

The "goaltending balance" is self-explanatory. No team has won anything lately without ultra-elite goaltending. The 2002 Wings with Dominik Hasek, 2001 Avs with Patrick Roy, 1999 Stars with Eddie Belfour all employed prior Vezina Trophy winners. The other recent champions – Martin Brodeur (World Cup 2004, Olympics 2002, Stanley Cup 2003, 2000) and Nikolai Khabibulin (2004) – were long before considered among the world's top few goaltenders. Using the average of about twenty-eight shots per team per game, a mere 0.07 difference in a goalie's save percentage is the difference between a win and a loss. In fact, that 0.07 figure was exactly the difference between first and fifth place among goaltenders in save percentages in 2003–04. From first to tenth was more than twice that. You can easily see how even slightly better goaltending could make a big difference in wins and losses. In 2003, Anaheim tied for the league lead in one-goal wins, snuck into the playoffs, and made it all the way to the Stanley Cup Finals. The next year, goalie J-S Giguere's save percentage dropped from .920 to .914, and the Ducks missed the playoffs by fifteen points. If they'd won the same proportion of one-goal games as the previous year, they would have had an extra, you guessed it, fifteen points.

Improvements in goaltending techniques (e.g., "the butterfly") were part of the rise in saves, but part of it was also enlarged goalie equipment. And trying to score, more goaltender interference was the antidote – often hard to see, and potential penalties were not subject to video replay – so it worked. With goals and chances being few, the difference between one extra save and one extra goal was often the difference in a game, so whoever could tip the goal-tending balance in their favour had a huge advantage. And again, this "net" game was distorted from the intentions of hockey, and unenjoyed by all.

The other major factor governing the outcome of games was the "peripherals balance." Peripherals are things that are part of the game but not central to it. The soul of the game is supposed to be teams at even strength, with players using their combined ability and resources to score goals and prevent them. Peripherals are the things outside of that: coaching, special teams play, raw physical attributes in isolation from overall ability, exceptional mistakes and fluke plays, etc. The balance of them means how you make them work for you versus the other team. Size and speed, as discussed, became major assets in plugging into systems, and had a strong correlation to winning, especially in the playoffs. That's why teams drafted big players. Coaching alone made a big difference through the superior ability of one coach to get his team to execute his system with discipline. This was really peripheral, as the coach is not even on the ice!

Another huge peripheral was special teams. Games that were played forty-eight minutes even strength but bottled up often instead came down to the relative efficiency of the teams in the remaining twelve minutes of special teams. This was especially true in the playoffs where they were often an even higher proportion of the goals (for example, more than a third of champion Tampa's playoff goals were on the powerplay, versus about 23 per cent in the regular season). And last are the fluke plays and unusual mistakes that so often influenced results, so that a team outplayed another for most of sixty minutes but then lost on one of these mistakes with the "hot potato." All of these factors have always been part of games and occasionally decided them in the past, but by definition their importance to a game's outcome should be secondary, with the soul of the game primary. But instead, in pro hockey in recent years, the exceptions overshadowed the rule, the peripherals outweighed the core – another distorted and widely dissatisfying result.

Together, this trio of factors (the officiating balance, goaltending balance, and peripherals balance) worked together determining games. Sometimes it was the goaltender, sometimes the officiating, sometimes the coach or special teams, and the vast majority of the time the combined balance of all of them – those who watched, this is what they saw. "Goaltending is a key in this business," said former Jack Adams Trophy winner for coach of the year Jacques Martin. "And a lot of times you're going to win with goaltending and specialty teams. If you win the specialty team part of a game, you really give yourself a great chance." Skill, hard work, and desire, the even-strength balance of play were dethroned as the measures of hockey, and these other things crowned in their stead. Hockey was supposed to be a contest of dashing, deftness, sense, creativity, energy, and passion, but that contest came to be dominated by engineering, execution, and ability to exploit the officiating. This wasn't true to the intentions of the game, and wasn't a development that benefited those involved: it frustrated players, coaches, and managers, and turned off fans. A sport born on that basis would never have got anywhere, and was on a road to nowhere if it continued.

STEPS TAKEN

The good news is, as the 2005–06 season begins, it appears some important progress is being made. A few of the rule changes announced for this season as part of the package to improve the excitement in the game should (not coincidentally) have a residual positive effect on the competition itself.

The most major of these is the crackdown on obstruction-harassment. "The coaching of illegal tactics in our game has gone on for twenty years. Fans have complained for years about the clutching and grabbing. . . . Well, the new standard of enforcement will address that," said director of officiating Stephen Walkom. The task is to undo the distortion in the fraction of infractions called, produced when obstruction spread and penalty numbers stayed the same. And the league understands that: "To us, it's not about statistics," Walkom said. "It's about a standard. If the players don't conform to the standard, then there will be penalties."

The question was, what should that standard be, what was the right fraction of fouls to call among those that happen in a game? In my opinion that fraction had to be "1" – that is, they should call *all* the obstruction-harassment *all* the time; indeed, this was what the league decided, announcing their new standard would be to tolerate zero obstruction. Others agreed as well: Tampa coach John Tortorella was said to have passionately argued for this in Shanahan's discussion-group; Toronto captain Mats Sundin said, "It's going to be good for everybody, whether you like physical hockey, or like a lot of scoring, or a higher-paced game." And NHL VP Colin Campbell said, "This is not something we decided to do. We've been told to do this by the general managers, coaches, players, the fans, the media."

Indeed, these fouls had no place in hockey, they just acted as a tax on skill and hustle, a tax not used to build anything positive in the game. And worse, like a cancer, when allowed to be there at all, they spread and couldn't be stopped from taking over the game – the only option was to eradicate them. These arguments extend to all fouls, not just obstruction-harassment. They should all be called without exception. Eliminating them would allow teams to use ability and exertion without interference, and be rewarded for it – making for a cleaner, fairer, and more enjoyable game to play, coach, manage, and watch. Indeed, through the 2005 pre-season, this is exactly what seems to be the case. "I noticed a big change in terms of the flow of the game," Walkom said. "More skating and open play," said Campbell. All of this is helping teams play the game the way it was meant to be played – without impediment – and to succeed by it.

Another important measure that has been put in for 2005–06 is to curb the enlarged goalie equipment. This will be discussed more in the next chapter, but excess equipment bulk beyond what's necessary to protect goaltenders should be eliminated. Goaltending has always been important, and it has been able to exert a larger influence over games through improved goaltending techniques, and goalies that are bigger themselves in nets that haven't changed size. We can deal with that, as long as the bar stops there and doesn't allow goalies to continue to use equipment that overgrows reasonable justification in protection. The reductions mandated by the league should help the remainder of the game regain more importance alongside goaltending. And that is something that should be appreciated not only by players and fans, but even by goaltenders, who, without the heightened primacy, were already playing one of the most pressure-packed positions in sports.

Another progressive move taken was to counter the problem of diving. This is one front on which NHL VP Colin Campbell should be applauded for his foresight, in that he began to target it even before the lockout, no doubt trying to ensure the problem did not keep growing until hockey ended up like soccer, which some hockey fans ridicule for its diving. As the fastest game on Earth, among other things, hockey is probably the world's toughest sport to officiate, so diving was an especial danger. The main thing that probably prevented diving in the past was the tough culture of the game that frowned upon it; but in this age, if it helps draw powerplays (which pleases coaches, and helps win games) frowning upon diving is no longer enough to keep it in check.

I understand the feeling that if fouls are allowed to run rampant it's unfair to target diving. "All they have to do is call the infractions, and guys won't have to dive. That's basically why they're doing it," Mario Lemieux explained a couple years back. But with the new clampdown to eliminate those infractions, there would be no excuse left for diving. And it has no place influencing games. It's acting, not hockey. Further, in a way it's deceitful and, at least in cases where an injury is faked, exploitative of officials' compassion and sense of justice, which is worse. It's like the fable of the boy who cried wolf. "It has to stop. This is a sport with a lot of history, and . . . we don't need that kind of stuff," Colorado GM Pierre Lacroix said.

Unfortunately, through the 2005 pre-season, one of the effects of the needed obstruction clampdown has been, inadvertently, to reinforce diving, as more is being called – which further supports the need for the anti-diving measures. One of those measures, I don't agree with: circulating a published divers list among teams, embarrassing players. (Besides, if you really wanted to embarrass those players, what you would really need to do is put out a video!) The other measures – warning letters, fines, and ultimately suspensions after several repeats – I think are on the right track. I would suggest adding an automatic 10-minute misconduct to any penalty for diving, and giving teams an added bench minor if they have a second dive in a game. I think most players and fans would agree that faking a serious injury should merit a stiffer fine and suspension. If the right calls are being made and someone still wants to dive, perhaps they should find a pool instead!

All of these are fronts on which actions taken should help make competition come back down to the intended and desired elements of the game. But as long as the squeeze still exists – and despite these initiatives it can – the way the game is played and the way games are decided will still be significantly affected. So there is further to go.

RETRIEVING THE KEYS

How can we really reestablish the right grounds of competition, return a team's game to what it should be, and restore victory's keys to their rightful hands?

The most critical thing that must be done has already been suggested in the "First Period" for a different reason, and that is to move to four-on-four. By ending the efficacy of the squeeze, four-on-four not only injects excitement back into the game, but deals the injustice in determining games a fatal blow. It is the squeeze that neutralizes the proper elements of skill, effort, and desire, that flouts any attempt to win by outplaying. But with just four players, space would not be tight enough to make the squeeze work, and teams would have to abandon it. Then the rightful rulers of the game would be liberated: Teams would once again be able to control the puck and manoeuvre into scoring position through skilful skating and passing, and they would have enough chances to beat goalies without having to interfere with them. Once again they could hope to pile momentum on the other team while playing at even strength, generate a series of chances out of it, and convert a reliable number of them into goals. Outplaying a team would, like a trump card, resume being the ascendant factor in games by and large, regardless of anything else happening.

Furthermore, demolishing the squeeze would cause its pillars to collapse. Coaches would not be able to systemize and control games, and coaching would return to a proper limited role in hockey. Size and speed would still be important, but only as part of the overall package of a player's total ability, as they should be. Obstruction would be less effective in a new style of play not based on clogging the ice. Thus even if nothing were done about the other factors distorting the competition in recent years, four-on-four would at least hammer the half of them present in the squeeze and its components, and the remainder would shrink in relative importance, overshadowed by the resurgence of the right factors made possible by four-on-four. I believe it is essential to the ultimate goal.

It is additionally important given the challenges expected and bound to arise down the road with the obstruction clampdown itself. One of those is whether the clampdown can be sustained over time, and the infractions kept from creeping back in as time goes on. In the past, previous intended crackdowns faded with time and under criticism. And already in this pre-season, there have been some players and others sounding off on the penalties being called, the consistency, and other complaints. "There's going to be bitching and whining when you do it. . . . Our guys will have to stay the course. . . . We have to hang in this time and support the referees when they call it," Campbell said. Indeed, hanging tough will be an important part of it. Another point people agreed on was that the clampdown had to be rigorous and consistent from the get-go so that the way the game was played would change before frustration with the penalties raised pressure on officials. "It will take a while because you're competing out there and looking for that edge. . . . But . . . if they're just consistent and make sure they call the penalties it's going to sink in," Mats Sundin said. "Every time a player touches another player with a stick, bang, it's a penalty. How long would it take for the players to figure it out and adjust? One month, two months?" asked Doug Gilmour. That's short-term pain for long-term gain, a principle participants and fans of professional sports are very familiar with.

However, as playoffs come and subsequent seasons come, and teams continue to push on the rules to see what they can get away with, one wonders about the fate of this campaign over the long haul. It will be difficult. One thing that can help is four-on-four: it's not so much that it eliminates the need for a clampdown as that it may make it considerably easier and really permanently feasible for arguably the first time. That's because four-on-four unclogs the ice, so there's more room to escape the fouls, and more room for referees to see them – which should result in fewer infractions. There would be less to follow on the ice, and scoring chances would be closer at hand, so fouls would be easier for officials to catch and justify calling. By changing the nature of the game back from closed and clogged to open and offensive, four-on-four may improve the long-term odds of the obstruction clampdown and make it a much better bet to endure and work in the long run.

Another initiative that needs to be undertaken is tackling goaltender interference. Not only is it an infringement upon the fairness of the game (particularly as goals are how the game's measured), it is dangerous: goaltenders can get hurt. The other measures undertaken should make it easier to beat goalies without resorting to goaltender interference. Specific measures to eliminate it will be covered in greater detail in the next chapter, but it certainly is something that must be specifically targeted for extinguishment. This will make the game safer for goaltenders, and give players, coaches, managers, and fans a better feeling about the measurement and outcome of games.

Together, all these changes would allow the game to once again be a game where hard work, ability, and desire comprise the core of the competition, and dominate outcomes. The best strategy would once again be outhustling, outshooting, and outchancing your opponent. The squeeze would disappear, and the influence of the three impostor determinants of the balances of officiating, goaltending, and peripherals would drastically diminish. There would be no shortcuts, no side doors, no tunnels, no scripted programs for victory. To expect to win, you would have to outplay the other team, and if you outplay the other team, you can expect to usually win. This would make the game feel more natural to players, coaches, and managers, and outcomes feel more right. Everyone would have a better feeling about the way teams play and the way the sport measures their performance. Fans filing out of an arena after their team is eliminated will still be disappointed, that will never change, but there won't be any other questions or complaints. All of this would be *just* great for the game.

WHERE HAS ALL THE SCORING GONE?

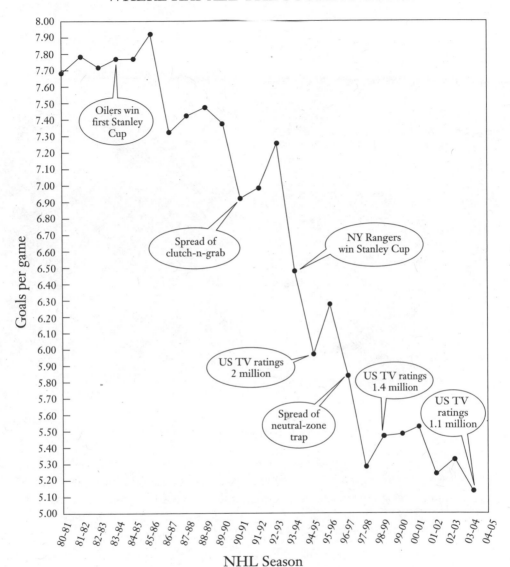

Decade	Goals per game
80s	7.63
90s	6.19
00s	5.30

This graph charts the recent steady decline of scoring in the NHL

Patrick Roy early in his career (at left) and late in his career (at right). Growth of goalie equipment not only contributed to changes in the art of goaltending and the art of scoring, but also affected basic methodologies of offence and defence. L:(*Paul Bereswill/Hockey Hall of Fame*) R:(*AP Photo/Jack Dempsey*)

CHAPTER 5

FREEING PLAYERS
TO PLAY

FIGHTING THE SYSTEM

The last chapter dealt with an important issue in hockey from a team point of view, in the grounds for deciding games. This chapter deals with a closely related issue, just as fundamental and important, but from the point of view of the individual player. It deals with the paradoxical and disconcerting fact that in recent years a professional hockey player could no longer "play hockey."

What do I mean by this? "Playing hockey," as I use the phrase and as other professional players would understand me to mean, connotes something more than just stepping onto the ice to compete in a game under the name of hockey. It corresponds to the way we played it as kids, the way our kids play it today, the way former pros play it in their old-timer games, the way we saw them play it in the NHL in their day, the way recreational players have always played it, which is something they would distinguish from their normal experience in professional games in recent years. It refers to the way the sport is played in its natural setting, the way it is meant to be played, but a way that it has not been at the professional hockey level in recent years with the radical rises in coaches' systemization, role specialization, goalie "inflation," and the seriousness of the stakes at hand. Everyone who has ever played hockey knows what it means to play hockey; only professional players of the modern age know what it means to step on the ice for a game under that name and do something quite different.

It might be best summed up as the difference between "playing hockey" and "playing the system." If that may seem nebulous in words, the gap is nevertheless night-and-day in experience: In recent years, the professional game was a set-systems oriented game, where there was little need for individual instincts and complex pattern processing. In a game of mistake avoidance, the risks inherent in creativity and improvisation made them things coaches largely frowned upon and deterred. In a game that mostly oscillated between a few predictable patterns, there was little room for anticipation or deception. It was, above all, a task of execution. Meanwhile, the scope of activities and opportunities within the game were narrowed. The art of stickhandling had little clay to carve, and the science of open-ice bodychecking was all but rarely locked out of the lab. The majority of passes were straightforward outlet passes and "chips" to open areas. And rarely did one see a player beat a goalie who was set and ready, fair-and-square. Nor was there almost ever time or space for dekes, so a lot of scoring was reduced to getting the puck on net before the goalie was ready, screening the goalie, or crashing the net to drive it in.

The flowing action of the game was disjointed; there were still a lot of transitions, but stuck in the neutral zone, back and forth and around in circles like an Abbott & Costello skit. Hustle, hard work, and desire were confined by the need to stay in disciplined posture. Each player's size or speed was predominantly utilized to perform their specific task provided for in the system. Players filled roles in it like parts in an engine, specialized by position on the ice and on the roster. Thus, many integral aspects of the sport "in nature" were removed or restricted in the modern pro game. The game could not be played the way it should be played. The professional player's ability to "play hockey" was thus unhappily impeded.

This transformation in the experience of the sport occurred gradually and progressively as one worked their way up. For kids (and recreational players of all ages), hockey has been the same as always – the same game that I fell in love with playing and watching on TV as a kid, the one that beat every other sport by a country mile. But for kids in competitive hockey in recent years, once you made it past minor hockey and onto the road to the pros, that's when the game began to change and be increasingly replaced by a systemized, restricted, bottled-up, watered-down game. In junior, every team would have a system, although with the dearth of practices, and the unbridled energy of teenagers trying to gain the attention of scouts at the next level, seldom would it be faithfully played. The teams that did, however, were generally more successful; and you started to get a taste there of the confusion and frustration of a different game. In college, with so many practices and so few games, the teams would play their systems with more discipline. But the culture of hockey in the United States is somewhat different, hockey is not life and death, so not too many teams played the squeeze system, which was considered stylistically repugnant to watch and little fun to play. Also college goaltenders typically were much better than at preceding levels, although there was still room to beat them. Nevertheless, the coaches could and would keep more control, because at this level the players were all good enough that mistakes could kill. So it was a much more regimented game.

Once you got to professional hockey, the change in the game would be dramatic. Players were a lot bigger, and the rink smaller, and on a crowded rink, the squeeze left little room "to play," in either sense of the term. Goalies were also a lot bigger, rendering even the net "crowded," with little place to beat the goalie. The stakes were higher, jobs on the line, and the business was to win, so the game came under increasing control from above, and the freedom to play was radically diminished. True inspiration, improvisation, and other things I loved, and other players loved about the game disappeared while system execution, obstruction, and other disagreeable components dominated. I understand as well as anyone out there the difference between playing for fun and playing for keeps, between shinny and organized hockey, between amateur and pro. But the top levels should still have the same basic character, still be substantially the same game. I doubt that any other major North American or European sport could have involved a change of this extent as you work your way up.

I also doubt that it used to be true in hockey. For most of hockey history, I believe at the highest levels, leaving aside the stakes of business and other off-ice stuff, the game wasn't really much different from what kids and everyone else played. In a sense it was – as it should be – the perfection of it. In fact, I believe this was true until not that long ago. If you watch a game replayed from Gretzky's heyday in the '80s, from what I can tell short of stepping through the TV screen and onto the ice, they're "playing hockey" as pure and passionately as you can find it. But then watch a game from the mid-'90s, and after that watch a game from 2000–04, and you can see the progressive changes occurring all within that same top level, right before your very eyes.

"It's a totally different game today. It's all defensive systems," Teemu Selanne, who broke into the league only as far back as 1992–93, said in 2003–04 while being a healthy scratch for the first time in his career. "It's just a totally different game than it used to be." The longer they'd been around, the more they saw their occupation transform. Look at the story of the great Paul Coffey, who entered the league in 1980, broke some of Bobby Orr's most unthinkable records, and retired in 2000 as the highest-scoring defenceman in NHL history. Coffey had won the Norris Trophy for the league's best defenceman as recently as 1995, and five years later he could still fly, but the changed game left little place for it to be used to advantage, and rapidly began to perceive a freewheeling style like his as a liability, so that just eighteen games into a new two-year contract with Boston, he was waived through the league and had to retire.

"I feel sorry for the guys today," Phil Esposito said recently while being interviewed after the publication of his book, *Thunder and Lightning*. "Not the money they're making, absolutely not, but they don't seem to have any time for fun any more. Players are over-managed and overcoached today, way overcoached." The money was there, but the game they fell in love with as a kid and spent a lifetime pursuing was not. And that was important. For pro hockey players not to be able to "play hockey" was not only wrong, but an absurdity. And not just for their sake, to be able to enjoy the kind of game that was their passion. But the top echelon of a sport must be its showpiece – a magnet, where the play of the game is so pure, and the experience of it so palpably fun, that it pulls people toward the sport as players or fans – the way the game of Gretzky's day or before did for us.

INTO THE SKATES OF A PRO HOCKEY PLAYER

So how was it that hockey players could no longer play hockey? Let's step into the skates of a professional player in 2004 to see just how this would happen. . . .

First of all, just by suiting up, you have a certain role reflecting your position and your place on the roster. Throughout hockey history, there may have always been somewhat of a blend of players on a team, partly by design but probably moreso by the limitations of the players available in those eras. But there is no question that roles were never remotely so specialized in any previous ice age as they are now, as you take your place on the bench, in 2004. The kinds of activity expected from each player, and even the kinds of players employed for specific roles, are quite specific. The defencemen's job is largely to move the puck quickly and safely to the forwards, to angle and pin opposing forwards to the boards, and clear them away from the front of the net. Of six defencemen, teams try to get at least a pair who are big and mobile (although they are hard to come by), because they can accomplish this task most effectively. These two play the bulk of the ice time. Then the team might have another three who are less skilled than the first two, but are even bigger and punishingly physical, and can be counted on to safely get the puck up to the forwards or off the glass and out. Then teams often have one smaller, more skilled defencemen who serves as a powerplay specialist. His job is to carry the puck, gain the offensive zone, and quarterback the powerplay. As a defenceman, if you try to do more than what your role is, you will (the majority of the time) break or get broken by the systems and end up accomplishing less. (And if you continue to do that, ultimately you might lose your job!)

Meanwhile, the forwards on a team have roles roughly corresponding to their lines. The first two lines are usually the most "pure skilled." They are allowed by the coaches to try to play more of a puck retention game because coaches feel if they can break through the defence, they will probably score. However, even for them, it is difficult – except on the powerplay, where many of the game's goals are scored, and where they are perhaps of greatest value. The third line usually consists of players with a blend of skill, physical size, and "grit." They are counted on to do the important but specialized job of shutting down the other team's top line, playing the system to a "T," and being able to capitalize when the opposition's top line makes mistakes trying to force risky offensive plays. The fourth line often boasts players who will play a hard physical game, not really expected to often score so much as just change the momentum of the game, and provide rest for the other lines while wearing out the opponents. These third and fourth lines are expected to try nothing too elaborate offensively, just get the puck in at every opportunity, get pucks to the net and go to the net, and always *always* stay on the defensive. "Do your job, don't do anybody else's job, and we'll be fine," players might coach each other. (Thank God nobody told Paul Henderson that in 1972!) Meanwhile, the goalie's job is the same as forever: to stop the puck. But even goalies are getting specialized in that more and more teams want big butterfly-style, positionally-sound limited-movement-style goalies.

Now step on the ice. You want to try to "play hockey." You have the puck and are facing up ice. In front of you, the opposition is set up in their squeeze. If you try to carry the puck up the ice, they will try to funnel you to the boards, cut you off, and check you. You can't use creativity and improvisation much, given that they are taking fixed defensive positions to steer you. You might try to use your speed, stickhandling ability, and agility, but unless you find a rare crack in the wall, it will be hard to get through. And the obstruction is there to close any such holes. Fancier passes are blocked by players and their sticks cutting off passing lanes. Usually, there is only one option open – the one the trap gives you – leading you down a path that's ultimately a dead end. The more you try to force something else, the more you increase the risk of a turnover, and where you're caught out of defensive position yourself, playing into their hands as they try to score on your mistakes.

If somehow you do manage to get by the trap and gain the offensive zone, it's more of the same. The defensive players set up in the middle of the ice and force you toward the boards. They race to take away your time and space, because those are what you need to beat a player one-on-one, to find an open man for a good pass, to aim a great shot. You try to get away, but it is to less and less dangerous areas, namely the corner, and now you're stuck in the vice. In the zone, expect to be hooked, held, crosschecked, and shoved so that it's difficult to get in a rhythm or execute a skilled play. The pass open is the "outlet" nearby, who defenders are just waiting to close on. Trying to force something else carries the same risks of a break the other way. So playing against a system like this, played with discipline, makes it hard to "play hockey," and usually better not to try.

Instead, you're forced to play a different kind of game. And it is your coach's job to make sure you do so. So he instructs you not to rely on your instincts or to improvise, but to play in tightly controlled ways. Don't expose the puck, don't hang on to it, no passes through the middle, don't try any one-on-one moves. Move it quickly to the nearest outlet, chip it by the trap, race and try to battle to get it back. In the offensive zone, same rules apply. Throw it at the net, then go to the net. The coach stresses safe plays, no turnovers. At worst, let the other team have the puck, let them make the mistake – then pounce. These are the only times you are free to play: when the other team makes a mistake and there is a break-down in their system. But since this is the way to lose, both teams doggedly try to avoid this by making safe, low-risk plays. You are under tight rein. "Playing hockey" is a no-no.

And meanwhile when you're playing defence, since the squeeze is so effective, your coach, like every other coach in the league, utilizes it too, and demands you play it. You're not to go off fore-checking with abandon, but take up your position in the system to steer, cut off, or block. Since opponent options are confined by your position, and your responses are dictated by your system, there's little need for real anticipation. It's about disciplined, simple moves. There are few odd-man rushes you'll need your instincts to stop, rarely anyone racing through you can catch with a clean, hard, open-ice check. Inside your zone, it's similar – as described earlier for the other team. This is the system. "Don't deviate from it," the coaches say. And so you don't, because it's playing the system that wins games. And the players reimpose discipline on each other when anyone falls out of line, because their collective efforts are invested in it, and their jobs are dependent on winning. The mantra in the dressing room between periods when a team is in a bit of a funk is no longer "let's just go out and play hockey," it's "stick to the system." It works; but it also isn't the way the game was meant to be played.

A special but important case of the game is the chance to score (indeed how the game is measured). Let's assume the opposition had a breakdown, and you finally have a scoring chance. With the other team rushing to cover, you might have at most a few seconds to work with. But worse, as you look for open net to shoot at, you proba-bly have only a few inches to work with! The last line of defence – the goalie – is a formidable one. Goaltending skill has improved, but as a shooter, your skills have improved too, perhaps in balance. Most players in the league can shoot the way only a handful of players like Mike Bossy and Mario Lemieux could just fifteen or twenty years ago. But the huge growth in goaltender equipment that occurred over the last several years, you could not keep up with.

While, if anything, improvements in materials and design made it possible to protect goalies with smaller, less bulky equipment, instead the equipment inflated (in volume and frontage area) greatly. Goalies themselves on average got bigger, but not in any way like the equipment. Typically the skinniest players on a team, the goalies look more like sumo wrestlers compared to the other players, when suited up in their equipment! And a number of the equipment features, such as pads that extend above the goalie's knees, shoulder pads that move up astride the goalie's head when he crouches down, chest protectors that fan out wide of the torso, and sails coming off the gloves, can't be for protection, they can only be to stop goals. League-leading snipers like Milan Hejduk and Ilya Kovalchuk, who are some of the best shooters in the history of the game, struggle to reach fifty goals, while only as far back as 1992–93, no fewer than fourteen players did. As you look at the net, you've got nothing – no "daylight," as Brendan Shanahan said. There might literally be no way to beat the goalie. Sometimes the equipment doesn't even have to make a save, it just presents such a huge visual deterrent that you don't shoot, and then defenders close in and you lose your chance.

It's very difficult to beat the goalie, even if you have a clear chance. Goals often go in when the goalie couldn't see, wasn't set, or was interfered with trying to make the save. Seeing this, again coaches change strategy. Why waste a lot of energy and take a lot of risks trying to elaborately manoeuvre into what seem like great chances, when from almost anywhere you can throw the puck at the net, get people in front, and in the mad scramble in front, try to poke it home? So the entire methodology of offence is changed, and you are told not to use the conventional way of trying to create scoring chances unless there is a breakdown, and instead just focus on getting the puck in, battling to regain possession, then throwing it at the net, and trying to crash it in.

Fans of the Toronto Maple Leafs might wonder how former defenceman Larry Murphy was found so useful in Detroit. It's because he excelled at getting pucks through on net. There are skills on the other end too – screening, deflections, physical tenacity in front, and timing on rebounds. It's their heightened importance that's new. Some of the key performers in the recent World Cup, including Canada's Ryan Smyth and Shane Doan, and the USA's Keith Tkachuk, are players who shine in front of the opposition net. And in the 2004 playoffs, where like other recent playoffs a huge proportion of goals was scored in this way, the superbly coached and physically tough Calgary Flames and Philadelphia Flyers were teams that excelled at this "in the paint" game. But although this is the way to score, it's not the way competition with the goalie is meant to be in hockey, or in the way it alters the entire approach to the game, of how it's meant to be played.

Now don't blame the coaches – it's not their fault – they're just doing what works the way things are, and their job is to win. Plus, as much as it's the coaches' systems that prevent you from truly "playing," in fact coaches have experienced a similar thing. The success of the squeeze and other systems have transformed coaching as well, from the major task being inspiring players to push the limits of their potential, to disciplining players not to try to exceed what the system requires them to do. Roles as mentor, motivator, and tactical adviser have shrunk in comparison with ones as personnel manager, drill sergeant, controller. But even the most successful coaches of the modern order, like Tampa's John Tortorella and Canada's Midas-touch Pat Quinn, want to see the game's possibilities opened up. Even as they thrive in the new game, they lament how the arborescence of their profession has been sharply trimmed. The rules of success restrict the fullness of coaching first, then move from the coaches room to the dressing room, and from the dressing room to the ice, restricting the fullness of playing second.

The rules of success don't exist in isolation, either. In recent years, hockey has become Big Business, raising the stakes involved and the pressure on coaches to succeed. They can't take chances, can't have a couple of losing seasons waiting for players to develop, can't even have too long a stretch of bad games. Even aside from the need to succeed, the new Big Business game influences them in ways that constrain play of the game: under immense stress, human nature is to react by reaching for more control – which means more systems and stricter adherence to them.

And as a player, you're under the same intense pressure as the coaches. You're either in the NHL making big money or trying to get there. You're a professional. You aren't going to step out of line to "play," but do what's asked whether you like it or not. The new culture of that business surrounds you – from special meetings, to the cadre of club executives and support staff, to the impeccable dress and facilities, to the frequent minor league call-ups. It underscores that the interests of a serious organization are on your back, and the collective emotion of a city on top of theirs. So you try to keep coaches and management pleased by doing what you think or know they want – even when they don't explicitly demand it. And the way the game is, the damage a huge mistake can do to you is greater than the benefit of a great play. Especially if you're a young player who can be sent down to the minors, or a fourth-line forward or sixth defencemen who can be sent up to the press box. Only the top few players can run afoul of the system's rules and get off the hook, and only to a point, and what is the point, since it is ineffective and many of them have the greatest desire to win of all.

DAYLIGHT

With the NHL's rule changes for 2005–06, things have improved for players trying to play hockey.

The promised clampdown on obstruction-harassment means players will be able to try to make plays with the puck without being immobilized or impeded. This doesn't just open things up for the one player with the puck at any given time, but for all the players all the time. It should buy a little more time and space for offensive players to play, instead of being stuck in a straightjacket as soon as defenders get a sticklength away. So far, through the 2005 pre-season, players are finding more room to skate and make plays: those holes in the wall can't immediately be closed with the obstruction like they were before. That wiggle room an offensive player may have in the zone can't be whittled down with harassment the way it was before. Some are complaining that with all the penalties being called, the game is all special teams – perhaps the most systemized aspect of the game of all – and that players that don't play special teams aren't getting on the ice to play *anything*, much less hockey. "Let 'em play," they say. But the whole idea is that by calling all these penalties early, the fouls will cease, and then the penalty calls will cease – and once both are gone, in the long run players will really be free to play.

In addition, reductions have been mandated on the goalie equipment. Some of the things that serve no protective purpose, like the sails on gloves, are slated to be eliminated. Leg pads have been reduced by an inch. Other equipment such as the width of chest protectors, and the circumference of the goalie around the pants had to be reduced too, which the league did catch and tried to cover with other cuts totalling "11%." Goaltending is only one element of playing hockey, but one very important element, because what hits or misses the goalie's pads is the difference between goals and no-goals. Scoring and preventing goals is what the whole rest of the game is configured to do. Goalie equipment "inflation" had to be stopped, or it presumably could have just continued until the day it filled the entire net! Just like engines in autoracing, bats in baseball, or clubs in golf, it had to be regulated to ensure the fair play of the game. With the reductions, skaters will have a better chance to score one-on-one with the goalie, and it will be more worthwhile weaving good hockey plays to set up chances, a fair number of which should be converted into goals. Through the pre-season, save percentages are down, goals against averages are up, but goalies don't seem to mind too much because it's across the board. Goals are being scored in ways they seldom were in recent years. And that's progress. "There's daylight again," said Brendan Shanahan.

In this pre-season, players have actually had more ability to play than the sum of the effects of the changes above. That's because, with all the new rules, and some inevitable inconsistencies in the application of them in early stages, teams and players aren't quite sure how to play in all situations. Players' old habits are dying hard, coaches are slowly trying to sort through the confusion of the new game – and the result is there have been lots of mistakes and breakdowns in the systems that can still be played, or played under some modification. Defenders are clearly on the defensive – and that hesitation is the worst thing for defence in hockey – so offensive players are running wild. But as time goes on, players will learn the ropes of the new game, and coaches will re-establish the cohesiveness of their systems. And although players will still be playing more hockey then than they have at any time in recent years, the gains will be more modest than at first they may appear.

In addition, there are some other fronts on which there is clearly still a ways to go. One is that, while the steps taken should help players play hockey while on offence, we also want players to be able to play hockey on defence. The current interference clampdown is focused on defenders impeding offensive players, but we also have to make sure defenders aren't interfered with by offensive players running picks, hooking defenders, or bumping goaltenders as they try to make saves. And both on defence and offence, the greatest impediment to players playing hockey is the systems – the squeeze – which can and are still used in the new game to govern players actions on defence, and constrain their options on offence.

There is daylight now, but there is still a screen that can be cut away.

LIBERATION

How can we further liberate the competitive instincts and creative expression of players, the fun and enjoyment of the game palpable to players, coaches, fans all?

The centrepiece of what prevents players from playing hockey is the squeeze, so once again we must start with four-on-four as its antidote. Four-on-four destroys the squeeze and so allows players to use their speed, stickhandling ability, and agility again to carry the puck up the ice. The defence would not be able to cut off the ice, so players could once again use their vision and passing ability, their creativity, improvisation, and skills of deception. In the offensive zone, there will be more time and space – enough to make plays, to set up chances as well as goals the way hockey was meant to be played. In defending, since the squeeze won't work, players will once again be allowed to rely upon their anticipation, instincts, and ability to read and react. They will be encouraged to use their energy and desire to forecheck hard and proactively. There will be less of instructing players what to do in every situation, and more inspiring them to use all of their resources, to *play hockey* to the fullest extent of their ability and reserves of energy.

In this more open game, it would be harder to employ and get away with obstruction-harassment, which would assist in the clampdown against this, particularly as time goes on and the rules are pushed on and it becomes harder to maintain those gains that help players play unchained and unencumbered. At the same time, that crackdown should be expanded to the other side of the puck – so that offensive players interfering with defenders are called tightly too. This will help players playing defence be able to play hockey, without interference.

In combination, four-on-four and the clean-up of obstruction-harassment wouldn't just free players to do what they're trying to do, but would more globally re-infuse fluidity into the game. "Skating is the foundation of the game of hockey. I don't know why we should punish good skaters by allowing people to slow them down," Colin Campbell said. Each player would once again be integrally involved in every aspect of the game. You would not be able to put out two lines whose given objective is simply not to be scored on, or be afraid to put out two lines who can score because of the higher risk they might try to force things and instead be scored on. Well-rounded players who can play at both ends of the ice would be the most effective. Defencemen would be able to be more involved in joining the rush on offence, taking calculated risks, and have more creative options on breakouts. Every shift would involve the possibility of a goal at either end, every player on the ice would be important in every situation. And that's the way the game should be.

Next, although the goalie equipment has been trimmed, if you look at the explosion in size that occurred over the last twenty years, it is obvious it has been considerably more than the 11 per cent it was just reduced by. Particularly with the upper body equipment. So although I would not suggest we go back to the sizes of the mid-'80s equipment, I do think there is more room to reduce the upper body equipment without jeopardizing goalies' safety. I can't say exactly what appropriate limits would be, but I would suggest that the Competition Committee create a permanent subcommittee comprising goalies, former goalies, skaters, equipment experts, medical experts, and league officials to develop limits and monitor the issue.

They could also experiment with different strategies of the all-important enforcement. One method would be to require all equipment be pre-approved by the league before it can be worn; there would be inspections, and if a goalie wears unapproved equipment, he receives a suspension. An alternative (or supplement) that I like is to give these issues a recourse within the competitive arena: teams would be able to call for measurements on any size limits pertaining to goalie equipment the same way they can for sticks. If it is illegal, it's a penalty, and the goalie must forfeit the piece of equipment (permanently, just like the stick) and actually serve the penalty himself (and not return till a whistle). If it's not illegal, same as with the illegal stick, the other team gets a bench penalty. Already, I have heard goalies say they are keeping an eye on their counterparts at the other end of the ice for potential abuses – here's a way to help.

I also think cuts would have to be gradually phased in, to give goalies a chance to adapt their style. I suspect today's goalies used to love watching the acrobatic saves made by a Vladislav Tretiak or a Grant Fuhr, and wouldn't mind slimmer equipment if it would allow them to play the butterfly a little less often, to showcase their incredible athleticism and reflexes in other ways, and give goalies a chance to enjoy playing hockey more too.

On the other side of the equation is the ongoing problem of goaltender interference. For the sake of both the fairness of the game and the safety of goalies, it is important that goaltender inter-ference be eradicated. And with the desire on the part of everyone for more goals in the game beginning in 2005–06, it is important that more goaltender interference not be one of the ways. To help stop it, we can look to soccer – which has even fewer goals, so the fairness of each goal is even more important. Soccer has good, tested rules that can be modified into something similar for hockey to adopt. First of all, we should make two creases (kind of like the two boxes in soccer): a smaller that one players are not allowed to enter without the puck and a slightly larger one where players can't inter-fere with the goalie while he is trying to make a save or play the puck. Outside of these, he is like any other player. In the smaller crease, if an opposing player is even partly in it without the puck, the whistle goes and a faceoff is held outside the zone (kind of like the key rule in basketball, for a similar reason). In fact, they have this rule in NCAA hockey – a player is not allowed to be in the crease without the puck, or there is a faceoff outside the zone.

In the larger crease recommended, if a player interferes with a goaltender trying to make a save, it's an automatic penalty every time. It doesn't just apply to deliberately running into goalies, but placing oneself in the way of where the goalie needs to go to make the save (as in soccer). These changes should be a fair (and safety promoting) tradeoff for goaltender equipment reductions. And it will reinforce the renewed use of conventional and appropriate ways to set up chances and score in hockey.

None of these proposals will take away the pressures present in the new Big Business modern game, but will change the way people react to them. A coach will still need to win, but he will have to accomplish that a different way, letting players play. Coaches would use more supportive, inspirational, mentorial methods of coaching and less controlling ones, simply as a prerequisite to having a chance to win. As a result, they will once again have the freedom and ability to coach in the fullest sense. Not only that, but this environment may result in more longevity and job-security for coaches, and less sleepless nights and grey hairs. An improved job description will spread from coaches to players, and be visible on the ice to those watching. Meanwhile, acting in a parallel manner, the same change would occur for players directly. There would be nowhere to hide from the game, and no way to avoid mistakes. You simply have to play hockey with everything you've got. I can't think of anything that would be better for the players in the game.

Together, all of these suggestions would once again allow pros not to be consumed with playing the system, but to play hockey – using all their skills of the game, finding room for creativity and improvisation, each player involved in all aspects of the game, and everything in the right balance. It would return the experience of the game to what made players fall in love with it in the first place, and pursue it as far as they have. Players will feel more connected to the game and less frustrated. Coaches will be less under the gun. Fans who relate to the experience of playing as they watch will enjoy doing so in the game they would see. Kids will too, and will aspire to be tomorrow's pros. Another restriction in the game would be removed, as we all delight in players "playing hockey" again.

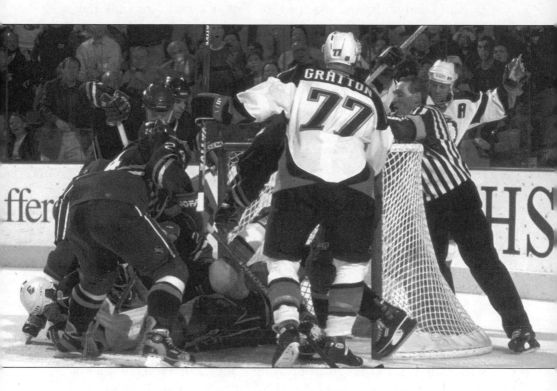

Was it interference? Or was it a goal? The referee has numerous factors to consider and a split-second to decide – with eyes watching him intensely from all sides. (*Dave Sandford/Hockey Hall of Fame*)

CHAPTER 6

CLARIFYING THE WAY THE GAME IS OFFICIATED

TOUGH CALL

E mbedded in the issues looked at so far were a number of items related to the officiating of the game: obstruction-harassment, diving, goalie equipment, and interference. And even beyond these, there have been concerns in the past about the way the game was officiated.

Consider these scenes: An offensive player has a great chance but is tackled from behind, and it isn't called because it's within a game's last few minutes. A defenceman is tripped in front of his own net by the player he is covering, leaving the offensive player open for an easy goal. One player roughs up another after the whistle, and they both get penalized. An offside is missed, the play continues, and the offensive team scores. How commonly did the game see examples such as these or others in recent years? Other observations may have been relative: Countless hooks are let go, then one suddenly is called. Two players slash each other, and they only call the retaliator. A player gets three penalties in one game for doing the same thing that was okay (seen but uncalled) the game before. There were many different examples.

The perception by those inside the game and out that there were too many of these errors and inconsistencies in the call of games was hard to dispute: when you watched a game, any game, you typically saw several obvious infractions let go, a few seemingly similar ones called, and some calls made that were in fact mistakes. There were regular patterns to certain missed calls, and a frustrating unpre- dictability to the call of others. Other sports were imperfect, but seemed to fare better.

The most senior hockey folks expressed concern about it. Pat Quinn explained, "If there is a dirty hit and it's not called and then there's a hit thirty seconds later, no worse or maybe not even close to the one that happened, and there's a penalty on it, you start saying, 'Hey, we're getting stiffed.' Those are the kind of thoughts that go through your head." How widespread this view was, was evident from the contention erupting call by call, game by game. You just didn't see in football, basketball, or baseball that constant tension over the officiating that you saw in hockey: virtually every game, people on one side or both furious at the referees; virtually every game, referees peppered with verbal abuse. On players' part, it was a recurrent frustration, not an isolated or heat-of-the-moment thing. Jeremy Roenick, Mike Modano, Joe Thornton, Teemu Selanne, and Joe Sakic were just a few examples of well-known players who had publicly complained about it. "Obviously when some of the best players in the league are talking the way they are, the league should listen," Thornton said. It's not that they should just listen to star players, but star players are often the only ones secure enough to speak out. On the other side, referees no doubt had just as much frustration and unannounced complaints of their own.

It was a pervasive problem, but it was also perhaps more pro- found than those of other sports. Playing in places in the United States where the game was new, I often heard novice fans express incredulity at how infractions that are in the rules, and which every- one in the building saw occur (including presumably the officials), were not called. The only conclusion many could draw was that hockey was something like pro wrestling, where this sort of official unfairness is part of the act. But that clashed with other messages hockey was trying to send them, and made it hard to take the sport seriously. From players to officials, from long-time fans to new acquaintances, there was a consensus question of whether the game was being called the way it should be called, or whether there was a better way for all involved.

It was important for a number of reasons: first of all, if something's wrong, it's wrong. Secondly, it's something we're naturally very attuned to. When we think something's happened that's wrong, we notice, and a stream of negative emotions ensue. In a major team sport, that stream can quickly build into a flood, as that emotional effect is multiplied by the twenty teammates, coaches, and other staff that automatically identify with their player, plus that team's thousands of fans watching. In addition, the fact there are so many calls to make also gives it a chance to build, if the officiating is anything less than speckless. More "tough calls" in a game make resentment build, and over a season or longer they undermine basic belief in the fair conduct of the game. On the ice, that contributes to disrespect for the rules, lawless behaviour, and abuse of officials – all of which we have seen. Off the ice, it hurts the image of the game, and thus ultimately its following.

Lastly, few things incite as fiery reactions as people perceiving themselves the victim of injustice, and sometimes those undesirable reactions themselves – while having to be the responsibility of those reacting – still added to the trouble. Embarrassment was the result in 1976 when the Soviet team refused to continue playing their exhibition against Philadelphia after a vicious elbow on Russian star Valery Kharlamov wasn't called. "They're going home, I don't believe it, they're going home," commentator Bob Cole memorably repeated. Eventually the Soviets returned – after being threatened the forfeiture of their tour money – but only went through the motions the rest of the game. Recently, there have been plenty of outbursts.

In the playoffs' first round against Detroit in 2002, Canucks GM Brian Burke held a press conference about the officiating, saying, "I didn't know that tackling was an acceptable tactic, I didn't see it in the rulebook." Burke continued, "Another point, our goaltender can be identified by the large pads and mask that he wears. He's also the goaltender on the ice that does not dive when he gets brushed. . . . We pay the same dues to the National Hockey League that Detroit pays and even though we're just a little Canadian team, we deserve a level playing field. We haven't gotten one yet and we're sick of it." Burke was fined for his comments, and the Canucks lost the next two games and were eliminated. The following season, the Leafs' Darcy Tucker and Tie Domi acted out some frustration in what they felt was an unfairly officiated game between the Leafs and the Ottawa Senators. "You put up with it for so long and after a while something is going to snap and this was a case where it was so frustrating, Tie and Darcy had enough and, like I said, if anybody is to blame for it, it's the referee. The other referee was doing a pretty good job," Leafs goaltender Eddie Belfour described after. Domi and Tucker were each suspended and fined.

The 2003–04 season saw an incensed Jeremy Roenick hurl a water bottle at a referee, then lash out after the game: "Terrible, absolutely terrible. [Referee's name omitted] did an absolutely terrible job. It's ridiculous." After being suspended, Roenick relented, sort of: "Our sport is a great sport, it's just ruled by Neanderthal people, that's all," he said. Later that season, Ottawa's Martin Havlat, frustrated while being hooked by Philly's Mark Recchi with no call, turned and swung his stick at the Flyer's head. "I was getting frustrated with all the hooking going on before that. I wanted to hit him, but not in the face," Havlat said before being suspended. Afterwards, Flyer coach Ken Hitchcock menaced: "Someday someone's going to make him eat his lunch. This is something in my opinion that the players should take care of." A few days later a brawl-filled rematch between the two clubs broke an NHL penalty-minute record, and gave the league a public black eye.

A short time later, after several other high-profile incidents and suspensions in a small space of time, NHLPA head Bob Goodenow said, "Player confidence in the officials' ability to control the game is diminishing. It does put an onus on the players themselves to behave in a different way. In some cases, people would suggest they take matters into their own hands. Others would just say have more respect for each other. I'm sure it's going to be an issue that's discussed widely at the meetings that are coming up this summer." To my knowledge, there was a lot of discussion about how to divide up business revenues at those meetings, but no direct consideration of the issues in officiating. And the trouble continued. Most recently, in the May 2005 World Championships, many witnessed the incident in which young star Rick Nash had an on-ice physical altercation with a referee and a linesman, in apparent frustration.

Undesirable reactions to perceived injustices haven't been confined to direct participants either. Fans may be less involved in the game, but that means they were also less bound to it, less obliged to be tolerant or stretch their patience. An extreme but important historical example was the Richard Riot on St. Patrick's Day 1955, in Montreal. A few days earlier, Rocket Richard had been suspended by the NHL for punching a linesman during an altercation with a Bruin player. At the next game in Montreal, a smoke bomb and other things were thrown by fans in the direction of NHL president Clarence Campbell, who responded by cancelling the game and awarding the victory to the visiting arch-rival Red Wings. An incensed mob spilled out of the Forum and joined others outside to riot and vandalize downtown Ste. Catherine Street for seven hours. More than sixty people were arrested, and the Rocket had to go on the radio to plead for an end to the chaos.

Fans have important emotional investments in the game too, and some calls can be tough to accept. Lately, there have been a number of such triggers of fan displeasure. Maple Leafs fans have not forgotten the highstick by Wayne Gretzky to Toronto's Doug Gilmour in overtime of Game 6 of their semifinal series against L.A. in 1993, which should have required an automatic four-minute penalty and a strong chance of a trip to the finals for the Leafs. But it wasn't called, and shortly after, Gretzky scored the winner, added a hat trick in Game 7, and Toronto has never been so close to breaking its nearly forty-year Stanley Cup drought since. Across Canada, many were livid over the controversial end to the World Cup 1996, when an apparent high-stick goal by the USA's Brett Hull immediately followed by an apparent kicked-in goal by Tony Amonte were allowed to stand with about three minutes remaining, turning a late Canadian lead into a sudden bitter defeat.

Likewise, many Buffalo residents had a lingering bitter taste in their mouths about the "in the crease goal" that gave the Dallas Stars the Stanley Cup in overtime against the Sabres in 1999, but which according to video replays should have been disallowed.

In last year's first round, Calgary led with under two minutes remaining in Game 7 when defender Andy Ference was called for slashing a Canuck player's stick. A minute later with the Vancouver net empty, Jarome Iginla's stick was slashed out of his hands, but the referee was busy picking up an object a Canuck fan had thrown onto the ice and missed it. Iginla tripped on his stick, and the man he would have been covering tapped in the tying goal with just seconds left! Would there have been riots in Calgary, instead of the now famous celebrations, if the resilient Flames hadn't rebounded by winning in overtime? Three rounds later, some angry Calgary fans *did* threaten a referee, make derisive chants, and rain debris down in disdain during Game 4 of the Finals.

Whether fans lose their temper, or lose respect for the game, ultimately a sport pays a heavy price for any troubles with the officiating. We have seen these kinds of things happen in other sports. Boxing is an example of a sport that has lost following due to perception of unjust adjudicating. And soccer is an example of a sport where the issue has bubbled over at times, including recently. For example, many Italians are furious about how they feel they have been treated in international soccer: A goal scored in seemingly unwarranted injury time lost them the Euro 2000 final, and "scandalously unfair" refereeing cost them in the World Cup 2002. After the World Cup, there were riots in Italy, politicians entered the fray, and broadcaster Rai reportedly threatened to sue FIFA. "It is perfectly normal for a referee to make one or two mistakes a game, but we are talking about three games with enormous errors. They have done everything they possibly could to stop us. We feel terrible. It is a disgrace. Episodes like the ones that occurred with the referee tonight are not part of football, they are not part of the sport I love," Italian defender Fabio Cannavaro said, more calmly and eloquently than anyone else at the time. Other players have reacted less calmly, including star striker Francesco Totti, who has twice erupted recently and been suspended. At the same time, the trouble makes life hard for referees too. Long-time Swedish referee Anders Frisk quit after receiving escalating death threats directed at himself and family members from Chelsea fans in the weeks following a match of theirs he refereed against Barcelona. Swiss referee Urs Meier was also receiving death threats following a match he refereed between England and Portugal, and subsequently retired. Club AS Roma was forced to play two home-field international matches without fans after a missile fired from the crowd hit and bloodied the referee, who had sent off a Roma player in a match against Dynamo Kiev. These are just a few among many examples.

To improve on the past, and avoid the kinds of ills these other sports have suffered, hockey would need to be vigilant about its officiating, and assure that any problems with it be confined and addressed. Frequently incensed coaches, frustrated players, bitter fans, and abuse toward referees were symptoms of an overarching issue of the way the game was officiated. It's difficult to measure how much this contributed to disrespect and bad behaviour on the ice, or what it cost in fans, since to re-use a famous Gretzky quote, "How do you count the fans that are *not* there?" But suffice it to say that ameliorating the officiating situation was another key challenge for hockey.

SCOUTING "STRIPES"

Some players and fans have gone overboard in criticizing and attacking officials – as in some of the earlier examples. Scapegoating officials is both unfair and nonsensical. At the other extreme are those who refuse to ever find fault with them, and dismiss without thinking all discussion of officiating shortcomings as the complaining of sore losers. That doesn't make any sense either: officials are humans, just like anybody else; they can and do make mistakes. And in overseeing games, officials play a huge and critical role. That's why every sport hires teams of professional officials in the first place. It matters who they are and how they do, as much as for people performing any other profession, including athletes and coaches. Just as hockey players and coaches must share responsibility when their team is in a slump, hockey officials must inescapably bear *some* – but certainly not all – of the responsibility for issues around officiating in hockey. Don't blame them, but don't hold them immune. That's just common sense.

That officials are both well intentioned and highly professional in their approach is beyond question. And I also don't think there's any doubt that the NHL boasts by far the best hockey officials of any league or association in the world. Where most of the trouble lay, it seemed, was in certain recurrent patterns, either of mistakes or of judgments that were ingrained in the way the game habitually had been called. For example, a large number of infractions were seen and ignored by a referee who adhered to the maxim "let 'em play," which meant to let teams play five-on-five. So obstruction-harassment and other fouls would be let go that were actually banned in the rulebook, to avoid disrupting the flow of the game by calling too many penalties.

But even though this may have been done evenly with respect to both teams, each time a player was fouled and it wasn't called, the player victimized was incensed, as well as teammates, coaches, and fans, because it was in the rules that it should have been a penalty. That was bad for the sport. The intentions may have been good, in that referees don't want to decide games. And you couldn't just blame a referee, because this pattern of officiating was widespread in the sport. The reason – which I sympathize with – was people don't want the game overrun by penalties and powerplays. But letting infractions go was not the answer: "Let 'em play" meant "let 'em foul." "It's 5-4 late in the game, or there's already a player in the box or it's in the last five minutes when a game is tied, we didn't make the call because it's the outcome of a game. But by not making the call the outcome of a game may be decided," Colin Campbell said. And not making the calls also just invited more and more fouls in the game, as things like obstruction skyrocketed, with a cascade of negative implications for the game.

Another thing that you heard people sometimes accuse referees of doing was calling a game "by the score," in order to keep games tight. "Any time you have a 2-0 lead, the refs don't call anything, unless it's against you," Joe Sakic said last season. " 'Gotta keep it tight.' That's what the league wants, I guess. Tight games." As well, people would complain that referees seemed to give teams a roughly similar number of penalties no matter what a game looked like or the balance of fouls occurring: "even-up" calls, broadcasters would label them on TV or on the radio. But an even number of calls for each team wasn't necessarily right; officiating should play the ball as it lies, and if there were ten penalties to two, so be it. If teams knew calls would be roughly equal, they would each have an incentive to foul more, overrunning the game.

Players and coaches were also very sensitive to what they perceived as inconsistency: things might be called one minute and let go another, called one day by one referee, but not the next day by the next referee. "We're clamping down." No, "we're letting things go." Players and coaches complained often of not having a clear and consistent line they knew they were allowed to play to. Another thing that often angered them was calls off dives, often by the same known divers game in and game out. "Maybe we'll call a practice tomorrow and practise our diving. I'm dead serious . . . It's disgusting. I should be teaching and I'm not doing a good enough job teaching diving," coach Ron Wilson said.

All of these were examples of patterns within the officiating that produced calls many people took issue with. And in my opinion, these patterns accounted for the bulk of any problems.

But as NHLPA head Bob Goodenow implied, many players in recent years, for right or wrong, had greater issue with the basic quality of officials. Maybe it was simply because in sports, officials are the face of justice – such a contentious issue – and hockey is a particularly tough sport to officiate. Maybe there was more to it than that. Either way, for players and coaches to so often complain about the officials was itself an issue that had to be spoken to. Forward Joe Thornton was for a while one of the most vociferous critics: "We have news conferences where we have to come out and discuss why we made that bad pass or missed a wide-open net. I'd like to see the same thing done with officials where they explain why they made a certain call or why they missed calls," he said. On another occasion, Thornton suggested NHL vice-president of hockey operations Colin Campbell be fined whenever referees miss calls. Indeed officials play a role in the game that is both important and sacred, and clearly their quality and players' confidence in that are both of material importance. To paraphrase the age-old legal dictum, "Justice must not only be present, but must be seen to be present."

BEYOND THE CALL

When it comes to officiating, for many people the thought ended with the officials themselves. But considering the issue in greater depth and examining the environment officials worked in reveals that what we have talked about so far was only half the problem. The position that officials were put in was the other. The job was very tough to begin with, automatically as a result of factors outside anyone's control. As in any sport where there are human arbiters, hockey officials were in a spot where they could never be praised, only vilified. In addition, hockey is the fastest game on Earth, so there are many things happening on the ice at all times, and only split seconds to make decisions. And it's a complicated game to officiate in terms of the number of line calls and infractions to watch out for.

With the way the sport traditionally operated, the predicament was even worse. Officials were put in a position of having to make complicated judgments when it was hard enough just to concentrate and call what they saw. Hockey's habit was of not enforcing the rules strictly; weak enforcement was the norm if not the expectation. This meant that before making a call, all kinds of other factors would be taken into account beyond whether a foul occurred: whether a foul was enough of a foul to call, the score of the game and the amount of time left, the number of fouls called so far, the balance of fouls between the teams so far, and so on. The officials had to try to weigh all these different factors in a split second. It was impossible. It put them into a situation where they just had to decide on impulse, because that's all they had time for, and automatically there would be plenty of mistakes and inconsistency as a result. This was probably the major reason for all the problems. Canadian writer Larry Scanlan has pointed out the irony of the fact that the black-and-white bars of the referee's jersey belied a job that was all about shades of grey.

Not only that, but by making every call a human decision rather than a function of eyesight and fixed rules, the officials were put in the position of being individual persons deciding games. They were on the spot, under the spotlight, centre stage with each decision of whether to make a call. This was unfair – the officials should be arbiters, not performers, in a literal sense. In a case for example where there was a blatant infraction with a minute left in a one-goal game – like the high stick that cut Martin St. Louis in Game 7 of the 2004 Final – what do the referees do? Damned if they do, damned if they don't, damned if they do something in between. The decision's on them.

The irony is that being front and centre like that is the one thing paradoxically everyone most wanted to avoid in "letting 'em play," but we ended up there afterall! That's always the case with weak enforcement: "For he who quells disorder by a very few signal examples will in the end be more merciful than he who from too great leniency permits things to take their course and so to result in rapine and bloodshed," wrote Machiavelli in *The Prince*. Not having officials call everything strictly from the get-go could only lead to an explosion of fouls, and from there to an impossible job of deciding when and which to punish, thereby incurring the ire of everyone. It is a horrible position the officials certainly didn't want to be in: the job was impossible, the stakes high, and the reaction neutral at best, and often fiercely negative. Referees thus became simultaneously but unwittingly the agents and the victims of the injustice in the game.

For those who believe it hadn't used to be as bad as it was in recent years, a major explanation would have been coaches and players continually pushing on the rules over time, seeing how much they could get away with. They did it with obstruction-harassment, with line changes, faceoffs, and most recently with other kinds of fouls. It's hard to blame any single individual for what's a natural and universal trend, part of what was mentioned at the beginning about how things spontaneously tend to disorder. But the effect was, with a skyrocketing rise in infractions that you couldn't call without ruining a few games, and with officials continuing to try to preserve the flow of games by only calling so many of them, there were way more things uncalled, way more officiating decisions, and therefore way more grounds for contention. Furthermore, the fact there were so many infractions going on and so few being called meant there would always be several particularly blatant non-calls, *and* the few calls that *were* made would always seem somewhat random or unfair. Further, the modern style of play magnified the stakes: a bottled-up game had few chances, few goals, and small margins in score. So each call had potentially major significance to the outcome of a game or even a season, and the perceived extent of mistakes seemed that much grander. These are key recognitions. Meanwhile, players had gotten bigger and the ice more crowded, making up for the extra pair of eyes provided by the second referee added.

Other recent unpredicted developments affected the lot of officials as well. For example, when goalie equipment exploded, goals became fewer, scores tighter, and the significance of calls and missed calls larger in the scheme of games. Also, goalie interference rose as an antidote, and became so prevalent it was hard to call – all the more because each decision meant the difference between a goal one way or a powerplay the other. A similar thing occurred with diving, exploiting a crowded ice surface where countless fouls were occurring, and it was impossible to keep rein of it all – so that what ended up being called was what stood out – which was someone falling, whether it was real or unfortunately sometimes a dive. All of this made the job of officials harder and harder in recent years.

All of these developments in the modern game increased the frequency and extent to which officials were forced to the centre of attention on the ice. A few years ago, the league took the names off the officials' jerseys – partly for security reasons, one presumes, but also to signal to players and fans that officials were not acting as individuals, but as objective applicators of the rules. However, the irony was that simultaneous trends in the game were resulting in a more personal, subjective, amplified, and impossible job for officials than ever before. A spotlight overhead and a seat in the eye of the storm.

There remained one more important contributor to the difficult environment officials worked in. And this consisted of the culture and attitudes of the game with respect to officiating. As a kid, you probably had an uncle tell you the joke that the referees got the uniforms they had by escaping from jail and turning the stripes sideways as a disguise! But the game's tradition (from kids' hockey up through the pros) of disrespect for officials, constant criticism and verbal abuse by players, coaches, or parents – as the case may be – is no laughing matter. This simply does not occur in other sports the way it has occurred in hockey. Abuse of officials is not strictly and consistently punished like it is in baseball, football, basketball, and other sports. Just "two minutes" (or ten without being shorthanded) – and only sometimes, of course. The game's tolerance of this abuse no doubt deters people from becoming officials and staying with it. No wonder a third of all hockey officials in Canada has been quitting each year. With an attrition rate like that, how can we expect to have good officiating in the future? In addition, allowing verbal intimidation and insults can potentially cause personality conflicts to enter into the officiating process, where they have no place.

Besides on-ice abuse, referees were quite often denounced by TV announcers accusing them of ruining a game by calling too many penalties, or blowing a game by calling an infraction they saw occur at a sensitive moment in the competition. This could embarrass them in front of thousands, and damage their reputation in the industry. Too pointed blame could ultimately even jeopardize their job, or heighten risks to their personal security – as in the above examples in soccer. In fact, hockey did make a referee substitution for Game 6 of last season's Cup Final, widely taken to be because of concern over threats and security. No doubt officials, as humans, were sensitive to this pressure, which could only distract them from freely officiating to the best of their ability.

VISION OF A NEW ORDER

What could be done to improve the way the game was officiated?

First of all, this began with whatever could be done to better the performance of the officials themselves. To its credit, even before the lockout, the league had already taken some steps to try to help in this regard. These included: video feedback sessions with officials covering on-ice issues, a training camp for officials that even included fitness testing, the disciplining or firing of underperforming referees and linesmen each year, and on the other hand the rewarding of top performing officials with playoff games and other bonuses. All of that should pay dividends in the years to come.

However, more can still be done. One thing officials can easily do themselves is target for elimination the patterns they have sometimes been accused of falling into, like "swallowing" whistles late in games, trying to call an even number of penalties, falling for the act of known divers, inconsistency of calls, and so on as mentioned earlier. Each of these patterns was part of common parlance on offi- ciating in the game, so their existence could not have been lost on the officials; it had to be more a case of these being ingrained almost like habits. As a result, it wouldn't take much for the officials to improve this, other than sensitivity to what's wrong with these, and attention paid to their avoidance. But in order to fully eliminate these wrinkles, the league will need to support the officials in that initiative – helping identify the most problematic patterns present, increasing officials' awareness of them, providing clear league direc- tives for their elimination, and distributing appropriate rewards and punishments for success or failure in doing so. Ironing out these wrinkles would do much to improve the officiating in the game.

On a more sweeping level, there are plenty of things the league can do to address some players' concerns about the quality of the officiating. One thing that can certainly be done more is to become more deeply involved with the recruitment and development of officials at amateur levels. Strong hiring criteria and professional- development programs the league may have for its own officials are one thing, but there's only so much you can do at that late stage. Just as more kids playing hockey and better skill-development initia- tives to cultivate their talents makes for better professional hockey players, attracting as many quality people into officiating as possi- ble and working with them from early stages of development to build their officiating skills ultimately means better officiating in the NHL. We market the game to young players, we have talent scouts, we have sponsors – all investing in the game's future players. Referees have an equally great importance to the conduct and pros- perity of the game. It seems that sports like football and basketball view things this way, so why not hockey? Making officiating a primary thought and not an afterthought may for some of us be a bit of a change in conception, but it's one that can only make the sport better. And that begins with investment in future officials back at entry-levels into the vocation.

Another strategy that can be used to try to improve officiating is to sweeten the job's rewards. In society at large, judges are very well paid and hold great prestige. Officials are the equivalent in sports. Although officials are by no means paid poorly, I can't imagine judges being laid-off as referees were during the player lockout, and having to sell used cars or install kitchen cabinetry, as some of them reportedly did to get by. And on the other side of it, just as high salaries and first-class treatment for players in today's NHL has in my opinion only induced the world's best players to respond by striving for ever greater and greater levels of skill and professionalism, similarly erring on the side of overpaying and overly well-treating officials would only encourage them to stretch the limits of their commitment and performance to new levels. Also in return for the greater rewards, officials could have duties that are full-time and year-round. Besides their work on-ice, they would participate in rule committee revisions, help train officials at lower levels, and bring the rules of the game and the message of respect and fair play to youth and amateur hockey. What I envisage is them serving as a kind of class of distinguished ambassadors touring on behalf of the league in their time off the ice to voice the message of the justice, integrity, and sportsmanship of the game. This would add to the profile, prestige, and respect of officials, while at the same time spreading a message that makes their job easier, and makes the game better. In trying to enhance the game, would that be a bad thing?

At the same time, many players and analysts believe that the league needs to do more on the other end with regards to standards and expectations of officials. Players, in making it to the NHL, have undergone a lifetime of training, risen to the top of intense competition, and captured jobs with elite standards of performance. The officials are on the same ice, and have power over them – they have a fundamental and vital role in the game. Players feel officials should have similar performance standards. The league can't duplicate the player-forging process with officials, but it can provide intensive "coaching" and have rigorous and specific standards of performance that officials are required to meet, analogous to those for players, but designed for officials. Professional development training such as the video feedback can be bolstered by ongoing "pro

scouting" evaluation and statistical analysis, as well as discrete initiatives for specific issues and specific officials, equivalent to players'
"practice drills." But perhaps at least as much an issue as the reality
is the perception. Why not make hirings, training methods, standards used, and development programs that are in place completely
transparent for players and others to appraise? This would tremendously improve confidence in the officiating, increase respect, and
improve the relationships that influence behaviour.

Accountability is another thing that critics of the officiating have
focused on as a needed weight on the scale of balance. Players and
coaches have the ultimate accountability – because their bosses are
in the competition, and have direct stakes on the line in that performance. Although officials are accountable to the league, the
league is not in the competition, and isn't affected by their work in
the same way or to the same extent. To have a similar accountability, we need to find a way to make officials accountable to those
directly in the competition – but in an objective and appropriate way.
Indeed, by near consensus among players, giving players and clubs
a say in assessment and review of officials is essential, so that the relationship is a two-way street. This could be accomplished by having
player-reps and club-reps sitting on a committee that evaluates officials on a regular basis (quarterly, for example) – a subcommittee of
the competition committee created for 2005–06 to oversee the on-
ice game. And *all* players could have a say in reviewing referees'
work through an anonymous survey at the end of each season, or
feedback cards they could put in a "drop box" for the league at any
time. As far as any serious misjudgments or egregious injustice,
teams could be able to file protests or grievances under certain conditions, with real remedies and repercussions. All of these measures
would induce players to have more respect for officials, and officials more respect for players.

The preceding initiatives can improve the officiating with
respect to penalties, line calls, and all other aspects of the job. But
ultimately, all of this is only half of what's necessary, because no
matter how good the officials are, they can't make up for what has

been an impossible situation where injustice was unavoidable and troublesome reactions to it all too common.

The real source of that was the sport's habit of loose enforcement of its own rules, which turned simple calls into complicated and uncertain judgments for officials of when to call something and when to let it go. And the most critical step needed to put a stop to this was to implement a "No Discretion" policy, removing the need for complex consideration by officials and placing officiating back in the hands of the rulebook. Refereeing ought to be a job for the eyes, not the cerebral cortex. If an official sees an infraction, he calls it, period. Everything is called by the book, all the time. No exceptions, No Discretion, no outside factors, no subjective judgments. Doesn't matter what the score is, the time left, the calls made already, the balance of calls, the people involved, the situation, the implications, none of it.

In criticizing officials in the past, people often mockingly said "the referees are blind." In a very different sense of that term, that's exactly what people wished they could be: blind – in making calls, blind as to when, where, how much, or what else, the only relevant question being "Did it happen?" With human officials, there will always be a human element and human error, but we still needed to strive to officiate with machinelike consistency, not constantly force officials into effectively personal decisions about game calls.

This objective essentially is what the obstruction-harassment clampdown announced by the NHL for 2005–06, as described in earlier chapters, strived for. There would be no more potential allowing of infractions that weren't too severe, or came at a contentious time in a game, or were committed by a team that had already been penalized several times in a row. If the foul occurred, it would be called. This plan, if it could be successfully implemented (and in the 2005 pre-season, it has looked to be on the right track), would be a truly momentous step for the game. Not so much on the excitement front, where it would still help, but on the fair and appropriate conduct of the game, where it would be a historic breakthrough. Some observers may have underestimated the significance of the change, because it involved no modification to the rulebook or had no novel moniker, but it was a revolutionary change in the application of the rules, and one that carried huge positive effects for the game and the sentiments of everyone involved.

Through the 2005 pre-season, there have been some critics condemning it – mostly (aside from some wrinkles that had to be ironed out) on the basis that it wasn't the way things used to be. No doubt "No Discretion" was far from the habit of the call of the game, and some used to that would have a hard time comprehending or accepting it. There was a time I would've counted myself in that camp. I remember watching one of my team's games while I was injured: two blatant infractions were let go in a row, the second one halting a half-breakaway, and the arena went up in arms – the sort of thing hockey was used to night in and night out. But the team doctor who was standing with me just behind the glass from where the second foul occurred turned to me after the crowd reaction died down and said, "You know, I never understood why in any other sport if an official sees an infraction, he has to call it, period. There's no deliberation, no decision. But in hockey, the referee sees a penalty, but he might not call it. They're expected to factor in all this other *stuff*. And I just really don't understand why."

Indeed, the game was in an area where football and basketball were big, and the doctor's sons played soccer, and none of those sports were like hockey in that regard. I searched my brain, didn't have an answer, and realized the doctor was right: there was no good reason. Why did we have discretion? Yes, factor in accidents, intent, and so on. But why factor in how much of a foul it was, the score in the game, the time of the game, the last five calls, the players involved? What was that but a devaluation of the rules? Discretion was a slippery slope that led to so many of the other difficulties we had. The other sports didn't have this: they called huge pass interference penalties in the last seconds of football games, they called just as many fouls on basketball teams whether they were down by a lopsided margin or ahead, they'd call ten fouls in a row on the same soccer team if that was what they saw. No doubt football and basketball would have been overrun by interference too if they didn't have the automatic and "unfeeling" penalties they did; same with other fouls, and same for the other sports.

I wondered whether there was some reason hockey was different and had to be called like this, but basketball had direct contact, and football was a physical game. The only difference was, hockey was way faster – and with so much going on at those speeds, that meant hockey should be the *last* sport to think it could make tricky computations and judgments like that. It was not even close to being appropriately possible. It was the biggest reason for the problems we had with officiating. And there was only one way to fix that: No Discretion.

If implemented and sustained, this would have a tremendous impact on the fairness of the game: it would create a clear standard for players to play by, and for officials to officiate by. If a call is wrong, it'll be a question of the eyes not the mind, and people won't get so mad at the official, because they'll know it wasn't done consciously. However, the clampdown undertaken by the league for 2005–06 pertained only to obstruction-harassment, and that particularly on the puckcarrier. For the sake of the officiating of the game, it is crucial that this be extended to all types of fouls, on all players, whether on offence or defence. Every infraction should be called by the book, all the time.

This would also dramatically improve the consistency of officiating by providing a clear and consistent standard that doesn't vary from moment to moment, game to game, official to official, and where things aren't always being measured not only against the rulebook but against every other call and non-call so far today and all-season beforehand, which will always provide a basis for dispute and the perception of injustice. No more comparisons to all these different things; just one measure – the rules.

In addition, as was the NHL's obvious intention with is clampdown, No Discretion would eradicate the rampant infractions that took over the game in recent years, which were illegal themselves and contributed to the bottled-up game where officiating calls were more significant and any mistakes in them magnified in importance.

Tough calls that might still unavoidably occur would then be less important and more easily overcome. There would also be less reason and opportunity for retaliation, or resorting to lawless vigilantism, as what's seen would be called, and the players would count on it. That makes the game safer and cleaner. In all, freeing the game of all these infractions would have an enormous effect on the level of fairness in the game, and equally or especially on the recognition of it by people in and out of the game.

Sustaining the change is going to be a key challenge. First of all, there is bound to be condemnations of the new order. "I'm not really thinking about the [complaints] and I don't really care," director of officiating Stephen Walkom said. "I'm just concerned about the implementation of these rules that I feel will help our game." That's a good sign. But even aside from criticism, as time goes on, games acquire more significance, and the rules are pushed on, it will be tough to maintain. "It's not going to be easy," Colin Campbell said, aptly likening it to trying to change "a culture." One way to make it easier, and given the struggle of past initiatives to tighten enforcement, is to go to four-on-four hockey, which would smooth the path for the implementation for No Discretion. It would help because it kills the effectiveness of the squeeze, which the obstruction-harassment and so many other widespread patterns of infractions enter the game as part of. Without them, what fouls remain would be easier for officials to see on a less crowded ice, so players would have no illusions about getting away with something. No Discretion could then come in and "bat clean-up." And that would make the game fairer and better, life easier on officials, and more enjoyable for players, coaches, and fans.

What about the composition of the officiating fleets we use? Another good thing about No Discretion is that it makes the standard the same for all referees, so we don't have to worry about inconsistency between one referee and another. And with four-on-four, there would be plenty of room on the ice, so sticking with the current two-referee system would allow one ref to keep watch on the play and one to keep watch on things happening away from the play.

Actually, most players I have spoken to favour the addition of still more officials, in the press box or stands. "Eyes in the sky," Doug Gilmour called them, kind of like the sideline officials in football and basketball, only they would have the benefit of video replay as well. These officials could signal down penalties in real time by pushing a button to turn on a light at ice level (sort of like throwing flags in football) or buzz down to the on-ice officials with a kind of pager during the play and then "huddle" by phone at the next stoppage.

Most players also supported expanded use of video replay capabilities; I think all goal-related plays should be reviewable for non-penalty calls plus goaltender interference, at the request of coaches, referees, or video officials from up top (going back to the last change of possession, or change of zone, or whatever). Coaches could be given a challenge like in football for a video replay on a goal-related play. But as discussed, it's less a question of vision than of approach to enforcement within the sport as a whole. The paradox of society applies to sport: that the right rules create freedom, that the more strictly they are enforced, the more they guarantee it, the more often they are updated, the better they preserve it.

This comes into play again regarding responding to new problem areas that have arisen in the game. There are a few specific steps that need to be taken for the rules to push back where they've been stretched:

- Goalie equipment: Reductions have been mandated for 2005–06. I would suggest adding a rule where a team can call a measurement like for an illegal stick, the result being forfeiture of the item, and a penalty the goalie must actually serve.

- Goaltender interference: If a player gets in the way of the goalie in an "outer crease" while he is trying to save a puck, it should be an automatic penalty; being in an "inner crease" without the puck should be an immediate whistle and faceoff out of the zone.

- Diving: The league should continue to target divers as it has before and again after the lockout, add an automatic ten-minute misconduct to the minor, and team repercussions for repeat occurrences.

But there will be new areas of concern in the future. As conditions continually change, and the rules continue to be pushed, there needs to be a mechanism to monitor changes happening and be able to respond to them before they reach breaking points. The same type of panel we talked about earlier for reviewing officials on a regular basis could do this in an annual meeting that tackles emerging issues.

Finally, we need to improve the way the culture of the game treats officials. Officials need to be accorded more respectful attitudes and better treatment at every level, from kids' hockey up through the pros. Supporting grassroots efforts, including the use of officials as ambassadors can help change the culture inside arenas from children's levels on up, so that an attitude of greater respect for officials and the rules is fostered in people as they grow up in the game. There is also nothing to be lost by instituting a tradition of players shaking hands with the referee as they skate out after the warmup, before games, like they do in soccer (and in tennis, they do it after). In fact, with two referees, we even have one to stand at each end where the respective teams come out!

When tough calls happen, I can sympathize with people's desire to berate officials. And there's no doubt that many players and coaches will feel the officiating needs to be substantially improved before they would consider yielding their "right" to berate officials. But through the measures above, it should be; and ultimately better behaviour toward officials at all levels is part of improving officiating in the big picture. Thus beyond arguing a call, actual verbal abuse of officials shouldn't "sometimes" or "in case of excess" result in a penalty, but immediately and always result in a penalty, just like in soccer, football, or baseball. And as with those sports, it should not be tolerated: you might get a warning to go with the penalty if it's nothing serious, but beyond that it's a game ejection. *Outrageous* reactions already do earn suspensions. With the proper channels proposed above for ensuring the accountability of officials to the parties in competition, there would be no excuse for official abuse. They could also consider having the league's officially licensed broadcasters be bound by the same rules regarding fines that players and coaches are: they could be allowed to state disagreement with a call, but not criticize the officiating (at least during official broadcasts), or face the same fines. Broadcasters are bound up with the league to a considerable extent, partners in so many senses, and allowing this criticism only contributes to the perception of in-house contempt on the part of the league for its own officials. Why not let others do the criticizing, if warranted? These steps would help command respect for the league and its officials, and for the sport and its rules.

All of these solutions would work together to radically improve the way the game is officiated and the way that officiating is perceived both inside and outside the game. There would be a sense of clarity and simplicity that would be a relief for all involved – not just team participants, but also and perhaps especially referees. The game would be natural, fair, fun, and free to play and watch without these things to notice or fret about. A culture of respect would develop and prevail. This new respect would go beyond officials to embrace the rules and the game itself, improving sportsmanlike conduct in hockey. It would be a landmark achievement for the sport – one with big benefits, and one that is critically needed.

EPILOGUE

Competition is central to sports, and the way we conduct sports' competition is – although not always obvious at that level – a very important influence on the feelings we get from participating in or watching them. Prior to this season, some important steps have been taken to strengthen the conduct of hockey's competition – and none more significant than the new "culture" with respect to calling penalties on illegal obstructive fouls. In addition, progress has been made on reducing inflated goal equipment, and trying to combat diving.

As time goes on, it will be an important challenge to sustain these initiatives – and to expand them. In particular, extending the new standard of officiating to all fouls – creating a "No Discretion" policy that cleans up fouls from the game, makes the rules clear, and the officiating more consistent – would help in numerous important ways. Aided in implementation by four-on-four, it would return the keys of the competition to the soul of the game of out-playing and free up players to play. No doubt when penalties abound, some would call for a return to the "old regime," but the "new order" is one that ultimately will make life easier for officials, and make competitors and fans happier with officials and the game. A number of other steps with regard to the way the game is offici-ated and seen to be officiated would also support this.

Strengthening the conduct of competition in all these ways and on all these fronts means more fun and enjoyment for players playing the game, and a clearer, more consistent playing field for coaches to coach in; it means a more manageable job for officials and greater respect for them, and a more natural, "likeable," satisfying game for fans.

THIRD PERIOD

HEALTH & SAFETY

"Every game, we've had ten to twelve players out of our lineup [with injuries]. That's about half our team."

– Los Angeles Kings coach Andy Murray

"If things continue, I'm not going to play any more. I still have the rest of my life to live."

– Dallas Stars Mike Modano after a vicious hit
from behind by Anaheim's Ruslan Salei

"Actually, this was twenty times worse than anything I've ever seen. You fight and you may get hurt but at least you have a fair chance. The kid never had a chance. This is not even hockey any more. . . . You don't go out and break a player's neck because he hit Naslund. . . . You just don't do something like that – hit someone from behind. Who knows if he'll play again? . . . I'm not the most innocent guy. It's bad, though, let's leave it at that. . . . Bad."

– Calgary Flames enforcer Kryzstof Oliwa after seeing
Todd Bertuzzi's attack on my brother Steve

"There are some cases . . . where the sense of injury breeds – not the will to inflict injuries and climb over them as a ladder – but a hatred of all injury."

– George Eliot

PROLOGUE

This third section of the book examines the issue of health and safety in hockey. There is nothing that casts a pall over the exciting momentum of a game, or the engaging drama of a competition, like an incident in which a person's health is damaged or endangered. Looking at it from the other end, health and safety are a precursor to any successful activity – especially one as physically and mentally engaging as professional sports.

But yet, two threats have long stalked health and safety throughout the history of hockey: violence and injuries. And in recent years, their prevalence has remained, while their danger has increased, both to the welfare of players and to the welfare of the game.

Recently, Hall-of-Fame goaltender, former Toronto Maple Leafs president, and current Canadian Cabinet minister Ken Dryden declared, "Hockey is at risk today of becoming an extreme sport." Confronting the threats of violence and injuries, and promoting the health and safety of players and their game, are the third major requirement of raising our game.

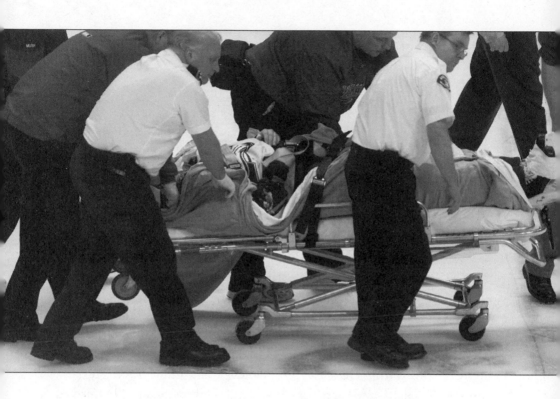

My brother Steve is wheeled off the ice on a stretcher accompanied by paramedics and trainers, March 8, 2004. Attacked from behind by fellow player Todd Bertuzzi, Steve suffered a broken neck and was knocked unconscious. (*CP PHOTO/Chuck Stoody*)

CHAPTER 7

EXORCISING THE DEMON OF VIOLENCE

IN THE GRIP OF A DEMON

One of the biggest issues in hockey recently, and certainly the most troubling, is the monster of violence. The disturbing attack by Bertuzzi on March 8, 2004, catapulted violence into the headline position of on-ice issues in hockey, ahead of the substantial issues already discussed in this book. And since then, violence has continued to remain an issue at the forefront, with what fodder available – from a dangerous high stick twelve days later, to the United Hockey League banning a coach for reportedly offering his players $200 to take out an opponent, to a crosscheck to the head that ended Peter Forsberg's storybook season in Sweden, to the NHL's reinstatement of Todd Bertuzzi and his invitation to join Team Canada in preparation for the 2006 Olympics.

Whenever I overhear people talking about issues in hockey, whether it be on the radio or in the street or in the stands of the arena, the issue of violence seems to often come up and involve the strongest reactions. The public clearly sees it as something that needs to be addressed. Is every new incident truly newsworthy on its own, or has the continued attention reflected a public view that too much has happened to accept, and not enough has been done to put a stop to it? "I think that Canadians feel that there is a problem with hockey, there's a problem with violence," said Canadian Prime Minister Paul Martin recently, "and that it should be dealt with . . . I'd certainly say [to professional hockey] clean up your act." For the general public, violence is one of the biggest on-ice issues of the game.

What constitutes violence perhaps merits a bit of explanation. According to the dictionary, violence is "unjust, undue force used to injure or abuse." Forces permitted as just by the game, including the bodychecking that makes it a contact sport, are therefore not violence. Hockey isn't the only contact sport – football, rugby, and to a minor extent baseball in the special case of a defender blocking home plate are, for example, as well. Good bodychecking is one of the things alongside fast skating and smooth stickhandling that makes hockey as thrilling to play and watch as it is. Like many fans and participants, I enjoy an intense, physical brand of hockey. However, the forces permitted must be and are restricted, and others are outlawed as unwanted violence. Punching, spearing, or hitting from behind are illegal forms of contact. Extents of force are also limited, as a bodycheck with too much of a run-up is disallowed as charging. And intent matters, as any deliberate attempt to injure is banned.

Any foul of these types must, by the definition, be considered a violent foul (as opposed to an obstructive foul like hooking or tripping). We may not be too concerned about every little hack or jab in themselves, but similar acts above a certain threshold are exactly what fill out the lists of bothersome violence. Within those, there are obviously still different degrees: penalties mirror severity of violence on a scale ranging from minor penalties (two minutes), to major penalties (five minutes), to misconducts (ten minutes or game ejection), to match penalties (ejection, and a report of the situation to the commissioner) for the very worst.

Violence hurts in many ways. Frequent and significant injuries are just the beginning. Over the long haul, a prevalence of violence discourages athletes from picking up and staying with the game.

And of course, the less people play, the less people watch. Violence also directly dissuades people from watching. Some have suggested that since acts of violence "compel" the attention of those watching, that it must attract fans. Not so fast: sure, people watch; but what about moments later when many are bothered by and lose respect for what they've been watching, or when it happens over and over and they change the channel or decide not to come back? Some fans like some violence, but there is no question that on the whole, violence runs against the current of the mainstream. Boxing has a following; but football – with plenty of contact but next to no violence – has a far bigger one. There may be violent movies, video games, and pro wrestling that are popular, but their violence is fake. How many of those would still watch if that violence was real, if a wrestler would have his "leg snapped" for real? The violence on the news is violence that happened on its own, viewers are just appraising themselves of those facts. How many would pay for seats in a store to watch thieves come in and beat a store attendant? Not many. Most people have no interest in being sponsors of real violence, or accepting a role not even as witnesses of violence but fans. Sports fans (myself included) like a hard physical game, but they don't like illicit and deliberate violence. They like a contact game, not a cheap game – which is what violence constitutes.

And of course, any extreme violence doesn't just do severe damage to its victims, but acutely harms the image of the sport. This is especially true as sports are played under bright lights, in North America's biggest cities, with cameras rolling, networks broadcasting, and the media machine moving full bore. A regrettable event can't be hidden away, with people pretending it never happened. If sh-- happens, it will hit the fan (and no pun intended). Even if, as other apologists say, extreme incidents are rare exceptions, society is not wont (nor should it be) to accept truly awful things, even if rare. I'm sure we can all think of powerful examples outside of sports of even the most uncommon of crimes, where public outrage demanded major reaction, the absolute assurance that everything possible be done to punish those responsible and prevent anything similar happening again. Rare isn't rare enough where a game's reputation is at stake.

In all these ways, hockey has been paying a price for the violence it has contained: a minor level of violence that's pervasive, a significant level of violence that's reasonably common, and extreme incidents of violence that have occurred. There have been numerous and serious injuries; there have been complaints by players about the conduct of opponents and the inability of league officials to stop certain things from occurring. Casual and potential fans have been turned away by the violence, long-time fans and former players have been disturbed by the physical recklessness with which today's game is played. Ratings have been poor – they've been beaten by bowling, poker, and arena football, among other things. As the lockout had only just begun, 83 per cent of Americans said they had little or no interest in the NHL when it returned. In Canada, polls found 37 per cent of self-described NHL fans didn't miss the game by February, and other polls predicted a 16 per cent to 30 per cent drop in interest in the future. Many factors have no doubt contributed to this (as discussed in this book). But one thing in common about other sports that have been doing well and growing in popularity is their ability to proscribe violence.

Obviously, hockey has also faced the fallout of severe incidents. It has been said the incident of March 8, 2004, received more media coverage than any other hockey story ever – more than the Miracle on Ice, more than the 1972 series, more than any Stanley Cup. That's a tremendously sad statement. For some people, it may be the only glimpse of hockey they ever see; for many others, it will be by choice the last. It was the scandal it was because of how outrageous and off the charts it was. But yet, it wasn't the first public black eye the game suffered from severe violence, or even the last: four years prior, the game had been dragged through a humiliating public trial over Marty McSorley's on-ice slash of Donald Brashear; and just a month and a half after Bertuzzi's assault, with the game's reputation already reeling and concerns of violence still burning up the airwaves, came a severe stick-swinging incident in the NHL's top farm league, resulting in more criminal charges and more embarrassment.

The biggest concern is not what has happened in the past, but what may happen in the future. Outside the game, society is ever moving toward values that have less tolerance for violence. Inside the game, violence persists. Not only does it persist, but it has the potential to expand. The bar of what can occur has been raised, weaknesses in enforcement have been exposed, and the forces of the game are greater than ever: psychological forces like huge financial stakes, massive media heat, and ultra-tight competition, and physical forces like bigger stronger players, faster speeds, and harder equipment. The atmosphere of the modern game has been pressurized, while its container is thin. So if things were to keep going that way – with violence in hockey persisting or potentially surging, and society's tolerance for it at the same time shrinking – it could only lead to the progressive marginalization of the game. For this reason, while violence may have long or always been a problem, the issue has gone from code yellow to code red.

Will hockey end up an "extreme sport," as Dryden worried, with marginal following, relevance, and respect? Or worse: Recently, an independent promoter organized a fight tournament called "Battle of the Hockey Gladiators" featuring no hockey, just hockey players fighting for prize money. It was cancelled in Minneapolis, then Winnipeg, after pressure from authorities, and eventually delayed, renamed, and moved to Prince George, B.C., where it went on in front of a small crowd. Was this really nothing but a parody of hockey, or was there perhaps a bit of prophecy in it as well? If hockey is to remain a significant sport that future generations will continue to play and watch, let alone achieve the wider popularity of a sport like football, it must shed its violence now. Other sports have faced similar problems in the past (basketball and Aussie rules football, for example), took action, made changes, and have largely exorcised the demon. Their popularity rebounded and increased. This is the challenge in hockey.

Hockey is a great game that can offer unmatched excitement, enjoyment, and artistry for those playing and watching; and progress recently made to improve the financial footing of the sport and the play of the game has raised hopes of a bright and prosperous future. But the violence that still stalks the game threatens all that, able in one moment, one incident, to kill hard-earned momentum, and endanger the future following of the game. Some have been calling for an answer to it for years, including Hall-of-Famer Mike Bossy, whose career was ended prematurely from injuries sustained by violence, and legal authority Roy McMurtry, former Attorney-General of Ontario, who appointed a special task force on violence in hockey during the notorious 1970s (headed by his brother William, no sissy, as a former hockey player, rugby player, collegiate boxing champion, and military man with reportedly twenty fractures, separations, and ligament tears to his name). Steps have been taken over time, but the violence remains, the issue remains. The only way to get away from the issue will be to confront the violence.

THE DARKNESS WITHIN

In a typical hockey game, dozens of violent-type fouls are committed (most uncalled). The majority are of trivial severity, yet it is notable simply how many there are compared to in other sports. How often in football are punches thrown, or is the ball carrier elbowed as he goes by? Not very often. Some violence occurs that is hard to detect – perhaps a basketball player coming down from a rebound "accidentally" landing on an opponent, or a soccer player cleating another player while "going for the ball." However, we can't count what we can't detect – and certainly anything evidently deliberate is exceedingly rare. But not in hockey: such fouls are frequent, and whether through excessive vigour, successive escalation, or prodding how far one can go, clearly they are closely tied to similar but more significant violence that occurs.

The violence that has most hurt the game can be divided into two categories: the common but costly, and the rare but severe.

The common but costly acts occur regularly and are significant in the injuries they potentially or actually cause. In other words, not trivial acts, but not extreme. This violence isn't new, but it did surge in recent years. The new prevalence of these dangerous fouls was visible to former players as well as fans who have watched the game over many years as part of a violently reckless modern style of play (fuelled by decreasing respect among players, some said, or by armoured equipment giving a false sense of security). The toll of it was evident from just watching, without having to read medical reports, walk into training rooms, or count the number of man-games lost to confirm. That also made it troubling to watch. A lot of it was also part of a cold new efficiency to the old strategy of trying to wear down your opponent physically – originally just by finishing clean checks, but evolved to include any means, including illegal violence. In addition, what used to be more minor violence became more significant as a result of the game's forces being amped up – tangible elements like size and strength of players, speeds of the game, hardness of the equipment, and intangible elements like money involved, organizational pressure, and a "professional ethos" – turning what might have once been stitches, bruises, or lost teeth into, recently, concussions, fractured wrists, and torn knee ligaments. Together, the surge in frequency and force brought a heavy toll for this "regular" violence.

Within this, certain *types* of violence have been notable for their commonality or danger:

- Checking from behind: There have been vigorous campaigns against checking from behind since around the time Mike Bossy's career was prematurely ended from back injuries caused by being checked from behind into the boards. Efforts made beginning about fifteen years ago led to significant inroads against it, but recently we saw these being eroded, at least at the professional level, where it was happening too frequently again. In fact, early in the 2003–04 season, NHL rules chief Colin Campbell felt it necessary to send a letter to all NHL players advising them of his concern about the number of hits from behind occurring and the serious injuries resulting. Checks from behind have been, since the original effort to curb them, cast as among the dirtiest plays that occur, because the recipient is in a compromised position and at risk of serious injury. These checks from behind usually take place near the boards, where the stationary recipient might be toppled forward and strike his head into the boards, causing significant back, neck, or head injuries. According to the injury prevention group ThinkFirst SportSmart, there have been 271 reported cases of spinal cord injuries in all levels of ice hockey in Canada from 1943–1999, nearly 37 per cent of which were caused by checking from behind. Recently, rates of these cases have been about fifteen per year. Examples of checks from behind some might recall include: Team USA's Gary Suter that knocked Wayne Gretzky out of the last Canada Cup; Claude Lemieux on Red Wing Kris Draper that broke Draper's face; Ottawa's Daniel Alfredsson on Toronto's Darcy Tucker in the 2002 playoffs that separated Tucker's shoulder.

• Illegal blows to the head and neck: These include ones inflicted by crosscheck, elbow, and what some call "extension hits" (where a player sticks out a limb at impact, rather than strictly checking with chest and shoulders). They also include high hits where the checker purposely targets his opponent's head, but they don't include clean checks, like most of New Jersey's Scott Stevens's hits, where a defender is just trying to do his job of taking the body, but the opposing player has his head in the way of where the check must come. But the high blows that are illegal violence are unacceptable, because they frequently cause concussions or other significant injuries that may include broken orbital bones, jaws, or facial injuries. These offences have been far too common in recent years. Sports doctors, including those behind the ThinkFirst campaign, say these illegal hits to the head have been a major and preventable cause of the alarming number of concussions occurring in hockey. NFL football changed its rules and began a clampdown in 1995 after injury rates among quarterbacks and receivers became a major concern; lately, this campaign has been intensified under NFL director of football operations and former wide receiver Gene Washington. To their credit, Colin Campbell and the NHL recently have begun to follow suit in trying to target hits to the head for enforcement. That's a good idea, and hopefully that focus will continue. Examples of such blows people may recall include: Gary Suter's cross-check to the head of Paul Kariya, celebrating a goal, that kept Kariya out of the Nagano Olympics; Montreal's Richard Zednik being knocked out by Boston's Kyle McLaren; and most recently a crosscheck to the head of Peter Forsberg in the Swedish elite league that ended Forsberg's season and knocked him out of the 2005 World Championships.

- Low blows ("submarining," clipping, and slewfooting): Again, this refers to illegal and deliberate or reckless ones, not accidents or clean hip checks. Any time players' legs are deliberately taken out or struck in a glancing manner, serious knee and lower limb injuries can occur. These can cost players whole seasons, damage critical leg strength and mobility, and even end careers. Of course, Bobby Orr's time playing hockey was sadly shortened by knee injuries caused by a career's worth of abuse, including a number of these blows. But this is another thing that we have seen do a lot of damage lately. Cam Neely's career was truncated. Mike Modano, Joe Nieuwendyk, Mike Peca, and Sami Salo are examples of other players who have been seriously injured by blows to the knee recently. Low blows are also a good example of a general property of the violence in the game, which is that a significantly large proportion of incidents are committed by the same few players, repeat or even continual offenders – some of whom (although I won't name them here) have acquired notorious reputations.

- Slashes to the hands: Many will recall Mario Lemieux had to overcome a broken hand from a slash to win the '92 Stanley Cup and Conn Smythe for Playoff MVP. But lately slashes to the hands have evolved into a tactic often used. In some games, you saw it almost constantly. Clearly, it has been a major cause of the number of wrist and hand injuries occurring. Joe Thornton, Adam Oates, Valeri Bure, Val Kamensky, and Jaromir Jagr are just some examples of the many players who have had their wrists, hands, or fingers broken by slashes recently. To its credit, the league took notice of this and started targeting it; but then it seemed the referees started to back off on the calls. It may have been because of the frequent and heated criticism they drew from coaches and players, because these slashes don't look very forceful, and sometimes it can be hard to tell whether the slash was on the player's hands or just his stick. The slashing was another issue Campbell sent a warning letter to players about last season. For Columbus star Rick Nash, that wasn't enough. After suffering a "two-hander" in a game against the Blackhawks, Nash said, "That's how guys get broken wrists. Broken wrists happen when the refs don't make the calls. No penalty. They hand out memos and talk about the slashing, but then they don't do anything." Even a relatively light hack, as the players know, can easily hurt or injure a player when taken on the hands. There is a gap there in the padding of both the equipment and the body itself, and wrists and fingers have a structural fragility. A slash of similar force higher up on the arm, or on the pants, would be harmless. And after all, it's hockey, not speed or figure skating, so hands are just as important as knees.

- Highsticks: Frightening and frequent, these may not often be deliberate, but are more often than not reckless or careless. The puck is on the ice, so why would sticks need to be up near people's heads or faces? Some players, even some who have reputations as clean players, seem to accidentally highstick a lot of people, whereas others almost never do. In any event, it's not the pure accidents that we're talking about here as violence, but all the others. Highsticks cause cuts, lost teeth, scars, swelling, broken noses, but also the occasional concussion, and, perhaps worst, scary eye injuries. Pierre Mondou's career was ended by a highstick by Ulf Samuelsson. More recently, Bryan Berard, Al Macinnis, and Owen Nolan have had eye injuries from highsticks. Last season significant suspensions were handed out to players Wade Belak and Martin Havlat for high-sticking incidents.

- "Jump" fights and suckerpunches: A sense of honour and penalties for instigation are supposed to protect against jump fights, but lately the lines of a "fair fight" started to become blurred or overrun as players wanting to seize the advantage of getting the jump were sometimes resorting to borderline or outright "jump" fights. The instigator penalty is infrequently called, no doubt partly because of the bullying denunciations of the rule by its opponents. But a clean punch to the head of someone unprepared to defend themselves can do a lot of damage (that's why boxers wear soft round mitts). Effects range to severe concussions or worse (recently, one hockey parent killed another in a fight in front of kids and other parents, in Massachusetts, with a punch to the head of a foe whom had been overpowered and was defenceless). Much more rare, but also even more dangerous, are suckerpunches. Here, the victim is not aware that he is being attacked, so the body's automatic bracing mechanisms are not even there to dampen the damage. Traditionally, suckerpunches have been rare, but lately we have seen a few of them occur. Examples people may recall include the one by Matt Johnson that ended Jeff Beukeboom's career, Tie Domi's on Ulf Samuelsson, and, last season, Brad Ference's on Martin Sonnenberg.

Of the violence in hockey, the preceding stand out as specific *types* within the common but costly violence that should be targeted as priorities to eliminate from the game.

GROSS MISCONDUCT

Covered so far, has been the violence in the game that ranges from trivial but prevalent to significant and regular. But there remains another category of concern: those few acts of *extreme* violence, where the method and circumstances matter less than the disturbing character, viciousness, and terrifying consequences. These are acts that make witnesses recoil in shock and horror; acts likely to, or which do, cause catastrophic injuries to the victim; acts that induce public outrage and disgust. Of course, these things can occur anywhere – in a bar, on the street, in a school, or on the ice. And while the particulars of the motivation, method, and other incidental details are dictated by the place, the critical fact – which is an act of extreme violence – transcends its location. That said, some places clearly suffer more "crime" than others – just like cities with historically high crime rates. And at the same time, every place in society has an obligation to do its absolute utmost to prevent such atrocity occurring within its borders. And they also have an incentive because of the immense damage they can do to reputation and interests (whether it is a neighbourhood or a sport). Moral obligation and practical incentive, players' safety and public perception, all demand the game take responsibility for doing everything possible to prevent even the rarest occurrence of extreme violence.

Let's look at some of the most major incidents of extreme violence (in terms of the severity of the acts, and the public furor they caused) in the history of hockey in greater detail.

On December 12, 1933, Toronto's King Clancy tripped up Bruins defenceman Eddie Shore, with no penalty being called. The angry Shore, the NHL's reigning MVP, rose and rushed to seek revenge against either who he thought dumped him or the nearest Leaf. He came upon the smooth and gentlemanly Ace Bailey, barrelled into him from behind, and flipped Bailey over his knee. Bailey went up in the air and came down hard on the ice on his head. The awful sound heard by witnesses was described like hitting a pumpkin with an axe. Bailey's skull was fractured, and he was knocked out;

he would lapse in and out of a coma and nearly die. In the meantime, bruising Leafs defenceman Red Horner, by his own account, came at Shore and said, "You can't get away with that, you son of a bitch," and knocked Shore out with a punch, so that Shore himself fell unconscious, hit his head on the ice, and was cut for sixteen stitches. For weeks, a saga ensued in the news. The NHL's Frank Patrick ruled that Shore's hit "was of a spontaneous nature with no malice behind it," and that Shore's record "does not class him as a vicious player. This is established by the fact he has participated in about 400 games in the NHL and has never been given a match penalty for injuring an opponent." Shore was suspended for sixteen games; Bailey never played again.

Some were unimpressed by the reaction. One reporter later wrote: "For twenty years, man and boy, this evil fellow [Shore] has been punching people, hitting them over the head with his stick, chewing their ears, butting, gouging, shoving and generally bedevilling his fellow men and always for handsome fees. . . . [He has] developed the role of Villain to such an extent that professional wrestlers gnash their teeth in envy." Present-day author Larry Scanlan, after thoroughly investigating the incident and the issue of violence in hockey, wrote of Shore in his book, *Grace Under Fire*: "His record surely says more about the NHL's reluctance to punish players for inflicting injury than it does about Shore's good character."

The NHL all-star game was originated as a benefit game for Bailey, to stave off a lawsuit threatened by Bailey against Shore, and pitted the NHL all-stars, led by Shore, against Bailey's former team, the Leafs. But meanwhile, Shore kept on playing, and the risk of more extreme violence continued right along with him.

On February 21, 2000, at GM Place in Vancouver, Boston's Marty McSorley, angry at Canuck Donald Brashear for allegedly embarrassing him and his team through certain actions earlier in the game, tried to force a confrontation with Brashear in the closing seconds, slashing him at the side of his head. Brashear fell backwards, his helmet coming off, and struck his head on the ice. He was knocked out and went into convulsions. Vancouver goalie Garth

Snow chased after McSorley, while trainers attended to Brashear. The incident sparked outrage in and out of hockey, and both McSorley in court in Vancouver and the game in the court of public opinion were put on trial.

"That was sickening to see. I haven't got another word that I can use. . . . There's no place in hockey for that. It was a despicable act, and I am sickened by it. I'm sick to my stomach," Canuck coach Marc Crawford said and later testified in court against McSorley. Canuck Markus Naslund said, "When things like that happen, you worry about a life. . . . The league has to make an example. We have to put a stop to things like this." "If McSorley plays another game in this league, then this league is a [bleeping] joke," Canucks defenceman Mattias Ohlund said. "It was the worst thing I've ever seen. That guy should be treated the same as if he tried to kill a guy on the street."

McSorley was suspended for the remaining twenty-three games of the season and any playoffs, and would have to apply for reinstatement. He was convicted at trial of assault with a weapon; the sentence was eighteen months' probation, community service, and not to participate in sporting events against Brashear. After the season, in response to McSorley's application for reinstatement, the NHL extended the suspension to a full year, eighty-two games. The aging McSorley, in fact, never played in the NHL again.

"Are we trying to make a statement? We're trying to right a wrong. . . . We don't want this to happen again, and hopefully, this has some input," NHL vice-president Colin Campbell said. "This is not how we want hockey portrayed. . . . It would be grossly unfair to suggest that his conduct is at all representative of the game, of the other seven hundred players who play in the NHL or of the countless others who play hockey at all levels." Commissioner Gary Bettman said, "I simply cannot in good conscience justify imposing a suspension of less. If this is interpreted as raising the bar, that's all right with me. . . . This decision will constitute an important statement about the game itself, and, more specifically, why parents should be comfortable knowing that their children can play hockey." Back in British Columbia, the prosecutor said, "My hope is, and I think probably, as a result of the amount of attention the trial has gotten, people will reflect on the way the game is played, and that is good."

It wasn't enough. With disturbing irony this point was mercilessly driven home: just four years later, on the same ice, in the same city, with many of the same people present, came another attack – far more terrifying, far more brutal, and far more devastating – and by a player who was a teammate and friend of the victim in the last one. In fact, after seeing Brashear's head hit the ice, Todd Bertuzzi had said afterwards, "Disgusting. Terrible. That does not need to be in the game of hockey. I've never seen anything like that in my life. . . . The league's gotta do something about it. . . . It's got to be taken care of. Sick."

The set of events that led to the attack began on February 16, 2004, in Denver, Colorado. My brother Steve was a rookie having, as Colin Campbell said, "a breakthrough season" with the first-place Colorado Avalanche. On this night, he had a bodycheck on Markus Naslund of the Canucks, who was hurt on the play. The check was ruled clean by the officials and no penalty called. The Canucks later scored and won the game 1-0, but afterwards and over ensuing days, the talk by certain people was of reaction to the injury to Naslund. Canucks coach Marc Crawford said such a hit "should not be tolerated . . . for there to be no call on that play was unforgivable." Most general managers, as high-ranking executives, stay above the heat of the fray and serve as voices of composure, but Canucks GM Brian Burke, also the president, took it alarmingly further, saying it was "complete garbage and that's not done to star players. . . . We can't afford to have players like that sitting on the sidelines because some grinder decides to take him out. . . . Star players get different treatment. . . . As cold-blooded as that sounds, it's the truth." Canuck player Brad May threatened, "There's definitely a bounty on his head. Clean hit or not, that's our best player and you respond. It's going to be fun when we get him."

Then there was Todd Bertuzzi, quoted in the *Vancouver Sun*: "That kid's a piece of sh—. We play them twice more, and hopefully they'll keep him [in the lineup]. It's called respect. Things like that kid . . . shows the respect we have around the league . . . ," he said. As Terry Frei reported in the *Denver Post*, Bertuzzi said, " 'It's unfortunate that the game was where it was at, because it would have been a different situation.' Meaning the Canucks would have retaliated? 'Absolutely,' he said." Bertuzzi, like Shore, had a history of violence. After some incidents in junior, the year 2000 saw him hit NHL star Peter Forsberg from behind, causing a concussion that knocked Forsberg out for five games. Two years later he received a serious ten-game suspension from the NHL for coming off the bench to join an altercation. In 2003, he suckerpunched Nashville's Karlis Skrastins with four seconds left in a game, breaking his nose. Months later, an illegal check into the boards on Minnesota's Willie Mitchell injured Mitchell's wrist during the latter's breakout playoff run, one reason why Bertuzzi was vociferously booed playing for the home team at the NHL all-star game in Minnesota the following season. "I just think it's fun leaving an impression on people like that," he was quoted by the Associated Press.

The threats against Steve by Bertuzzi and other Canucks became a big story in the media, playing in sports headlines across Canada and the United States. In the meantime, at the request of the Canucks, the NHL reviewed Steve's check on Naslund, and again ruled it clean. Several of the Canucks also saw the replay and said it was clean after all, and Steve was just doing his job. Steve was surprised to find himself in the middle of a controversy. He told reporters: "I'm sorry [Naslund] was hurt on the play, but I just finished my check the way we always do. Sometimes that happens." However, the promises of revenge were not recanted, but reaffirmed as the rematches approached. Alarmed by the extraordinary threats, the NHL took various steps to try to prevent retributive violence. Top league executives Bettman and Campbell flew to attend the next game in person, and reportedly delivered direct warnings to those involved. "You know what? Games will come," Bertuzzi explained to reporters about why not much happened at the first rematch March 3 in Denver. "Situations will present themselves. . . ."

The second and last rematch of the season between the two teams was a few days later, on March 8, this time in Vancouver. Early in the game, hoping to put the issue to rest, Steve accepted a challenge to fight from Matt Cooke (Steve's first pro fight), which seemed to go fairly evenly. Later, Steve scored a goal, which, with Colorado flying and the Canucks seeming distracted from playing hockey, set an NHL record of the four fastest goals by a team in NHL history. Just over eight minutes into the third period, with the Canucks now trailing 8-2, Steve was skating with the play when Todd Bertuzzi came up behind Steve and began following him at slow speed. Down they went, the length of the ice, and then back the other way, Bertuzzi not seeming to watch the play, but Steve, from a few feet behind. In an interview on *Hockey Night in Canada*, Ken Dryden later compared it to watching a lion stalking a gazelle in a *National Geographic* film. Then suddenly Bertuzzi dropped his stick, grabbed Steve from behind with one hand and pulled him back while leaning in with both feet to swing a ferocious suckerpunch into his defenceless head. Steve was immediately knocked unconscious. As he slumped limply to the ice, Bertuzzi continued to attack, falling upon Steve's back, pushing his head down, and driving Steve's face into the ice. Steve's neck was broken, and a pool of blood was spreading on the ice. Bertuzzi then grabbed Steve by the back of his neck and tried to punch him again. The punch was deflected by Colorado's Andre Nikolishin, who arrived at the last second to save Steve from an even worse outcome.

Trainers rushed out to where Steve was lying face down, immobile, and attended to him for several minutes. The TV feed switched to the stunned expressions of players not knowing what to do, and traumatized fans holding both hands to their face. Colorado coaches Tony Granato and Rick Tocchet were screaming at Crawford. "A television closeup of Crawford showed him smirking after Bertuzzi had smashed Moore's face into the ice," *Toronto Sun* reporter Steve Simmons described. Still unconscious, Steve was removed from the ice on a stretcher and then taken by ambulance to the hospital, where he was diagnosed with a broken neck, bad concussion, and other injuries. Back at the arena, appalled Vancouver fans phoned the police from the arena to have Bertuzzi arrested.

Over the next few days, millions saw the video footage over and over, as the shocking incident made round-the-clock coverage on CNN and news networks worldwide. The public recoiled, the media railed, and the image of an already fragile game was shattered. In ensuing days, it only increased as excuses being made by certain people clashed with what viewers saw in disturbing slow-motion replays. In total, the damage would be severe: not just Bertuzzi or the Canucks, but the sport itself was again put on trial in the court of public opinion, and this time near-universally condemned. "It's a dark day for hockey. We're trying so hard to publicize the NHL in the Unites States and the whole country has to see this terrible exhibition of sportsmanship," Florida Panthers goalie Roberto Luongo said.

As far as the issue of violence in hockey, the question was, "What would the response be?" Despite what authorities thought would be strong deterrents issued in the McSorley case, this had happened – and by a team and a player with direct experience of that incident, and full awareness of both the punishments handed out and the damaged reputations. Indeed, this act was far worse in several respects – the premeditation (three weeks since the promised threats), the irrelevance to the game (unprovoked, and with a lengthy stalking away from the play), the viciousness (a maximum-force initial blow, plus a succeeding piledriver, and then another attempted punch), and the cowardliness (a suckerpunch from behind). "It never crossed my mind that somebody [might do that]," said NHLer Matthew Barnaby, no stranger to the game's physical dangers. ESPN writer and *Horns, Hogs and Nixon Coming* author Terry Frei wrote: "Bertuzzi's act was among the most despicable ever seen during a North American pro game, and the attempts to wave it off as anything but that are laughable in their disingenuousness." In addition, the damage caused was significantly worse – both the severe injuries (a broken neck and a much more serious concussion) and the game-damaging public fallout. And it had also been done in defiance of numerous warnings, by a player with a history of offences and suspensions. The NHL's Campbell also "was more adamant than ever that the [Canucks] team, and specifically Burke and coach Marc Crawford, didn't do nearly enough to defuse a potentially explosive situation," said the *Vancouver Sun*'s Gary Mason, who interviewed him.

The NHL announced its decision. The Canucks were fined $250,000 for their role in the affair, but neither Crawford nor Burke were suspended. Bertuzzi would miss the balance of the season (twelve games) and playoffs (another seven), and reinstatement would depend on the progress of Steve's recovery. The extent of the NHL's response on Bertuzzi would be put off until a later date. The next question was the law – this was obviously a crime, a serious assault. Police were investigating, and charges were laid. Although there was videotape of the incident, the B.C. prosecutor agreed to a deal with Bertuzzi allowing him to avoid a trial, as well as even a criminal record, in exchange for a $500 fine, community service, and a year of probation.

How would these responses affect the game? In the next few weeks after Bertuzzi's attack, there were a slew of other on-ice incidents: a spear, a vicious high stick, a kick, and a suckerpunch that looked eerily patterned after Bertuzzi's but that thankfully only grazed the head of the intended victim. And then on April 30 came the incident in the American Hockey League, in which Hamilton player Alexander Perezhogin sent Cleveland's Garrett Stafford to the hospital with a concussion, seizure, and twenty stitches with a slash that coach Roy Sommer said "makes the McSorley–Brashear thing look like Girl Scouts." Since then, while the NHL was idle, a number of NHL players went to Europe, and it seemed violence was increasing over there as well. A brawl was triggered after Joe Thornton's hit on a goaltender in the Swiss league. Then there was the crosscheck to the head of Peter Forsberg, abruptly ending his celebrated and attendance-record-setting homecoming season.

During the 2005 European playoffs, International Ice Hockey Federation president Rene Fasel wrote in an editorial: "From what I have seen myself and from the reports I have been getting from other leagues I must draw the conclusion that the image and public perception of our sport is deteriorating. The playoffs in several European nations are showing the ugliest part of our game. Fights and incidents leading to severe injuries are occurring almost on a daily basis. Coaches are inciting the players and fans by calling a playoff match-up a 'war.' . . . The atmosphere . . . is starting to resemble the one at a wild-west saloon where unshaved men are exercising frontier justice. . . . I have seen sickening incidents in the Swiss playoffs and relegation games, with vicious two-handed slashes to the head and mindless attacks on goaltenders . . . Just a few weeks ago a game between two of the most skilled teams in the Russian league erupted in a massive brawl, resulting in 322 penalty minutes, a new record for the Superleague. . . . Do we need another Bertuzzi incident for people to come back to their senses? Or does anyone need to be killed before everyone realizes that this has gone too far? What we need is a collective cooling-off. The image of our great game calls for that."

With the lockout over, and the NHL looking to resume in the fall, next on the agenda was the decision the NHL had put off on the complete punishment for Bertuzzi. A hearing was scheduled, where according to Bettman, Bertuzzi's lawyer argued to him for Bertuzzi's reinstatement. Steve was there to answer questions from league doctors and officials about the status of his attempted recovery. He remained unable to play hockey. By Bettman's account, his counsel, Tim Danson, suggested that the ruling "could be a defining moment for the NHL, which will be judged on how the matter is handled." Bettman said he agreed. Three months later, the decision was released: "Conduct such as Mr. Bertuzzi's simply has no place in the game of hockey. There is no question that Mr. Bertuzzi's actions clearly went well beyond what could ever be considered acceptable behavior in the National Hockey League. Mr. Bertuzzi must be held responsible for the results of his actions, and the message must be delivered loudly and forcefully that the game will not tolerate this type of conduct," Bettman said. The public and press had speculated about what the punishment might be. Four years before, Bettman had extended McSorley's suspension to eighty-two games – yet this subsequent incident happened, and was far worse. So what would the punishment be this time? The decision came: It was reinstatement. Effective "immediately." The *New York Times* noted that, "anticipating a torrent of criticism, Bettman issued a lengthy [approximately ten-page] email message explaining his decision." "Some might think there needed to be a harsher punishment," Bettman said in it, "but I am satisfied with the result."

But how would others interpret the signals the decision sent about violence in hockey? "THE THUG IS BACK," read a headline in the *Toronto Sun*. "NHL GREEN FOR BERTUZZI TO PLAY," said China's *People's Daily*. *London Free Press* writer Morris Dalla Costa wrote: "Imagine what would have happened if Bettman, after investigating the attack, had told the watching world, fans and non-fans alike, that he was suspending Bertuzzi for a mere 20 games . . . Bettman has sent the message that the NHL . . . didn't care what happened to Moore. . . . And what about the message sent out to the other players? . . . Your league just gave a guy who broke another guy's neck, gave him a career-threatening concussion and damaged the precious reputation of your league throughout the world, a 20-game suspension." "Finally, the bar has been set ankle high," the *Toronto Sun's* Mike Ulmer said. "So here's the message," the *Toronto Star's* Dave Feschuk wrote, noting the simultaneous new crackdown on hooking and holding. "The new NHL won't tolerate obstruction. But frontier justice? They're fine with it."

The detrimental effect to the image of the league from this response to what had happened was also clear, as an avalanche of criticism and lost respect came down: British Columbia's *Kamloops This Week* wrote: "It's a sad day for hockey . . . The sympathy shown for the power forward by Canucks fans has been embarrassing, but not as much as the sellout by the league not to tack more time onto the suspension. . . . The incident was a mugging. If it happened on the street, he would have done jail time. The punishment severely erodes the respect and credibility for which the league should be striving. . . ." The *Globe and Mail's* Allan Maki wrote: "The NHL may be trumpeting this season as a fresh start, but today it looks a lot like the old NHL, which is to say narrow-minded, manipulative and disappointing. . . . The league . . . continues to be its own worst enemy. . . . Go to the penalty box and sit in shame . . . a game misconduct for leniency."

Meanwhile, Bertuzzi was invited to join Team Canada's training camp the following week, in preparation for the Olympics in February. The national program had been founded by Father David Bauer to foster fair play, sportsmanship, and player safety, declared its "primary interest is the well-being of its participants," urged parents to "understand that children learn from adults" and players to "play by the rules and to resolve conflicts without resorting to hostility or violence." There were plenty of other great players available, including those who had won Canada the 2002 Olympics and 2004 World Cup while representing these values well. Instead, the *Toronto Star*'s Damien Cox said that Hockey Canada president Bob Nicholson & Co. were guilty of "hypocrisy" and "embraced the outlaw element in the sport and turned their back on many of [their] principles" by immediately welcoming Bertuzzi. Fans seemed to agree: a Sun Media poll found a majority of Canadian sports fans did not want Bertuzzi playing for their country's Olympic team. A Decima research poll had also shown 25 per cent thought Bertuzzi should have been banned from hockey for life. Yet, the next week. there was Bertuzzi wearing a Team Canada jersey and track suit, speaking to the media for the first time in seventeen months, and preparing for the start of the NHL season.

In the grand scheme of things, Cox noted, "Despite the enormous hits in revenue and reputation the game has absorbed in recent years, the NHL has done nothing substantive to curb systemic violence in the sport since it was last open for business." Indeed, among the league's lengthy list of rule changes for 2005–06, only a single item was addressed to reduce violence, and it was so small it wasn't even reported in most news summaries: a player who instigates a fight in the last five minutes of a game would now be suspended the next game, and his coach fined. That was a rule that has been in place for several years already in most junior and professional leagues where fighting occurs. In addition, Cox said, "Nothing has been done that would prevent an incident similar to Bertuzzi's attack on Moore in the future."

For hockey, violence is something that has taken a great toll. Violence that is regular has turned prospective players and fans off of the game, and extreme incidents like that of March 8, 2004, don't just wreck lives, they devastate the reputation of the game. Already preventing the game from breaking into the mainstream in the United States, and now jeopardizing the ground held in traditional places, the biggest concern about violence applies to the future. Competitive pressures have mounted, incidents spiralled, enforcement failed, and excuses been increasingly unaccepted as tolerance shrinks: so what will the future hold? Also, player safety is at issue. "When this thing happened with Bertuzzi, I didn't even want to go on the ice any more," Teemu Selanne said. "The players were saying the same thing, 'Let's just stop this game right now.' A lot of guys were talking about it, saying, 'Let's just stop this game. It's not a safe place.'" "I read what Selanne had to say and those were some pretty strong comments," Toronto's Joe Nieuwendyk said. "I think maybe a lot of players feel that way." Most of the time, players might not worry about it (and I'm sure Steve and Donald Brashear never did before what happened to them either), but what about players' wives, families, parents, children? As IIHF President René Fasel asked, "Does anyone need to be killed?"

COMING TO GRIPS WITH TRUE CAUSES

Ultimately, to find answers to the conundrum, we need to delve deeper and understand why there has been the violence there has been in the game, why it has surged, and why there is reason to be concerned about the future.

First of all, we should clear up some red herrings you sometimes hear, which are not the true causes. For example, one of these is that violence occurs because "hockey is an emotional game."

Indeed, hockey *is* an emotional game – all sports are emotional games, business is an emotional game, families are emotional games, life is an emotional game: there are huge tensions, conflicts, and strong feelings on an almost daily basis in all of these. And yet we don't see the level of violence in them we see in hockey. Another excuse is that "hockey is a physical game." But football is an intense physical game too, and yet there is very little violence in football, probably even less than in the non-contact sports of baseball and basketball. In fact, football players have probably been guilty of far more violent behaviour off the field than on, as pointed out in the book *NFL Pros and Cons*. So how do you explain that football players are exceptionally well behaved and perhaps "on their best behaviour" while playing their "physical game," whereas hockey players are not? This brings us to another surmisal – that hockey is a sport that "breeds animals" or somehow selects people of inalienably violent constitution. In that case, Wayne Gretzky, arguably the best player of all time, and five-time winner of the Lady Byng Trophy for gentlemanly play, must have been one hell of a mistake, to have been so good while being so unviolent! And many other of the best players ever as well. Also, despite some recent incidents, on the whole the perception is that off the ice, hockey players are among the most well-behaved, laidback, and congenial athletes in any sport. Why is it, unlike football players, they're more violent when they're playing? The answer to all the on-ice violence isn't in the nature of players or of the sport itself. It isn't a function of reasons or motivation, but of two other things: imperative and opportunity.

Let's begin with the question of opportunity, because without it, violence can't occur. In hockey, as in life, there are free wills, freely moving bodies, and few walls between – so opportunity cannot directly be taken away. But laws in society and rules in sport are supposed to barricade what is not acceptable from what is. Since they are theoretical, not physical, they require real punishments on offences in arrears to make them work as deterrents to opportunity in advance. Barricades that are weakly upheld are easily overrun. And hockey is generally felt to have had a history of inadequate enforcement of its rules on a consistent basis. The late Scott Young, celebrated Canadian writer and hockey enthusiast, and father of rock musician Neil Young, wrote in 1959, "Some provisions of the league's rulebook are enforced, others are sometimes enforced, others never enforced. If one took the 10 Commandments and decided to ignore the ones on theft, murder and adultery on the grounds that they are extremely popular, and too hard to stop anyway, one would have an exact definition of the way the NHL regards its rulebook." Some fouls were habitually let go, and more severe things often underpunished. This all resulted in a certain amount of illegal violence being effectively tolerated (unlike in other sports).

This apparent disregard for the game's own rules, and the inevitable inconsistency in officiating that it led to, would all encourage an attitude of disrespect and defiance toward officials and the rules themselves, fuelling still more violence. In addition, the ability to get away with small things just invites players and coaches to do more, to see what they can get away with, to push the envelope, so to speak. So there was an ongoing escalation of the level of violence – more and more, and worse, infractions. But as the boundaries were pushed, they didn't push back: penalty calls stayed the same, creating a disconnect with a changing game. We got to a point where countless infractions (including both obstructive and minor violent fouls) were let go without penalization every game.

More serious violence was then called in proportion. Each level of the rules was watered down so that it was insufficient as a deterrent: substantial acts would receive minor penalties, severe ones five-minute penalties, and ejections only for things too awful to accept. And this extended beyond the ice as well. Suspensions of a few games over a long season (including eighty-two regular season games, plus exhibition, plus playoffs), a gruelling season at that, and with players far from being in any danger of starving due to disciplinary fines, weren't enough either. Rough sports especially need tough enforcement, because the potential is there for them to boil over from "hot" to "explosive." For example, look again at football. For any even minimal act of violence, you are out of the game. For a medium-level act, you could be suspended for a quarter of the season or a lot more. And if you did something severe, well, we haven't seen it, which means you'd probably disappear from the sport. The same holds for every other sport. Even boxing – despite common perception of it as extreme and corrupt – has very strict penalties for illegal violence: headbutts or low blows, bites or other acts of violence result in disqualification, and one loss on your record could easily ruin your career. On top of that, you could lose your licence, and face huge fines. But hockey is a rough sport with traditionally weak enforcement, a bad mix.

In addition, teams wanted (and paid) players who got penalty minutes (as many evaluators used them as a rough or lazy measure of "grit," something they wanted). This was both the result of (and proof of) the inadequate enforcement of the rules, as teams felt that a level of illegal play by their players, weighed against the penalties that that play accrued, was a balance tilted in their favour. If the rules were enforced more strictly, that balance would change, and that kind of play would be a liability. And the result and the proof would be in player contracts. Factoring in the employment rewards for penalty minutes, the meek enforcement seemed to create as much of an incentive for violence as it did to dissuade it.

Lately, a disturbing corollary has evolved to the weak enforcement in the game, and that is the often weak enforcement by *society* of its laws, upon athletes and other celebrities. Lawyer and author Jeff Benedict, in his best-selling book *Out of Bounds: Inside the NBA's Culture of Rape, Violence and Crime*, details how off-court misbehaviour of NBA players results from those players being conditioned from a young age to believe that because of their sports stardom, they are special, unaccountable, practically above the law. The general public has been concerned about the outcomes of a number of celebrity cases lately, wondering whether usual or appropriate legal repercussions were evaded thanks to good lawyering and a bit of luck. The McSorley and Bertuzzi cases had considerable "celebrity or high-placed pressure" on authorities to soften the response, and many no doubt wondered about what impact it had. Weak enforcement sets a dangerous tone, and provides inadequate disincentives, so that when motivation arises or an incentive is found for violence – which will always happen – then violent acts can and will occur.

A related fact is that there are weaknesses and loopholes in the rules themselves – low sections or gaps, even in the *theoretical* barricades. Never was this more clear than with Fred Shero and the Broad Street Bullies in the 1970s, who employed violence as a team strategy, badgering and battering their opponents into submission. "If we can, we'll intimidate our rivals. We try to soften them up, then pounce on them. There are lots of ways to play this game. Our way works," Shero admitted in the midst of the Flyers' Cup-winning heyday. In 1972, forward Bobby Clarke famously knocked the Russians' top player, Valery Kharlamov, out of the Summit Series with a slash to the ankle. Some had perhaps thought that rules had changed, and eras with them, and that that violence could no longer yield an advantage in the modern game (or perhaps in some "bush league," but not in the NHL). But although it may not often be used as brazenly as in those days, it certainly still can be and is. Often, roughing (where there is no clear signal like the glove-drop in fighting) is used to intimidate or rough up opponents. Although rare, more severe things sometimes happen too – for example an "agitator" engaging a star player – where if that player doesn't react by fighting in self-defence, he risks severe injury; and if he does fight the two get equivalent penalties. These examples highlight problems around the issues of fighting and roughing in the game.

Likewise, some exceptionally vigorous examples of "crashing the net" show that a two-minute goaltender interference penalty, even if called, is insufficient deterrent for action that may result in the loss from a game of a team's most important player. In a playoff series, that may even be true for a five-minute major. Same with charging on a star player. These examples show how violence as a tactic can still enter the game, "hiding" as legal or less serious common plays of the game.

Another omission pertains to the fact that a relative few account for a disproportionately large number of the incidents of violence that occur. Without explicit rules for repeat offending (apart from considering a player's prior suspensions in deciding subsequent ones), frequent offenders can go on playing the same way. Same with teams. And not holding coaches and GMs responsible as a general rule allows those inclined to repeatedly incite violence. In five years of studies, research firm JustPlay (recently hired by the City of Toronto's youth league to help combat the growing problem of "rink rage") has consistently found that coaches are the primary instigators of violence, responsible for about 43 per cent of all "critical incidents." "We have found a strong correlation between poor coach behaviour and subsequently player and spectator conduct. The coaches are where all three are looking to as role models," the company said. René Fasel, president of the IIHF, points out: "The national associations and the [pro] leagues have a good and pretty consistent routine for suspending players for violent conduct. They are not nearly as good when it comes to suspending or fining coaches or managers for inciting." After the Bertuzzi incident, the NHL finally took a step toward making them responsible, reportedly sending a memo to teams advising them that coaches and managers will be held accountable for the actions of their players, according to Bob Grove of the *Pittsburgh Sports Report*. But coming near the end of the last season played, there has not been opportunity as yet to see what this will mean.

Besides the issue of external barriers to misconduct, the other important restraint that should be in place is the one in a player's own mind of what he ought or ought not to do. But again, in some cases these have not been sufficiently present in hockey, or have been overruled by other internal imperatives *toward* violence.

Contributing to this are what many have called "backward" mentalities that exist in some places in hockey, distorting what a player "ought" to do. Some talk in the press has speculated as to the existence of a "code," but there is no code, or perhaps there are several codes that are vague, overlap, and contradict each other. Different people have different versions, each selectively applied. What they really are is just mentalities – attitudes, in other words. And some of these attitudes have had enough adherents in the game to contribute to violence. For example, alongside sportsmanship that is so dominant in a sport like golf and prevalent in most sports, hockey has a strong contravening streak of approaching the game as all-out-competition or open conflict. (This perhaps reflects a society where we value success at any cost, but sports are supposed to be different, and more pure.) Football players help opponents up between plays; in hockey, some coaches frown on players even talking to opponents they know on a faceoff, and teams famously won't reveal injury details during the playoffs for fear opponents will target them for aggravation. A corollary of this flows from the observation that a substantial amount of violence in the game seems to occur when scores are lopsided, which is of course no coincidence, but flows from the idea that you should try to "get something out of the game" or "send a message" of some kind, if a win is out of reach. In other sports, this would be unequivocally and universally derided as being a poor loser.

Another mentality, less common but held by some, is that any big hit, any injury (fair or not, accidental or not), requires retribution, some resorting to illegal means. By contrast, in football I have yet to see an offensive lineman chase after a safety and club him for doing his job and hammering a receiver, or even sacking the quarterback (of which there is no player of equivalent importance in hockey). What are other problematic attitudes some held? One is the idea that young players have lesser rights. I always found this one not only wrong, but something that undermined the ideal team concept of a brotherhood. A similar attitude that stars have special rights, and are not subject to the same rules of the game everyone else is, contradicts the fundamental principle upon which our whole society was founded: equality before the law. And at the same time, there was a simultaneous but opposite attitude of deliberately targeting the other team's star players for maximum physical punishment.

Some had an attitude that players could and should police themselves (e.g., proponents of removing the instigator rule). But that would be a tribal system, which despite its romantic appeal (in certain movies or television shows like *Survivor*), anthropologists use the end of to mark the birth of civilizations. Likewise, the idea of retribution is not unique to any sport, it's human nature, and the problem with such vigilantism arises in the lack of objectivity to judge, which is why it's illegal. Yet the culture of self-policing and vigilantism are an ingrained problem for the game at every level through to recreational leagues. For example, one popular league in Toronto markets itself as the Adult *Safe* Hockey League. Within these ideas of self-policing is the mentality that fighting is a way to solve problems, or diffuse tensions. Clearly, society does not share that view. There are also macho attitudes: if challenged, one should fight. If abused without retaliation, one is a coward. (But yet Europeans don't have to, and stars don't have to. They can have someone else do it for them.) Sometimes, you even see television analysts seeking to "educate" the public about these various attitudes, commentators celebrating violence as a sign of grit, and networks including dirty hits among clean ones in their promo highlights (I assume those selecting them don't know the difference), which can't help.

Many hockey players don't hold these attitudes, many hold opposite attitudes – and more and more, particularly at the NHL level – but there are significant numbers who do subscribe to these various mentalities at certain times. And attitudes are passed on as one adherent makes another, and one generation drills it into the next. So, as long as this is happening, these attitudes will continue to have sway over minds. And since the mind controls behaviour, ultimately, they continue to influence actions on the ice. With these "imperatives" arising in people's minds, it is easy to see how violence occurs. And of course, it's most tragic when these mentalities flow down to kids, as they do, spoiling the enjoyment and endangering the safety of hundreds of thousands of people, miles away from making livings as pros.

Recently, the pressured environment of the modern game only amplified the effects of these factors and skewed further the "shoulds" in players' minds, contributing to the rising violence. The amount of money involved and attractiveness of the major league lifestyle certainly affects players' thinking. A heated struggle to make the playoffs with thirty teams fighting for sixteen spots increases tension. The immense importance of hockey in Canada and the importance of success in general leads to a compulsion to win by any means available. This is exacerbated by the pressure from club organizations, fans, and media on coaches and players. Then throw in the increasing size of players, and the decreasing room on the ice, which creates constant contact within a static game and no room for escape. Animal studies, published in John Calhoun's famous article "Population Density and Social Pathology" from *Scientific American*, found that in rat populations that grew above a certain population density, even as food remained abundant the animals would undergo a "behaviour sink," engaging in increasing violence, rape, gang behaviour, cannibalism, infanticide, and so on. And then there are whatever stimulants, supplements, and other chemicals being used by players that can affect them physically and moreso mentally – concerns about "roid rage" or the like. A media amplifying things, the entertainment side packaging things, the business side sanitizing things – they all weaken the recognition that this is real life, real people, real consequences, not superheroes, videogames, or cartoons. All of these things raise tensions high, making for a heated environment where the balance in the mind is more pressured toward violence than ever before. So when something happens, and violence escalates, things can quickly reach scary levels.

Related to this is the risen "professional" ethos of the modern game: players no longer think of themselves as they did twenty or even ten years ago as simply athletes or sportsmen at the highest level of their sport. Today's players think of themselves as "professionals" who have a job to do, for which they are being paid handsomely, and which they do without hesitation and without scruple, according to the expectations of their organization and its need to win.

Sportsmanship, respect, humanity, and all personal principles are pushed aside; a professional's sole concern (and the expectation of him) is to "get the job done." Players feel in a way like machines, soldiers, or some kind of special-forces troops sent to carry out an operation. The "professional" ethos creates an air of impersonality that leads to a lack of respect. The armoured equipment adds to it by concealing your and your opponents' humanity and vulnerability.

Ultimately, there isn't enough either in the rules and their enforcement, or in the imperatives of the mind, to keep the violence, which is always there as a possibility, at bay. And as a result, it can and does too often, and too awfully, occur.

EXORCISING THE DEMON

So how do we get from here to Avalon?

Well, first of all, hopefully the incidents that have occurred, the public outrage against them, and the time off during the lockout have given those competing within the sport, on and off the ice, an opportunity to take a step back, reflect, and "cool off," as Fasel said. Likewise, hopefully relief at the game's return, and what I expect to be a strong initial return of fans to the game, will also foster a sense of appreciation for the game and its supporters that can counter the will to act on a motive to violence that could harm it again. But ultimately, even if these hopes bear true, their effect is temporary, and their ability to deter an act of potentially catastrophic damage to the game is far from enough to rely upon. Action must be taken against the sources of violence in the game.

The specific types of violence we listed as being of particular concern – hits from behind, high hits, low blows, slashes to the hands, high sticks, jump fights, and suckerpunches – should be specifically targeted for removal from the game. This strategy of honing in on especially dangerous forms of violence was used successfully to put an end to brawling, through severe automatic suspensions on players and coaches. It also made good inroads on hitting from behind, in that case via increased player awareness and stiff penalty calls (before the initiative and the results recently faded). The league has begun to target additional fouls, which is good, and more must be done.

At the same time, we have to be smart about it. For example, a crackdown against hits purposely striving to strike the head is needed. But some have campaigned for hockey to deem illegal all hits to the head, and some amateur leagues have adopted such a rule. However, unlike checks from behind, a puckcarrier skating forward is an offensive threat, and body contact, which is the foundation of defence in hockey, typically requires the defender to come in on a certain line to make his check. So it must be the offensive player's responsibility to keep his head up and out of the way of that proper check. The alternative is to remove bodychecking from hockey – and maybe some would support that too – but that's not the hockey that most of us know and want. By making strong but smart rules to target particular types of violence of concern, and using both enforcement and education to support them, we can make important progress. We can't remove every kind of foul in this way, but if we are always knocking off the ones at the top of the list of worst kinds, we should be moving in the right direction. It's not like if you got rid of one form, another would simply take its place. There might be a few more, but people commit particular acts of violence primarily because they can, not because they need to.

On the whole, clearly violence is too pervasive and varied in form for initiatives aimed at specific types on their own to be sufficient in cleaning up the game. A blanket approach is needed in tandem, battling the issues of opportunity and imperative behind all violence in the game directly through enforcement and re-education respectively. Campaigns very much like this have been successful in other sports.

The sport of Australian rules football went through a similar trial by fire about fifteen years ago. A story by Chris Zelkovich of the *Toronto Star*, written in the midst of the recent uproar over violence in hockey, describes how Aussie rules football used to be synonymous with fighting and violence. In fact, increasing violence had driven families out of the stands, and attendance began to drop. Meanwhile, young athletes turned away from the mayhem they saw and took up sports like soccer and rugby instead. The Australian Football League was in danger. To Zelkovich and many hockey fans, the story seems familiar. But then, as Australian football veteran and Canadian national team coach Greg Everett said, "They decided to take [the violence] out of the game and it's worked beautifully."

They did it by toughening up punishments and by stopping the promotion of violence. Previously, fighters weren't penalized but simply given a yellow card, and hearings produced few suspensions, most of them short. But rule changes meant fighting is now met with a referee's report and often an ejection from the game. Perpetrators of violence must appear before a tribunal that routinely hands out suspensions for three to eight games in a season of just twenty-two, depending on the severity and the offender's history. Also, a "melee rule" allows for suspensions even when no punches are thrown. The league reviews video of all games in case the referees missed any vicious tackles or plays, and acts on them. In addition, violent tackles were removed from promo materials, which instead show action and speed.

"It's changed the focus of the game from being big and mean to being fitter and faster," Everett said. It is still a physical game, a tough game, but today, "the violence has been toned down and fights are so rare they aren't even an issue," Zelkovich says. How did that change work out for the sport? Attendance is back up, families have returned, and more than 135,000 kids are enrolled in "footy" programs in Australia. "There's been a huge change in the crowds," said Everett. "Instead of the rowdies we used to see, there are kids and families."

A little closer to home is the sport of basketball. Some may be surprised to hear that basketball once had problems with violence strikingly similar to that of hockey, but it did: "In those days [the early 1970s], brawling was a common occurrence in the NBA. Most teams had an enforcer . . . whose primary job was to protect his teammates when the going got rough," wrote legendary coach Phil Jackson in a section titled "A brief history of NBA warfare" from his best-selling book *Sacred Hoops*. Shortly after a brawl between New York and Atlanta, Jackson wrote, "The NBA started taking steps to reduce violence on court. First players were fined and in some cases suspended for coming off the bench and joining a brawl. Next the league clamped down on throwing punches: anyone who struck another player was immediately ejected and suspended for at least one game. Hall-of-Fame enforcer Wes Unseld argued that the no-punching rule gave the bullies in the league licence to hammer away at players and get away with all kinds of treachery without having to worry about retribution. In the 1980s, the era of the Detroit bad boys, the NBA instituted a new rule severely penalizing players for committing 'flagrant' fouls, malicious acts away from the ball that could cause serious injury. That helped, but some teams in particular the New York Knicks still found ways to intimidate their opponents with brute force. So the league changed the rules again in 1994–95 restricting hand-checking and double-teaming in certain situations."

Believe it or not, basketball had a kind of Bertuzzi incident as well, except that it was a spur-of-the-moment swing that the thrower said was in self-defence against a charging opponent. John Feinstein's book *The Punch* chronicles the incident and its effects – a devastating punch by the Lakers' Kermit Washington on an unprepared Houston player, Rudy Tomjanovich, that demolished Tomjanovich's face and nearly killed him.

Fans were shocked, a public furor erupted, and Tomjanovich's Rockets joined him in suing Washington and the Lakers. It was basketball's worst incident, and it was a breaking point for violence in the sport. "This was a monumental event when it occurred, because it appeared to symbolize everything people were saying about us. And it got so much attention at the time," said David Stern, who was then legal counsel to the struggling league. "The violence was without question a major issue, something that had to be dealt with." And the NBA did deal with it.

Commissioner Larry O'Brien was able to use the incident and all the public fallout to convince owners and others involved with the sport to support bold steps to wipe out the violence that many thought was dragging down the sport. "The message had to be sent to the players that what had gone on before was no longer tolerable," Stern said. According to NBA number-two man Russ Granik, "I would say most of the rules we have today governing violence and fights really grew out of that incident. We were aware before then that we had a problem, but this incident made it crystal clear the potential dangers of letting men this size take full swings at one another. . . . We had to take steps to keep these sorts of things from happening again." Those bold steps worked – the violence was cleaned up and the NBA went on to prosperity far beyond anything it could have imagined in the days of Washington's attack on Tomjanovich.

Today basketball continues to thrive in a post–Michael Jordan era. There are still occasional incidents – the Ron Artest & Co. fracas with the fans in Detroit, for example. But they're quickly dealt with so they don't happen again – in that case with a seventy-three-game, year-long suspension for Artest that will cost him nearly $5 million, other player suspensions totalling another seventy games, plus the institution of a player and fan code of conduct designed to prevent recurrence. "The line is drawn and my guess is nothing like that will happen again – certainly not by anyone who wants to be associated with our league," said now commissioner David Stern. There were probably basketball fans that liked fighting and certain violence – but the NBA decided they could go watch boxing or another combat sport, and if they came to watch basketball, they would just see basketball. They bet that more fans and potential fans were interested in their sport without it, and they were overwhelmingly right. The truth we have to accept is that hockey isn't as different as some may think. Hockey is facing the same questions about the future as the NBA and Aussie rules football did at their critical junctures – what kind of following will it appeal to, what kind of future does it want?

To enjoy similar success as the NBA and Aussie rules football have had, hockey must toughen up enforcement. The first step required is something suggested previously to combat rampant fouls and perceived officiating inconsistency, and that is: No Discretion. This means a policy of consistent enforcement of the rules with no leeway. If you see an infraction, you call it. No discretion, no exceptions. Indeed, a slice of this – targeting obstructive fouls – was announced by the NHL for 2005–06, and through the pre-season it seemed to be working. Not only was it cleaning up obstruction, but the attitude of strict enforcement itself, through that crackdown, seemed to be having a carryover upon violent fouls, reducing those too. This was an extremely promising sign, and shows just how much of a positive impact strict application of the rules has. However, to counter violence more comprehensively and long-term, the No Discretion crackdown must be explicitly extended from obstructive-type fouls to all fouls, including violent-type fouls.

This is critical, because when you tolerate low-level violence (i.e., anything other than a clean bodycheck), a bad example is set, and it becomes a slippery slope to more and worse acts, each harder to stop. Similarly when the tolerance is at a level or of types of acts that can't be strictly defined and policed, it opens the door with a slight twist in a grey area around something dangerous to things no one would ever want tolerated in the game. As well, tolerating more serious things and things far apart from the actions of playing the game makes for less of a jump to terrifying extremes, whenever things escalate. The suggestion that some leeway prevents escalation to more serious acts occurring through "venting" is nothing but a form of the intriguing but untenable "appeasement doctrine" (notoriously discredited leading up to the Second World War), which, it has been consistently proven, fundamentally misjudges human nature. Calling the rules with consistency, diligence, and vigour will establish the rule of law over the game and create an atmosphere of respect for the rules and discipline that will decrease the number of violent acts. The limits will be clear, and players won't be testing them, or trying to stretch them, leading to worse violence.

Hand in hand with No Discretion must be Zero Tolerance. Zero Tolerance, as I mean it and as it is widely used, is actually a policy of strict and severe penalties for violence. Under Zero Tolerance, if certain rules are broken, the perpetrators face immediate, automatic, and overwhelming punishment. This is the enforcement strategy that has been used with great effectiveness lately to rein in long-time, persistent, and tough-to-crack problems such as schoolyard bullying, weapons possession, and other violence in schools, as well as sexual harassment, discrimination in the workplace, drunk driving, and a wide assortment of other problems. If the offences targeted by the Zero Tolerance policy occur, offenders face immediate and guaranteed expulsion, firing, or stiff jail sentences or fines, as the case may be. Zero Tolerance is, although perhaps without the name, the essential policy that keeps football and other tough sports successfully under control.

There are two components to implementing Zero Tolerance in hockey. One is to strictly interpret and enforce the rules already in place. The two main levels of penalties in the rulebook should be interpreted and utilized as in basketball and soccer: that the two-minute minors are for essentially harmless violent fouls, and more serious ones – the "common but costly" (that are deliberately or recklessly dangerous) – instead of being called as an "upper level" minor as they are now, would get the five-minute penalties. Beyond that, what are called as majors now should get ejections, what get ejections now get the other more serious penalties that are in the book.

Equally important is the question of supplemental discipline. How many times do we hear players and coaches, having acted out frustration, say to reporters "I don't care if the league fines me. I don't care if they suspend me"? If that isn't proof that those fines and suspensions are not feared, and are not enough, I don't know what is. Warnings should be sent out before the season that the penalties will be much harsher than in the past. Something that gets an ejection now should get a suspension of one to three games, something that gets two games now should get ten, something that gets ten games now will get half a season. In a season with eighty-two games (plus up to twenty-eight playoff games), suspensions of a few games are just not sufficient to deter the kind of violence that currently warrant suspensions; they need to be measured in tens of games. The NHL upped the ante in this way when they gave Dale Hunter an unprecedented twenty-one-game suspension for hitting Pierre Turgeon after a goal in 1993, but the effect of that warning shot has long faded, and consistently stricter enforcement is needed to have the needed effect. We must strengthen the repercussions for violent fouls to where the penalties are more than an inconvenience, they are a clear sign that violence is intolerable.

Nobody wants all these tough penalties, but the whole point of Zero Tolerance is that if players know really stiff punishments await, they will not want to mess around with them by committing violent fouls, so those tough penalties will seldom have to be used, and meanwhile, the game will be cleaner, safer, and more widely appealing. "Sometimes we have to suspend people in situations where it hurts us," the NBA's David Stern said. "But [the violence against Tomjanovich] was far worse. We can't ever let that happen again."

That brings us to the matter of extreme violence. For hockey, the overwhelming focus (through the punishment of lesser fouls above) must be on prevention of it ever happening again. If it does, courts will inevitably intervene. Suggesting it's part of the game would only degrade the game. Arguing the game can police itself won't matter if authority's larger responsibility is for the message to the public watching. And at a certain point, even pro athletes need protection from criminal behaviour – for example, as depicted in the opening scene of the movie *The Last Boy Scout*, where a football player pulls a gun and shoots opposing players on the field. "Hockey – no sport – is immune from the laws of the land and the authorities will decide if they should apply," Prime Minister Paul Martin said. Court intervention has happened several times already. In the 1976 playoffs, fans in Toronto were so furious over the Flyers' roughhouse tactics, and particularly an attack on Leafs defenceman Borje Salming, that scuffles broke out between the Flyers and the crowd, and four Flyers were charged with assault. Coach Fred Shero worried about the safety of his players from the fans; meanwhile, two Flyers were convicted. In 1988, the Stars' Dino Ciccarelli was sentenced to and spent a day in jail after twice hitting Luke Richardson in the head with his stick. Then there were the recent charges against McSorley, Bertuzzi, and Perezhogin. Sentences have not been harsh, but just days after Bertuzzi's plea bargain, a recreational hockey player in Edmonton got ninety days in jail for a suckerpunch that broke another player's jaw. At some point public outrage over perception of soft treatment of celebrities will create an opposite incentive to make an example.

If that fails, the authorities may go further. Prime Minister Martin said he might discuss the issue with the Minister of Sport. The minister, Stephen Owen, said he felt "we should be making every effort as a country and as sports teams and as coaches and as referees and leagues to enforce rules . . . much more stringently than we do." In the U.S., there were congressional hearings held in 1980, and a Sport Violence Act introduced to punish "unreasonably violent" activity with a $5,000 fine, a year in jail, or both. It never went through, but as the strict steroids legislation expected to be soon passed by the U.S. Senate demonstrates, next time it might be different. To prevent all that, Zero Tolerance enforcement by the sport, as you see in football, as has evolved in basketball, is the only way.

Together with tough enforcement of existing rules, hockey needs some rule changes. What do we do about fighting? Proponents argue that leagues without fighting have more other dangerous violence like stick fouls and checks from behind, and that fighting keeps a league cleaner as the threat of getting beat up by the opposition "enforcer" deters "cheap shots." But at the same time, fighting is itself violent, so by having it, although we may curb some forms of violence, we are incorporating another. Somewhat contradictorily, supporters of fighting also sometimes say that nobody gets hurt in fights. But that's a cultivated myth; they do: "You do get hurt. I pulled out a shoulder in a fight. I've pretty much broken every finger in my hand. Tore ligaments in my wrists, my hands. I've been cut many times. Lost two front teeth. Had my jaw displaced," Marty

McSorley said. Former Leafs fighter Nick Kypreos's career ended when a fight left him with a severe concussion. Steve Smith's leg was broken in two places; Cam Russell reportedly nearly died. The list goes on. Well at least it's voluntary, fighting's proponents say: if two guys decide to go at it, and one gets hurt, it's his own fault. Usually, fights are between two enforcers, and often that could be said; but some would argue that when a weaker combatant is drawn into a fight, the watching eyes of teammates and thousands of fans constitute duress.

In addition, it's tough for fighting to work very effectively as a deterrent if fights are completely voluntary on both sides. Where's the threat if the cheap shotter can simply avoid a fight? This has caused some players and others to argue that the NHL should remove the "instigator" penalty whereby if one player is the instigator of a fight, his team gets an extra two-minute penalty and he is ejected. "In the good old days before the instigator rule," the party line goes, "nobody cheapshotted Wayne Gretzky because they were afraid of Dave Semenko." There's another popular myth. First of all, people did cheapshot Gretzky despite Semenko's presence. Gretzky also played twelve of his twenty years in the NHL without Semenko, and seven with the current instigator rule. The real reason Gretzky got some respect was not because people were afraid of Semenko, but because they respected Gretzky! They respected the level of ability he had reached in the game, and the great things it was doing for the game. An ultimate testament to that was Bobby Clarke, leader of the Flyers and their anything-to-win hockey, coming in to the Oilers dressing room after Gretzky scored five goals against them to say, "I just wanted to tell you, a lot's been written about you, and I don't feel any of it's adequate." In fact, on a more general level, at that particular point, it seemed that there was more of a code of honour and respect in the play of the game than immediately before or after.

In reality, instigation allowed the brutal old days of the Broad Street Bullies more than it allowed the good old days of Gretzky's Oilers; it allowed players and teams free licence to use fisticuffs to do any kind of violence and to ruin the game. That is why the rule was first introduced (in its original form) in 1976–77 after the Flyers led the league to arguably its most brutal year of violence yet in 1975–76. The NHLPA had urged the league to consider a trial year ban on fighting; the league rejected it. Things kept getting worse. "The way things are going, someone is going to get killed," tough Minnesota veteran forward Dennis Hextall said. Even the man behind the mayhem, Freddie "the fog" Shero, said after the playoff war with Toronto, "of the 17,000 [in Maple Leaf Gardens tonight], I bet 1,000 of them aren't all there. They let their emotions get to them. They spit on players, curse at them, throw things at them. Some night a guy is going to come in here with a loaded gun." The league was going out of control, hockey fans were appalled, and some believe only the dominating skill of the Montreal Canadiens saved the sport from ruin. Instigation doesn't just allow wrongs to be made right or deterred, it allows fighting to be used for any purpose, right or wrong. And instigation also allows one player to attack another who is unprepared, one of the most dangerous things possible – and even moreso with the amplified forces in today's game. Removing the instigator rule is not an option.

In fact, even without instigation, 2004 was another '76 for violence in the game. I have joined the number of current and former players who believe that leagues without fighting like the NCAA used to have more other violence, but no longer. With pro hockey's ultra-high stakes – the stickwork, hits from behind, and all the dirty play are now as bad or worse – plus you have the fighting on top. A lot of people don't see a problem with a fair fight between evenly matched tough guys; a lot do. "One of these days, a guy's going to get the upper hand in a fight and he's going to land a bomb in the wrong place . . . and someone could die. And then all hell will break loose because everyone will stand back and say 'how did we ever let this happen?'" said Phoenix GM Mike Barnett.

The biggest danger is that by allowing such a high level of violence into the game, on the rare occasion when things may go outside the lines . . . or by allowing something so hard to define and circumscribe, when acts drift into those shades of grey, the consequences can be harrowing. That's what happened with the incident in basketball. "Back then, fights broke out in the NBA every night . . . We were used to fights," *Houston Post* reporter Thomas Bonk said. "And then in an instant [with the punch on Tomjanovich] it all changed and it became terrifying." And in hockey lately, more and more "honest tough guys" have been losing jobs to players less scrupulous about how they use violence.

In 2004, Pierre McGuire said it was time to ban fighting in hockey, pointing to the playoffs as the NHL's best hockey, and hockey with virtually no fighting. For those used to fighting in professional hockey, this is a big change. One way to give people time to adapt would be to phase it in, by modifying the fighting rules so that no player can make contact with another player in any fighting-related manner until both players have first separated so that neither is touching the other and secondly dropped their gloves. This means no punches, no grappling, or any other type of fighting unless and until the two players have dropped their gloves while completely separated. If that happens, then they can fight with the usual penalties. Adding these conditions is the only way to ensure that both players are aware and prepared, in other words that it is truly a mutually voluntary and fair fight. After all, dropping the gloves has really become a signal, more than anything anyway. So let's be clear about it, to avoid some potentially much more lethal situations. And if any player breaks this rule, in any way, it has to automatically result in a hearing with the commissioner and a severe suspension.

However, even a fully fair and voluntary fight, as Barnett said, is certainly not without danger of serious harm. And so this proposal is intended only as a step toward ultimate elimination of fighting as soon as the game feels it is practically possible.

What is essential is to ensure that by the time fighting is to be eliminated that other kinds of potentially more nefarious acts of violence are under control and not to increase in its absence. Clearly it makes no sense to ban fighting and continue to allow other kinds of violence like hits from behind, elbows to the head, and high sticks.

Why single fighting out while letting these other things – which have probably been doing more physical damage than fighting – continue to grow? The answer is to ban all equivalently dangerous or serious kinds of violence across the board (as the NBA *eventually* did, but as hockey needs to do all at once). This means not just penalize, but ban through ejection and suspensions all dangerous violence including hits from behind, illegal blows to the head, violent stickwork, and others. Any force outside the boundaries of a clean bodycheck and beyond the severity of regular penalties must be removed from the game, by ejection and suspensions, not tolerated in any way. Another proposed rule change would divide fouls into the two categories they reflect: obstructive and violent. All violent-type fouls (even two-minute minors) should be automatically accompanied by a ten-minute misconduct. After all, violence is misconduct.

Other rule changes need to target the use of violence as a tactic. Making injuries resulting from deliberate acts of violence a factor in suspensions has been undertaken, and is a sensible and appropriate step. However, for this to be credible and meaningful as a deterrent, it can't just be called "a factor"; the relationship must be publicly set out more, and there are lots of options. There should be tougher penalties to protect goalies, kind of like in football with "roughing the passer." Also, many players and coaches feel that coaches need to be held more responsible for violence that occurs, particularly the kind that fits into a pattern. Obviously, any coach or team personnel that directs or incites an act of violence should be severely suspended – whether the act is carried out or not – say for a year, at minimum. The coach in the UHL was given a life-time ban. And players or personnel aware of such incitement should, as in law, be compelled to help stop it and bring it to the league's attention, as Derian Hatcher was praised for reportedly doing again in the UHL case (where Hatcher was playing during the lockout).

To further discourage the use of violence as a team tactic, another important change I recommend adding is something equivalent to the "team foul" in basketball, or being a "man-down" in soccer: after a team commits a certain number of violent-type fouls – say one per period – that team automatically incurs an extra two-minute bench penalty on top. If the "over-limit" penalty occurs in the last period of a game, or when the margin in score is more than three goals, the coach is ejected and suspended for the following game.

A related area where the rules must be bolstered pertains to repeat offending. There should be tracking both by human rules officials and by statistical records – and looking not only at past suspensions, but all violent-type fouls committed, of players, coaches, and teams. And in addition to taking account of past conduct through discretion by the league's disciplinarian, there should be automatic stepped suspensions for repeat offenders of violent-type fouls, even of things that seem accidental like high sticks. These automatic suspensions would provide minimum lengths to which the disciplinarian at his discretion would be able to add but not subtract. So, for example, after five violent-type fouls, or two majors, an automatic two-game suspension might follow. As repeat offences pile up, the automatic suspensions rapidly "step up" (say double) each time to: 4, 8, and so on. There are again lots of options. Coaches of teams who are repeat offenders in sustaining team fouls or majors should face the same kind of automatic and stepping suspensions for failing to keep their team under control. And their teams would have the team foul stepped to 4, 6, 8 minutes and so on. As these penalties quickly accumulate, violence would turn from a potential advantage to an unsustainable detriment, and those who employ it regularly would have to turn away from it to be successful and stay in the game.

Together, these strategies of No Discretion and Zero Tolerance will go a long way as deterrents to violence, so that – without all these strict penalties often needing to be called – the violence won't occur.

Besides all these methods of tightening enforcement, the other major thing necessary to curtail violence in hockey is to change attitudes within the sport. Attitude changes have clearly been effective in countering specific acts like spearing or previously hitting from behind, but they need to be undertaken more comprehensively with respect to pervading mentalities behind violence of any kind in the game. We need to reform, repackage, and celebrate hockey through changes in supervision, education, and marketing – as they did with Aussie rules football. The breadth of hockey's appeal and the brightness of its future are greatest if the sport puts fun and sportsmanship first, and competition second – as opposed to being something that is "life and death," or all-out conflict. Hockey heroes like Bobby Orr, Mike Bossy, and women's Olympian player Cassie Campbell have been involved in positive programs like Safe and Fun Hockey that make great efforts to promote this. But meanwhile, when kids watch professional games on TV, they've seen very different behaviour and heard very different messages. Attitudes supporting retribution, player-policing, and outlaw conduct on the ice have to go. The rules are the same for stars, young players, and everyone else. There can be no more mixed messages, no more *mauvais melange* of the rule of law and the rule of the jungle.

From a grassroots level, we need to focus on role models, leadership, and the way the game is taught and portrayed. It is critical that at those levels too, bad apples be banished, responsible education be insisted upon, and the culture and oversight of the sport be consistent with its needs. The sport should demand that those who wish to become or remain involved in it conduct themselves appropriately according to its desired values, just as other areas of society will not tolerate defiance or detrimental conduct. All the measures discussed will help ensure that people can only respond to the modern game's pressures in constructive ways (i.e., playing better), not in destructive ways (such as engaging in violence). This will help change the mentalities that strongly influence conduct.

The play of the game can also have an effect. The obstruction crackdown for this season that should provide a more open, free-skating game makes violence somewhat less usable. The larger end zones that will boost powerplays should make violence somewhat less useful. And on the motivation front, an antidote is available for the overcrowded, overheated quarters of the modern ice: four-on-four. Lowering player density on the ice means more space per player, less collisions, less static time in contact, less conflict, less tension, and less violence – if we're like animals from studies done. It means more skating, more skill, and less place for goon tactics. And referees can see clearer everything that's going on, so little is missed, no retaliation is needed, and no escalation comes about.

Together these changes would help hockey escape the shadow of violence, solve an old problem that has never been adequately dealt with, and that lately surged as a concern. They would address both the violence occurring regularly that accumulates such a toll, and the devastating extreme incidents – hopefully preventing that next incident, the one everyone is afraid of – where someone might be killed or the game never recovers. For the future, it is critical to take these steps, for all that's at stake: the welfare of today's players, the peace of mind of their families, the inclination of the next generation to pursue the sport, fans' financial support, the respect and interest of the wider public, the sport's meaning in society, and its freedom to stay on the ice and out of the courts. And if an incident happens, the public will know *everything possible* had been done to prevent it, so that the incident will be reported, the individual may be derided, but as with other sports, no issue to do with the sport will go on. How much more should we wait before taking these steps? The answer is zero, and the time is now.

Player equipment is not as "friendly" as it used to be. L:(*Frank Prazak/Hockey Hall of Fame*) R:(*Matt Polk/Hockey Hall of Fame*)

CHAPTER 8

SLASHING THE TOLL
OF INJURIES

A PAIN IN THE ICE

Injuries happen, particularly in contact sports. But even at their least significant, they are no fun, and some are truly awful. From a participants' point of view, although you rarely think about them while you're playing (and it has to be that way in order to best avoid them), they remain probably the worst fear in the back of your mind and, when they happen, the biggest unpleasantry in the game. Nothing puts a downer on the spirit of an athlete, or the fun of a game, like being stalled by an injury. Pain is often the least part of it, behind associated physical impairment and absence from the game. We have a duty to prevent injuries in the game to whatever extent we can and, beyond that, to minimize them as much as we can.

But injury figures have been high in recent years, and some serious ones have in fact been increasing: the epitome has been the rising, raging concussion conundrum – concussions have tripled in less than twenty years, so that suddenly epidemic numbers of players getting this significant injury to the body's most indispensable (and irreparable) part. Most concussions shortly subside, but getting

223

another one adds up. And then there are a few that are not so co-operative in clearing up. There are other significant injuries occurring quite commonly as well. We can see the scene in our minds: Two big bodies collide, a wrist is jammed, a snap; one player drops stick and one glove, leaves the play, and skates to the bench clutching his bare hand with the other in pain. A forward tries to make a cut around a defenceman at the blue line, knees collide, the forward tries to get up but his leg collapses under him; the whistle goes and he is helped to the bench, teammates on each arm, one leg dragging limply behind. A player skating with the puck, another chasing him from behind, trying to hook him, his stick glances off the puckcarrier's shoulder and hits him in the face; he falls to the ice, clutching his face, while the trainer rushes out, and everyone in the building holds their breath hoping it is not his eye. With respect to these, and to all the others – to injuries as a whole – the cost has been increasing, and proven difficult to counteract. What do the future trends portend both for those who play the game and for the nature of the game itself? With all the forces of the game (size, strength, speed, equipment, pressure) increasing, where is the game "headed"?

Hockey players are trained like soldiers to plow through pain, stay focused on the battle, and not be distracted by wounded comrades. But in confronting the issue of injuries, macho attitudes are really not where it's at. Every time we see one of the game's colossal-sized players shattered by injuries, that point is made to us in graphic terms. And it was also made with an irony that spoke volumes when the favourite symbol of macho cultists, the NHL's ultimate iron warrior, Scott Stevens, retired this season due to a career-ending injury. He whose thunderous bodychecks that KO'd Eric Lindros, Ron Francis, Shane Willis, and Paul Kariya earned him the nickname "the concusser" had quietly succumbed to post-concussion syndrome. Similarly, a dismissive stance advances us nowhere either. I once had a perspective something like that: not a lack of concern for others, but as far as myself, I thought I was invulnerable, as most players I played with had been knocked out of action by injuries at one time or another, while I hadn't yet missed a shift. But years later, in one moment, one injury, my career was over, my life changed, my self changed, my family strained. There have been numerous others besides me: some whose names everyone knew, such as Bobby Orr, Cam Neely, Mike Richter, or Al Macinnis; but many more whose names we knew not, or not yet – and now we never will. That's because in part the famous ones are those who survived physical injury and the psychological impact of them to make it as far as they have (especially in intensely competitive hockey hotbeds like Canada). Just think how many beyond those well known must have been felled along the way. Whether their names are known or not, the damage is equally difficult to bear. Major injuries can sever careers and alter lives. And all injuries, taken collectively, are a serious issue for the sport.

Not long ago, Peter Forsberg's father, Swedish coach Kent Forsberg, said, "The NHL has to do something. You put your life in danger to play in the NHL. This has to stop. It's not just about Peter. It's about everybody." The current professional game is one in which players are no longer simply at risk throughout their careers of a major injury to a knee, shoulder, head, or some other part, but almost assured of one. The risk now is whether that major injury will turn out to be career-ending or permanently disabling in some way. Just among the players I embarked in pro hockey with, a large number were stopped by career-ending injuries, good players whose names most fans never got to know. Rising insurance costs reflect the trend: over the short span of my career, insurance premiums skyrocketed while benefits plummeted, across the board. On a more basic level, a fundamental purpose of athletics is to express physical prowess and sponsor physical fitness (that's why we teach them in schools). The rising prospect of incurring a physical impediment or disability instead is a disturbing result for an activity that should be "health-promoting." "I decided to walk away now rather than crawl away later," I remember Dale Hawerchuk saying when he retired.

But there is more to this problem than all the damage being suffered by the pros. Ultimately, participation at every level is affected, because youth that see an injury profile they are uninclined to face instead turn their aspirations and focus to other sports. Perhaps even more significant over the long term are the concerns of parents. I know that numerous parents are deciding their kids will not play hockey because the game is becoming too dangerous. Further, spectatorship is intimately tied to participation in sports, in the sense that generally a populace doesn't watch sports it doesn't play. As such, the injury problem threatens not only the next generation of participation in the game, but of public following as well. The issue of injuries may not be a very sexy one . . . or if the success of so many recent television shows like *ER* is a measure, maybe it is. Either way, the direct pain, associated costs and complications, and influence on future participation and following all make player health and safety from injury a real and important issue hockey must face.

ASSESSMENT OF INJURIES IN HOCKEY

Some say revealing in itself is the fact the NHL does not reveal its figures on injuries. However, a number of studies published concerning figures for other competitive hockey leagues help paint a picture of pro hockey's injury profile. For example, a study by Dr. Jouko Molsa and colleagues looked at injuries at the top level in Finland, and was published in an article entitled "Injury Profile in Ice Hockey from the 1970s through the 1990s in Finland." The study found that the injury rate per game increased significantly from 54 per 1,000 player-hours in the 1970s to 83 per 1,000 player-hours in the 1990s. In concluding, the authors noted "an alarming increase in the rate of ice hockey injuries." Another study of junior A hockey by Dr. M.J. Stuart et al., published in 1995 as *Injuries in junior A Ice Hockey: A three-year prospective study*, found a staggering injury rate of 96.1 per 1,000 player-game hours.

An NCAA Division One collegiate hockey study conducted by Flik, Lyman, and Marx and published in the *American Journal of Sports Medicine* in February 2005 found 113 injuries in 23,096 athlete exposures, including 13.8 per 1,000 game-athlete exposures. Notably common injuries included knee medial collateral ligament (MCL) sprains and high ankle sprain. Concussion was the single most commonly sustained injury (18.6 per cent) and was responsible for nearly one-quarter of all game injuries. "Concussions are a main cause for time lost and remain an area of major concern," the examiners concluded. The NHL, of course, is the world's most intense league, where the greatest forces of every kind are present. Authors Greenberg and Wilton, in an article on injuries published in the hockey encyclopedia *Total Hockey*, tabulated all injuries in the '97–98 NHL season, counting a total of 1,404 injuries for 3,992 man-games lost. In 1999–2000, there were 104 concussions, which in a league of about seven hundred players represents about one out of every seven players *per year*.

Among the injuries of concern are less serious ones like abdominal strains, groin pulls, dislocated shoulders, sprained ankles, hip pointers, and charley horses. From the player's point of view, these injuries are frustrating in that they frequently cause players to miss games, or to play through them nagging and hampering performance, and weakening resistance to further and more serious injuries. From the point of view of the team, they are costly also. Missing players leave holes in lineups, increase the pressure on existing players (which can lead to more injuries), and ultimately affect the bottom line – through medical and insurance costs and hits to performance and fan interest. Several teams have had entire seasons wiped out by man-games lost lately, including the Montreal Canadiens, who had a staggering 563 in 1999–2000, and the Los Angeles Kings, who lost a record-breaking number of man-games the last two seasons in a row. Other times, they can catch teams in a pinch, in which huge portions of their lineups are out of commission or rendered ineffective at key times of the season or the playoffs, which can ruin a season's work and deflate a city of expectant fans. In 2002, the Toronto Maple Leafs, whose fans have not seen the Stanley Cup since 1967, began the conference finals missing eight players from their lineup, and succumbed not just to Carolina, but to sheer physical collapse.

Figures indicate that these types of injuries have recently been going up. A study published in the *Clinical Journal of Sports Medicine* by Emery, Meeuwisse, and Powell noted a total of 617 groin/abdominal strain injuries in the NHL over six seasons of play. The cumulative incidence rate in the NHL increased over that time from 12.99 injuries/100 players/year in the 1991–92 season to 19.87 injuries/100 players/year in the 1996–97 season, for a rate of increase of 1.32 injuries/100 players/year. A conservative estimate of the impact of groin and abdominal injury on each NHL team was 25 player games lost per year; "The impact of groin and abdominal strain injury at an elite level of play in hockey is significant and increasing. Future research in this area is needed to identify risk factors and potentially implement prevention strategies," they concluded. Equally importantly, all these lesser injuries clearly bear relation to the more serious injuries, not just by an upwards trend of numbers, but in the kinds of injuries occurring and how. For instance, recognizing patterns concerning shoulder dislocations – how they're occurring, how they can be prevented or minimized – should help us confront shoulder separations, a more serious injury knocking a player out for a couple months or more and perhaps requiring surgery. Less obviously, rises in things like groin pulls and hip pointers may point to things to help us to understand and diffuse the "concussion crisis."

But of greater direct concern than the preceding injuries are the more serious ones that do wipe out seasons, and damage or end careers. When these occur, the game suffers from the loss of its players, including some of its greats and the interest and passion they garner for the sport. What else might Bobby Orr, Mike Bossy, and Cam Neely, for example, have achieved for themselves and for their sport if their careers weren't darkened and halted by injuries? At one point in the 2004 season, all of the following stars were sidelined by injury at the same time: Rob Blake, Mario Lemieux, Peter Forsberg, Jeremy Roenick, Pavel Bure, Jason Allison, Adam Deadmarsh, Al Macinnis, Derian Hatcher, Markus Naslund, Marty Straka, Ziggy Palffy, Keith Primeau, Sheldon Souray, and Eric Daze. That had to be an unprecedented group, for hockey. Some serious injuries, as terrible and sometimes even life-threatening as they are, are very uncommon in hockey (for example, a fractured neck, ruptured spleen, or collapsed lung), and I don't know if they can tell us much, apart from what we learn by looking at the details of each case plus the panorama of injuries as a whole. But there are other serious injuries that fit into recurring patterns of result, and sometimes of causation. They occur more frequently, and merit direct examination. We have an opportunity to try to understand them, and the sport has an obligation to try to do something about them.

Among these recurrent serious injuries are the following:

- Knee: Injuries can include MCL, ACL, and PCL strains or tears, meniscus tears, and fractured kneecaps. These can be very bad injuries that cost players whole seasons, and may permanently hamper their mobility, even with cutting-edge surgery, rehabilitation programs, and high-tech knee braces. In addition, players with certain injuries may be at greater risk of difficulties with arthritis later in life. Bobby Orr, Mike Modano, Joe Nieuwendyk, Pavel Bure, Derian Hatcher, Steve Yzerman, and Doug Gilmour are just a few well-known players who suffered serious knee injuries that affected their careers. According to a 2001–02 study by the Injury Data Collection Program for the Hockey Development Centre for Ontario (HDCO), which logs and compiles statistics in that province, knees were the third leading body part (behind head and shoulder) injured in hockey, occupying 8.43 per cent of all injuries. The percentage would be even higher, strictly within injuries that are considered serious. Wounded knees are often caused by glancing collisions, low blows, falls, or injury-causing movements by the player himself.

- Wrist: Injuries can include fractures to the two big bones entering the wrist (the radius and ulna) or the numerous smaller carpal and metacarpal bones that form a kind of matrix in the middle of the wrist, as well as sprains and tears and dislocations, which can sometimes be worse than fractures. Wrist injuries have cost several players almost entire seasons and threatened careers. In hockey, a lot of force has to be wielded in many different ways through the small and unstable form of the wrist. Weakness in it is a consistent problem for many hockey players, despite advanced surgical techniques, therapies, and the old standby of taping them up for added support. Chris Pronger, Sergei Samsonov, Ladislav Nagy, and Sheldon Souray are some well-known players who have had serious wrist injuries. Wrists were tied for fourth on the HDCO's list of commonest injuries. Leading causes include collisions where the wrist is jammed or overextended in flexion or extension, slashes on the hands, falls into the ice or boards, and fights.

- Shoulder: Common injuries include dislocations, grades of separations, and tears to the labrum or rotator cuff. They often keep players out for a couple months at a time, sometimes less or more, depending on the severity. They generally have a good prognosis for recovery; however, they are a good (or should I say *bad*) example of injuries where there seems to be an added susceptibility for them to recur with greater ease and worse severity. Barrett Jackman, Gary Roberts, and Darcy Tucker are some players that have recently had to deal with difficult shoulder injuries. They are often caused by bodychecks into the boards or the ice, or sometimes in open ice, or other falls and collisions.

- Eye: Eye injuries are not common (occupying less than 1 per cent of all injuries), but when they happen they are often devastating, and in recent years there seem to have been a number of cases. In the year 2000 alone, twelve players sustained eye injuries, including Bryan Berard, whose eye injury forced him from the game (from which he miraculously returned, but with limited vision in the injured eye). Only a few years after losing Berard to a serious eye injury, the Leafs alone had recent scares with Owen Nolan, Darcy Tucker, and Tie Domi all in the same season. St. Louis's Al Macinnis was most recently forced to retire after recurrent problems. "I couldn't see a thing. You wonder if you'll ever be able to play again. It's the worst thing you could ever go through," Macinnis said of the experience. Steve Yzerman ended the 2004 season with a scratched cornea and broken eye socket after a puck struck him, in what, at the time, was slated to perhaps be his last game. According to ophthalmologist Dr. Tom Pashby of Toronto, over the past thirty years, there have been 1,914 injuries to eyes in hockey in Canada, causing loss of sight in the injured eye 311 times; more than forty NHLers have been forced into retirement. Scratches to the cornea, torn or detached retinas, and fractured orbital bones are some of the eye injuries that can occur. Besides those mentioned, others who have shown great courage to overcome tragic eye injuries include Pierre Mondou, current Phoenix GM Michael Barnett, Carolina Hurricanes assistant GM Jason Karmanos, and Toronto Marlies coach Paul Maurice. The most common causes are sticks and pucks to the eye.

- Head: Concussions have achieved a bad combination in that they are among the most serious and now among the most common of injuries. Players who have suffered complications from concussions include Michel Goulet, Dave Taylor, Pat Lafontaine, Mike Richter, Brett and Eric Lindros, Alyn Macaulay, Paul Kariya, and numerous others. According to the HDCO, head injuries were by far the most common injury at 15.78 per cent, and that's excluding eye, ear, dental, and facial injuries. In 2004, *The Era-Banner* reported concussion injury rates in the NCAA have increased steadily from about 0.7 per game in 1986 to 2.6 per game in 2000; Canadian major junior saw a similar rise. But don't let the increasingly common diagnosis make this scary injury seem mundane. It is among the most serious of injuries in several ways: area affected, span of effects, potential danger, cumulative danger, and difficulty of treatment.

A concussion consists of a traumatic injury to the brain (sometimes called TBI); when people get head injuries from a car accident, or being hit with a baseball or a bat, or being knocked out in boxing, this is usually the basic injury they have. One recent definition for sports concussion is "a complex patho-physiological process affecting the brain, induced by traumatic biomechanical forces" that may be caused by a direct blow to the head, or a blow elsewhere that causes an impulse to the head "that results in impairment of neurological function" and "a graded set of clinical syndromes." In other words, after being struck with a physical force, the brain doesn't work properly for a period of time, how much and how long depending on the severity of the concussion. Common symptoms include headaches, pressure in the head, neck pain, balance problems or dizziness, nausea or vomiting, feeling slowed down or fogged mentally, sensitivity to noise and light, confusion or a sense of "not feeling right," and more. Sometimes a person may lose consciousness (i.e., be "knocked out"); almost always there is a period of amnesia (holes in memory) extending either before the event or after, or both. It can result in long-term syndromes of headaches, cognitive dif-ficulties, difficulties with sleep, emotional disturbances, vision problems, and other neurological-related complications.

Even when the concussion resolves, studies have found that people that have had a concussion before seem to have an added susceptibility to having one again. And they "add up": the symptoms may be worse or take longer to resolve as a person has more concussions. Other possible complications include fractured skulls, bleeds into the brain, or coning that can cause severe disabilities or death. In 1967, the Minnesota North Stars' Bill Masterton (for whom the NHL's trophy for perseverance and dedication to the game is named) tragically died after falling and striking his head on the ice. Another possible asso-ciated syndrome, one that has become all too common in hockey, is post-concussion syndrome, where symptoms, abnor-malities, and impairments may linger for an indefinite period afterwards. By far the greatest cause of concussions have been collisions with other players, totalling 65.87 per cent (including bodychecks 20.63, pure collisions 28.57, and checks from behind 16.67), followed by the boards at 22.22 per cent and the ice at 6.35 per cent.

As far as providing deeper insight into the nature of injuries in sports and their potential effects, the injury that ended my career offers a good illustration of what in many ways is common, and in other ways of what can happen in a worst case scenario. From the age of thirteen to twenty-three, while playing on both club and school teams each winter, early on in that stretch being about the smallest player on the ice, and later making it through the tough competition of junior hockey around Toronto, and four years in the intense NCAA, I never missed a single game due to injury – or even a period. I'd also made it through twenty years of hockey without a concussion or even a question of one, despite obviously having been hit in the head hard plenty of times. Later in my career, an increasing number of players around me had been getting them, some several, often from seemingly unspectacular blows. With the widespread talk about susceptibility in connection with NHL stars like Eric Lindros or Paul Kariya, as well as certain players on each team I played with, I figured "concussions are something that happen to other people."

But one morning I woke up and went to practice at the Civic Centre in Wheeling, West Virginia, as the fog was still sitting over the Ohio River. During the practice, we did a standard drill where the puck is shot around the boards and the defenceman tries to hold the puck in while the forwards try to knock him off the puck and get it out of the zone. On one of the reps, a smaller forward came around and, as he hit me, his head was down, looking for the puck in my feet. Unintentionally, his helmet hit me in the jaw, its raised edges on top catching me almost like knuckles in an upper-cut punch, whipping my neck back violently and causing my head to immediately feel screwed up. I had trouble keeping my balance, was dizzy and disoriented, and felt pressure in my head like it was going to explode. I didn't know what was going on yet, since I'd never had a concussion before; but I knew instinctively not to absorb another hit, so I drifted out of my position, interrupting the drill, and switched positions with the other defenceman who starts the drill by passing a puck off the boards. The first two passes, the puck didn't make it. The coach asked me what the hell I was doing – can I not make a simple pass? I tried again, the third time, it went nowhere near the forward. The coach said, "What's wrong with you?" By now, it had been probably almost a minute since I got hit, and I was feeling worse and worse. "I feel dizzy," I said. "In fact, I feel like I'm going to fall over." He said it looked like that was the case as well, and to get off the ice and go see the doctor.

The next few hours, I don't remember, the next few days not much more. The doctors call this "post-traumatic amnesia." Little episodes are all I recall: being crushed when the doctor said I wouldn't be able to play the next game, feeling awful that the team had hired me to do a job, and was counting on me, and instead I couldn't play. Watching our team play from the stands, my eyes feeling like they were ten feet back in my head. Having trouble following the play, as though the fog over the river had permeated into my brain.

My symptoms included things like dizziness, headaches, pressure in my head, nausea, vision problems, and many others. Sometimes they would get better, as they were when, months later, I began talking to the Canadiens, and I would be optimistic of being able to come back for the following season. But then they got worse again.

The tryout with Montreal's top farm team in Hamilton wasn't the NHL camp, but I'd already been to three NHL training camps and had an available invitation to a fourth, but for various reasons, I felt this was a much better opportunity, and was really looking forward to it. Montreal coach Claude Julien knew me, and I knew the type of player he was looking for. The organization was managed by Bob Gainey and Andre Savard, two of the most highly respected people in the business. I'd always wanted to play for the Canadiens since I was a kid; the mystique still held huge power over me. It seemed like everything was finally coming together – perhaps fate? – if only my health would hold up. But in the end, the concussion symptoms got worse again, and the doctors would not clear me to play. With no end in sight, out of time, wanting to give someone else a chance in my place, I had to call Andre Savard; it was the most difficult thing I'd ever had to do. "Are you sure . . . ?" was his stupefied reply; there was a pause while insane, impossible ideas flashed through my mind. Meanwhile, he explained what a great opportunity this was. Slowly, the impossible thoughts in my mind left, replaced by the crushing realization that I couldn't. It was the break I was waiting for, and I couldn't play. My body was literally pulling my mouth away from the phone, and I could hardly find a voice to say that I was sure, that there was nothing I could do . . . I would've played through any amount of pain, I would've risked my life in a second; but how could I play through the spells that come where I can't see straight, can't think clearly, so disoriented I could barely stand up?

Who knows what would have happened, there was still a ways to go, and things might well not have ended up the way I hoped, but it was very frustrating and disappointing, for sure, not to be able to pursue it. In the meantime, I had to sort out the future and the past of my life and the game   how we got here, where we would go from here. When I was first injured, as disappointed as I was, I counted on being back for sure the following week. But next week became the week after, and then next month, and then the month after, and then next year. I did what the doctors said: rested longer and longer, was referred to higher and higher experts; did more and more tests; tried more different tips from people who'd recovered – but it wouldn't go away. I never played again. I never retired, never had a final lap, never quit, never had a final make-it-or-break-it chance and lost, as a sportsman at a minimum expects out of life; never had a chance to realize my dreams, or have them dashed; it was more like someone called a timeout early in the game, the contest was put on pause, and just never resumed. Like Douglas Macarthur's old soldier, I never died, I just "faded away."

I also began to learn more about my injury: that it doesn't so much matter what a head injury looks like from the outside, but what happens to the brain on the inside; that a concussion may not really be one injury, but a variety of different injuries under the same name, sharing in common that they are traumatically induced, function-altering injuries to the brain, but potentially very different in nature, effect, and outcome. Each at the moment elusive in understanding and impossible to predict. Much of what I found out was about what wasn't known. The brain – inaccessible, unbelievably complicated, unclearly differentiated, and absolutely vital – is still largely "one big grey area" to science. The mind, it's co-inhabitant, is even more mysterious and, if it is not axiomatically unfathomable to itself, must certainly be our most undiscovered frontier. Now try making sense of them both in conjunction. Or for that matter, what was the relationship between ongoing concussion symptoms and whiplash, which in addition to myself, others like L.A.'s Jason Allison and the Senators' Brian Pothier had reportedly also had? Why, as Bobby Clarke observed: "I saw lots of guys get knocked out while I was playing and we never heard one player saying he had yellow vision or disorientation. If they had it, they couldn't have played with it for long. I don't understand why we never saw it."? Why were there more cases of players suffering worse cases of post-concussion syndrome? Was it some change inside the game that was increasing effects, or some change outside the game that was impeding healing? Few answers were known.

In the meantime, I learned of the many more players with similar kinds of injuries, and similar problems, from similar kinds of things. Forward Adam Deadmarsh, who was injured three days after me, announced his retirement prior to this 2005–06 season, unable to shake the effects of his second concussion after close to three years and counting. "I've kind of been holding on and hoping and praying that I'd recover from this concussion issue that I have and I haven't been able to do that," Deadmarsh told the Canadian Press. "I think it's time that I faced the fact that my brain doesn't want to play hockey any more." And there are others suffering from other injuries too: knees, hips, shoulders, wrists, backs, elbows, etc. An army of injured swelling along the sidelines, or in the background, suffering largely in silence, while the game goes on without them. Many of them dealing not only with pain, but disablement, psychological effects, career uncertainty, financial difficulty, legal hassles, treatment challenges, strained or broken relationships. Professional hockey players are people schooled in toughness and character; they deal with injuries as courageously and effectively as anyone. But ultimately, there is only so much they can control. And they can't stop their suffering from burdening their family and those that care about them, or stop their team from missing them in their absence.

Too often lately, the swollen sidelines have cast a long shadow over the ice. It is critical, from the point of view of player health and the future health of the game, not to let the current casualty rates become accepted. No matter what medical advances may or may not be on the horizon, the game must heed the ancient adage "an ounce of prevention is worth a pound of cure."

WHAT ARE SWELLING INJURIES?

This has been especially clear in what has happened with injury rates, despite major advances that have occurred already in medical treatment and general fitness. Leading-edge training methods and resources have helped today's athletes reach levels of physical fitness higher than ever before. There are more and better treatments for underlying health conditions. There have been revolutionary advances in the field of rehabilitation. Medically, a knee injury that would have been season-ending, and perhaps career-ending in Bobby Orr's day, today's doctors can repair with arthroscopic surgery, and the player can be back playing in a matter of weeks. Similar improvements have been made in surgical repairs for other joint injuries. Modern medical staff for hockey are among the best in the world, as are plans for coping with on-ice emergencies, and protocols for injury management and return-to-play. Yet we have not seen a corresponding plummet in injury rates or the cost of them. And some serious injuries – especially head injuries – have sharply risen. So the first thing we need to try to answer is, what is swelling the game's serious injuries? How do we explain that while medical treatments have enormously improved, the profile of injuries in the game hasn't?

The basic physics of the sport give us our first clues. Injuries typically arise out of collisions. Collisions, which include basically any time two bodies come together, are governed by the physical quantity of momentum, which is the product of mass (weight) times velocity (speed). The rising quantities of the game – speed, size, strength – thus increase the momentum of collisions, which results in more and worse injuries. The size of players has grown enormously: thirty pounds over half a century, including half of that and two inches taller since about 1980. As Doug Gilmour noticed and authors Greenberg and Wilton confirmed in *Total Hockey*, the equipment most players wear has grown by an even greater amount proportionally. The added mass directly increases the momentum of collisions. The speeds of the game (the other factor in momentum), both of players (perhaps two-thirds faster than in Rocket Richard's era) and shots (now over 100 mph with the invention of the slapshot, better sticks, and stronger players), have also grown. Even more significantly, as Ken Dryden has drawn attention to, player shift times have dramatically decreased over time, from two minutes in earlier eras to little more than thirty seconds today. This means that players are out for short full-speed shifts and then go off, so that the whole game is played at full speed, which substantially increases the speed of collisions. Although I said in earlier chapters that carrying the puck with speed had become less effective (or evident) than it once was, players were still skating fast, indeed faster – they just wouldn't get as far on a rush before they would get hit. And speed certainly also could be and has been used by checkers taking runs at players that do have the puck.

Together, the simultaneous increases in both velocity and mass have a combined double effect on increasing the momentum of collisions. And if there are two players involved, each heavier and moving faster, then there are four increases in one collision. The greater strength of the players through improved strength training and physical fitness plays into both of these quantities, as it increases the mass of the players and allows for the generation of greater speeds of impact. This is how hip pointers (which are occurring because players are taller, and their hips are now coming into contact with the ledge on the top of the boards) and groin pulls (proliferating because players have bigger muscles, and move them suddenly and explosively over short full-out shifts) point the way to increased concussions, caused when big fast bodies collide. (Please see table on page 259.)

At the same time, the increase in these same factors has led to an overcrowded rink where there are big bodies moving everywhere and no room or time to avoid them. This makes for far more collisions, and therefore far more injuries of which collisions (including unintentional ones) are the overwhelming cause. It's just like there are far more car collisions in heavy traffic than on empty roads, only in hockey, where you don't have to stay within lanes in straight lines, heavy traffic and high speeds can coincide. With these two fundamental changes – far more collisions, and far greater impact momentum in each collision – it is simply unavoidable that there would be a huge increase in the number and severity of injuries. The basic physics of the game then, aside from more conspiratorial, compli cated, or creative explanations, go a long way, perhaps the furthest, in explaining the rise of injuries.

There are other important factors, however, as well. One of these is that the way the game is played in recent years became much more physically gruelling, even playing within the rules. There simply was a lot more punishing physical contact than fifteen years ago, or ever before. There were more hits now, and the hits were harder. Why did the style change in this way? Part of the reason was the pressurized atmosphere of the modern game – with high financial stakes, huge media attention, and close competition. Also, there were more trade-deadline deals and off-season free agents, which means players had less secure positions; playoff success was critical to job security, and since the playoff format (a series of games against the same opponent in a short space of time) prizes a strategy of physically wearing down the opposition, players would have to try to show their fitness for this kind of battle, starting long before the playoffs actually began. Adding to that is the fact that with recent expansion barely half the teams in the league make the playoffs now, versus more than three-quarters as recently as fifteen years ago – so for all but the top few teams, each game is seen as a do-or-die scenario from very early in the season. As a result, almost every game from the halfway point of the season on has had the air and intensity of a physically tougher playoff game, where each player is expected to finish every check, hard, at all times.

Further amplifying physical play was a growing cult of "heart" and "grit" within North American hockey, ever since the "European invasion" in hockey took away North Americans' ability to hang our pride on superior skill. TV has helped sensationalize this. Spectacular collisions are compelling (people don't remember who scored the winner for the Devils versus the Flyers in the 2000 playoffs, they just remember Scott Stevens knocking out Eric Lindros with a body-check). And they are so extraordinary to spectators, compared to their own way of life (as captured by those humorous ESPN commercials where hockey or football players slam into officeworkers sitting at their cubicles or desks). Since skilful plays are often visually obvious, physical play and its contribution to winning is one thing numerous television expert analysts have fixated on highlighting for viewers, and the result of all this was that physical play was glorified and inflated beyond the real importance that it has.

I also believe the new "entertainment" presentation of games inside arenas – complete with pre-game laser light shows, thousands of fans wearing your licensed uniform, chants and taunts over the PA system, and scoreboard cartoons depicting the opposition being squashed – affected the way players played. The spectacle grew about the sport, and the larger-than-life atmosphere encouraged players to play with a recklessness for their own physical safety that belied the fact for all their amazing physical prowess, professional hockey players remained all too human, and therefore vulnerable to injury. Of course, the sport of hockey itself, like other games, has evolved over time. "Boarding" is a relic of an age long gone when hitting a player into the boards used to be a penalty. Now, most of the hits – and 40 per cent of the injuries – take place along the hard boards and glass, or into them. At the same time, the spread of the squeeze made in recent years for a more static, physical game, for a game played along the boards and in front of the net, where players clustered. There was little open ice to get away to in the play – it was all highly physically contested space: battling, hitting, jockeying, so that lots of injuries occurred.

When you combine the more physical style with the increases in size, speed, and strength, the injuries really started to pile up. You can see this at work on a case-by-case basis in acute events (like Scott Stevens hits), but moreso you see it over a long season where people get worn down, miss games, and there are few ironmen left. In this context, an eighty-two-game schedule made for too many games. Don't forget hockey used to have fewer games until not that long ago: recently two less at eighty and, prior to that, seventy (plus fewer exhibition and playoff games). With the modern game, the season became too gruelling, players got worn out, and like a repeat rolling of the die with bad odds, eventually injury was bound to happen.

But there was more behind the risen injuries than evolution of things within the rules of the game. Players also got away with more outside the rules. As described in the last chapter, the number of violent fouls occurring – from slashes and crosschecks, to charging and hitting people without the puck – had been increasing for years, without penalty calls going up in tandem. Injuries were often a direct result of these plays. Even fighting is a good example of illegal play that leads to a lot of injuries. In the March 9, 2004, edition of *The Hockey News*, the NHL said it reviewed the first twenty-five concussions of the season, and four were caused by fighting. And there might have been more, if some enforcers got concussions but didn't want to disclose them because of their role, and the thinking they could get by until they got better. The same study found six of the twenty-five concussions were penalized (i.e., caused by illegal blows), and the reviewing group felt another one deserved a penalty, pushing the total slightly higher to almost 30 per cent of the total concussions caused by illegal play.

Even when fouls don't immediately cause injury, if they occur frequently, as crosschecking, slashes on the hands, and charging did in recent years, they could wear players down, leaving them vulnerable to injury by other means. Or sometimes the fouls might cause only minor injuries, but those minor injuries accumulate into more serious ones, or cause players to compensate in a way that lead them to be injured more severely. Insurance companies recognize the cumulative effect of injuries and often put "exclusions" on body parts that have been injured before, such as a knee that's previously been operated on, because of the high risk they perceive of further and more serious injury. The classic example is concussions, where a player may get one from an illegal hit, recover, but with added susceptibility, get another one innocently and not recover. Tolerance of too many minor fouls allowed escalation, and although a more serious subsequent foul may draw a penalty, it may at the same time cause a serious injury, which that penalty call was too late to prevent. In all these ways, violence was another cause of concerning injuries.

Another significant factor – which may or may not seem surprising at first blush – has to be the equipment. It isn't something we often think about, it's something we normally take for granted; we wear what we're given, and we assume that it's getting better and better and we're getting safer and safer. And in some ways, it obviously has, and we have. But at the same time, as protective equipment has got "better and better," there have been more and more injuries. In fact, it is often said that there are more head injuries now than when players wore no helmets! How do we explain that? Partly factors mentioned earlier, partly better recognition (although some would argue that's offset by worse disclosure in an age where immense concern on the part of employers about recurrence can hurt player employability). But these can't be all. An obvious and quite common belief about how equipment actually contributes to injuries is that the bulky, plated "gladiatorlike" equipment, as people often call it, gives players a false sense of security, so that, fostered by the illusion of being protected from serious harm, players play more dangerously with respect to themselves and others wearing the same equipment, causing injuries the equipment has failed to prevent. Any benefits gained from potentially better equipment are thus overshadowed by the way players play in it. Surely it's no accident that in U.S. college where full facemasks are worn, there are even more concussions occurring than in the NHL where they are not, a staggering 2.6 per game in 2000, according to the *Era-Banner*. "I think [the injury problem]'s tied to the players having less respect for the risk because of a false sense of security with the newer equipment . . . There is a reckless abandon," Devils GM Lou Lamoriello said.

But in two more direct ways, some have concerns whether the equipment design is hurting more than it's helping. One is that, as the equipment is made of increasingly hard and strong materials designed to protect the wearer, those materials in colliding with others are seeing other players injured on the ice. And, of course, it ultimately impacts the wearer too, because the others he or she is playing against are wearing that same equipment. As a result, we can end up with more injuries, instead of more safe. "Pads used to have a soft leather feel, now they're almost like steel," Lamoriello said. Yet those "protective" hard surfaces often omit covering most of the stomach, lower back, neck, and other areas that house the spinal cord and most of the vital organs. "The protection itself may have become as dangerous as the false sense of security it inspires," said Greenberg and Wilton in *Total Hockey*. In twenty years in hockey, my three major injuries were not caused by any dangerous play that was part of the game, or by acts of violence, or by the boards, but by other players' equipment on innocent plays: two wrist fractures, both caused by having my hand hit the hard and squared surface of another player's pads and snap. And the concussion, which similar sights are familiar enough in football (think of Troy Aikman, Steve Young, or Ed McCaffrey being felled by helmets to the jaw). The NHL has itself started to recognize the problem, announcing a ban on the hard-shell elbow pads. The potential dangers in striking the boards are clear to everyone associated with the game, even though boards are stationary and players can usually position themselves before impact to avoid injury. But the hard-surfaced equipment is almost as hard, moves fast and unpredictably as the players wearing them do, and *tries* to hit you, as hard as it can. Maybe the equipment was designed for gladiators after all!

In another way, the equipment reminds me less of gladiators than of medieval knights. In all their shining body armour, Europe's knights of the Middle Ages could hardly move, so that when the virtually armour-less Mongols under Genghis Khan and his successors invaded, the knights were slaughtered. By comparison to the knights, look at what soldiers wear today – almost no body armour. But in hockey in recent years, we went the opposite way, to equipment reminiscent of the knights of Europe's Dark Ages. "Hockey armour" featured rigid, plated, bulky parts, whereas softer, lighter, more streamlined equipment could absorb or deflect impacts and allow movement to avoid injury.

Many serious injuries in hockey are joint injuries, where having heavy equipment on limbs places more strain on them, like torque about a nexus. When I was at a major equipment company's offices for some equipment work, I asked the rep why they didn't make equipment resembling that of speed-skiing or fencing, a kind of "padded wetsuit," that was easier to move in but still protective. (At the time, I asked because I was interested in something easier to play in, not because of anything to do with injuries.) His reply shocked me: he said they did. Their design staff came up with prototypes very similar to what I was describing, he said. But here was the reception they got: they were scoffed at and ridiculed by the sponsored pro players they showed them to, who said they looked absurd and vowed they would never wear them. And they were rejected by consumer parents in test-marketing, who statistically always preferred the biggest, bulkiest, most armourlike equipment offered, for their kids. And so we have kids struggling to skate beneath heaps of restrictive equipment, at levels where there is no checking and little force generated. And we have pros in their gladiator garb barrelling into each other, injuring one another with each other's "protections." I believe cutting-edge technology is often being used with little common sense in hockey, through some of what the equipment companies supply, and some of what we tell them we want, buy, and put on.

A very different category of products are also used by some athletes, some of which may have serious health consequences: stimulants and other chemical "supplements." A substantial amount of concern has been raised recently about athletes' use of ephedra, amphetamines, and other stimulants that can alter body metabolism and chemical levels, and some of which carry risks of causing heart attacks, seizures, strokes, dehydration, and other complications. Earlier this year, defenceman Stephane Quintal estimated 40 per cent of NHLers use stimulants. Although most of them are over-the-counter, that also means in many cases players who use them do so without expert supervision (and therefore detailed knowledge of the product and its potential implications). Use of ephedra in particular was linked to recent deaths of some college football players. Athletes who rely on these or on "pseudies" (pseudoephedrine), high-dose caffeine "sport" drinks like Red Bull or Jolt, or other "uppers" often also must then rely on "sleepers" or "downers" like Ambien, Benadryl, and Valium to bring them back down again and enable them to sleep. The third group is painkillers. Many of these can be addictive as well. The cycle of uppers and downers, the long-term reliance on medications that have adverse effects can take a heavy toll on athletes' health. Another commonly used substance in sports is the strength-building and recovery-speeding supplement creatine. By many accounts, creatine is thought to be safe. Yet there have been some questions raised since the sudden deaths of three college wrestlers in a short space of time in 1997–98, all said to have used creatine. At the Pittsburgh Penguins training camp in 2001, trainers advised us there was some concern that creatine may be associated with abdominal muscle tears, which have become more common and aren't exactly a traditional hockey injury. It may be that these concerns have faded and creatine is fully safe. But in my opinion, the recent discovery of dangers in long-term use of the popular (and government-approved) anti-inflammatory drug Vioxx is a poignant reminder that we should be cautious in using new chemicals extensively or in extreme situations such as the training and competition of elite-level athletes.

An even brighter spotlight has been shone recently on athlete use of steroids, related chemicals like "andro," and other illegal performance-enhancing substances. A number of hockey players have recently gone on record to say that steroids are indeed being used in the sport. Long-time minor league enforcer Dave Morrisette made some waves with his detailing of this issue in his recent book, *Memoires d'un dur de cuir*, where he admitted with regret having used them himself. Other "tough guys" including Rocky Thompson and Dennis Bonvie have said that while they don't use them themselves, they have noticed steroid use in players they have had to fight. Sabres enforcer Andrew Peters was believed to be the first NHLer to admit using a performance-enhancing supplement, telling the *Buffalo News* he legally used the steroidlike chemical androstenedione (made famous by baseball slugger Mark McGwire) before the U.S. Food and Drug Administration banned its sale in April 2004. But don't stereotype enforcers, unless it's to say they seem to have been the ones with the most courage to talk about the issue as it may exist in the game. "There were steroids before me, and there will be steroids after. The system is such that young people are ready to do anything to get maximum performance," Morisette said. So how prevalent are they? "You see guys come into the league and the year before they were 220, this year they're 245," Thompson said. "How many people can put on 25 pounds of muscle in a summer? I've tried for years and I'm still 200 pounds . . . I'm not going to name names because I don't know for sure, but it's awfully suspicious. . . . Common sense would tell you that." Talk goes around, but as Thompson said, you don't know for sure, so it's hard to say. And all the technology of the game is changing so fast – including substances used to aid performance – that being just two years out of the game, I would be in no position to estimate. But there is sufficient concern about substance use that Gary Bettman has been called before U.S. Congress twice this year (alongside commissioners from other sports) to testify about the issue in hockey. And Congress is threatening to legislate a government crackdown on performance-enhancing drug use in professional sports if the leagues can't stop it themselves.

Some may wonder whether clamping down on performance drug use is necessary. Many athletes are given the impression they are not particularly dangerous or unhealthy (or give it – such as Jose Canseco, who said in his book, *Juiced*, that "steroids, used correctly . . . will make you healthier") if used according to expert protocols. But the very lists of banned substances published by the World Anti-Doping Agency are intended to mark out those that are known or suspected by medical authorities to be dangerous or unhealthy. And indeed, the public has seen so many of those rumoured in the press to be users blow out their careers with a series of spectacular joint injuries, surgeries, and debilitating conditions. Football player Lyle Alzado and baseball's Ken Caminiti blamed steroids for rapid downward health spirals that ended in their tragic premature deaths. And even if those taking them know and accept the risks, what cannot be accepted is the pressure that puts on others who don't accept those risks to take them as well to keep up, or on kids aspiring to be like their heroes, who are at greater risk, and without having the understanding or maturity to make those decisions, playing Russian roulette with their health for fantasies mathematically no more realistic than winning a lottery.

But it's not just the safety of the players *using* these various chemicals that we have to worry about. Many are also worried that use of these steroids, stimulants, and other substances put players into states where they can harm *others*. "The guys are so fired up. I don't know if they're taking Sudies or ephedrine or whatever, but guys are not thinking clearly and if that's the case, we've got to fix that problem," Teemu Selanne said. They believe that some of these chemicals create a state of excitation or frenzy (for example, "roid rage") that contributes to the reckless on-ice play and senseless over-reactions that can cause injuries. Not to mention inhuman levels of strength and power, which other humans will be on the receiving end of. I believe that the majority of pro athletes who take substances do so "defensively," because they know or think others are, and they don't want to be at a physical disadvantage that may imperil their safety or their job security. Nobody wants to go into battle "unarmed," and so some join the group taking them – to protect themselves, not because they want to get ahead by cheating. And on it can go, like an arms race – which is why even among mature and sensible athletes, there is a danger for it to grow, and frighteningly escalate. To have hockey players be conducting chemical experiments on their bodies is not something anyone wants.

A HEALTHY FUTURE

So what do we do to reduce injuries and safeguard player health and welfare?

From a treatment point of view, I believe the NHL and its teams are largely doing everything they reasonably can – there is very high-quality medical care, along the best guidelines available. This includes not only the team doctor and the (two or three) team trainers, but a full set of affiliated specialists, chiropractors, physical therapists, and rehabilitation experts. That's one of the good things about how sophisticated hockey organizations have become in recent years. At the same time, the NHL in conjunction with the NHLPA had implemented a substance abuse program to help players recover from health issues outside injuries. Such excellent treatment is good for players' health, and it's also shrewd for business, because clubs have so much riding on the players.

But ultimately, once things happen, there is only so much that even the best available medical treatments can do to repair damage or speed recovery. Prevention and minimization have to be the focus of efforts to improve the safety and health situation. Over recent years, preventative steps have been taken. Comprehensive physicals comb from head to toe – poking players in the eye with a device to measure pressure in the eyeball, and scraping the bottom of players' feet with the blunt end of a knife to test nerve function – looking for potential problems before they occur. For specific injuries, medical prevention programs have been put in place: for example, on the head-injury front, lengthy neurologic baseline testing and club-affiliated neurologists try to reduce the risk of premature return and re-injury; a "post-concussion syndrome project" study has been set up under Pittsburgh Penguins physician Dr. Chip Burke; and a one-week mandatory layoff has been put in, which is a leading-edge protocol in professional sports.

However, clearly a lot more can be done. Recently, post-lockout, the focus in hockey has been on trying to make the game more exciting and entertaining for the fans – and that is of course a worthwhile and essential goal. But we can't afford to let issues of player health and welfare get lost in the shuffle. Unfortunately, in the package of rule changes and other initiatives announced for the 2005–06 season, no item (at least announced publicly) was designed to address the issue of injuries. In fact, a rule that most other leagues in the world have, and that many people, from doctors to Don Cherry, had hoped and anticipated the NHL would put in for that purpose – "no touch icing" – was instead specifically rejected: "Touch icing will remain the practice," the announcement read. That means dangerous full-length chases to the end boards (just for a defenceman to touch the puck before icing is called), such as that which resulted in the broken leg that ended the year of San Jose leading scorer Marco Sturm last season, will continue. The league said extending discretion to wave off icings from referees to linesmen "should have the effect of reducing the number of situations in which a race for the puck might result in an injury to a player," but waving off an icing only makes the puck live, meaning the chase continues, whereas blowing the play dead as soon as the puck crosses the line ("no touch") is the only thing that would avert the injuries. The advantage of touch icing is for fans – being able to watch the chase, and having a few less stoppages in the game and more flow. But I don't think it's worth it. Sometimes "shortcuts" don't take us where we think they will – like the seamless glass some teams put in to aid spectator sightlines, but which was accused of increasing concussions to exciting star players, before the NHL mandated it be taken back out. In the past, hockey was sometimes accused of catering to the views of insiders while being callous to the desires of fans, but the opposite would also be unsuitable: We must find ways to satisfy both needs – a more fan-friendly and player-healthy sport – at the same time.

Another rule that many thought would merit more discussion in the new CBA was mandatory eye protection. Minimum half-visors are mandatory in junior hockey and recently in pro hockey's AA ECHL (and full facemasks in amateur hockey and the NCAA). The half-visors on the market have improved immensely in recent years, and while I'm not sure we're in position to say all players should be forced to wear them, I think we should at least set a deadline of say two to three years (grandfathered if necessary), putting pressure on manufacturers and players to get to a solution for eye protection by then that is satisfactory to players. There is also some concern about some of the new rule changes and focus on offence opening the door to more injuries from things like charging and goaltender interference. "I don't know what you can do if you don't have twenty defencemen to play the year," Ken Hitchcock said. The solution, of course, is simply to focus with equal vigilance as on calling obstruction and inflated goal equipment on calling charging and goalie interference.

This leads us to a more general required step – and the most straightforward and obvious one of all – in the campaign against injuries, and that is to counter illegal play and violence that cause or lead to injury. These are all the things we talked about in the last chapter: Continuing and expanding the crackdown on hits deliberately targeting the head, as they have in football, as well as slashes to the hands. Renewing the crusade against hitting from behind that can cause terrible back and spinal injuries, and adding the constant crosschecking to it. Clarifying and consistently calling extension hits, which cause concussions and separated shoulders and all kinds of injuries. Calling all violent fouls without discretion, whether the particular case at hand led to injury or not. Stricter enforcement with greater punishments (Zero Tolerance) for more serious infractions that can cause more severe injuries, along the stepped penalty scale in place, but with the deterrent in line with the damage (or potential damage from certain acts) and the consistency of application never in doubt. Rule changes to ban all forces beyond those permitted or regulated as truly minor, eliminate grey areas in the rules, and allow for the tracking and punishment of repeat offending players, coaches, or teams. Changing mindsets such as "anything to win" and frontier justice. Confronting the violence in the game that takes such a toll on players will allow the reduction of injuries, including some of the worst and most horrific ones. Certainly, they are the most inexcusable and unacceptable injuries, and the ones we have the most direct control over. For this reason, stamping out violence is an obvious important step to reducing injuries in the game.

Less obvious but more far ranging and important to solving so many of the problems of hockey is four-on-four. The changes in the basic physics of the game have made the injury problem we have seen recently as practically unavoidable, in the current five-man configuration, as it is staggering. And further, without a change, it can only get worse: insufficient space leads to a clogging style of play, a demand for bigger and bigger, faster and faster players, which leads to less space, and so on. It's a vicious circle, with injuries spiralling upwards. We can't legislate smaller, weaker, or slower players, or, worse, less competitive coaches. It doesn't seem possible (or ideal) to build bigger rinks. And I'm not about to recommend removing body contact from hockey. So what is the only alternative, as the game is drifting from an already unacceptable casualty rate to an unsustainable one? Four-on-four.

As I've said before, with four-on-four there is far more space available on the ice, which leads to fewer collisions, which leads to far fewer injuries. This simple fundamental adjustment may do more to reduce injuries than anything else. In the August 2004 *Canadian Journal of Neurological Sciences*, an article by Dr. Richard Wennberg of the University of Toronto Hospital found an average of 170 collisions per game on wider international surfaces, versus 264 in the NHL: "If the findings of this study are replicable," he wrote, "it would suggest that . . . the larger international ice surface . . . could reduce the number of collisions, and by extension, concussions that occur in the sport." Four-on-four on an NHL-sized rink would increase the amount of ice surface per player *even more*. We don't want to decrease the forces of the game (eg., skating speed, shot speed) that help make the game exciting, but in that case, we need to create more space out there for us to get out of the way of them. Also significant is the fact that four-on-four would change the way the game is played, rendering "squeezelike" clogging schemes ineffective, so that there would be more wide-open, flowing, open-ice play. The static, constant physical contact along the boards and net front that contributes to so many injuries would now drastically diminish. Four-on-four is a crucial cog in the positive-feedback wheel of decreasing injuries.

But more needs to be done to protect players' health, particularly from the kind of injuries that don't "happen" but "accumulate." Currently in hockey, there are eighty-two games a season, plus a half dozen or more exhibition games and up to twenty-eight playoff games, not including training camp and practices throughout the season. Compare that to football, the most similar sport in terms of physical contact and injury toll: NFL teams play only sixteen games, the games are a week apart, and the season lasts only four months. And remember that in a much less physical era in hockey, with smaller players and slower speeds, the NHL played fewer games than they do today. Even though modern players have far superior physical conditioning, training, and medical treatment available, there are no true ironmen any more: the longest streak in the league going into this season is owned by Karlis Skrastins at 351 consecutive games played, barely a third of the 964 Doug Jarvis compiled from beginning to end of his career (1975–1988) or the previous record-holder, Garry Unger with 914 (from 1968–1980). With almost every player guaranteed to miss games every year, it is obvious the season is not just hard, but unreasonably so. Players can't sustain the punishment, the wear and tear. I'm sure most players would agree. Some of them, especially older players or players at less than full health, but who were able to come back, were at least partly relieved to have the lockout give them a year off to recuperate.

With the way the game is now, the season needs to be shortened to perhaps seventy-two games. A few less games, a little more time in between, makes a big difference in recuperating from injuries, having the energy to avoid them, rather than having them accumulate or leaving a player vulnerable to a worse one. Even one less game every couple weeks makes a big difference. In addition, players don't use training camp to get in shape any more, they come in shape, and are expected to, and typically all but a few roster spots are already set. Shortening training camp, having less exhibition games, and moving the season up, which will also help by improving ice conditions at the end of the year (and besides, some people won't watch hockey into June anyway), should all help reduce injuries. A shortened season is a sacrifice the NHL can make in order to protect its players and its own investment.

Another piece of the puzzle, I believe, has to be smarter, better equipment. The NHL did the right thing in mandating the removal of the hard glass and replacing it with flexible glass systems. And to their credit, they have recognized the parallel problem with the equipment, and begun the process of doing the same thing on that front, by banning the hard-shell elbow pads. Now the initiative needs to be extended to other pieces of equipment. More forgiving equipment benefits everyone – as opposed to using hard equipment to protect one player at a time when it can injure the other nine skaters on the ice, and doing this for each by turn. If hard pads are necessary, why not have them covered with softer materials on the outside for the benefit of opponents like they are on the inside, the side closest to the wearer's body? Similar to equipment there used to be in hockey, and to types still used in some other sports such as fencing, or the headgear used in Olympic boxing? And I mean for all the equipment: elbow pads, shoulder pads, helmets, pants and others – regardless of whether it causes injury intentionally or unintentionally. And why not weave it in, like the protection for speed-skiing, for example? This would create a more streamlined, less square or angular surface, making for less collisions, and less jarring collisions. In the last year or two, there seems to be some movement toward equipment offerings and choices more in that direction, but only incrementally. There have been rumours the NHL has plans to unveil new streamlined uniforms in the near future, but until they do it is unclear to what extent that will also include the equipment. But it's time for those prototypes to be dug out, refined, and introduced. Based on the number of injuries caused by collisions, the majority, at 55.53 per cent, according to the HDCO (including bodychecking at 26.28 per cent and other collisions at 29.28 per cent) this should reduce injuries considerably.

In addition, softer, lighter equipment would better protect the players *wearing it* from the real injuries that are common and significant – not cuts and bruises, but joint tears and concussions – because they would be able to move more freely and quickly (with less weight) to avoid injury, and the softer equipment would absorb impact rather than create jarring and/or force-concentrating ones. No doubt in the process, it would allow players to play better and more freely too. In addition, less bulky, armoured equipment would reduce the illusory sense of being protected like a knight, and playing like a gladiator, so that players feel more responsible for their own safety, and play safer and less recklessly, reducing injuries.

The players need to be made aware, and parents buying equipment for their children need to be made aware, that like the knights, all that equipment still might not save them from injury, certain kinds of equipment may in fact increase risks of injury to them or others, and that they have to consider how best to protect themselves alone and in unison. In designing, we need to start matching modern materials and technology not just with one-dimensional force-tests, but with more common-sense understanding of the game it's used for, how it works, and the experience of playing it. Leagues, players, parents, and manufacturers, in conjunction with medical personnel, must take the initiative and responsibility jointly.

More generally, there needs to be a component of injury awareness education from minor hockey to the pros, to inform players and families about prevention, recognition, and treatment – as well as get feedback from them, about their experience and observations. Educating people on how common significant injuries like fractured wrists, torn knees, separated shoulders, and concussions occur, and on how to avoid those situations would surely help. If we can tell people how to diminish the chance of injury in a factory, or a pool, or in other situations, we can do it for on the ice. Educating about various injuries themselves, how to recognize them and manage them so that they don't drag out, recur, or get worse will also help. In particular, concussions or other internal injuries that are not as obvious as a broken limb need to be well described and explained so they can be recognized. Grassroots efforts toward fostering sportsmanship and clean play, play within the rules that keeps everyone safe, must be part of the plan. Educating players and families on how the equipment works, what it can and can't protect from, when it needs to be replaced, and of the advantages and disadvantages of different kinds available means people are more informed, and safer.

Some of these are starting to happen through the efforts of groups like Safe and Fun Hockey, ThinkFirst, Dr. Pashby's Sports Fund, USA Hockey, and others. It would be great to have the NHL on board, using its "superpower" to help lead the effort both directly and by example in these initiatives to protect current and future players. But the communication must be two ways. All the groups responsible for safety in the game need to listen more to players, parents, and other people in the field about what their experiences, concerns, thoughts, and desires are around injuries, equipment, substances, and the play of the game.

Although, as mentioned, there are generally excellent and leading-edge protocols for treatment by teams, medical staff, and coaches in professional hockey, some effort and energy is required to have this make its way down to lower levels, where there are less means, and where lies the future of the game. I hope we are past the point of teams pressuring players back into action too soon (as there are plenty of nightmare stories of in past eras), but if not, there should be programs to protect against this scenario, and players should know what they are undertaking or risking.

As far as performance-enhancing supplements and drugs, clearly there needs to be both better education and tougher enforcement. Having experts explain to pros and aspiring pros the facts on the various chemicals out there – what the risks and concerns are, what good and safe alternatives are – is the first part. And programs to deal with use of illegal and dangerous substances is the other part. "We need drug-testing. That puts everybody on a level playing field," Bonvie said. Whereas in the past, the performance-enhancing substance use issue was largely ignored by professional hockey, the new CBA of 2005 has corrected this deficiency. The policy outlined calls for "up to two" no-notice random tests per player per year. For a first positive test, a player would receive a twenty-game suspension, for a second offence, a sixty-game suspension, and for a third, a "permanent" ban (but the player can apply for reinstatement after two years).

This was obviously an improvement over the situation before. However, when announced, it did not satisfy the heads of the Congressional committee studying the problem, who held hearings with players, management, and union officials from the various sports. The Congressmen wrote, "We have serious concerns about the effectiveness of this new policy. It appears to contain numerous loopholes that might allow players to circumvent the testing regime." Their complaints included that no minimum number of tests was specified, there was no independent administrator, no "clear and comprehensive" list of banned substances, and days when testing could be administered were sharply restricted. The policy referred most issues of substance (no pun intended) to a committee to be formed between the NHL and NHLPA on the drug issue, with no specifics or deadlines set in stone at the time.

In baseball, delays on specifics led to embarrassment: working with Senator Jim Bunning, a Hall-of-Fame former baseball pitcher, Senator John McCain told baseball's union leader: "Are you and the players living in such a rarified atmosphere that you do not appreciate this is a transcendent issue. Don't you get it? Don't you get that this is an issue greater than collective bargaining. It's about young [people] who are tempted to take these substances into their bodies and some of them commit suicide. Don't you understand that this is an issue of such transcendent importance that you should have acted months ago." To hockey, the Congressmen wrote: "Your efforts to develop your own policy appear to be inadequate and to provide additional evidence of the need for our legislation."

One alternative is to have the NHL/NHLPA hammer out specifics that would be acceptable to Congress. But given that Congress already has two bills on the table – the Clean Sports Act and the Professional Sports Integrity and Accountability Act, with specified terms (including a two-year ban for a first positive test, and a lifetime ban for a second), it seems what they view as acceptable is quite clear. Thus rather than have hockey go through the same embarrassment as baseball only to come up "on their own" with the same terms already outlined by Congress, why not just accept the legislation, as baseball's Bud Selig eventually offered to do? The legislation would extend the anti-doping power over Olympic sports onto the professional sports including hockey, charging third parties (the U.S. anti-doping agency, or Montreal-based World Anti-Doping Agency, led by IOC member Dick Pound) with the task, rather than leaving it up to leagues to supervise their players. So it would be further difficult to reject a policy already accepted for the Olympics, without just making it look like you must have something to hide. Surely Congress will not accept a proposal where sports leagues administer the programs on their own. But even outsourcing the testing, the argument could be made that professional sports leagues have enough on their plate. Leagues have enough to worry about in the business of the game, and the officiating of the game, and don't need extra headaches. Having testing administered by dedicated expert agencies already in place for Olympic and other sports seems a sensible plan. It means players won't be counting on leniency at any level to get them off the hook, which forces users to go clean, eliminates suspicion and accusations, and ultimately results in less people being caught and less embarrassment for the sport.

In addition, since among those who use substances, I believe far more do so "defensively" because competitors are, it would be the best way to make everybody clean across the board, so they are no longer forced to use substances to keep pace. For the kids emulating pro athletes, this is the best way to send them the right messages that using them isn't right, isn't necessary, and, with absolute assurance, is not being tolerated. Together, these education and enforcement initiatives will prevent harm to players, opponents, and admirers all. "We want drug-free sports for sure. Both for our guys here and for our kids all over the nation," Pat Quinn said.

Together all these measures would make a huge difference in stemming the surge of and ultimately reducing or minimizing injuries and improving health and welfare. Hopefully, together with our modern medical techniques and treatment protocols, it should allow us to reduce the physical and associated cost of injuries significantly even below traditional levels. That's what hockey should be – a tough game, a game on the edge, a game where you frequently get hurt but rarely get injured. And almost never permanently. We owe it to the players of today and tomorrow, to the families they depend on, to the teams and leagues that depend on them, and to the fans that want to and pay high prices to see them, to do everything possible to limit injuries. Saving just one player from a life-changing injury makes it worth it. The future of the entire game demands it.

CHANGE IN THE BASIC PHYSICS OF THE GAME

Most injuries in hockey are caused by collisions between players. Collisions are governed by the physical quantity of *Momentum*.

Momentum (p) is the product of *mass* (m) times *speed* or *velocity* (v).

Over the last 20 years or so, players and their equipment have gotten considerably bigger, stronger and heavier while the speed of the game has increased through improved skating abilities and shorter shift-times.

This makes for more "momentous" collisions.

Below are calculations of the approximate momentum of the players in two imaginary collisions: one, a typical collision from 1984, and two a typical collision from 2004.

Collision 1: 1984: Forward Rick Vaive is carrying the puck up ice, as bruiser Denis Potvin steps up to hit him.

Rick Vaive's momentum:
p= (180lbs + equipment estimated at 10lbs) x
    (15mph, a minute into his shift)
p= (190lbs.) x (15mph)
p= 2,850 lbsmph

Denis Potvin's momentum:
p= (200lbs + equipment estimated at 10lbs) x
    (5mph, a minute into his shift)
p= (210lbs.) x (5mph)
p= 1,050 lbsmph

Collision 2: 2004: Forward Eric Lindros is carrying the puck up ice, as demolition-man Scott Stevens steps up to hit him.

Eric Lindros' momentum:
p= (240lbs + equipment estimated at 20lbs) x
    (30mph, 10 seconds into his shift)
p= (260lbs.) x (30mph)
p= 7,800 lbsmph

Scott Stevens' momentum:
p= (215lbs weight + 20lbs equipment) x
    (15mph, 30 seconds into his shift)
p= (235lbs) x (15mph)
p= 3,525 lbsmph

Increase:	4,950 lbsmph	2,475 lbsmph
	274% of collision 1	336% of collision 1

The players have an additional 7,425 lbsmph of momentum going into the second collision, a total of almost 300% of the original collision.

Result: Collision 1- Rick Vaive gets a shoulder bruise. Collision 2- Eric Lindros gets a concussion.

EPILOGUE

Health and safety are fundamental prerequisites to playing a game, and to enjoying it. Time off for hockey during its lockout has hopefully provided a cooling off period that should dampen violence in the game for a period of time. But then it will be critical to take action to keep it out, not only for the welfare of players, but that of the game, as the sport tries to maintain and build positive momentum on other fronts. At the same time, injuries have been taking a great toll on players and their game, and ways need to be found to reduce them.

Strengthening enforcement against violence across the board through the team of "No Discretion" and "Zero Tolerance" is the most critical step to reducing violence. New rules to fill gaps – including automatic tracking and punishments for repeat offending, and penalizing teams and coaches for consistent violence – would support this. Not tolerating violence at any level not only directly makes for a cleaner and safer game, but gives the sport the best chance of preventing an extreme incident such as what happened to my brother Steve from ever happening again. Working to foster attitudes in the sport that clearly frown on violence and misconduct within it will also help prevent violence from within. To cut down on injuries, we have to uncrowd the ice and shrink collisions, which cause concussions and so many other injuries. Four-on-four would fix the broken physics of the game that lead to so many broken bones, careers, dreams, and teams. It would allow hockey to again be what it should be – a flowing game with a component of toughness and an element of risk – but nothing more. Fewer games, softer equipment, and drug testing could also provide for more sanity and *santé*.

A safer game is a better game for players and their families, and a more appealing game to the families of children from which future generations of players must come. A cleaner game, unmarred by disturbing scenes, and with as many of the best players as possible healthy and playing is the game most attractive to the widest group of fans.

OVERTIME

THE FINANCIAL SIDE OF SPORTS

"Regardless of how they got there, they are on a treadmill to obscurity, that's the way the league is going. So something's got to change."

— Former chairman of the U.S. Securities and
Exchange Commission Arthur Levitt,
after concluding economic study of the NHL

"Grown men who behaved like . . . spoiled kids fighting over a toy only to see it break."

— *The Hockey News* editor Jason Kay on the dispute
that eviscerated the 2004–05 NHL season

"We've already lost the blue-collar fan, I'm worried about the white-collar fan."

— Leafs coach Pat Quinn

"Money is the root of all evil."

— The Bible, 1 Timothy 6:10

PROLOGUE

The fourth major issue of the game, unlike the preceding three, is primarily an off-ice issue. However, nothing has been having a more pervasive effect in changing so many things in the game, on and off the ice, in recent years as the evolving financial side of sports.

The painful lockout of 2004–05 was the epitome of the influence of financial issues over the sport. But it wasn't the first, and won't be the last. Previously teams had lost millions, and there had been bankruptcies. Trying to breakthrough to a wider following was and remains a key objective. And today, money issues of many kinds are affecting the nature of the sport, for those involved, and the meaning of sports, to society.

Guiding the financial side of hockey to greater heights of prosperity, in ways supportive of the sport and good for the public, is the fourth and most sweeping challenge of raising our game.

NCAA hockey action. The wild and patriotic atmosphere of college sports is a great place and a great time to make new fans. (*Tom Dahlin/Hockey Hall of Fame*)

CHAPTER 9

BOOSTING FINANCIAL FORTUNES

STRADDLING THE RED LINE

On February 12, 2004, in a much publicized announcement, Arthur Levitt, former chairman of the U.S. Securities and Exchange Commission, hired by the NHL to review its books, pronounced NHL hockey a "dumb investment" and said "the results are close to catastrophic for the size of this business. . . . They've got a serious problem." According to his findings, the league had lost more than $1.54 billion over the preceding decade, including $273 million the year before, where nineteen of thirty teams lost an average of about $18 million each. Four teams had recently moved; three went bankrupt (Buffalo, Ottawa, and Pittsburgh). Two teams, according to Levitt, were in "perilous shape." Later, the league claimed losses of another $224 million for the 2003–04 season, on revenues over $2 billion. The financial woes were dire, the league insisted; the conditions unsustainable for ownership. "Regardless of how they got there," Levitt said, "they are on a treadmill to obscurity . . . so, something's got to change." That bottom line was the basis for the league ceasing operations and losing the entire 2004–05 season, trying to drive down salary costs.

These loss figures were not accepted by everyone, however: the NHL Players' Association disputed them, alleging them to be inflated by accounting tactics geared toward the pending showdown. Reacting to Levitt's findings, PA boss Bob Goodenow said that he himself had only been allowed to conduct a thorough review of the finances of four teams, and "on those four clubs alone," he said, "we found just over $52 million in hockey-related revenues and benefits not reported." To argue that claims of desperately poor hockey teams were simply not credible, Goodenow pointed to the fact that the big-market New York Rangers were one of the teams the league reported to have lost the most money. At the same time, a number of players pointed to several well-known and savvy businessmen, investors, and corporations such as Disney, Comcast, and Turner Broadcasting that had invested in NHL franchises in recent years (including new owners for the Canucks and Ducks after the lockout started) to say that these people haven't become mega-rich by being foolish with money, so the business can't be too bad.

So what was fact and what fabrication? What was accurate and what exaggeration? Established and well-respected business publication *Forbes* magazine conducted an independent study of the league's finances, and *Forbes* concluded the league did lose a considerable amount of money, but far less than it claimed: $96 million in 2003–04, and $123 million the year before. In other words, less than half what the league claimed, but still a sizable $3 million to $4 million per team per year average. Uncounted associated revenues from things like cable deals, arena luxury suites and concessions, sponsorships and related real estate developments made up the difference, according to writer and senior editor Michael Ozanian. In addition, *Forbes* pointed out that team franchise values had been rising continuously for several years – up 31 per cent over six years, including 3 per cent over the previous year (despite the looming lockout) – a claim confirmed, according to *Forbes*, by a number of actual team sales. So owners were realizing capital gains that, up to a point, offset operating losses. If you factored in all those things, the picture was not quite so bad. "The National Hockey League is hemorrhaging money. But the economics of owning a team can still be quite good," summarized *Forbes*.

As far as teams in trouble, Gary Bettman himself had vehemently emphasized at the time of the bankruptcies in Buffalo and Ottawa that insolvency had arisen from ownership factors unrelated to hockey. He and others also argued that suffering Canadian teams, including the departed Winnipeg and Quebec City franchises, had been victims of a weakened Canadian dollar. Other observers additionally made the point that there have always been teams in hockey – from the Montreal Maroons to the California Golden Seals – as well as enterprises in every field of business that fold or move from time to time; no business has ever been guaranteed to be prosperous or without risk. Some, including Don Cherry, even said they hoped the NHL would lose a few of its "weak sister franchises."

Adding it all up, however, the bottom line was, granted the mitigating facts and factors, business has still not been good. There has been too much in the way of annual losses, recurring operating-finance issues, and player transactions being made mostly over financial considerations for the sport's situation to be sustainable. It's ultimately not a truly healthy business-of-sport scenario. Further, it seems to me, that to a wealthy team owner, the "opportunity cost" of not investing in any of the numerous lucrative business opportunities available to people with great capital, as alternatives to a money-losing hockey team – including more profitable sports, real estate, private businesses, and countless other things – is enormous. How many of these titans of business can be expected to bear that opportunity cost, and for how long? It is not a sustainable situation for the game to continue to cycle through owners as fans (with by far the most expensive seats in the house!) until they've had enough of the financial sacrifices and move on: there are only so many people who have both such means and such a passion for hockey.

For this reason, I believe the game needs owners to be able to do more than lose a little or break even; it needs them to have a *chance* to make a good, if not superb, return on their money. So the $2-billion question is, Why hasn't that been the case in hockey? How did the NHL end up in these financial straits?

PITFALLS IN THE ICE

Is hockey simply a bad business to be in? A look at other sports suggests otherwise. NFL football is one of the best businesses around, as teams made an average of $26.6 million in operating profit in 2004 (a 16 per cent return), according to *Forbes*, while at the same time, franchise values are rising through the stratosphere, with teams valued at a whopping average of $733 million, a 17 per cent increase in just one year. Baseball made $132 million, or about $4.4 million per team, again with double-digit capital growth; NBA teams pulled in $277 million, or about $9.6 million per team. Sports are more popular than ever, and the entertainment field in general is huge – a growing industry of enormous potential. Among other mass entertainments, musicians on tour can rake in more than $100 million annually, movies remain as lucrative a business as there is, and videogames have grown rapidly. Meanwhile, an increasing number of other entertainment offerings, including some new or newly emerging sports, have proliferated to feed the seemingly insatiable appetite of western culture.

If we take a historical look at hockey, we also find what was pretty good business: "After World War II, hockey was thriving – firmly established in what was then the six-team NHL, as much an institution as it was a league, along with secondary pro leagues like the AHL – while pro basketball was still struggling," wrote the *New York Times* in a retrospective after the NHL's 2004–05 season was lost to its financial dispute. In fact, the NHL remained largely prosperous through the 1970s and 1980s until a recent salary explosion changed the numbers. Even today, a number of other hockey leagues are doing well – minor professional leagues, European leagues, and junior hockey loops are growing and thriving. Based on all these facts, it wouldn't seem to make sense that hockey just by nature does not make good business.

Has there been some extraordinary outside negative development that is to blame? None that I have seen. There has been no large-scale economic depression, no overarching natural disaster, no sudden sociological shift, no radical new competition or other outside calamity that have damaged the business of hockey. If anything, external conditions have probably mildly improved over the time that the NHL has developed its financial problems – the economy has grown, the population has grown, sports have gotten bigger and more popular, and awareness of hockey has increased dramatically as well. So there's no major unexpected outside adverse development responsible.

That leaves only one possibility. Internal business developments must be the cause of the NHL's financial woes. Although industries are very different, at their most fundamental level there is no complicated or mysterious formula to what makes a business in any field successful. They all operate by the simple arithmetic: add up revenues, subtract expenses, and you have your bottom line. If revenues are greater, you have a profit, if expenses are greater, you have a loss. In professional hockey, the major expense today is player salaries, and they have skyrocketed in recent years – *tripled* in just ten years, according to the league. Most fans would say the escalation has been "out of control." The major revenues in sports, meanwhile, come from TV rights fees and people at games. League-wide attendance had a jump through expansion, and gate revenue increased through jacked-up ticket prices, but those have now been stretched as far as they can go. Meanwhile, TV revenues have been very small in comparison with other sports, and will fall further in the newest deal. The result is, revenues haven't kept pace with increased expenses. Prior to the lockout, *Forbes* said the percentage of revenues that went to pay player salaries (never mind all the other expenses) rose from 59 per cent to 66 per cent over five years. That was higher than other sports, which ranged from about 58 per cent (NBA) to 64 per cent (NFL). It didn't leave much room to cover other expenses and stand much chance of turning a profit. That's how the game's financial problems arose out of the internal arithmetic going askew.

In the book *Money Players*, author Bruce Dowbiggin makes the point that the players shouldn't be blamed, they've just done what anyone would, in taking what they can get. (If someone came along and offered you $5 million to do your job, would you say no?) Dowbiggin also argues that the Players' Association and player agents can't be faulted for doing their job and fulfilling a legal obligation to further their clients' interests as best they can. It didn't make sense to blame "the system" either, because the system was just a word for the collective bargaining agreement (CBA) that had been freely negotiated and accepted by the league in 1995 and renewed twice since. Dowbiggin's point was that ultimately it had to be business management's responsibility that more was spent than could be afforded, or that not enough was made to cover what was spent. Management oversees the production of revenues, and management signs the contracts of salaries it pays. "Nobody puts a gun to their head," player Peter Worrell is quoted. St. Louis Blues general manager Larry Pleau agreed: "I don't blame the players, the agents, or the players' association. That's what they're there for. We're the ones who've driven it. We have to get it together in our local markets." "The only people dumber than us are the people in baseball" said Bruins executive Harry Sinden, no doubt thinking of the $252 million (that's not a misprint) contract baseball's Texas Rangers gave Alex Rodriguez a few years ago.

But if hockey was once good business, what specifically happened inside to make the math go awry? To investigate this question, we need to divide the business of the game into two parts: the business of individual teams (organizations) and the business of the league as a whole.

INSIDE THE BUSINESS OF TEAMS

Since expenditures are mostly player salaries, and salaries are negotiated between a team and a player, problems on the expenditure side must have arisen mostly at the level of the business of teams.

Although it is true that at the league level, a CBA is negotiated that sets general rules or guidelines governing the marketplace of teams and players, in fact the CBA negotiated in 1995 (as well as the one before) was quite favourable to cost control, certainly as compared to the average business environment. It contained a number of salary-restraining conditions not present in the overwhelming majority of businesses, and exceeding those in most other sports. These included a nine-round draft, caps on entry-level contracts, fixed qualifying offers to be able to retain players' rights, and heavy free-agency restrictions that basically locked up players to one team until age thirty-one. Every agreement has imperfections and loopholes, but from an objective point of view – and from the point of view of the lawyers (Gary Bettman & Co.) who on behalf of the league negotiated and accepted the agreement, and later renewed it – it should have been a good framework for cost control. So what happened on the level of teams, where actual salaries were negotiated – that salaries soared too high?

The escalation can partly be understood as the product of a recurring cycle of a few "inflationary" signings (radical price raises over the previous market), followed by a succeeding upwards rescaling of player salaries across the whole league in comparison. The surge began with Gretzky's move to Los Angeles in 1988, and former Kings owner Bruce McNall's decision that an elite athlete like Gretzky should be paid an elite salary in society. After giving Edmonton $15 million for Gretzky, McNall gave Gretzky a deal worth $2.5 million a year for seven years, an enormous deal at the time. "It had a major impact. It started a trend," Devils GM Lou Lamoriello said. Brett Hull's agent at the time – Bob Goodenow – then linked his player's value to Gretzky's, during his negotiation on behalf of Hull, and that "marked the genuine beginning of the salary spiral," wrote Dowbiggin. "There's no doubt the Gretzky deal catapulted the salary structure. There is an ability to pay that's been unlocked," said Goodenow at the time.

Soon after Hull got $7 million for four years, Mario Lemieux got $2M, Steve Yzerman $1.3M, Patrick Roy $1.2M, Ray Bourque

$1.2M, Paul Coffey $1.15M, Chris Chelios $1.1M, and so on down the line. Then from 1990–92 came inflationary free-agent signings of Scott Stevens, Brendan Shanahan, and Adam Graves, and an enormous entry-level contract for Eric Lindros, that paid the untried rookie a $2.5 million signing bonus and $18 million over six years. Again, there was a reverberating effect as other free agents like Chris Gratton, Mark Messier, and Pat Lafontaine left their teams to sign with other clubs for big money, and subsequent high draft picks like Alexandre Daigle and Joe Thornton exceeded Lindros's contract numbers. Soon, the whole league was again rescaled up in comparison. By 1994, the average salary was $733,000.

Then in 1997, the agents for Sergei Fedorov exploited a rivalry between Detroit-area businessmen Peter Karmanos (owner of the Hurricanes) and Mike Illitch (owner of the Red Wings) to extract a $14 million bonus, $2 million a year for five years, and another $12 million bonus for advancing in the playoffs. All told, that gave Fedorov $28 million for one year, and more than $7 million a year over the life of the deal. Again, teams scaled up other players in comparison: stars Jagr, Forsberg, Kariya, Bure, Hasek, Pronger, Blake, and Leetch all moved within range of an unfathomable $10 million a year.

Then in 2001, free agent physical forward Martin Lapointe signed for $20 million over four years, and the following year, defensive centre Bobby Holik signed for five years and $45 million. By the time of the last NHL season, the average salary was up to $1.8 million.

Clearly, this was an inflationary trend. League-wide player expenses had gone from $195.2 million in 1991–92 to $1.477 billion in 2003–04, more than a 750 % rise. Why did this happen? To begin with, any time a player signs a contract, the terms are disclosed, and it becomes for others a benchmark for comparison. In the negotiations, they call them "comparables." When an inflationary contract is signed (for whatever reason, and lots of things can play into that, as in the examples above), the agents for other players push it as the comparable in their contract negotiation, and ask that their player be compensated equitably (better if better, equal if equal, scaled with if worse). Teams can and do put forth their own comparables, low comparables, and in the end both sides try to reach an agreement. So why were contracts continually rescaled upwards in line with the highest ones?

One of the major reasons is that *merit* valuations get mixed together with *market* valuations. A market valuation is the price the market arrives at for a player's services through competition in supply (other players) and demand (teams) for those services. A merit valuation is fixing a price of what a player, based on his ability, "deserves." These are two completely different systems of valuation. Each would work on their own: the market would dictate high prices where there is high competition for a player, but offset these with cases where the CBA restricts competition for a player and he basically has to take what his team offers him; with merit as the guide, teams would take what they can afford to pay in total, divide it into a payscale that mirrors the scale of players' abilities, and pay players by where they are pegged in the scale.

But mixing the two types of valuation is dangerous business (it should have those "caution" labels from chemistry attached)! In hockey (and to some extent other major sports), market and merit valuations have been mixed together, and a salary explosion was the result. In situations where there was a high market valuation, the market valuation prevailed: teams competed for an available player everyone wanted, bid each other up, and the player got a huge salary. But in cases where the market valuation was low (because of restricted competition, which under the old CBA was the vast majority of cases), instead a merit valuation was used: the player's agent found similar players who were paid in a more competitive market and used them as comparables with the player's team, focusing on the players' similar ability.

To club managers, it seems fair (that's what merit is all about) that comparable players get comparable salaries, or that the scale of compensation reflect the scale of ability. In a sense, merit valuations are natural. Not only that, but historically pro hockey salaries *were* primarily merit valuations: there were far fewer teams (at one point, only six), a restrictive "reserve system" whereby clubs permanently owned a player's rights, no effective union or agent representation, and no disclosure of contracts – teams could basically pay players what they want, and they gave it out according to a scale of merit (famously starting with Gordie Howe at the top and moving down from there). The majority of managers today played professionally in eras where things worked that way, so it's not only natural, it's life experience, it's in the blood.

On top of that, since salaries today are a matter of public record, GMs have to worry about players' feelings on who deserves what – if their players' salaries are out of line with each other or below those of other teams, their players might harbour resentment, harming performance or disrupting team chemistry. For all these reasons, managers agreed to salaries much higher than the market would dictate in given cases. And then the whole thing became circular, as the next time a highly sought player entered a competitive market, he had these raised merit valuations as a launch pad to start the bidding, so the price went still higher, and salaries across the league were rescaled up again. Over and over in this way, a few top market valuations fuelled a salary spiral across the league.

Why couldn't it work the other way, rescaling downward? It could, but not so easily. On a personal level, it's legitimately hard for a manager to tell a player who did everything he was asked that he should make less on his next contract (if market conditions warrant that) – it seems insulting, unfair – and there are issues of pride, ego, and loyalty involved. And it's hard to say to a returning player he should take less than an inferior player just brought in on the open market. The result is, salary street was one way, going up.

Another way some teams ran into cost problems was by over-reliance on free agency. The conditions of the free agent market – thirty teams vying in open competition for a small pool of eligible players each year – made it an expensive place to acquire players. It was so difficult to get good value, it only made fiscal sense as a rare "luxury" expense (e.g., to fill a key hole), not for fleshing out most of a roster. Yet some teams relied heavily on free-agent signings, while making less use of all the other more cost-effective sectors to acquire players, perhaps as if you were to buy most of your household needs in luxury boutiques and only a few items through warehouse direct. Why would teams do that? Free agents have their allures. They are usually veteran, proven players – and managers whose jobs are on the line as well – who don't like to take risks, like to know what they're getting. Many are well-known players: hockey's version of "brand names." Others may have played for a Cup winner or a team that had playoff success, and the hope is that similar success can be imported through acquisition of these players. All of these attractions, without having to give up any players in return, explains the allure. A few teams (such as Detroit, New York, Philadelphia) had the money to play the free-agent game. Most didn't, and ran into financial problems when they tried. Meanwhile, the more teams relied on free agency, the more it drove up the price of free agents, like an intense auction. And the more player acquisitions were made on that market, the more pressure it placed on managers to compensate non-free agents comparably.

Costs were also inflated by large amounts of money lost on unproductive players. One obvious case of waste is millions spent on high draft picks, many of whom don't turn out to be useful players. The draft is so uncertain, it is tantamount to gambling rather than true investment. But that's not teams' fault, it's a function of an unreasonably low draft age (discussed in the next chapter), which forces teams to try to divine which eighteen-year-old kids will become NHL-calibre players in typically about five to six years (aside from a few rare exceptions). Considerable amounts were also lost on players at the tail end of their careers. Society prizes seniority, and hockey is no exception – but that came at a price: older players almost invariably cost much more than younger equivalents, and also were appreciated more – so teams relied on more of them, inflating costs. The perfect example was a team spending $2 million on an older veteran to fill a spot on the bubble or as a spare, when a young equivalent might cost $350,000. In addition, sports is one of the few fields where at a young age, you start to become less valuable with time and often at a certain unpredictable point suddenly "washed up." Yet with many contracts, even for older players, being multi-year deals at fixed salaries, that meant a lot of money was lost. Indeed, more generally, with mostly fixed salaries and less proportion of bonuses, was this a risk. When performance beat expectation, players already under contract often renegotiated a higher salary (sometimes applying pressure by holding out), but this couldn't work the other way. Players on the payroll that didn't perform to expectation also meant teams had to go out and get extra players (in advance or after the fact), which would improve team performance, but only add to the expense. There isn't a way by which it has been measured, but the amount of money lost on unproductive players had to have been immense and a major factor in excessive salary costs.

As an antidote to high free-agent costs, and as a means of universally getting the most "bang for one's buck" out of salary investments, player development was another key issue. If a team was good at developing players, they could rely mostly on these affordable homegrown players and others obtained from them through trades and largely avoid costly free agents. Indeed, some of the most consistently successful teams in recent years (Ottawa, Colorado, and New Jersey, for instance) used this formula to win without breaking the bank. Yet for some other teams, the outside salary spiral pulled the focus toward buying and budgeting and away from player development. Development – hockey's version of R&D or self-investment – refers to a lot more than signing prospects and hoping they turn out, but rather to a whole sophisticated plan of initiatives and expenses to maximize the potential of players an organization has. Wide discrepancy in these programs and in successful development ratios from team to team reveals it as another major reason for excessive costs. Development could be compromised by a team not having a minor-league affiliate of its own, or having limited say in it due to the arrangement with the affiliate. Some affiliate coaches with NHL ambitions would elect to forsake development for wins, when they conflicted. Not many teams had special player development coaches, even fewer sports psychologists. Most had physical trainers and nutritionists, but in rare cases did they work with players and development overseers on individualized bases. Drafting players in whom they see so much potential, but so often having the development of it compromised or cut off by lack of resources, must have driven more than a few scouts crazy!

Also, some key developmental resources (permitted number of contracts, roster spots, ice time, draft picks, etc.) are limited – in many cases even more limited than money – so the way they are utilized becomes crucial. Some teams have spent virtually all these resources trying to make a few high draft picks who were "supposed to be good" turn out, while other players showing promise got little opportunity, patience, and leeway. But meanwhile, the draft was just a ranking at one snapshot in time, far in the past – and having such sharply divided "inside tracks" and "outside tracks" cramped developmental efficiency. In all, spending big dollars on salaries, while having anything short of the best development plan possible (which costs "peanuts" by comparison), might compare to buying a luxury car and foregoing a good warranty and maintenance package. The most cost-effective performing teams haven't been the teams that bought the best, or drafted the best, but the teams that developed the best – developed a higher percentage of players into useful components of winning teams. On the other hand, poor development ratios did more than just raise costs, they have been the seed of franchises' competitive demise.

On a deeper level, it is probably fair to say that cost control problems have been exacerbated by the set-up of organizations itself. Owners typically have been enormously wealthy individuals or big corporations, for whom the team was not the principal business. So in many cases there has been absentee ownership, which is not uncommon, but not ideal for business – I'm sure all of them would agree. Generally speaking, owners also weren't "hockey men" who knew the ins and outs of that industry – and one thing they likely concluded in being successful in other businesses is that in order to be successful, one has to really know one's industry. So they haven't interfered, and they let things be run the way they were always run, which was a GM (who was a hockey expert) having the responsibility for contracting players.

But things changed radically from the time when salary costs were comparatively minuscule and the only real concern of a manager was to win hockey games. Over the last fifteen years or so, as hockey followed other sports in becoming a sophisticated corporate business, salary oversight became a critical component of management, and overspending on salaries became something that could actually ruin the business. According to Bruce Dowbiggin, this meant: "Hockey-men-turned-GMs . . . were thrust onto a high-stakes tightrope with no net. Men unschooled in salary negotiation found themselves up against a motivated force of lawyers and businessmen [agents] who combed the small print of the CBA, and a Players' Association that would back them to the last comma." Agent J.P. Barry said, "They didn't have the background to deal with many of the new legal issues. A lot them had no technical expertise at all. They just looked at a guy and said, 'What do you think he's worth?'"

GMs' expertise was in player evaluation and roster management, other executives (often club presidents) typically were the business experts in the fold. But even though player costs became a major business concern, the traditional structure of management still had player contracts under "hockey operations," meaning the GM generally had the authority to decide how much to spend. And the authority of presidents or executives who supervised all other aspects of the business was very limited in this key area.

Having GMs continue to bear the responsibility also meant GMs now faced the difficulty of being judged on two different bases: success on the ice and financial frugality. If a GM ran a profit but didn't win, he could be fired. So out of natural self-preservation, if these two job responsibilities diverged, the GM would be pushed to spend more than could likely be afforded, and sacrifice business to trying to win games and keep his job. In this way, the very structure of management incorporated a competitive incentive that runs against fiscal judgment.

What about the owners? Why would they allow that to happen? According to Dowbiggin, "One key failing . . . has been the NHL's policy of allowing men trained as skaters and fighters to assume responsibility for spending the owners money . . . this reliance on the hockey culture has been total. Even the owners who sign the cheques cannot overcome the immortal putdown 'how many games did you play in the NHL?'" So teams would approve what a GM thought he needed to spend to win. And even occasionally an aggressive owner might encourage expenditures, pushing for an admired star player, or breathing down a GM's neck to "win win win," whatever the cost.

Together, these issues in the business of teams explain the mystery of why player costs skyrocketed in professional hockey. That's half the picture – the expenditure side – to the financial woes challenging the sport.

So what could teams do to restrain costs?

Mainly, use available advantages. If teams declined to pay players falling under restricted-market conditions salaries in line with those signed as expensive free agents, and used their leverage instead to pay them the minimum necessary to prevent them from pursuing their limited alternatives (going to Europe, or sitting out a year to become a free agent), that would save immensely. This would include not renegotiating with holdouts, as Ottawa successfully did with forward Alexei Yashin. There might still be a few high free-agent signings, but these would be recognized as the product of open market conditions, and the majority of players' salaries, set in restricted markets, would not be scaled up in tandem. Having done this, the market-merit mixture would work the other way: teams would say, "We have most of what we need at low cost through restricted-markets, why pay a lot more for little gain?" Then the limited-market salaries would bring down the free-agent salaries. More than anything, that would push the scale of salaries down, and get teams back in the black. In fact, in the last two years before the lockout, management successfully started to use the system this way, and the salary escalation halted.

Teams could also avoid overspending on free agency by resisting the costly allure of things like brand names or pieces of past success, instead building from within. Trying to buy a team through free agency didn't work very well anyway. It's easy to see why – most of the allure is illusory: veteran players are known quantities, but that doesn't necessarily mean they're better than untried players. "Brand names" are no guarantee of quality in hockey, where a player's performance goes up and down. And most of the players available off past winners weren't key players, and sometimes offered little more than the hope of some hidden, intangible, or even talismanlike effect on success. Meanwhile, market restrictions allowed a team to grow and sustain a strong core without having to venture onto the free-agent market, except for that special piece to put them over the top, as recent history consistently bore out.

But this means teams had to excel at player development. Indeed, development was a key tool for maximizing salary investments anyway. One step would be hiring special development coaches to work with players individually, closely analyzing their progress, shoring up weaknesses and improving strengths. Better communication within an organization between different staff and especially with players themselves would keep everything in line. Psychologists, nutritionists, specialized trainers along with training facilities and other material resources would help each player push the boundaries of their performance. Optimizing limited development resources, including a more streamlined and efficient system than an inside track and outside track for different players based on draft order in the distant past, would also help. All of these things would cost a tiny amount to make the large amount spent on salary much more productive and, in the end, would result in major cost-performance savings.

Savings could also be achieved by slashing the huge proportion of payroll wasted on unproductive players. Part of this is beyond teams' control, in that the NHL should raise the draft age to when players are about to turn pro, so that there is less future in the expense, and it becomes more investment and less gamble. Utilizing cheap young players in place of expensive older players for roster fringes and spares would also pay. Comprehensive, systematic approaches to personnel management – like that of baseball's consistently low-paying high-performing Oakland Athletics, as described in the popular recent book *Moneyball* – may have analogous forms applicable to hockey as well. Greater use of incentives and performance bonuses (on a range of individual measures, and team measures) alongside completely fixed salaries would cut risk and ensure that payouts are never too far from income-determining performance. Just reducing payroll "dietary fat" through these measures would do wonders for clubs' financial waistlines.

Some adjustment to the structure of management might also help improve the cost profile. One way would be to transfer the authority over total salary costs to the "business operations" side (as some teams have already done), letting GMs concentrate on the hockey aspect, which is their real passion anyway, without too much rope or a second basis of judgment to worry about. Alternatively, for issues like this and others that are significant to both the business and hockey sides, teams could have responsibility be truly shared rather than essentially divided.

In all these ways, the expenditure-side problems of recent years could be dramatically improved, allowing clubs to thrive on given revenues, simply through addressing a few issues in the way teams do business.

However, as things went, a very different method of seeking cost control was pursued: this was the league making radical revisions to the CBA – and it would come at the price of an intense and ugly dispute with the players, and a lost season. In the end, the league got what it believed was the answer – "cost certainty" through a salary cap.

But yet, without doubt, smart agents and accountants will find new loopholes in this "fixed" CBA, and any future one. This includes even the vaunted salary cap: for example, NFL teams under a salary cap have used deferred monies to spend more in the present, crippling their team in the future with salary cap commitments for players already gone; receiver Raghib Ismail signed a lucrative contract for "personal services" to owner Bruce McNall of the CFL's Toronto Argonauts, while getting a regular salary from the team to fit under its tight cap; and minor league hockey teams, operating under minuscule salary caps, have given players houses and cars as "gifts," separate salaries to serve as playing "assistant coaches," and other means of skirting caps to get the top players available. Similar things are bound to happen in the NHL when an agent gains the necessary leverage and a team can afford to pay. Cost "certainty" may not be as certain as it is cracked up to be.

In the initial period of "the new system," it also didn't seem to yield spectacular cost savings: twenty-one-year-old Rick Nash, emerging from his rookie contract, was handed a five-year $27-million deal by Columbus. Anaheim signed Scott Niedermayer for four years at $6.75 million per season. Edmonton signed Chris Pronger for $31.25 million over five years. Ottawa inked Marian Hossa for three years at $6 million a year. Calgary's Jarome Iginla got three years at $7 million per season. "Did anyone expect, 25 days into the free-agent frenzy, that some players' wages would rise so rapidly under the new salary-cap system? Wasn't this system supposed to temper the temptation that some general managers have to overpay the game's elite? And how about how swiftly the market was set for young players?" asked the *Globe and Mail*'s Tim Wharnsby in an article titled "Salary Hikes Raise Eyebrows." Carolina Hurricanes owner Peter Karmanos was himself not impressed, telling the *Raleigh (N.C.) News-Observer*, "Has everybody lost their hockey mind? Some of the GMs have a short attention span."

The salary spree had NHL negotiators already on the defensive before the ink was dry on the new CBA. "Right now, there is a bit of a false economy in the NHL," an unnamed NHL executive told Wharnsby. "You see teams [such as Pittsburgh, Columbus, Florida, and Nashville] that have really pumped up their payrolls and they were among the league's seven or so lower-salary teams [in 2003–04]. And don't forget nobody knows what the league-wide revenues are going to be. How much money could the players lose in the escrow account [based on projected league revenues]?" Some defence that was: the teams that already couldn't afford things before have pumped up their payrolls, and there was hope players might not get all they signed for, if the league could fall short of revenue projections!

The CBA deal certainly was not favourable to players, and did have the potential to be good for teams (as described in the next chapter). But by having the effect of giving managers a "coast is clear" sign, after the fiscal caution everyone had painfully learned leading up to the lockout, it seemed that some potential gains owners might have made under the new deal might be undone. In fact, just with the same revenues as before, the salary cap (equal to 54 per cent of revenues) would be $48.2 million per team, and if teams spent that freely, more money would be spent than before.

But assuming the new deal completely solves all the problems from before, still those were yesterday's problems; tomorrow there will be different ones, including some inevitably caused by the new agreement (discussed in the next chapter). There is no such thing as a loophole-lacking code, nor a foolproof business. New CBA or not, good business will still and always require good management. And good management will mean finding ways to address the new problems of the day.

INSIDE THE BUSINESS OF THE LEAGUE

Expenditures are one side of the financial scale of balance; revenues are the other side – there's an equal symmetry there. Both are the result of actions, neither are givens. When you're scrutinizing financial disappointments, you could just as easily say "revenues are too low," as say "salaries are too high." After all, hockey players are not paid that much compared to peers in other sports. For example, football players make slightly less at an average of $1.25 million, but their teams have to pay fifty-three players versus only twenty-three in the NHL, and they play only sixteen games versus eighty-two in the NHL. Roster sizes in the NHL are between those of basketball and baseball, yet hockey salaries are considerably lower than both, with the average NBA salary being $4.92 million and baseball $2.5 million. And those sports are not in any financial crisis supporting those salaries.

So why aren't there the revenues in hockey to support them?

By most objective and independent criteria, revenues *should* be soaring. Sports continue to enjoy a huge, although not untroubled, place in society. The essence of hockey has all the ingredients that sporting participants and entertainment consumers thirst for: it's fast, forceful, highly skilled, distinctive, stylish, and full of emotion. It's rules are simple and straightforward, yet its action is boundlessly creative and unpredictable. Where other sports have inherent weaknesses and repetitiousness, hockey has strengths and versatility – it has everything. Up until the lockout at least, hockey players were also well liked. And business experts have often noticed the game's ability to appeal to both sexes and to key demographic groups. The fact that people across the world play it and love it (which can't equally be said about football or baseball) also gives an objective indication of the merits of the sport. And hockey has another big advantage over the other North American sports in that it boasts serious international rivalries (like soccer has with the World Cup), a huge bonus opportunity to really stir up interest in a sport through patriotic feeling.

But instead of leading the sports world, hockey has been far behind: American TV audiences of about 600,000 on ESPN before the lockout, and 350,000 during the World Cup, were expected to dip further when the game returned. By comparison, ABC's prime-time NFL games in 2005 averaged more than 16 million. Many economic and media observers called hockey's a "fringe" or "niche" audience, and one that was shrinking. In terms of revenues, the NHL took in about $2 billion, a billion less than the NBA, half as much as baseball, and far behind the NFL's $5 billion.

Hockey has had its opportunities to break through in the U.S. market, where twenty-four of thirty teams and most of the available revenues reside: Ten years ago, with Wayne Gretzky in Los

Angeles, and the Rangers winning the Cup, the NHL looked to be "on the verge." *Sports Illustrated* ran a cover story: "WHY THE NHL IS HOT AND THE NBA IS NOT." And national network Fox signed a new TV contract to carry NHL games. But instead of walking through the door, the sport turned around and retreated. "We thought the NHL was poised for growth – nothing but upside," says Fox Sports senior vice-president Lou D'Ermilio. Instead, Fox's ratings went progressively down.

More recently came another great opportunity with the 2002 Winter Olympics in Salt Lake City – the first on American soil since Lake Placid in 1980, billed as "the sequel to the Miracle on Ice." Headlining the games as the sole major team competition, the hockey tournament was among the most anticipated events in the sport's history, and given some seeming malaise with other sports, and hockey's campaign casting itself "the coolest game on Earth," everything seemed to be in place: this time, how could things not go right? Capturing rave reviews, the Olympic tournament didn't disappoint; a record 11 million Canadians watched the final, and similarly strong audiences in the United States. But somehow when the NHL resumed, the momentum didn't stay on the tracks and the game quickly and frustratingly slid right back to where it was before. Now, the other big sports are riding strong again, some other sports and games (car racing, wrestling, even poker and cycling) have come on, and there isn't a red carpet being rolled out to hockey anymore on the U.S. entertainment scene.

I believe the opportunity is still there, in that while other sports are prospering and more ingrained, they all leave something to be desired to the quintessential American appetite, which hockey at its best – with its speed, physicality, flashiness, constant action, and personality – best fits. But now, hockey lacks the advantage of being perceived as a sport on the way up, instead fighting the perception it is a sport on the way down. Lately there have been more predictions of hockey's disappearance off the list of major sports than of it being the next big thing in American sports. The game has been cool all right, but not in the sense that the marketing campaign intended.

Why is this the case? That it's the lay of the land or the weather of the times is no reason. Certainly it makes no sense to blame the fans, who pay more than enough, or non-fans, whom it's the sport's job to sell itself to. Within the business of the game, it can't be the players fault – they play hard the way they're asked, co-operate with promotional plans, and haven't had a say until now in how the game is played, packaged, marketed, or exposed. Neither have agents or the Players' Association to any great extent.

Teams may have had problems controlling expenditures, but they have had no trouble maximizing their revenues. They have certainly maxed out, in my opinion, what they can squeeze from fans for ticket prices, parking, concession, and so on. They have built new arenas full of luxury boxes that companies pay fortunes for, and have covered the buildings in and out with advertising. Most fans you see at games are decked out head to toe in their team's licensed paraphernalia. I'm not sure what else teams could do. Besides, they already seem to quickly seize and use any little new idea used effectively in any other sport or entertainment, such as scoreboard music and movie clips, stopwhistle and intermission entertainment, third jerseys, ever more creative items of licensed merchandise, bobblehead dolls, player card sets, cable specialty channels and pay-per-view, seat licences, corporate sponsorships, arena naming rights, etc., etc., etc. What's left – aside from those ad-covered uniforms they wear in Europe – which we've mercifully been spared?

Ultimately, revenues come from people, and in the sports and entertainment world, that means audiences. Looking at comparable entertainments, a major component is television. But the revenues hockey has got from television have been very low, placing the NHL way behind the other major sports leagues, and behind the entertainment business eight-ball. National TV revenues in 2003–04 were about $4 million per team, compared to $25.5 million for teams in basketball and an enormous $75 million in the NFL. Hockey's national TV contracts (from both countries combined) contributed just 6 per cent of revenues, compared to about 24 per cent for the NBA and 45 per cent for the NFL.

Recently, those TV revenues have fallen further: the NHL's new contract with NBC (similar to those the network has with Arena Football and the National Lacrosse League) provides the sport zero guaranteed revenues; long-time cable partner ESPN also declined an option to continue broadcasting the NHL for roughly half the price they did before, meaning the NHL will now be carried on OLN. The league will get $65 million this year, and $70 million next year (about half what national TV revenues were before) from OLN's parent company, Comcast. Comcast also get rights to a cable specialty channel and Internet streaming. Despite the reduced rate, ESPN still thought that was overpriced. Said ESPN and ABC Sports president George Bodenheimer: "We worked very hard to build and sustain our relationship with the [NHL] and would have liked to continue. However, given the prolonged work stoppage and the league's TV ratings history, no financial model even remotely supports the contract terms offered." Perhaps everyone in the industry should send a thank you to Comcast owner and Philadelphia Flyers owner Ed Snider. But meanwhile, compare what is happening in hockey to football, where the NFL recently signed new deals that, starting in 2006, will see their already lucrative TV revenues grow by at least another *56 per cent!* That gives an idea of how fast and how far hockey is falling behind.

Historically, the bulk of hockey revenues have been gate receipts from attendance. But recently attendance has shown some signs of weakness too, threatening the most critical and reliable revenue source the business has had. Before the lockout, attendance was down for about a third of the league, long-time hockey homes like Chicago and Pittsburgh were way down. Further falls were projected in the aftermath of the omitted season both in crowds and ticket prices. Back at the time of Levitt's announcement, the league said that over the prior twelve years, overall revenues had gone up from about $400 million in 1991–92 to more than $2 billion. However, those figures were partly inflated by the addition of eight new teams through expansion, boosting league-wide revenue, but not revenue per team, which is what counts for teams balancing against player costs. Also, the building of twenty-four new arenas since 1990 – with all of their revenue-maximizing luxury boxes, club fees, seat licences, corporate sponsorships, naming rights, and so forth – provided a one-time quantum leap in revenues that cannot be repeated. And ticket-price rises were another major contributor to increased revenues, and another initiative that cannot be sustained. So revenues from live attendance leave little room to grow, and have perhaps more chance to fall. Some have even predicted some "soft" markets may not long survive.

Adding it all up – with TV income small and declining, and expansion and attendance fees perhaps overstretched – the revenue picture doesn't look good. There was a jump in the 1990s, but now that growth is proving hard to sustain. There are serious challenges on both primary revenue fronts. Both of these challenges are predominantly ones for business at the league level. The league oversees the conduct of the sport that is the fundamental product, which either attracts or repels people watching. The league also has the responsibility for setting and carrying out the primary strategies for building awareness and familiarity with the game, to spread and support ongoing interest. They choose the marketing strategies, handle public relations, and manage partnerships with sponsors and broadcasters.

So why have breakthroughs not materialized, and successes been less than hoped?

There are really two categories of answers: on-ice issues, and off-ice issues.

On-ice issues primarily have to do with the actual on-ice product sold as hockey. These are all the things discussed at length in the first three periods of this book: The style of play has deteriorated through schemes of clogging the ice surface, choking out excitement. The fair and natural play of the game has been undermined, and overshadowed by infractions, coaching, officiating, and other peripherals – frustrating and disillusioning many. Violence has continued to give the game's image black eyes (or worse), preventing the game from gaining mainstream acceptance in the United

States, and causing it to lose ground elsewhere. Excessive injuries have cost the game in many ways – including on the revenue side – from missing the draw of top players sidelined or forced to retire. These on-ice issues are a big reason for the struggle.

The public and media have been on these issues for a while. In the past, some accused the league of underreacting to them. However, comprehending the nature of each of the problems, recognizing solutions, and gaining support for them, are all complicated processes. Never would I agree with anyone who says they are easy. There have been disappointments in the way of hoped-for revenue growth in the past, but at least now we are at a point where some of the on-ice issues have been acknowledged and have begun to be addressed. Steps have been taken which should help in that regard. But clearly to grow revenues or make the breakthrough that has been elusive, the game needs to be as fully great as it can be.

What about issues in the off-ice business of the league?

Hockey has long-established roots in several American cities, including Original Six homes Boston, New York, Chicago and Detroit. But as far as deep roots and pervasive involvement with the sport below the professional teams, these are really at the deep level they are in Canada only perhaps in the cities of Boston, Buffalo, Detroit, and Minneapolis-St. Paul. Even great hockey towns like Philadelphia and Denver don't have the widespread participation, and universal familiarity and tradition that a sport like football does to have huge followings across America. In a system that "automatically" works to reinforce extant economic disparities, without huge followings you don't get prime TV slots, and without prime TV slots it's harder to gain huge followings. So in terms of building revenues, a key objective has been to increase the popularity of the game in its great untapped land of milk and honey, the United States.

As far as off-ice business strategies, the question is, How do you do this? The strategy the league has followed has been clear from their actions: First, court big-time businessmen as owners of teams, to benefit by their wisdom and connections (Michael Eisner in Anaheim, Ted Turner in Atlanta, Wayne Huizenga in Florida,

Eugene Melnyk in Ottawa, etc.). Second, create a national presence by having NHL teams in every region of the country (achieved by recently setting down teams in Nashville, San Jose, Dallas, Florida, Columbus, and Carolina). Third, increase television exposure (which they did through deals with Fox, and then ABC/ESPN). Fourth, sleek the league's image through marketing moves (a "commissioner" to replace the old "president," new geographic conference and division names, slogans like "the coolest game on Earth," exotic all-star game jerseys, an NHL film division, a slick Website, etc.).

These are all helpful ideas, but not sufficient ones. It's great to have such outstanding owners, but these owners came in because of the promise of a league taking off. It didn't happen, and now some have started to leave: Eisner, Turner, and Huizenga are gone and the Lauries (heirs of Wal-Mart's Sam Walton) have put St. Louis up for sale. Establishing NHL teams in every corner of the country hasn't made hockey a national sport either, in terms of depth through society, anyway. There is still very thin support in many of the newer areas, and that is perhaps shrinking as the novelty wears off. Some observers believe the league has now begun paying a price for the temporary boon of expansion, with teams struggling to survive on the harsh frontiers of hockey dragging down the others. Good TV exposure hasn't led to any breakthrough either, and some would argue was counterproductive considering the on-ice quality of game fans were first introduced to. The sleek public profile is left – and as the league emerged from the lockout, it has renewed its commitment to this – announcing a new "invigorated NHL shield," whose "upward-reading letters project a vibrant, optimistic image" and with silver replacing orange "in homage to . . . the . . . Stanley Cup." There was also a new slogan, "my NHL," and an elaborate ad series created by music-video producers. But ultimately we need more than marketing to make major inroads.

Missing are the meat and potatoes of the business. The meat is the game itself – to make significant inroads in the United States requires the most exciting high-quality game the sport makes possible, but that has been absent in recent years, as discussed earlier.

The potatoes is getting out in the field and growing roots for the sport in participation, experience, and familiarity in places where these haven't been. TV executive Ralph Mellanby, part of a group asked by the league to look into how to make the game more appealing in the United States, said, "Our feeling was that to enhance the game for television, you had to have a better product on the ice." And colleague Neal Pilson, former head of CBS sports, said, "Hockey's real problem in the U.S. has nothing to do with camera angles or more player access. It's that so few Americans have played the game and have no appreciation of the skill levels and the degree of difficulty."

On that score, some of us in hockey complain frequently about the fact that people in the United States don't grow up with our game like they do football, basketball, and baseball, without asking ourselves how did those sports get to where people grew up with them? They climbed their way to those positions, in some cases supplanting previous pastimes in the nation's heart. In fact, basketball was invented by a Canadian, and first staged professionally to fill arena dates when hockey teams were on the road. But as the *New York Times* put it, "This was an instance of a child outgrowing the parent." More recently football grew out of the long shadow of baseball as Americans' favourite sport, and now surpasses it by a 2 to 1 margin in surveys. It's time *the way things are* stops being an excuse and starts being the evidence that there is work to do.

As far as efforts to build a broader, deeper base of support, there have been some initiatives in this regard, but not ones successful enough to have the revenue growth and stability hoped for. At the same time, many fans the sport already had have been pushed away by things that have occurred. Teams were moved away from loyal fans in Canada and the northern states, which have been the game's long-time lifeline. Disaffection with the direction of the on-ice product, and uproar over incidents of violence, have plagued reactions in established hotbeds and mainstream markets. Rising prices for live attendance, and to a much lesser degree television viewing on special cable channels or pay-per-view, has meant short-term revenue increases through extracting more from those who can afford it, but in the meantime, many long-time fans and participants have been priced out, narrowing the game's base. As Pat Quinn said, "We've already lost the blue-collar fan, I'm worried about the white-collar fan."

The increasing divide between the average person and multi-millionaire players, and between the very different versions of hockey they play, are eroding lifetime fans' ability to relate to the professional game. Spiralling costs of participation at amateur levels are also creating a barrier, as a poll in the winter of 2004 found 66 per cent of Canadians feel the sport is becoming elitist in who can play due to the high costs associated. And then of course was the crowning insult – the lockout – in part embraced because of cracks already opening on the revenue front, but also severely exacerbating them, as an entire season was lost, and fan alienation reached new levels.

All of this has occurred while an unprecedented number of alternative entertainments have been made readily available to people in an age of digital technology (TV channels, cable, Internet, video games, DVDs) as well as other cultural activities in an age of mass media and mass travel. As a result, instead of gaining ground in new areas, the sport is losing ground in old ones.

As hockey ceases to be something novel in expansion markets, and the long-term fallout of the lost season unfolds, the full extent of the challenge will become clear. But the question is the same: What can be done in order to solidify revenues and realize their potential?

On the ice: The greatest thing hockey has going for it is the sport itself – how incredibly exciting a game it can be for fans and participants alike. As discussed earlier, what it has to offer, its appeal on so many grounds, to such a wide audience, leaves it completely unmatched by any other sport out there. Entertainment industry observers saw this in rolling out opportunities to hockey over the last decade; they saw how well suited in theory the sport is to the American thirst, how stacked it is with attributes other entertainments can only dream of. But all of this has been in chains, paralyzing the sport's excitement and appeal.

So the first and most important step of unlocking revenues is unchaining the game from the things that have encroached on and corrupted it, so that the game can capitalize on its own assets. Freeing the game, opening it up, and cleaning it up will come from all the things talked about earlier: increasing the offence, creativity, and excitement; improving the just conduct of the game; stamping out violence and injuries. This has to be the greatest thrust in the drive for revenues, along with the hope that enough people will notice, that second chances will be given, and that hockey will finally exploit them. Short-term marketing strategies must be *comporté* by a thoroughly robust game, invigorated by a long-term vision of what is possible with the game's best on display. What more could you ask for, in trying to capture the hearts (and not just the momentary attention) of new followings, and win back old ones, than a thrilling exhilarating spectacle? The most important step of realizing revenue potential is for hockey to realize its sporting potential on ice.

Off the ice: The above on-ice steps will create a fondness for the game for those who get to know it. The other crucial step is getting people to know the game by building familiarity in the United States. The sport needs a comprehensive strategy to create lifelong experience, whether for fans or participants or both. The sport of golf has provided an excellent model of how to successfully build participation, starting with kids. The PGA Foundation, begun in 1954, allowed golf to capitalize on the TV popularity of Arnold Palmer and turn a small, elitist game into a game for the masses, which grew exponentially through the '60s, '70s, and '80s. Recently, they have renewed this focus on grassroots efforts through their "Play Golf America" program, and again, golf is enjoying fantastic growth, not just in America, where 50 million people now play, but worldwide.

In hockey, we need to get out in the community and do things like visit schools – not just visit them but really push for participation in them. We need to get arenas built, youth programs founded, foster the creation of local house leagues, travelling teams, and middle and high-school teams. We need to provide instructional clinics, exhibitions, and special events around the country. We need to make equipment and ice affordable so that more than just the elite can play; and where ice can't be available, promote in-line or street hockey.

To do this, the league needs to use players more in outreach initiatives organized both by teams in their communities (standard contracts require players to fulfill such duties) and by the league to meet its own needs and goals. More significantly, I think the league should set up and manage a national network of former pros to live in different communities and serve as teachers, coaches, and "salesmen" for the game, supporting participation programs, putting on clinics, and organizing exhibitions and special events on behalf of the league. If you think about the status pro athletes have in society, where people line up just to meet them or get an autograph, you can imagine the advantages they have in striving to work with community and corporate figures to help create and finance these programs, programs with charitable intentions: before they even arrive, prospective partners are probably already half-sold.

And golf, again, has shown just how well the interests of corporate sponsors, business groups, and community leaders can dovetail with those of a sport trying to grow participation and experience. All this is hard work, but while the main costs would not be on the part of the league, the benefits would. Being able to successfully implement grassroots initiatives like these is essential, and will help tremendously to grow youth participation and allow the game to put roots down in new soil.

Another very pivotal point of developing lifelong experience in the battle for the American market is college. College ball was a crucial cog in how football and basketball grew from peripheral status to become mainstream American sports, alongside or surpassing the American original, baseball. College is a rite of passage through which the majority of the population goes. It's a time when people have the freedom to make choices of their own, the inclination to experiment, and are young enough to be impressionable. The comparatively small, tight-knit highly partisan atmosphere of college means that there is a great deal of support for college sports, with a captive audience that is encouraged to go in support of their school. And they can afford to go: attendance may be free or very cheap for students. With no price barrier, it's extremely easy for students to go as an experiment. And when they see the game, especially in the supercharged college atmosphere, they get hooked.

Hockey – like college basketball and football, and unlike many college baseball teams – has the advantage of being played in enclosed, loud, noisy, raucous, stadiums with screaming students and marching bands. People first exposed to the game in this highly patriotic and exciting atmosphere begin a lifelong relationship with the sport, or at least get that early familiarity that is so crucial to supporting pro teams later. We've seen it happen in football and basketball, and I've personally seen it in hockey, in places in the United States where I played like Clarkson, Cornell, and recently Omaha, Nebraska.

For these reasons, probably *the* most important off-ice strategy the NHL requires for growing the game in the United States is to foster NCAA varsity hockey programs in as many American schools as possible across the country, and create a widespread national college league with a tournament that can mirror the enormous excitement generated by the "March Madness" NCAA basketball tournament.

The NHL should set as its goal within ten years that every major U.S. college should have a Division I hockey team, and that two-thirds to three-quarters of basketball schools have a hockey team in Division I, II, or III. Again, it's a strategy with highly favourable financial conditions: no players to pay, an audience of students and alumni always there and always dedicated, and arenas already built for basketball that could fill open dates and draw more revenues by accommodating hockey. So the NHL would have a strong case to make in going to these schools and convincing them to add a hockey program that at worst would be economically viable, and at best could duplicate the windfalls they've made through basketball. The remainder of the NHL's role would just be supporting the schools, and helping with corporate sponsors.

The other issue is players to fill those teams. Unlike football or basketball, very many of hockey's good young players forego college and instead play Major junior hockey until they turn pro. Without the players it would need, it would be tough to initiate this Division I College expansion suggested, for the NHL to use college as a springboard to new popularity the way the other sports have. On the other hand, I respect the fact that for many professional hockey players, junior hockey was a phase in their lives and their careers they look back on with great fondness, and view as a key part of their athletic development. Accordingly, a way to potentially satisfy everyone involved would be for Major junior hockey to continue, but as a *precursor* to college – for 17- to 19-year-olds (not earlier), and with no pay except high school tuition, room and board. It would actually be the recruiting grounds for college, similar to prep school loops in the United States.

As it is, players' junior eligibility runs out at age twenty or twenty-one, and few players crack the NHL at that age without having to spend time in the minor leagues first. By ending junior at nineteen, players could then go to college instead of the minors, and get an education, all while reaching a fuller stage of development at no expense to NHL or junior teams. And then at the end of college, the draft would be a more predictable and efficient investment. Throughout college, players could continue to hone their skills (and allow businessmen to sell tickets) by playing in summer junior leagues, as there is in basketball. Indeed, college plus summer-junior is a system that has worked well for development in basketball, which is similar to hockey in all respects relevant here.

Besides helping its own business, the NHL, by shifting its direct recruiting grounds to college (and college's to junior) would also help each generation of hockey-playing kids get a free education through the game they love. Colleges have started to offer a variety of alternative programs geared toward students less interested in canonical academic subjects. Things like business, sports management, kinesiology, physical therapy, and nutrition may be alternatives that appeal to more hockey players. And for those worried about kids leaving Canada, there is no reason why Canadian colleges could not join this initiative too, making it a cross-border program.

All of this is to help hockey make inroads with youthful fans who will catch on to the game, stay devoted to it over a lifetime, and pass that passion on to their children. Fostering the sport at the college level is the crucial missing link that explains how football and basketball have emerged from the shadows of baseball and conquered the United States, while hockey hasn't. College is the key to the door, the rite of passage the NHL must pass through on the road to greater and sustained professional prosperity.

The final key piece of the puzzle of how to build a solid support base for the game is so basic, it may escape attention. It has been my experience, playing in different places in the United States, that business – even the business of a pro sports team – is a whole lot more personal than you might expect. Support is not automatic or based on the product alone – at least not in the long run and through thick and thin. Rather, by fans getting to know the people involved, a mutual friendship and loyalty develops that is the safeguard of the sport's business. The sport of Nascar racing, for example, has recently enjoyed phenomenal growth, and analysts attribute much of the unexpected success to the personal accessibility of the drivers, who fans feel like they are able to form a bond with.

This can only be more important when dealing with the relationships between a team and its fans. To use a dramatic example, in the '72 Summit Series, many believe the passionate speech Canada's Phil Esposito made, laying himself and his teammates personally out to the Canadian public, was the turning point in getting the country back behind the team, and getting the team the support it needed to get back in the series.

On local scales, one interaction or one interview at a time, the "personal touch," is what allows most minor league hockey teams to survive, and I believe it would greatly enhance the business of the NHL. Having a lot more TV interviews of players and coaches, autograph sessions, school visits and community and business group functions would all help achieve this goal. When people feel they know and like you, they support you; and chances are they'll get other people they know to do so too. Word of mouth, shake of a hand, and even a face on TV are important ways to grow the business of hockey in the United States. And the impetus for this strategy is an important component of the business of the league.

As far as television broadcasts in the United States, I think the game has also missed some fundamentals, while some telecasts preoccupied themselves with gimmicks. "In an effort to break out of its position as a third-tier sport sharing air time with the likes of taped curling and dog shows," the *Toronto Star*'s Chris Zelkovich wrote, the league introduced various new initiatives: exotic camera angles, HDTV broadcasts, microphoned players, and full length pre-game shows were all being planned. These ideas are fine, but I think we may have somehow missed the forest for the trees. "Mikes on the players, that's just cosmetics," Ralph Mellanby said. There are two simple and fundamental things needed to fix the American TV viewing experience: one is the too-high camera position, and the other is the lack of crowd noise.

On Canadian broadcasts such as *Hockey Night in Canada*, which has perfected the art of televising hockey, low camera positions give great visibility and a sense of being in the game, and the crowd noise is almost as loud as the commentators, intensifying the drama. Many people, especially in the United States, go to NHL and NBA games as much for the loud and emotion-charged atmosphere in the arena as for the game itself. But hardly any of this noise is captured in most U.S. broadcasts, and with the high camera positions, watching the players silently glide around way down below is like watching minnows swimming around a fishtank.

"We'd love to have the low centre-ice position they have at the Air Canada Centre, but that means taking out seats and they're not willing to do it," said Doug Sellars of Fox Sports Net, which owns the regional broadcast rights for most American NHL clubs. And what would a movie be like without music? So is a sports event without crowd noise.

With regards to frontiers, the NHL more than any of the other major sports, has more to do than to look south to the United States. It also has to look east and west, seriously, and do something about that other frontier, overseas. There is rising competition from Europe where salaries are tax-free, and hockey is more popular than ever – and especially from Russia – a huge country like the United States, but unlike America, one where hockey is czar. As the economies of the former Eastern bloc's hockey-playing countries increasingly rise out of the ashes of communist deprivations, and their quality of life as well, within the powerful European Community, this will only increase. Is the NHL content to someday become just one of a number of top-level pro leagues, like there is in soccer with the English, German, Italian, French, Portuguese, and Spanish leagues, among others? Or should the NHL, like the NFL – but for a totally different reason, and in a different way – proactively move into Europe soon and extend its brand there either through expansion or absorption, to increase revenues and diffuse potential competition?

Given recent disaffection and demographic changes, it also wouldn't hurt for hockey to work to shore up its traditional base areas of support and the revenues relied upon there. Perhaps a return of the NHL to some of hockey's most loyal patrons is in order in the form of ticket prices within reach of middle-class and working-class families. Also, Winnipeg, for example, has recently built a state-of-the-art new arena, hoping for an NHL team again. Some of the sun-belt teams might perhaps best relocate to Canada or the northeast and leave expansion in the south for when these areas are a little more ready (as Colorado did). The prices of attendance and viewership need to be dropped so that the game is accessible to more fans, not just the corporate elite and urban rich. Making sure equipment is affordable, and the game is enjoyable for kids, are important too.

Shortening NHL training camps and the season by a few games would allow the season to start sooner and end sooner, before even the most devoted fans lose interest and move into "warm weather mode" during the NHL's best potential audience hook, the dramatic Stanley Cup Playoffs.

Although some consideration could be given to allowing more teams to make the playoffs, giving more fans some hope (but shortening early-round series, so the whole playoffs aren't longer) I have an alternative plan, which may at first seem a bit novel, but I think is superior in several respects. This is to create two to three more tournaments during the season (like kids' hockey, and provincial junior, and college hockey have) in addition to playoffs. For example, NCAA hockey's annual Beanpot tournament in Boston for two weeks puts the sporting spotlight in New England on college hockey, and gives it a rare foray onto the national sports scene. The newspapers give front page coverage of the event, alumni come to town to cheer on their team, and fans watch to see which school will win that year's tournament bragging rights. It gives teams who may not have the best season-long record a "fresh start" for that tourney, and gives fans something to look forward to. One year, my Harvard team had unexpected success in the Beanpot, despite an otherwise disappointing season. Yet all the fans later remembered was the exciting run in the Beanpot. Having that extra tournament doubled the grounds on which fans and media could look back and perceive a successful season, helping create good feeling around a program, both inside and out.

Looking at successes other sports have had, golf and tennis have their four "majors," and European soccer (which is the biggest big-league sport in the world) has a league championship, a club championship, and European international club tournaments. Each generates a fresh opportunity for teams and fans, as well as a considerable buzz for the sport.

The tournaments I propose would include the sixteen teams with the top records over the immediately preceding twenty-five games of the regular season. The tournaments would be single-game elimination (with shootouts after a five-minute overtime), and would be played over a four-day weekend (or perhaps the first round would be played a week in advance at the homes of the top-eight teams, and the surviving eight teams would go to the tournament venue for a final weekend playdown). I would have one tourney to kick off the season (based on the last twenty-five games of the pre-vious year), one around Christmas, and one around Valentine's Day (in non-Olympic years), just before the trade deadline. And then of course, the Stanley Cup Playoffs are the fourth and ultimate tour-nament, in the spring.

These other tournaments would not detract from the lustre of the playoffs, but would create more "specials" – broadcasting and media are all about special events, events that capture and concentrate uni-versal attention. And sports TV breakthroughs are all about a chance to hook people with a great memory or experience, which is just what the NHL needs. Currently all there is besides the playoffs is the all-star game, which goes head to head with the Superbowl!

The tourneys could be a mixture of ones that are fixed and ones that move around (like in golf), in order to reward and make use of hockey hotbeds, but also spread the honour and help grow the game in frontiers (including ones without teams yet). Regardless of the venue, revenues would be shared. Names and personalities would be devised for each of the tournaments, as there is in tennis and golf (think of Wimbledon and The Masters), to give them each a draw and appeal beyond the "sudden-death playdown madness" that draws interest to things like the NCAA basketball tournament. For example, the one to kick off the season could be called the "Canada Cup," whose site moves throughout Canada, including cities without teams like Winnipeg, Quebec City, Halifax, London, Regina and Kamloops; next could be a "Winter Ice Games" every year in Toronto; the third could move throughout the US and be called the "President's Cup" as it would fall around President's Day. If those ideas aren't ideal, the NHL's marketing experts could surely come up with other ones. The all-star game would then move to after the season (like the NFL's pro bowl, which makes more sense in giving us the full season to decide who the all-stars were, anyway), and could be held in conjunction with the NHL awards.

The tournaments would also mean that teams and their fans would always have something to play for and look forward to, more hope going forward and more potential success to reflect back on.

New tournaments would give teams the chance to create the stories and fabled traditions that form an important bond between city, fan, and team. Shortening the regular season by about ten games, as I previously advised, would mean it's not more games over the season as a whole, but a few less.

With these changes in the business of the league and in the business of teams, it would be possible to greatly strengthen the financial situation and grow profitability – and without resorting to work stoppages. The business of hockey – and that of players, owners, and the league itself – could thrive.

NHL commissioner Gary Bettman (at left) and NHLPA head Bob Goodenow (at right)
faced off in a financial dispute between their respective sides, as hockey was
benched for all of 2004 – 05. (*CP PHOTO/Tobin Grimshaw*)

CHAPTER 10

LEARNING FROM
THE LOCKOUT

BENCH BRAWL

lready with a lot on its plate, beginning in the fall of 2004, a labour-management dispute led the NHL to shut itself down altogether. Games were not played, the season was cancelled, rinks sat empty. By initiating this "lockout," management (league executives and owners) effectively said "we're temporarily closed for business – no jobs, no pay" in an attempt to try to pressure labour (the players) to accept financial concessions. But of course it also meant no revenues for business during that time.

A shutdown such as this is an extremely hard-line, high-risk strategy that creates huge division and resentment between management and labour, strains the finances of everyone involved, and drives away customers who may not return. It is the "scorched earth" policy of labour negotiation – perhaps something like the Russians burning Moscow in 1812 to deprive the invading Napoleon of its supplies, or a company swallowing a "poison-pill" to prevent a hostile takeover. In sports, there is a third party: the public, who are caught in the crossfire, and deprived of their sport. Those fans are alienated by what they see as greed by both sides in going to such lengths to fight over the spoils of something fans themselves supported because it was supposed to mean something "fun" and "pure." The legacy of major league baseball's cancellation of the World Series in 1994 showed how the public can hold it against the sport when the dispute is over. "If there's a work stoppage it's going to hurt everybody, not only the owners, but also the players," hockey's Mario Lemieux (who is actually both) said two years in advance. "We might lose some fans that have been supporting us throughout the years. It would be devastating."

Indeed, in hockey, where there were already considerable financial challenges at hand and ahead, in the eyes of many, the use of this tactic had a nuclear quality to it. Several commentators expressed amazement that the league would even consider such a strategy in such circumstances. NBA commissioner David Stern (who later settled basketball's dispute without resorting to a work stoppage) said as hockey's lockout neared, "It's too bad the parties can't model the pain that is going to come."

Some were further surprised by how aggressively and how far the lockout was pursued, resulting in the loss of an entire year – the first time in history a North American sports league had cancelled a season. "[The two sides] were like two children holding their breath until they turned blue. But even children know when the game has gone too far," wrote the *Toronto Sun*'s Al Strachan. Indeed, the widespread disillusionment, declining interest, and apathy reflected in numerous polls taken during the lockout had many worried. "A sport that can be exhilarating, when played the right way and managed by reasonable men, is committing suicide because the employers and employees can't figure out how to divide what once was a $2 billion pie. And what's scary is, not even the Zamboni machines give a puck," appraised the *Chicago Sun-Times*. Front-page treatment in the New York City papers the day after the cancellation offered, "R.I.P. – THE DAY HOCKEY DIED" (*New York Post*) and other similar declarations. Many industry insiders had also used the term *armageddon* in referring to it, including Don Cherry and Pat

Quinn: "How these two sides couldn't get it done is quite frankly still unbelievable to me. I can't understand it. All the work done by us and the players to tell the world what a great game we have, and now it's all gone," Quinn said.

Many wonder whether certain vulnerable markets such as the "sun belt" teams and other small-market teams will survive in the long run after the damage incurred, whether the game, vulnerable itself, could truly reclaim its status as a major sport. "Down in the States, they'll lose about four or five franchises, guaranteed," Cherry predicted.

THE STORY OF THE LOCKOUT

How did we get to such an extreme course of action? The root of it was the financial troubles discussed in the last chapter: teams were losing money at a rate they felt they could not sustain. They blamed player salaries, which they said ate up 75 per cent of revenues and were inflated beyond what the business could support. The league claimed salaries could not be corrected and controlled through the contracts teams negotiate and sign with players, but had to be brought in line by changing the collective bargaining agreement (CBA) between the league and the union, a set of basic rules under which the business works. The other major basis of the dispute was that the league alleged a finance-based competitive imbalance between rich teams and poor teams – and said it needed to address that through changes to the CBA as well. The players, meanwhile, sensed they would have to give something up, but didn't want to give away the farm, and clearly expected to get things in return: greater transparency in the teams' financial books, revenue sharing for teams to help one another, more free agency perhaps. That set the stage for a battle.

The existing CBA expired in the fall of 2004. For a couple years leading up to it, the sides engaged in public posturing, pronouncing themselves fit for a long fight, and disseminating information to the public – such as the league's Levitt Report, which tried to paint for the public their version of reality. Early discussions ultimately yielded no progress toward an agreement. It seemed clear that, barring a last-minute collapse by the Players' Association, a lockout was inevitable. In fact, back in 1998, the league had reportedly sent out a memo asking teams to set aside $10 million each for what some called a "war chest" in case of a lockout. As early as 2002, some had started using the terms *the war of 2004* to refer to what they expected to be a long and intense labour battle.

As the deadline approached when the old CBA would expire, negotiations on a new one failed almost before they started. The day after the World Cup ended with Canada rejoicing its victory over Finland, Commissioner Gary Bettman announced the initiation of a lockout. Thirty rinks slammed shut, training camps were cancelled, referees and front office staff were laid off, reporters and thousands of others – from security staff to local bar and restaurant owners – whose livelihoods and families' livelihoods depended on one level or another on hockey entered into limbo. And fans were angry with what they perceived as an unreasonable "rush to war." Critics said it was a fitting way to cap off a string of self-inflicted troubles since hockey's peak at the 2002 Olympics. Pro hockey entered its "darkest hour."

The league began the lockout with demands for "cost certainty" (i.e., a salary cap) as a *sine qua non* demand, a prerequisite to any deal and to resumed operation. The PA, meanwhile, was focused on greater revenue sharing between teams. With the league being the one locking out and pushing for a new CBA, and the PA prepared to continue to operate on the basis of the old CBA, naturally the league's demands became the focus in the dispute. And with the PA steadfastly opposing any kind of salary cap, this quickly took over the negotiations, turning it into a "philosophical dispute" and an interminable game of collective-bargaining "chicken."

A few events stand out in the course of the lockout. The league's "cost certainty" ideas were set out in a meeting on July 21, 2004, in six different ways, including salary slotting along a scale, and contracts being negotiated with the league directly. These were rejected by the union as tantamount to a salary cap, which they deemed unacceptable. On September 9, the Players' Association countered with an offer of their own, including a 5 per cent salary rollback on existing contracts, scalebacks on rookie compensation, and a luxury tax on team spending. The league rejected them as failing to achieve the required cap on costs. On September 15, the existing CBA expired, and without a new agreement, the NHL would not start the season. Hundreds of NHL players played in Europe instead, while others sat at home.

From then until December, both sides traded public barbs, pointed the finger of blame at each other, and played for public opinion, including successive appearances by Gary Bettman and Bob Goodenow on CBC news programs where they presented their sides to host Peter Mansbridge and to fans. Then, on December 9, 2004, the PA came forward with a new offer, including a 24 per cent roll-back in pay, a cut in rookie pay and limits on rookie bonuses, again a luxury tax, and team rights to arbitration. The league rejected the offer, and again countered with a demand for a salary cap.

Meanwhile, on December 14, it was reported that Canadian Prime Minister Paul Martin approached both sides to offer help to resolve the dispute; he was rebuffed. On January 4, 2005, American writer Russ Conway, author of the book *Game Misconduct* that examined the business dealings of the league and PA under the leadership of Alan Eagleson, published his own proposal to solve the lockout; it was ignored. On January 12, former Atlanta Thrashers president Stan Kasten wrote to both sides with an idea to resolve the dispute, and an offer of help; he was declined. But the play for the public continued, "Let's be clear on where the responsibility lies for where we find ourselves today: it lies exclusively at the feet of union leadership. . . . The union's chosen strategy in this process [is]: ignore the economic problems, delay in offering meaningful relief, and refuse to negotiate over an economic system that will ensure that the problems will not be repeated," the NHL's Bill Daly wrote to the Associated Press. NHLPA senior director Ted Saskin fired back:

"To date, the NHL has chosen not to negotiate. Instead, the league expends its energies on initiatives like setting and then cancelling Board of Governor meetings to great fanfare but no discernible reason. The league should spend its time doing something other than trying to justify its ongoing owners' lockout and refusal to negotiate with us [to the public]."

On January 19, a series of meetings began, without Bettman and Goodenow, at the request of NHLPA president and Vancouver Canuck player Trevor Linden. The meetings went nowhere: "We still have very strong philosophical differences," summarized Daly. Meanwhile, on January 31, a group of NHLers led by forward Kris Draper signed to play for a team in the "A" minor league UHL loop for $500 a week. This was denounced by many observers, including Don Cherry, a proud long-time former minor-league pro player himself, and national sports radio host Bob McCown as a betrayal of the supposed brotherhood of players. All-time minors goal-leader Kevin Kerr told reporters: "The hypocrisy of it is unbelievable. They don't want a salary cap, but they'll come to a league that has one and take somebody else's job . . . I wish I could play in the NHL for a fraction of what they make. . . . They probably make more in a week than I do in my whole season." Saying he made $700 a week in-season, and had to take a job with a swimming pool business in the off-season to stay afloat, indeed they did make more in a week in the NHL than Kerr did in his whole season.

On February 2, the NHL made the NHLPA another proposal, including a team payroll range of $32 million to $42 million, player compensation limited to 53 per cent to 55 per cent of league revenues, team rights to arbitration, limits on rookie signing and performance bonuses, and a profit-sharing plan. It was rejected as a cap. A week later, the league proposed trying the players' December 9 proposal with the condition that if certain economic triggers are hit, they revert to the league's offer. The union said the triggers would be instantly met, and rejected it. On February 10, talks took a downturn when the union pressured the league about its revenue-sharing plan; Bettman and Daly reportedly left in a huff and flew back to New York.

On February 13, a meeting was ordered by and held with government mediators in Washington, D.C. It produced no breakthrough, though the league learned that the union might accept a cap if the league dropped its link to revenues. On Valentine's Day, Daly and Saskin secretly met in Niagara Falls. Alas, it was only to discuss the possibility of accepting a salary cap without linkage! But they remained far apart at $40 million versus $52 million. However, news leaked out, and people on both sides questioned the sudden change in their group's respective positions. On February 15, Bettman wrote a letter to Goodenow raising his offer to $42.5 million, a final offer, he said. The union wrote a counter-letter offering $49 million, no less. Both rejected the other's "final offer." And on February 16, the rest of the season was cancelled, marking the first year the Stanley Cup was not awarded since before the Second World War and the Great Depression, when in 1919 it was felled by the Spanish Flu epidemic.

Afterwards, back-channel discussions by people on both sides feeling that the respective positions were too close to a resolution to let it go, resulted in an attempt to "uncancel" the season, and there were reports that a secret deal had been struck. A meeting was held in which Wayne Gretzky and Mario Lemieux were invited to participate, but when other details of the league's final offer were revealed, the players quickly retreated, both sides announced they were further apart than they previously thought, and the season was effectively "re-cancelled."

In all, the fallout was harsh: "This will be remembered as one of the strangest, most mutually destructive labor battles in the history of professional sports," wrote Jeff Gordon of the *St. Louis Post-Dispatch*. "I could care less if [NHL] hockey ever came back, to be honest," the Canadian Press quoted David Gilmour, a Vancouver season-ticket holder who said he would never subscribe again. "I think it's tough on a country to have what (was) really a kind of civic religion undone," especially by unaccountable forces, added Bert Hall, a professor at the University of Toronto. Meanwhile, fan polls in the United States continued to show increasing apathy. "Let's be honest – Toronto, Montreal, Vancouver, places like that, people are going to be mad and disappointed and upset, but eventually they'll come back," Gretzky said. "But that's not our project. Our project now is places like Phoenix and Miami and Los Angeles, where we've been on the back burner, where we've worked so hard for so many years to try to establish a foundation. We've disappointed a lot of fans," he added. "From the business point of view, we've probably disappointed a lot of corporate sponsorships, so only time will tell how we're going to win all those people back over."

On March 1, Bain Financial Capital Corporation of Boston, together with the help of GamePlan Financial Marketing, formally offered to buy the whole league for roughly $3.5 billion; they were rejected. Around the same time, the NHL hinted at using replacement players if a deal could not be reached with the NHLPA on time for the start of the following season. But the league recanted after surveys apparently made them fear such a move would backfire. On April 25, a disgusted Bobby Orr published an editorial in the *Eagle-Tribune* saying, "The collateral damage caused by [the sides] refusal to compromise is a disgrace. Our fans have been used and abused. Those associated with our game have had their careers severely damaged or ruined. Most of us are sick and tired of the way the sport is being strangled by those responsible for serving it. They've made no progress in two years, and they have no excuses." He called on "both sides [to] immediately put an end to this nonsense." On May 5, the league and union agreed to at least set a new aggressive schedule that would see them meet frequently until a deal was reached.

But meanwhile, as late May rolled around, with no deal in sight, ESPN announced it would not renew its option on the NHL's TV deal, and the league said its corporate sponsorships were at risk if a deal was not imminent. "It doesn't matter about the $5-million and $10-million players and owners," Walter Gretzky said in June. "The people who really lost out and really got hurt are the ones making $6 and $7 an hour at the rinks – the people who needed those jobs to pay for their schooling or just needed that money to live, to pay for food. They're the ones who lose, not the greedy ones. It's sad. I never, ever, ever thought I'd see this. I'm stunned."

Just over a month after the season was cancelled, NHLPA executives at a four-day powwow in Pebble Beach, California, agreed to adopt new concepts as the basis of their stance in future negotiations. This included a salary cap – as the league had wanted – but also a salary floor: a minimum team payroll. Presented with this proposal, the league accepted the idea. For the next two months, however, the sides went on negotiating and fighting over numerous other details of the prospective agreement. Finally a month after the 2005 Stanley Cup Final that never was, a deal in principle was announced on July 13, and the following week, players and owners ratified a new CBA.

ASSESSMENT OF THE ELEMENTS OF DISPUTE

During the lockout, public opinion polls showed that a majority of Canadian fans faulted NHL players more in the dispute, and Web blogs and radio call-in shows were filled with fan anger at "greedy players." What did American fans think? Well, mostly they weren't even paying attention any more. The majority of players obviously didn't think of themselves as overpaid, a fact reflected in how hard they fought in earlier negotiations to get those salaries and their reluctance and frustration when they offered salary rollbacks during the lockout. In fact, when Brett Hull made his famous comment that "probably 75% of the players in the league are overpaid," Doug Weight had said, "The thing is, probably 90% of the players think they're in the 25%." So what is the reality of player salaries?

There are more facets to the question than one might at first think. The players are the best in the world in their field; if you compare their compensation to the top people in other fields, in some cases hockey players make far less compared to high-ranking business executives, other entertainers, or other athletes. People may feel that some of these positions deserve more. Others, they certainly will feel, deserve less. In the year that Alex Rodriguez signed his mind-boggling baseball deal for more than $25 million a year, the top paid hockey player was Peter Forsberg at $10 million. At the same time, Oprah Winfrey made $80 million, and Tom Cruise made $75 million – for one film, *Mission Impossible 2*. I expect none of them absorbed the kind of punishment that Peter Forsberg did as part of his job, which included losing his spleen. What do hockey players deserve compared to them? Or as Bruce Dowbiggin wrote in *Money Players*, "Until the Enron and Worldcom stuff, nobody was bothered that one CEO took home $750 million in salary and stock options [from a public company] in one year." There just hasn't been the attention and public scrutiny on other fields that there is on athletes, where salaries are disclosed, and debated on sports magazine shows. (Please see graph on page 344.)

On the other hand, there are many fields that people may think deserve way more than an athlete, but get way less – perhaps scientific researchers, or university professors, or even other artists, athletes, and entertainers. Most writers, theatre actors, classical musicians, marathoners, and freestyle skiers, among other examples, make a lot less than NHL players. The median income in Canada in 2002 was $24,300. Compare that to the average NHL salary in 2003–04, which brought in $59,341 for one week's work. Or the $21,951 for one game, or about $1,317 per minute of ice time. In a separate line of thought, the public feels there are thousands of people playing the game somewhere, that they think are pretty good, that would love to play for just a fraction of NHL salaries. Indeed, players in the American Hockey League, just one level down, make an average of only $50,000 a year (almost forty times less than the average NHLer's $1.8 million), and AA and A pros make even less. Should NHLers make the millions they do, while many players doing the same job, just outside the NHL, may not make enough to raise a family? So both ways, when you try to measure what an NHL player deserves by comparison to how other groups are paid, things aren't so clear.

The players can use a number of arguments to support their view that they deserve a large salary. One important thing I think many people often forget or fail to fully appreciate when they are evaluating player salaries is that most professional athletes – certainly the ones I know in every sport – have trained seriously their entire life, unpaid, leading up to the few years in which they are paid as a pro. If you ask the average NHLer when in his mind he turned pro, he'd probably say at the age of ten. While other kids are hanging out, watching movies, or just being kids, future pro athletes are spending virtually all their free time and energy building their skills, their careers. It's not always fun, more often it's work: practising drills, shooting pucks in the garage, lifting weights, and running hills. All of this work is put in unpaid year after year – and at immense financial expense and time commitment for parents too; at this level, these constitute investments in the hope of a future career. Some other fields have training phases as well, but even professionals like doctors and lawyers invest about 5 years, not the fifteen or so of a professional hockey player.

Meanwhile, the average NHL career, according to the union, is five and a half years. Thus in a sense hockey players are paid over about five years for twenty years' work, plus all of the financial investments made along the way. From this point of view, the average salary works out to about $500,000 – still high, but similar to what a fairly prosperous lawyer or doctor might earn, which casts it in a different light.

Furthermore, while the hockey player's career is now finished after those five years, people in other professions can continue to practise their career for another forty years until they reach retirement age, or in some cases longer. Although a former professional hockey player can find another job, the reality is when that player's career is over, perhaps in his late twenties, or later if he is luckier, he is now behind the eight-ball with respect to pursuing other careers. The time and energy and money he put into his sport was at the expense of investing in other careers, building other skills and resumés, in many cases even completing an education. He can't turn the clock back, many of those opportunities are closed off permanently, others compromised – it's just not the same as a young kid with his life in front of him and all the time, energy, and freedom in the world. And for every player who made a fortune in the sport, there are many others who had short NHL stints, and mostly played in the minors where they made little.

Another thing people may underestimate is the physical damage players often accumulate as well. In a hard physical sport like pro hockey, suffering a number of serious injuries, or even a permanent limitation of some kind, as a result of one's career, is not uncommon. And that's not including the additional risk of major injuries like those suffered by a Pat Lafontaine or a Brett Lindros or a Trent McCleary, or even death, as befell Bill Masterton. As far as studies of retired players, more work has been done following players in football, the most similar sport to hockey in terms of physical play. A 2001 study by the University of North Carolina of nearly 2,500 retired NFL players found 16 per cent said they had suffered arthritis so severe it "often" limited their activities, 87 per cent of the players said they suffered from depression (which is correlated to concussions), and 46 per cent were on anti-depressant medication. Former Chicago Bears offensive lineman Dan Jiggetts explained, "You play in the NFL, you're just beating yourself up. It's like handing your worst enemy a baseball bat and asking him to whup on you for a couple of days nonstop. I think the typical player feels like the game takes eight to ten years off his life." There is an ongoing study by the U.S. government's National Institute of Occupational Safety and Health examining NFL players' concerns that they have a decreased life expectancy, an issue revived after the recent death of legendary defensive end Reggie White at just forty-three. With the growing size of NHL players and other changes in hockey today, multiplied by much faster speeds and five times more games than football, just imagine the physical toll hockey takes on a player's health. The professional game is simply not the same game as the sport people play for a hobby, and with each passing year, the divide is getting wider.

Many of these issues are factors people may not fully appreciate in judging what they feel hockey players should make.

On the other hand, the fans that contend players are overpaid can make strong arguments as well. No matter how hard the job is, no matter how different the professional game is than the one people watching it play for leisure, it's still fun in many respects: it's still competition, with adrenalin pumping and a crowd watching; it's still the fulfillment of a lifelong dream. I'm sure for most hockey players, there isn't anything else they'd rather do. The public also recognizes that players get to be celebrities, and in our society, celebrity has a value, a big value – sometimes they get special treatment, or other off-ice business opportunities, that others may not. Public opinion is that having a job that's fun and where you get to be famous ought to count for *something*.

Indeed, with the status of sports in our society, many people put years of dedication and sacrifices into dreams of sports stardom, yet only a very few make it to the professional ranks. Those who do have had superior talent and efforts – that's a prerequisite. But they have also had to be lucky to have the right opportunities, and to avoid injuries and other conflicts. To get one of those prestigious and hotly sought-after positions, the public that plays the game feels the players have in a sense already "won the lottery" in society – gaining glamour and notoriety. Beyond that the public says "sure let them make a lot, but how much is no longer a lot, is more than enough, or even outright ridiculous?" "Today I might be making eight or ten million bucks. But that's okay. You can only eat one steak at a time, drink one beer at a time and play one round of golf at a time," 1970s star Darryl Sittler is quoted in the book, *Shooting from the Lip*.

Of course, an economic thinker would say "in a capitalist society like ours, no person can judge how much someone deserves, the 'free market' judges how much they deserve." In other words, competition in supply and demand provide consumers (fans) with what they want at the cost (in player salaries) of what it's worth to them. But the truth is, free markets with unfettered competition in supply and demand really only exist in the imaginations of economists. And the NHL, which practically has a monopoly in its field, and a CBA that places numerous restrictions on both players and teams is anything but a free market. In fact, the whole reason why the CBA is at issue in the lockout is because of the influence it has over salaries determined by "the market." And often GMs are explicitly *not* paying players according to the market, but by how much they think the player deserves. So, with all these restrictions and impurities mixed in, how could we possibly interpret what "the free market" says players deserve?

With respect to the level of salaries, the bottom line is no person and no market give us an absolute answer to what NHL players should make, and that's one reason why the dispute has been so protracted. Fans' basic feeling is "Why should anyone need a huge excess of income?" and who can disagree with that sentiment, as long as it is applied not only to NHLers, but everyone – players in other sports, other highly paid entertainers, business executives, business owners. Common sense tells us NHLers should be paid very well, to reflect that they are at the top of their field, have invested a lifetime in the game, and will pay physically over a lifetime afterwards – but not to a point far beyond any reasonable need. Business sense tells us NHLers should be paid as much as the business can afford, but not beyond all means of the business so that the game suffers and the business teeters and fails. Where that point is is hard for anyone to say – particularly as the lockout itself pushes the business of the game onto an unknown road ahead – suffice to say it is a primary matter of dispute. But on one point, all (including players with their offer of rollbacks) agree – at the time of the deal, that point would be below the last level of NHL salaries.

So where do you lower them to? The league sought deep cuts, the Players' Association less. But in the meantime, that negotiation was hijacked by a dispute over the "how" of controlling salaries. The league insisted that the primary mechanism for controlling salaries had to be the implementation of a salary cap. Equally adamant in opposing the cap, the PA suggested an across-the-board salary rollback plus a luxury tax. The fundamental "philosophical" difference between the "cap-no cap" positions on how to reduce salaries dominated the dispute for several months. A salary cap, sometimes called a hard cap, or what the league called "cost certainty," basically means a limit teams are allowed to spend on player salaries (and a ban on spending above that). That limit is either fixed at an arbitrary dollar figure or else fixed at a per cent of league income. In rejecting a hard cap, the PA took the position that "market forces" should be allowed to continue to play a role in determining salaries, rather than price-fixing in the ultimate form of a fixed maximum for all player costs combined. Instead, the luxury tax they proposed, sometimes called a soft cap, is similar except that there are financial penalties (taxes) on spending above certain limits, rather than an outright ban. The rollback was a one-time reduction in all existing contracts for the balance of their span.

What do we make of these respective positions? Actually, both of them were potentially effective ways of achieving the stated goals. Among the other major sports, a hard cap is used in football, soft caps in basketball and baseball, all of whose economic situations are far superior to that of hockey. At the same time, it cannot be said that either method would guarantee the side proposing it what they wanted, or even guarantee them a better result than that proposed by the other side. A salary cap at even a moderate level would not help the bottom line of the poor teams purportedly most in need of cost control (the maximum would be far above what they were already paying). And even if they could get an NFL-style hard cap like they wanted, was a system where the NFL's small-market Indianapolis Colts paid Payton Manning a $34.5 million signing bonus, and a $99 million contract, with another $19 million in potential performance bonuses, the panacea perceived?

On the other hand, what was so wrong, from the players' point of view, of a salary cap in the form of a fixed per cent of revenues – so long as those revenues were independently and accurately calculated, and the players are given more power in generating them? It would protect the health of the business and thus the player jobs that depend on it, and allows salaries to grow if owners are bringing in more money. Instead, the NHLPA wanted this "linkage" off the agenda. My point isn't that each side took a position that was worse for them than what the other side offered; my point is simply that either solution could work to the benefit of either side, or for both or neither, and that a wide number of other factors (a cap's dollar figure and how it compares to revenues, luxury tax rates and thresholds, independent auditing, the involvement of PA representatives in league business decisions, and various salary-determinative provisions) come into play to determine who ends up benefiting most.

From the point of view of "principle," too, it was hard for either side to justify the rigid stance they took in this philosophical dispute. How could the league blame player salaries for the high cost of fans attending games, demand a cap on what they pay players, but not guarantee the fans a "cap" on what they pay for tickets and other associated costs in return? And would the PA have insisted on "market forces" as a matter of principle if – to use an extreme example to illustrate the point – the league had been offering every player in the league guaranteed ten-year contracts at a fixed salary of $50 million a year? One of the real tragedies of the cancelled season was all the time lost in a hollow philosophical dispute that wasn't a determining factor in economic realities. And this was proven when the sides subsequently moved on from this logjam in discussions after the season's cancellation, but still spent months and months going through other issues. The cap "concepts" weren't life-and-death in the reality of the business of hockey or of salaries, and to the extent they were perceived to be life-and-death on any other front, that clearly got in the way of progress.

But the cap–no cap issue was not the only item of dispute regarding salary control. Part of the tradeoff for discussions of salary caps was discussion of salary floors – a minimum that the PA requested in order to consider a cap, and the league at first refused. Another issue was "arbitration," a process whereby players at a certain point in their career could opt for a hearing before an independent arbiter to decide their salary for the coming year. The league called the process inflationary and unfair; the PA disagreed. And there were other issues.

But the most significant remaining issue was that of revenue sharing, which the PA insisted had to occur as a complement to any schemes of salary reduction they agreed to toward the goal of helping poorer teams stay afloat and compete. Revenue sharing means that either rich teams share revenue with poor teams, or all teams pool a proportion of revenues and divide it up equally, to support each other and narrow the rich-poor gap. The NFL shares two-thirds of its revenues, the NBA about 35 per cent, and MLB shares its entire national TV contract plus 34 per cent of local revenues. Meanwhile the NHL's Bill Daly said the NHL shared 11 per cent – and that's accepting the league's figures – which, on other counts, *Forbes* magazine and others didn't. The players insisted NHL teams do more to help each other – they wanted higher revenue sharing on par with the other sports, but the league sharply refused.

What do we make of this? On the one hand, the league's position was hard to defend, in that how could they demand negotiated concessions from the players, trumpeting their solidarity in the fight for them, while at the same time not putting their money where their mouth was in supporting their own brethren? If the two problems were so serious, how could they defend not doing what the NFL does in this regard, while blaming players for wrecking the business of the league, and pointing to the NFL's hard salary cap as what they needed? On the other hand, there remains a notable difference between hockey and football or other major sports in that the overwhelming majority of revenues in hockey are local, not league-wide in the form of national TV deals. So revenue sharing could create a situation where you're literally taking money from one owner running his business well and giving it to one who is not, or is trying too hard to keep a team in a market that really can't support it.

In addition, what do you do about the fact that different owners paid far different prices for their franchises in an environment where there was little revenue sharing? How do you compensate for that? It might require a complicated major compensatory restructuring. Also, if a salary cap has already been committed to as a necessary demand, then on what basis would a big-market team, already losing a potential competitive advantage through greater means, wish to further agree to sponsor the competition through greater revenue sharing?

As far as evaluating the overall respective sides in this dispute, we can't do it on the basis of one issue at a time in isolation like this, and divorced from actual figures. We need to look at everything together and with the amounts mixed in to get a sense of the practical implications, the compensating tradeoffs, and the ultimate fairness of the deals offered by either side while the dispute raged. Let's look at the final (presumably best) offers, before the season was terminated because no deal was made. Both included the 24 per cent rollback on existing contract salaries, stiffer caps on rookie compensation, team rights to arbitration, and elimination of mandatory 10 per cent increases in qualifying offers to retain players' rights. On top of that, the league's best offer was a $42.5 million salary cap (no linkage), with a 50 per cent luxury tax on spending above $34 million. The PA offered a cap of $49 million, with two exceptions allowed per team every six years to exceed the cap by 10 per cent, and a scaled luxury tax starting at a 25 per cent rate at $40 million and reaching a 150 per cent rate for the over-$49 million exceptions. That's as close as they got, and the season was cancelled.

Observers noted that the difference between these two cap figures seemed a relatively small amount – $6.5 million per team – and wondered why they couldn't saw it off somewhere in the middle, compromise in their mutual interests and those of the game, and resume playing. In the last day leading up to the cancellation, there had been a letter-writing exchange between Bettman and Goodenow rather than the two sides talking by phone. To many, it seemed odd. They couldn't figure out why, if they were trying to make a deal, they wouldn't just pick up the phone and chip away at the $6.5 million gap. The only thing that seemed to make sense was that in the twenty-four hours since word leaked out of the

details of the "almost-deal" in Niagara Falls – where the leadership, pushed by pressure from moderates on both sides, had taken
steps of compromise – both leaders were then confronted by more
militant factions of their membership and backed off. The theory was,
the leaders each decided they had gone too far, wished they could back
off the ground that they had taken. But of course they couldn't "reject
their own offers," so they simply refused to stretch enough toward
the other to reasonably get a deal. What happened a few days later
seemed to confirm that. Another meeting was scheduled, fuelled not
by the leaders, but apparently by back-channel discussions held by
some on the players' side who felt it looked as though a deal was close
and could and should be made. But when player representatives met
with the league, instead of getting closer, the sides got further apart.
The league maintained an unyielding stance on other issues pertaining to the amount of signing bonuses and minor league player
contracts to be included under the cap, the amount of revenue
sharing increases, provisions for escalation of the cap figure over time
(with inflation or as revenues rise), and the possibility of providing
for a minimum team payroll. The players left without saying any
more, other than the deal was much worse than they had previously
thought. The season remained terminated.

So what was fair, of these two positions before "T-day" on
February 16? Given all the new salary restraints offered by the union,
including a rollback that would have placed the salary percentage at
57 per cent of previous revenues (in line with or lower than the other
sports), as well as elimination of many of the mechanisms of salary
increases (such as one-way arbitration and automatic 10 per cent
raises in qualifying offers), plus a hard salary cap on high spenders,
and no salary floor to prevent frugal teams from spending as little as
they want, and the dropping of the demand for stiff increases in
revenue sharing – I believe an argument could be made that the league
should have taken the deal.

Before the expiration of the old CBA, it already seemed that
the need to control salary expenditures had been burnt into the
brain of everyone in the league. And before receiving all these added

concessions from players during the negotiation, it seemed teams had finally learned in the two years immediately preceding the lockout at last how to exercise fiscal responsibility, use the restrictions of the old CBA to their advantage, and stop the escalation of salaries. With all the bonus restrictions offered by the PA to get a deal, it is a virtual certainty that salaries would have by and large been significantly below the PA's proposed cap figure of $49 million per team, and that with that figure in place as a worst-case scenario for those who could and wanted to spend it, it would have been a livable deal for teams. By that logic, the league would have taken the deal, salvaged the season, and minimized damage to image, relationships, and revenues. However, obviously, it wasn't exactly what the NHL wanted. And after they had already gone that far, they clearly felt it was worth it to sacrifice the rest of the year, run out some expensive player contracts, and get an even more favourable deal – which the feeling certainly is they did. Whether it was worth the sacrifices, time will tell.

Meanwhile, an argument could be made the NHLPA should have accepted a deal some time earlier. Why accept all these restrictions including abandoning the demand for salary floors and greater revenue sharing, and even propose restrictions of their own like the stricter rookie cap and the 24 per cent reduction in actual signed-contract salaries (and all the rest of them combined), rather than accept a negotiated fixed percentage cap of revenues ("linkage") that would grow in line with the business, and move on to focus on getting other conditions to make it work advantageously? It seemed like a steep price for players to pay to avoid a cap. But having adopted an anti-cap stance at the outset, and asked for support for that stance from all players, for the PA executive to later accept a cap after sacrifices had been made risked seeming like a shameful surrender rather than a potentially sensible deal. So it may not have been seen as a good option, and more and more other concessions were made instead – ultimately in vain, as a cap ended up being accepted after all.

In the end, the deal that was agreed to included the fixed link of salaries to revenues, with players to get 54 per cent (or slightly more if revenues exceeded certain targets). A salary cap at $39 million and a salary floor at $21.5 million were established for the following season, based on revenue projections. The league would hold a portion of player salaries in escrow in case errors in those projections led to an overpay on the 54 per cent. On the other hand, if salaries paid amounted to less than 54 per cent of revenues, the difference would be handed out evenly to all players at year end. Also included were the 24 per cent salary rollback on existing contracts, a stiffer rookie cap, a single player cap of 20 per cent of the team cap, and team rights to arbitration. Meanwhile, players obtained a higher league minimum salary, and would see greater revenue sharing between teams. And unrestricted free agency was expanded so that by the summer of 2008, a player at age twenty-eight who has played four seasons, or any player who has played seven seasons, would be eligible for unrestricted free agency.

This deal was not far off from the offers made immediately prior to the cancellation, or from earlier proposals, or those suggested by third parties before the season was lost. "Unfortunately, it had to take a whole year to get to a point where we could have been last year," Jeremy Roenick said. Indeed, the players agreed to a cap figure below the one they rejected in February. The league agreed to a cap figure that was $6 million *more* than what the average team salary from the year before the lockout would have been with the 24 per cent rollback that players first offered way back in December. The league gained the linkage to revenues they wanted that wasn't part of the final offers in February, but it came at the price of that fixed link also being a salary floor, so that the league would be obliged to pay the players this amount, which at $39 million was only $5 million less per team than what they paid in the last season played – and that's factoring in a projected revenue decrease due to the lockout that shrinks 54 per cent to $39 million. That would be surprisingly modest savings, given how deeply unaffordable the situation was said to have been before, and how far the lockout had had to go. It seemed the big-market teams that spent $60 million or $70 million before – but weren't the ones complaining – could see the biggest windfall.

In short, the deal finally made was a deal reasonable for both sides, but it's hard to say it was a huge improvement over what was tabled earlier. "There was no reason to go through all this hell and frustration to get a deal they could have done in February. I think we let our game slip. It's broken right now," ESPN hockey analyst Barry Melrose said after the deal was completed. The new deal is fixed for four years. Hopefully then the "War of '04" will not be followed up with the "Annihilation of '09!"

A FAIR AND EFFECTIVE LABOUR-MANAGEMENT AGREEMENT

Stepping out of the perspectives of each of the two respective sides now, from an objective point of view, what would a fair, appropriate, and effective labour-management agreement look like, and how would it differ from the deal the sides signed?

There certainly isn't the space here to spell out an entire CBA – the new one is six hundred pages, which is about twice the length of this whole book! And the truth is, there isn't one ideal deal, there are countless possible combinations – we are talking about a number of issues, and elements, and tradeoffs – a package deal. And there are lots of packages that can work to produce generally fair and good results. But following are some elements I think are important to an effective agreement worth discussing, and the extent to which the CBA scripted provides for or precludes them.

The most important thing, surely, is to forge much more of a partnership or "teamwork" understanding between the players, on the one hand, and between the teams and the league, on the other. This doesn't refer to some phantom feeling, but real practical financial arrangements. This includes the link created in the new CBA between revenues and salaries. I have always liked this idea (even before it was revealed as one of the concepts tabled) because it makes sense from the point of view of all parties, removing risk, and protecting the health of the business itself (and therefore player jobs), and providing a shared goal to grow revenues, to grow the game. Both sides are then using their energy pulling in the same direction rather than against one another, trying to take money out of the other's pocket.

A number of conditions are necessary, however, for this to work. First of all, the percentage that goes to salaries has to be a number that leaves both sides with sufficient incentive to focus on trying to grow revenues. At 54 per cent (with the potential to be 57 per cent if certain targets are hit), the figure in the new CBA is a bit low for players (compared to other sports, for example) but is within the range needed to leave both sides with the incentive to grow; it's not too heavily tilted to one side. The other stand-out point in the early negotiations was that all the talk was centred on versions of a salary cap, or "ceiling," with no mention of a corresponding salary "floor," a figure for total salaries that players would at minimum be guaranteed. To act as a fair and meaningful incentive for players, a link with revenues had to not merely be a link to a salary maximum, with other mechanisms in place that could prevent salaries from reaching that level, but had to be linked to compensation *actually paid out*. The new CBA accomplishes this, by making 54 per cent the players' fixed and guaranteed share. Profit-sharing with employees is used in the business world by many of the world's most successful companies; even entry-level employees are in a sense partners or associates in many businesses. Under this arrangement, players are like shareholders in the league as a company – not in franchise values, which is the privilege of owners who put up the capital – but on the operations side.

A third necessary condition is that players have a say in how the business is run, in the decision-making on everything from the way the game is played, to how it is marketed, to broadcasting and media deals. This helps ensure rule changes take into account the on-ice realities that only players understand. It's also important toward the NHL and its players working together when it comes to the use and exploitation of individual players and personalities for marketing the game. This type of promotion has been crucial to the success of Nascar and pro wrestling, which have been surprisingly successful in recent years compared to the NHL. If players are to share in the risk of the business, owners should share in the authority of running it. Again, the new CBA has provided for this with the creation of a joint competition committee to assess how the game is played, and a broadcasting/marketing committee to deal with capitalizing on it. The details of things like these are important, however, and it remains to be seen how they will be implemented in practice.

Also as part of a future as partners, all the books would have to be open, business practices transparent, independent auditors in place to oversee the calculation of revenues, and rules established to prevent abuse. An atmosphere of mutual co-operation, trust, respect is also crucial: how could any business work effectively over a sustained period with the extreme division, mutual distrust, and even disdain sometimes evident during the NHL's lockout, or in the past? This will be an ongoing challenge to overcome, and regardless of what CBA provisions or public relations pronouncements may say, only time will tell the extent to which this is successfully achieved. A new atmosphere of mutual trust and respect is crucial, and regardless of what CBA provisions and public-relations pronouncements say, only time will tell the extent to which this is successfully achieved.

Another critical step is greater revenue sharing among teams – extending the partnership approach between the league's franchises themselves. Revenue sharing, in the opinion of many analysts, is a bigger reason for the NFL's success than its salary cap. Sharing revenues is an effective method of reducing any financial-based competitive imbalances, and of dissuading teams from trying to beat each other with dollars and ending up just beating each other up. It is also a good method of getting teams to work together to grow revenues, being part of the same league as they are. But again, there shouldn't be an excess so as to discourage teams from running their business well because it would all be siphoned away by this "tax." The revenue-sharing plan in hockey's new CBA is not on par with that of the NFL, but it is a step in the right direction. And it may be sensible to proceed in steps, like this, in order to gradually compensate for a past where owners paid very different prices for teams in an environment that had little revenue sharing and while the league tries to find a way to build up national TV revenues that are more naturally apt to be shared.

Another element that would contribute to a fair and effective market in hockey is a heavier proportion of bonuses in the pay structure. *Universal* bonuses are a good way to make up any difference between salaries paid out and the fixed per cent of revenues guaranteed to players as their share. The new CBA indeed provides for this by stipulating that any such deficit, as well as the players' share of any revenues above projections, be distributed evenly to all players. These universal bonuses are effective in that they give every player an incentive to help grow revenues league-wide. Another important category of bonuses is *performance* bonuses. Many businesses – especially in highly competitive fields – use group or individual performance bonuses as sizable parts of their employee compensation packages. It motivates, focuses, and reduces risk for everyone, keeping compensation in line with performance. Contracts that are wholly and entirely fixed may diminish motivation. And in hockey, they can place enormous pressure on GMs and coaches if those players perform below their pay level. With errors in projecting performance inevitable, several players will be seriously overpaid and others underpaid each year. And then next time – another round of unavoidable guesses, another round of unavoidable errors. A system that commits all future pay based on past performance can not only be perilous to a team and its management, but, in a salary cap environment, to players themselves: money going to players that are overpaid comes out of the pocket of others that must be underpaid – or be sent packing.

In order to retain other key players, the defending Stanley Cup champion Tampa Bay Lightning had to let go star goalie Nikolai Khabibulin. "It sucks," playoff MVP Brad Richards said. "We've already lost one of the best goalies in the world who we could have signed without a cap and now we don't know what's going to happen with our Hart Trophy winner [Martin St. Louis]." The Lightning were able to find cap space to keep St. Louis, but now will there be room to keep Richards himself, when his contract is up in a year? I'm certainly not suggesting non-guaranteed contracts as an alternative – such contracts are effectively meaningless. But just having in addition to the fixed base salary, a higher proportion of bonuses for personal and team success both in the season and in the playoffs, might be a helpful plan. Unfortunately, hockey's new CBA not only doesn't provide for more performance bonuses, it *precludes* them (except in the cases of rookies, players who have been injured for long periods, and veterans over thirty-five). This rule was obviously intended to seatbelt managers from getting carried away with bonuses, but it may only put more GMs unfairly before the firing squad, as inevitable mistakes in fixed-salary commitments take on added significance in a salary cap environment where there is no room to escape.

Another important issue is entry-level players. Stricter caps on rookie compensation were one of the first things discussed by both sides in the labour dispute. Indeed, in recent years, an incredible amount of money has been wasted on high draft picks who haven't turned out. Teams sign these picks for big money based on draft position, as they do in basketball and football. First-round players have seen around $2 million, second rounders close to $1 million, and third rounders in the neighbourhood of $400,000 – all of this guaranteed, and before ever setting foot on the ice for their organization. The trouble is – unlike those other sports – few of even hockey's first-round picks turn out. And of those that do, sometimes it's because organizations give them chance after chance to try to salvage the investment. Yet to have a future, and to support their scouting department, teams are compelled to sign their top draft picks. And they are compelled to sign them for big money, because it will take several years to evaluate whether the player will turn out or flop, while if the player is not signed within two years of being drafted, they go back in the draft, and the team loses them.

Meanwhile, if later round picks pan out, those expenses are extra.

The NHL's solution to this in the new CBA was to lower the rookie compensation cap to $850,000 per year. This means teams won't lose $2 million a year like they did before, but the previous rookie cap seemed just to provide a figure for agents to immediately demand and get teams to agree to. If this continues, is $850,000 a year plus bonuses (for a minimum of three years as per the CBA) on a player who turns out to be completely unproductive a small amount to lose? Clearly not. Some have also said it was unfair to young players for the NHLPA to have offered this concession, exploiting the fact that the players affected are not even part of their union yet (and those that shortly will, will be at the bottom of the seniority-based pecking order). But to the extent it cuts costs for young players who are actually productive, ironically the veterans at the other end of the pecking order may be hurt more, as teams would have financial incentive to replace them with cheap young players. I don't object to having a rookie cap, but I wonder whether the new stiffened rookie cap is significantly going to improve the lot of anybody.

To me, the real issue here is perhaps being missed: the draft age is far too low. The NHL is drafting literal kids at eighteen and nineteen, in all but a few exceptional cases, several years from even potentially being able to play in the league. It's "guesswork at best," *Money Players* puts it. Yet big money must be spent on all these totally unproven players to secure those who someday will turn out. The fortunes wasted on the many that don't is one of the most costly wastes in the game – and it doesn't benefit anybody in the game, except perhaps agents. Big money on "future maybes" is not a good investment, but a bad gamble.

Looking back, the reason the draft age was set at eighteen, after previously taking place at age twenty, was because in the 1970s the WHA was stealing young players from the NHL by having a lower draft age. But that rationale is long gone, and today more than ever, players that young have a very hard time sticking in the league. In every other sport, the draft occurs when a player is imminently turning pro – usually at the end of college. The player is twenty-two to twenty-four, or sometimes older in football. Teams know who to sign without requiring extras, they have a good idea whether a player will turn out, and know what they're immediately going to get, and where that player fits into their short-term plans. This is a relatively clear, safe, good investment. That explains why the NHL has had to have nine rounds (now seven in the new CBA), while the NBA has just two and the NFL – filling out a roster of fifty-three players – needs just seven. The solution is to raise the draft age.

Another important issue is free agency. Hockey's 1995 CBA was one of the most restrictive in sports. Entry-level contracts were followed by virtually player-mandatory renewals, and a player was bound to the team he started with until finally qualifying for free agency at age thirty-one. The problem with that system was that players could get stuck with a team where they were underappreciated – or simply want to go somewhere else but not be allowed to for the bulk of their careers. On the other hand, the advantage of it was that cities didn't suffer the loss of marquee players in the prime of their careers, like Orlando did in the NBA when it lost Shaquille O'Neal.

Likewise, hockey teams that had invested in the development of prospects into quality players could count on recouping that investment over several productive years before that player might move on through free agency. But in the new CBA, free agency has radically changed. In exchange for players bowing to the league's salary cap demand, they asked for and received a system with much more free agency. Now players will become free agents just as they are reaching the cusp of their development and entering their prime at age twenty-eight. The league's rare true protégés who have played in the NHL since they were eighteen will accumulate the seven total seasons necessary for free agency by age twenty-five!

The result is we may have gone too far the other way – with some unfortunate consequences: Small-market teams that still can't afford to pay the top amount of the cap will have somewhat less time to benefit from players they develop before those players can leave – as a way of making up ground against higher spenders – unless they sign them to long-term deals at fixed prices (which many seem to be preferring so far). Second, the hope that low-finishing franchises have been able to sell to cities in the form of a highly touted top draft pick will lose some lustre as fans realize that by the time most of these players are ready to lead a team to a championship, they will be free to move to another city.

More free agency also means more player movement every year, which hampers the bonding between players so important in a sport like hockey, as well as bonding between players and fans, so important to the business of the game. The initial free-agent frenzy that followed the end of the lockout was exciting, as it seemed to open up new worlds of possibility to fans in all places, with Peter Forsberg signing with Philadelphia, John Leclair with Pittsburgh, Eric Lindros with Toronto, and Chris Pronger ending up in Edmonton. It was a novelty. But typically fans are at least as interested in continuity – players like Steve Yzerman and Ray Bourque that played two decades in a city have been invaluable in creating a community bond to grow and sustain the business. Wholesale change from year to year undermines a key foundation of sports, as discussed in the last chapter: players already aren't typically from the town they play in, so if they are all recently arrived and quickly moving on, there is little relationship left with players, and ultimately their uniforms then become meaningless as well. More modest expansion of free agency – say from age 31 to 30 – may have been better, along with more provisions (based on games played by a certain age, salary versus the league average, or even ice time) protecting players truly not getting a fair shake.

Another issue is minimum salaries and "two-way" contracts: The new CBA boosted the league minimum salary from $175,000 to $450,000. But the significance of this is shrunk by the fact the players most likely to be making the league minimum can be sent to the minors, where their "two-way" contract pays them at a different rate, usually about *ten times* less than what it pays them while up with the big club. With such a huge disparity in rates depending on where a team chooses to send a player, two-way contracts are like non-guaranteed contracts.

What would be much better for players at the bottom of the pay scale and pecking order is not a higher minimum NHL salary per the CBA, but a minimum *total* salary, factoring in both pay with the NHL team and when assigned to their affiliate, say of $100,000 for all players under contract to an NHL team. With fifty contracts permitted each, should NHL teams be able to each lock up thirty players outside the NHL for a total of $1.2 million, while the average NHLer alone makes $1.8 million, and some stars make almost $8 million? Or would even a slightly more reasonable amount of social justice benefit all players over their career (since the vast majority now come through the minors), and improve organization chemistry? It might also have an important side benefit: having organizations guarantee their signed prospects a stronger living would improve their development by ensuring they stay fully committed to developing as hockey players, and not have to split resources to supplement income or cover the risk of not ultimately making it to the NHL. (Don't worry, there would still be plenty of motivation to make it to the big leagues.) The future of an NHL team is their prospects today, and I think this step is well worth it to both teams and players over the span of their careers.

As far as other issues:

- arbitration: Arbitration in itself can't be a problem. Awards made by arbitrators reflect only the salary market already out there, and how convincing a case each side makes to the judge. Arbitration (like bonuses) can benefit everyone on the whole by eliminating risk, and keeping pay in line with performance. What was unfair and has been corrected in the new CBA was to allow not just players, but teams the right to go to arbitration. Beyond that, if the process needs to be fine-tuned, then it can be without discarding it altogether.

- playoff revenues: It would be fair for these to be fully shared with players, as regular season revenues are. Paradoxically, this would help teams too, by decreasing their incentive to make bad gambles on expensive salaries in the hope of recouping the money by going far in the lucrative playoffs where teams don't have to pay players.

- the entry draft: Once the draft age is raised to when players are imminently ready to turn pro, the number of rounds should be cut down to three. It was at nine, and the new CBA has trimmed it to seven.

The elements described above form the basis of what in my mind would be a fair and effective CBA. The new CBA gained ground on a lot of these issues, lost ground on a few others, and did not affect some others. But looking back, at least as important might be the approach: a CBA negotiation doesn't have to be conceived of as a legal dispute between divergent interests, it can be conceived of as the co-operative design of a blueprint for effective business by convergent interests. Hopefully when the CBA is up next – as well as for the many other issues that will involve various groups within the business of the game – a less confrontational, destructive and more collaborative, constructive approach can be embraced.

THE LARGER PICTURE

One thing that may be lost in the lost season's bitter story is all the countless hours of labour, the intense stress, and sleepless nights endured by the negotiators on both sides – most of all Gary Bettman and Bob Goodenow. The leaders of the two sides demonstrated a level of zeal that made most observers exhausted just watching. No doubt they exhibited a similar amount of industry: how many people can imagine reading a six-hundred-page legal document, let alone drafting one, line by disputed line? And through it all, they suffered virtually nothing but criticism and abuse from everyone outside the parties they were hired to represent, and sometimes from some of them too. Their many long-time critics saw the long lockout as an opportunity to kick them while they were down.

But ultimately, these Herculean efforts in pursuing this war, this unwavering perseverance under question and criticism, the tense and lengthy dispute itself, what was it all for? All of it was for revisions to the collective bargaining agreement – a document in unionized businesses that sets out basic ground rules between management and that sector of their labour force – from the previous one negotiated in 1995 and renewed twice through 2004. That previous one was said to be "fatally flawed," and indeed there were well-chronicled financial problems, but much of that had been exacerbated by the new era of Big Business Hockey, which management was initially unprepared for, but more recently (in the 2 seasons immediately prior to the lockout) seemed to be successfully adapting to. Changing the CBA was a way to try to correct those problems in "one fell swoop," something which had a compelling logic and attraction to it, especially given the ongoing financial-related frustrations before. But there was at least something to be said for how much less contentious it would have been if it was able to be successfully dealt with on the level of teams. Indeed, the new CBA resulting from the year-long disruption is fixed for just the next four years, so if players are then as displeased and driven to change it as the league was in this case, what would happen then?

Actually, it's not the idea itself of changing the CBA that was so much the real issue. In this case, both sides agreed from the outset that changes would have to be made to it. What became a problem for everyone was the lengths that had to be gone to to achieve it. Early on, missing games was seen as a potential strategy for one side, and likely a necessary sacrifice for the other. Of course, neither wanted it to happen, and both had to prepare for the possibility of it, since they only controlled half the agenda. But to some, if not most fans, and seemingly even some members of each side, they wondered whether it was accepted perhaps too readily. Likewise, to reach a point of cancelling the entire season, many questioned whether the players could have achieved a similar deal without fore-going a season's salary. Or why the league wouldn't shoot for more modest concessions in a shorter deal, and more again next time – perhaps a more navigable proposition in something as difficult as collective bargaining. To many on both sides, I think the trauma of the year of lost income, the uncertainty over the industry, and the negative feelings produced by the sport's disruption were more painful than anything in the proposals themselves.

Adding to this pain, were elements of the methods used. Each side seemed put off by "overhanded" moves by the other – talk of replacement players rankled players, and union certification moves upset the league. Certain public statements alienated people, and made compromise more difficult. Knowing how players think, I par-ticularly believe that if the league had strived to reap hockey players' famous loyalty, rather than threaten their famous pride, things might have happened quicker and easier. At the same time, after it was over, a number of players challenged their union leadership for keeping them too much in the dark, or excluded from greater input, contributing in their view to a disappointing result. Plays for public opinion on both sides only seemed to irritate fans and media, and embarrass the game and those involved.

In the larger picture, one wonders whether some deeply involved in the process got so caught up in it, that the significance of what it is they were trying to achieve, or trying to avoid, became inflated. A salary cap was accepted and survived. And cost certainty came at a price of some revenue uncertainty, arising out of the shut-down, for the short term and long. "The economics of the game" were said to be "fundamentally broken," and needed to be fixed. But the primacy of the issue of revenue growth over revenue distribu-tion is itself a fundamental of economics.

Prior to the lockout, hockey's revenue future showed cracks – decreasing TV ratings, attendance losses, decreased satisfaction with the game, and public relations hits. The lockout of course would exacerbate this, disillusioning fans by sacrificing the spirit of sports and fan goodwill to what they perceived as the greed of those involved. In 1994, Major League Baseball's labour dispute wiped out only two months and the World Series, yet it "sent attendance spiralling down the toilet," described sports writer Randy Sportak. Average attendance sunk more than 5,000 per game across the league, and was slow recovering. The home-run chase in '98 helped, as attendance came back above 29,000 per game, but that was still 2,200 fewer than before the cancellation. Hockey's fans are famously loyal, and all signs point to a strong initial rebound for the sport. But in the longer run, some are not so sure the lockout may not still have fallout. Inevitably, some casual fans will have found it's "not passion but habit" as Ken Dryden said; others that it was passion but not compulsion – it was something they could do without, something they had a choice about. And that could have an effect. Gary Bettman himself said "I think there will be a tremendous amount of damage."

Baseball's stoppage also contributed to its losing its status as America's "No. 1 sport," to football. In hockey's case, it may have been more practical ground that was lost: TV space. Replacement programming for hockey on long-time broadcaster ESPN outdrew prior NHL ratings, and ESPN VP Mark Shapiro said that was "not a good prognosis": when the NHL came back, ESPN decided to stay without it. A number of NHLers also went to play in Europe during the lockout. A veritable NHL all-star lineup including Ilya Kovalchuk, Vincent Lecavelier, Alexei Kovalev, Dany Heatley, Nikolai Khabibulin, Alexei Zhitnik, and Brad Richards all played for one team, Ak Bars in the Russian league. Although certainly no imminent concern, strengthened competition from those leagues may continue to rise in the future, or even a rumoured pan-European superleague seek to challenge the NHL's status as hockey's sole "No. 1 league."

We often heard people describe the financial dispute as a tug of war between players and owners. But in the big economic picture, an increasing number of other significant and complex challenges – from satisfaction with the core product, to status of key revenue streams, to public image, to outside competition, to changing demographics – are on the radar as well. Overabsorption with the tug of war could only detract from tending to those other challenges. In all, Wayne Gretzky said: "Everybody lost. We almost crippled our industry. It was very disappointing what happened."

On the other hand, a number of positive developments also have arisen in the larger picture as a result of the lockout. Recognizing the suffering baseball went through, and spurred by opinion polls during the lockout – hockey mustered deep motivation and wide support coming off it to take action on some long-running problems or criticisms, and win back the support of fans. This of course includes trying to restore excitement to the game, begun with the package of rule changes put in for 2005–06, and the work of the new Competition Committee as time goes on. It also includes striving to improve the television broadcast experience – particulary in the United States – partly under the watch of another committee. And it includes the new initiatives at improving player accessibility and using personalities to bond with fans and build deeper relationships in communities.

Just the break and "cooling off" period provided by the stoppage – as many hoped – provided the opportunity to make a fresh start, and chart new directions for the game on the whole and on particular issues. This, more than the simultaneous marketing campaigns or any push for positive press, looked to really give the NHL the opportunity to create a new image in the public eye, one better than ever, and one founded on reality. Also, an attitude of fresh appreciation for the support of fans and media was on display, striving to make up for opposite messages given off by the lockout – and it seemed to be well accepted by those groups, who initially are responding well. At the same time – perhaps surprisingly, but beneficially – it has also seemed that many followers of the game in the public and media have a new appreciation for their game, having been deprived of it for a year. Many *did* find it was a passion. Many realized it was not as boring as had perhaps been said, and that despite problems, there was still a lot about the sport to like.

Within the NHLPA, some were spurred by what happened to fight for greater openness and accountability from their leadership. "It's just so goddamn rotten it's unbelievable," Detroit's Chris Chelios said. The final straw, according to the *Toronto Star*'s Rick Westhead, who broke the story was "union president Trevor Linden . . . without consulting the 37-member executive board, sacked former executive director Bob Goodenow, agreed to an $8 million severance package for Goodenow, and hired Ted Saskin to a $2.1 million a year contract as Goodenow's replacement." "If someone did things this way at the united auto workers, they'd be lynched," Brett Hull said. Legal action was being taken, and the goal of more player input into decisions and directions was being pursued.

In the end, was all that happened worth it? Of course, only time will tell. If you look at it strictly from the point of view of the actual matters of economic dispute, my guess is that that may be unlikely. Players lost a whole year of salary, and accepted a deal many of them thought was not much different than they could have had without doing so. The league will almost certainly make cost savings and gain cost security, but against that you have to count diminished TV revenues and increased revenue uncertainty. Competitive balance was already fairly OK, and overall the new deal fixes only four years. To me, it is in the larger picture where the game has the best chance of making what happened worth it. There are some compounded challenges as a result, but there is also new motivation and support to act on and improve fundamental issues – from the quality of the game, to relationships with fans and media, to the image of the game in the larger public. "The best thing that I can say to our fans is we're back, we're going to be better than ever, and we're going to make it up to you." And there is a new opportunity to do so, a fresh start following the interruption, so to speak, and a fresh choice.

When baseball went down after the lost Series and came back with the home-run chase, I believe people in that sport learned the hard way that the right strategy is decisive fixes to malaise with the game, and gradual tinkering with economic agreements, while making sure to avoid another cancellation. Indeed, in 2002, a potential stoppage was averted by last-minute compromise. I hope and I think that as a result of hockey's lockout, people in our sport have learned a similar lesson too.

And with respect to those other issues in the larger picture, the challenge is to continue the positive change and the positive momentum, so that it outweighs the negatives, and makes what happened worth it. Much as injury and other hard experiences pushed me to write this book to try to help the larger game and salvage something positive out of a lost career, now everyone in the game has a similar choice or opportunity coming off the lockout. "When you look back in a year, five, 10, this era in history . . . will be viewed as a pivotal point in time" Gary Bettman said. Indeed it will. Hopefully when posterity takes its look back on the lockout of 2004–05, it will be to say that in the larger picture, it turned out to be a key catalyst to being something better than it had been in a long time, maybe something better than ever. And for *that*, it was worth it.

EVALUATING EARNINGS

2004 earnings

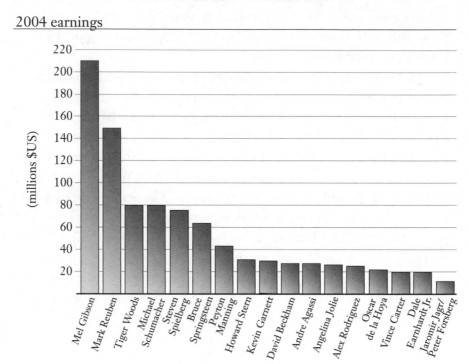

2002 approximate average earnings

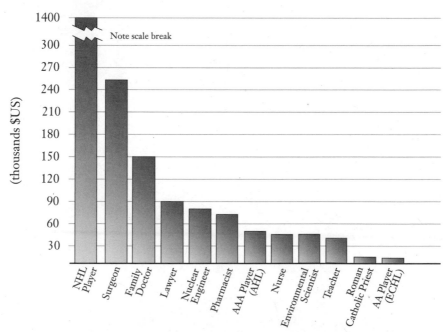

Defending Masters champion Tiger Woods places the Green Jacket on succeeding champion Mike Weir. Could you imagine hockey's defending champions handing the Stanley Cup to its new winners! Golf's strong governing bodies help preserve the sport's integrity and sportsmanship amidst major business influences and competitive impulses. (*AP Photo/Elise Amendola*)

CHAPTER 11

BALANCING BUSINESS
AND SPORT

PLAYING BOTH SIDES

Hockey's financial issues go far beyond the lockout of 2004–05, far beyond collective bargaining, far beyond the sport's financial bottom line of today or tomorrow. They go to the very nature and identity of professional hockey – what it is and how it works.

In fact, the issues of this chapter and the next are issues of the world of professional sports as a whole: many of the details and examples apply strongly in hockey; some apply more in other sports, and may not apply in hockey at all, or not yet. But taken as a group, the issues of these chapters are very important both to hockey and to other sports, now and in the future. Professional hockey, like other professional sports, has a fundamental dual identity – like the comic-book superhero Batman with his alter ego, the ultra-wealthy entrepreneur Bruce Wayne. Pro hockey is both a larger-than-life spectator sport and a big and ever-branching business. These two identities, and their relationship, are involved in every facet of professional hockey, every decision made, every factor determining its ultimate fate.

On the one hand, hockey is a sport. We all know what sports are about; there's supposed to be something pure and wholesome and healthful about sports. They offer us an incomparable blend of fun, good-natured competition, exercise, and opportunity to strive to realize our potential. All with a positive spirit that is more than idealistic fantasy (it is a word in the dictionary) – *sportsmanship* – a real and attractive thing about sports, in contrast to more unsmiling forms of competition. Billions of people all across the world play sports: people of different ages, backgrounds, circumstances in life, and levels of ability. They play sports of all different kinds, as different as bowling from boxing, or rugby from rhythm gymnastics. What unifies all these assorted people and all these various activities is the nature and spirit of sports – it impels them toward sports from such disparate points of origin.

And sports' importance goes beyond their attractiveness to people. Athletic pursuits offer opportunities for learning valuable lessons in character not strictly part of the traditional curriculum of academia: things like striving, sacrifice, co-operation, and perseverance. And many others. In a culture of conformity, sports offer people a chance to distinguish themselves through pursuit of a chosen athletic activity. Against what medics are calling an "epidemic" of obesity, sports offer a critical forum for physical exercise in the modern, urban world. And the benefits are not just for participants. Sharing in the athletic activities of children is a natural way for parents to bond with children, and sporting pursuits are an effective "anti-drug" and prophylactic against other kinds of mischief for idle adolescent minds and bodies. On a grander scale, major spectator sports are one of the few remaining things that bring large numbers of people together, behind a local or national team, and in friendly (instead of hostile) rivalry with people from other places. The popularity of sports is not without reason; the importance of sports is not without justification.

Hockey is just such a sport, invented more than a century ago as a winter pastime for the sake of fun and leisure: young men gathering together whomever they could in the neighbourhood to play an informal contest, outside, with "road apples" for a puck, no uniforms, and no fans. It emerged in post–Second World War Canada as *the* popular form of sports competition and athletic striving, as Canadian athletes were eagerly drawn by the fluidity, creativity, vigour, and spirit of "the game on ice." The speed, skill, and straightforward simplicity of the game caught on with Canadian spectators too, above and beyond other sports like baseball, football, cricket, and curling. Hockey attained huge significance in Canada – because of these attributes that set hockey apart from sports, and because pursuing it with phenomenal skill and to fanatical lengths set Canada apart among nations.

But inherent in this importance of hockey is the importance of sports as a whole, growing throughout the past century for the reasons mentioned above – albeit sometimes different sports in different countries. But hockey has had great moments in other places too, like the United States with the Miracle on Ice; as much as larger political issues were bound up in the meaning of that triumph, it couldn't have happened without sports, and without a sport that meant enough to be played at a high level by peoples at opposite ends of the Earth and of the political spectrum. From the frozen rivers of Canada, to the cement and rollerblades of California, to the icefields of Siberia, millions play (and watch) hockey for no other reason than their love for it as a sport. It's everything that we love about sports: physical, fun, challenging, competitive. It's an exhilarating and intense escape into a world of super-action, of costumed competition, of heroes and villains . . . like the billionaire Bruce Wayne stepping into his Batcave, donning a cowl and cape, and ruling the night as the superhero Batman. Hockey is fully a sport, for what they are and mean, described above – and a distinguished one at that. Without staying true to its nature and spirit as sport, hockey doesn't make sense, and would not exist.

On the other hand, at certain levels, hockey is a business. We know what businesses are, the same way we know about sports. For all their sometime size and complexity, and everything involved and undertaken – there is a fundamental simplicity about businesses –

what defines and drives them is a financial bottom line, a measuring of accounts, and a dollar figure plus or minus, big or small. Everything a business does, in some minor or major, immediate or long-term way, is supposed to be for that purpose. And that bottom line doesn't count what was done, how it was done, what its effects were on others, or on the world. Businesses that do well by the bottom line survive, thrive, and grow; those that don't, disappear. People that help business generally are promoted, people that hurt business generally are let go. Owners are involved to make profits, employees because they are paid, customers because they are getting more of what they want at a better price than alternatives.

Hockey is such a business. Professional hockey, in particular, is a business – where owners pay players to play, and charge customers to watch. Major junior hockey is also a business. College hockey is a business too (except that the business is part of a not-for-profit institution, a school, where scholarships are suggested to be appropriate and sufficient compensation for players). And there are a whole slew of derivative businesses radiating off from the business of hockey: hockey equipment and licensed apparel, arenas, broadcasting and media, agencies and career management firms, trainers and training facilities – even hockey publishing (although I'm told there's no money in that). The NHL alone when it last played was a $2 billion-plus-a-year business. All of these businesses use hockey in some way as their product. To survive, to succeed as businesses each of these entities need to make money, and make enough money to cover the salary costs of players or other employees and satisfy the owners or investors with the return. To maintain partners and patrons, hockey businesses must continue to be able to offer them what they need at a price they can afford. Hockey is as fully and regularly a business as any other. Professional hockey is, the organizations that comprise it are; this is also their identity: the Bruce Wayne ego.

There is a duality present, as professional hockey is both a sport and a business unto each. And professional sports such as hockey are not *part*-sport, *part*-business, but *fully* both – because sports can and do fully exist where they are not businesses, but yet in cases where they are a business, they are no less so than any other. This fundamental, irreducible duality is uncommon, and a bit hard to understand. It puts pro sports in a special category shared with a few things – painting, music, theatre, acrobatics, etc. – which have a complete ethos and logic apart from business considerations. There may be a certain pride in craftsmanship and service within every business, but sports go beyond this in being associated with purity and other values that we find it hard to put a price on, and are really in a different category, as mentioned, where this duality is full. As a result, the duality is ever present in our minds, ever ready to confuse us, or to lead to potential conflicts. This is at the root of many of the conflicting feelings, unresolved confusions, and recurring errors to do with professional hockey, and at the heart of many of the issues that have recently threatened it or will do so in the future.

In general terms, what is good for hockey as sport is what sustains the fun, the fairness, the healthiness, and the sportsmanship within the game. On the other hand, as business, the bottom line is the bottom line: what makes money and increases the monetary value of the business. These are two very different perspectives from which to look at hockey. And although teams and leagues may each divide themselves into a business department and a hockey department, in reality the two perspectives don't apply independently in separate spheres – each are complete "theories" governing everything involved with and affecting the sport. So what happens when the two motives come together over a particular issue? Sometimes they pull in the same direction: a team tries to win for the sake of competitive pride, and the business wants the team to win because winning brings in more fans and therefore more revenues. Sometimes they work together synergistically: a team makes a profit, they use it to buy good players, the fans like watching them, they make more profit, and so on. But sometimes these two different motivations may collide, and point in different directions on the same issue: whether to re-sign a player who is unproductive but popular; whether to rid a team of high salaries after success, to make it more attractive for a lucrative potential sale. There are countless examples.

These conflicts can create problems for hockey and all involved. A manager may be torn by competing responsibilities and desires: does he try to put together the best team he can, when it may lose his organization a fortune? Sometimes an owner may incur the ire of fans if the direction the business charts is unpopular with fans – such as when former Oilers owner Peter Pocklington was rued for Wayne Gretzky's trade to Los Angeles. There may be a certain player or coach who will resort to questionable tactics, because it wins hockey games, and ultimately pays off.

Whenever there are conflicts, these are real issues – they are hard things for one involved and others watching to understand and judge. There is a complex relationship between the two identities within hockey coexisting and co-commanding at the same time. The sport and business natures of hockey are mutually interdependent, with the health of both necessary for the other: If there isn't a sport, there isn't a business. If there isn't a business, there isn't a professional sport. And if there isn't a professional sport, then the whole strata of that sport below suffers. Without the release of being Batman, the troubled Bruce Wayne couldn't cope with his inner demons in order to do business as Bruce Wayne; and without Bruce Wayne's billions, there is no money for a Batcave, a Batmobile, no way to afford the time and money for pursuing ideals in the escapades as Batman. The dual identities of hockey need to be figured together in the whole: not to forget or neglect one out of preoccupation with the other. When we sacrifice or neglect one or the other, or mess up the way the two come together, it leads to big and wide-sweeping problems.

A NEW AGE

To some extent, as long as professional hockey has been around, so have these issues been around. As long as hockey survives, managing these issues will be an ongoing task and struggle. But what is of concern here is that something big has happened, has changed over the last fifteen years or so. There has been an enormous, swift evolution of the business of hockey. It has gone from small-time to big-time, local to global, mom-and-pop to corporate. This has led to huge, unchecked changes in the relationship between hockey the sport and hockey the business.

In the early days, this balance between sport and business was mostly weighted toward sport, business just stringing together what it could to sustain it. Many smaller sports still are that way at their highest levels. Hockey lived longer than some other major sports in an old-fashioned, small-time business mold. But recently and rapidly, it has been transformed with a vengeance into Big Business. What was essentially a business built to support a sport, and whose culture was predominantly determined by the idiosyncracies and cultures of the sport, has over this short space of time become a big entertainment business, with the latter's insatiable appetite for profits and control. Millions of dollars are at stake for players now, tens to hundreds of millions for owners and for associated businesses.

Teams became more frequently corporate owned and integrated with other businesses (including arenas, other local sports teams, cable networks, and real estate developments) as part of highly sophisticated, developed, and mature organizations. Salaries rose astronomically: Since 1967 when the average was $19,000, salaries have grown to an average of $1.8 million today. The average tripled in the past ten years. Meanwhile, league revenues have grown from $400 million in '91–'92 to more than $2 billion in '03–'04 and revenue sources branched out beyond ticket sales to include substantial national and local broadcast rights, licensed apparel, luxury boxes and seat licenses, arena-naming rights, corporate sponsorship, and other advertising, to name a few. Franchise values rose enormously: in 1990, Norm Green bought the Stars franchise for $38 million; five years later, he sold them to Tom Hicks for $84 million; at the end of 2003, *Forbes* valued the Stars at $270 million. In 1990, the San Jose Sharks expansion team cost $50 million; in 2002, the owners sold it for $147 million. *Forbes*'s latest valuations placed the average at

$163 million, up 31 per cent over six years ago, and much more than that since the change in the business complexion of the game began in earnest about fifteen years ago.

The fans have seen the change, not only through new names for arenas, but new arenas, huge rises in ticket prices, and other costs. Around the sport was built a complete "entertainment product," combining videotron animations, fireworks displays, and fuzzy mascots firing souvenirs into the crowd. Coaches have seen their salaries rise, but job security lessen; unusual new aspects have been added to their work, including needing to look good for TV (ESPN analyst Barry Melrose even had a best-dressed and worst-dressed coaches segment!) Managers have seen a new importance to contract negotiation and budgeting emerge alongside traditional responsibilities of scouting, development and evaluation, as well as a separate and sometimes conflicting scale on which they would be judged besides winning: profitability. Organization size and structure has radically changed, not as much on the hockey side, but on the business side, where there are now dozens of front-office employees with specialized tasks ranging from community relations co-ordinators to the Webmaster of the team Internet site.

Ownership has changed in that the high costs and amalgamation means more corporate ownership and typically deeper-pocketed and wider-invested owners who are more hands-off than in earlier eras. The business of owning a sports team has also changed from when it used to be a small investment with small risk. All the while, outside competition for entertainment dollars has increased with the proliferation of new and alternative forms of entertainment, including TV exposure for a wider variety of sports, video games, Internet, and DVDs. The insatiable appetite of broadcasting and media for content to package and sell means sports have been more than ever in the spotlight, and coverage has become enormous.

In other affiliated businesses, similar things have happened. The once-numerous hockey equipment companies have been consolidated and come under the control of Nike and Reebok, and the prices of equipment have gone up astronomically. Superagents and financial management companies have evolved to replace the family lawyer helping out a player part-time on the side. Camps and instruction have turned into big-business operations, with higher and higher prices, paid by parents thinking or hoping they are just small investments compared to the return on a child's lucrative future NHL career. An entire city's business is affected . . . from local bars and restaurants and retailers, to the media, to tourism, to the image and appeal of a city courting new businesses, employees, or residents – which is partly why we have seen so much public money shelled out to get or keep major league sports franchises lately.

Why has all this happened? It is part of general trends in all industries toward consolidation under specialized management, and also reflects the growing importance of entertainment in our society. The explosion of mass media, cable, and communications that drive the entertainment business is a big factor. Another reason is new business-driven management hired by the NHL and NHLPA a decade ago. And the growth of athletes' salaries that pushes the bar of what is needed in revenues, forcing more professional and aggressive management of the business. But the ultimate outcome is huge changes in the business side – unmonitored, unregulated, unchecked from the point of view of the sport side – translate into huge effects on the relationship between the two sides, and on hockey itself. There has been a radical tilt in the balance between sport and business to a point where I think financial issues are altering and transforming the sport.

DOUBLE TROUBLE

The development of this drastic change in the interplay of the two identities of hockey flows like a river tributary into a cascade of problematic effects. For example, the transformation has resulted in a huge rise in the amount of money on the line, intense media exposure, and public scrutiny of performance. All of this in turn has tremendously raised the pressure on individuals, teams, and organizations to succeed. At the same time, the transformation has also meant margins of error have dramatically shrunk: Astronomic salary costs leave little room for other business reverses, if an organization is to stay afloat. And there is more intense competition than ever, breathing down people's necks. For management, that competition arises in trying to qualify for the financially all-important playoffs where there are no salaries to pay, huge gate receipts, prestige, and reputations on the line, and millions to be made in future tickets and sales of paraphernalia. But expansion means only sixteen out of thirty teams make it today versus sixteen out of twenty-one teams fifteen years ago, and greater parity means more of those teams are in the hunt. For players, the competition is in more people playing (especially the rise of players coming over from Europe), training harder, pushing the envelope further in competing for player jobs. With a big corporate machine on their backs, players, coaches, and managers must win, must succeed – now and constantly. With all that's at stake, they figuratively and sometimes literally can't afford not to.

So then the approach to the competition becomes "anything to win, anything to succeed." And that in turn has contributed to each of the major issues covered in this book. It may not be immediately obvious because of the lack of attribution and the gradual, indirect, sometimes insidious means of affectation, but look and you find it in the background of every crisis the sport has recently faced: for instance, it has forced the adoption of the successful but derided defensive schemes and obstruction, whereas in college and amateur leagues, and even international tournaments featuring NHL players and coaches, these have not been played so frequently. The high-stakes of the business were the difference between competitive impulse and compulsion, and overrode counteracting impulses of how they might like to play the game, or how they ideally think the game ought to be played.

The altered style of play and bottled-up game then affected what factors games came down to. The pressure to succeed also led to the rules being pushed through things like the growth of goalie equipment, goalie interference, and diving – even if some of these things ran against sportsmanship. These in turn enhanced the pressure on referees, and inflamed the reaction against them when they made real or perceived mistakes. The altered style of play also meant less room on the ice, so there were more frequent and harder collisions, and more injuries. A more physically intense game to the point of recklessness toward oneself and one's opponents was fed by less respect for safety than for the jobs and fortunes on the line. Fierce competition for the all-important playoffs and all the benefits that resulted from success in them pressured teams to overspend or outspend each other, and a lockout ensued to bring salary costs under control. That lockout then had its own substantial fallout.

The increase in pressure and alteration of the approach to the game is just one way among many in which the broader transformation of the business of hockey contributed to the major issues covered in this book. As a whole, the problems this transformation is causing can be seen across virtually every aspect of hockey: It leads to teams losing superior players they can no longer afford, which frustrates the team concept of a team sport, for teams, players, and fans alike – and no matter how many times the mantra "Hey, it's a business" is repeated. It has led to scheduling aberrations where teams have been forced to play at a tough time to accommodate a television schedule. It has led to internal strife between organizations and players over holdouts, arbitrations, and above all the lockout. It has led to a gulf between players and fans: "The money is astronomical now. Its hard for the average person to fathom," Gretzky said – and resentment toward millionaire players by those watching or playing at other levels. Special treatment has contributed to bad behaviour, on and off the ice – with kids watching and bound to emulate. It has led to an uncertain ownership situation, as small owners were priced out and big owners were tired of the headaches, getting out and potentially leaving a void.

Even when decisions made for business reasons turn out bad for business, it is sometimes still the result of the transformed game forcing new decisions, some of which will inevitably be mistakes. So many of these things happening have damaged or distorted the sport of hockey. Untended to and unchecked as they have been and continue to be, the integrity of the sport into the future necessarily is at stake. While hockey's survival as a business depends on its recognition as a sport, more and more, people involved are looking the other way, and even justifying decisions based on business principles. The sport is getting lost in the shuffle.

This overarching issue of business versus sport and the particular problems it causes are one thing that hockey is not alone among sports in confronting. All of the major league sports (or Big Business sports) are facing these. Some compelling practical examples and their significance include:

- in baseball (which was the earliest Big Business of any sport), basketball, and European soccer, for example, the same big-market teams like the New York Yankees, Los Angeles Lakers, Manchester United and AC Milan seem to dwell on one "tier," competing year after year for championships, while a score of others are on a lower tier, occasionally breaking out, and quickly falling back down

- in football, team owners have been sued by and sued the league; star players have been released (such as Drew Bledsoe by the Buffalo Bills) to save money in a league where contracts are nonguaranteed

- the Olympics, which presents itself as the torchbearer – literally – of everything that is supposed to be good and clean and pure about sports, has been racked by financial corruption scandals

- boxing has faced allegations of fixed outcomes or improper decisions

- track and field, and cycling (as well as the North American team sports) have been tarnished by allegations of steroid use or doping

In general, the transformation of each of these various sports into Big Business, over the last fifteen to thirty years or so, has created a panoply of problems distorting the dynamic duo of business and sport within each game, and undermining many of the fundamental meanings of sport. It has led to radical changes in the character of a pro athlete's profession and the way he or she approaches it. It has put in jeopardy the meaning of athletics as something that promotes physical health, as athletes may now also risk or sacrifice health through increased injuries or performance-enhancing drugs, for what's at stake in the Big Business competition and high-stakes environment. It has led to deterioration of "sportsmanship" in favour of an alternative attitude of "win at all costs" – threatening the good-natured character of competition that made sports appeal to us over other things that were merely institutionalized conflict. It leads to money and other kinds of influence interfering with athletic decisions and undermining the equitability of the playing field. While still in many ways fostering good character through self-development and self-realization, pro sports now in other ways spawn bad character through spoiling, special treatment, and unaccountability for non-performance related behaviour.

And all of these trickle down from the pros to aspiring pros, to kids. Thousands of kids are not having enough fun because it's too-serious business, and there's too much social pressure from coaches (even movies celebrate depictions of coaches screaming at kids), parents, school, and other sources to succeed. Enjoyment is being sapped by overtraining, excess structure, hostility, and dangers like drugs and violence. As an industry, we have to ask ourselves, "Is this sustainable"? As a society that supports these sport-businesses, people (and lawmakers) already are asking themselves, in what they're becoming, are they worth it?

Economic interests have come to dominate everything else: do what is right for business, don't worry about what matters to sports. But in the process, fundamental secrets of success, and important things about sports are being obscured or lost. And as time moves forward, the industry's direction is in question, as the twin-engines are out of sync: changes are increasing the steam of business, while nothing sustains pressure on the side of sport.

A QUESTION OF BALANCE

You can compare it to juggling: some psychologists portray the art of living as the juggler's art. Or you could compare it to tightrope walking. I like to think of it as question of balance between business and sport – the one founded on the other, the other supported by the one. A delicate balance allows them to coexist and thrive simultaneously. I remember reading former U.S. vice-president Al Gore's book *Earth in the Balance* about the balance between human society and the natural environment, between human activity and life-sustaining natural processes: you can't preserve a healthy society on the foundation of a sick planet. It strikes me that that is a way of understanding what is happening in sports: that sports are drifting out of balance, up and away from their roots in the nature and spirit of sports, into the air and clouds of Big Business preoccupation. An ever more intricate "entertainment" business construction upon an increasingly cracked foundation of sports. No wonder Washington Capitals owner Ted Leonsis called "a fundamentally broken industry."

It doesn't seem like the plainest, biggest, most urgent problem in any given sport at any given time, it doesn't seem like the concern that must be tended to *now* (just as environmental dangers have been continuously overshadowed by the Cold War, terrorism, and other "hotter" foreground issues). And just as with those environmental dangers, we have to fear whether this threat to sport will ever be tended to until it's too late, because it's in the nature of these kinds of things that they move in the background gradually, indirectly, "imperceptibly," whereas it's in the nature of human beings to turn attention to what's obvious, sudden, and acute. The problem is, though they operate more slowly and invisibly, they are also wider threats, just as cancer gradually, quietly claims far more victims than earthquakes or tornadoes in all their sudden and spectacular fury. The weight is building up top, unbalanced from below, and the game is getting caught in the avalanche that results.

What is at stake is the meaning of sports. Not just at the professional level, because at lower levels, although not to the same degree, problems trickle down from the top. Will they not continue to offer healthy pursuits physically and mentally? Will their integrity be beyond issue? Will they continue to represent the spirit of sportsmanship that makes them what they are? If they lose some or all of these things, what will ultimately happen to them down the line?

Perhaps there are some who would shed no tears at the prospect of the fall of sports, that view sports as an insignificant preoccupation of an idle society. Not me, and chances are not you, if you are reading this book. The explosion of sports after two World Wars had something to do with them being a healthier form of competition and rivalry than war, after we had pursued that about as far as we cared to go. Sports' appeal, whether you're playing or watching, has something to do with them being a healthier, good-spirited preoccupation than other diversions in our society. The future of sports relies on them remaining a healthy alternative and a counteraction to other trends in our society. They are special for all they offer: fun, good-natured competition, fairness, physicality, health, self-development, self-realization, character – things people often are not getting elsewhere in our postmodern world. For all these reasons, the importance of participating in sports in general – in Canada, in the United States, in western society, in the world – is tremendous, and only increasing. They must survive.

But what about hockey, what is so important about this one "little" sport? Obviously for people like me who love hockey and are devoted to it, that importance is simply there, on a personal level. But beyond this, for the general public, I think there are primarily two answers to this question. The first is that hockey really is by nature an amazing, special sport. It could and should be such a great embodiment of all the good things that sports offer, such a complete and perfect test of athletic prowess, such a distinctive presence in the world of sports – a truly special game. Second, hockey's plight is the plight of sports as a whole, together ailing from a dangerous imbalance between business and sport. Hockey's fate represents the prognosis for the other major sports suffering similar illnesses. What makes hockey the test case? Not that hockey has a worse case, but that for various reasons, among the North American "major" sports, it is the most vulnerable. Thus, although perhaps not by choice, hockey seems destined to provide a model of either how things can go wrong, or hopefully how to purify sports and achieve for them a more brilliant future.

FINDING A NEW BALANCE

So how do we face up to this fundamental issue and restore the balance between sport and business in hockey?

We can't, nor should we want to, turn the clock back to a bygone era to achieve the balance. We have to reconfigure the relationship of sport and business and find a new balance in the world of Big Business professional sports (with new weights on each side of the scale, but they are in balance once again).

On certain issues within the larger trend, in some cases steps have been taken that should help, as discussed in earlier chapters. For example, the revenue sharing provided for in the new CBA should help reduce financial-based disparities between teams, which could result in an uneven playing field in competition. And the various measures to modify the level of salaries should limit the extent to which cost concerns overwhelm conduct of the sport. On the ice, the announced clampdowns on obstruction, goalie equipment, and diving should improve fair play and sportsmanship, and increase excitement and enjoyment for participants and fans of the game.

Other changes suggested throughout this book can help on these and other particular fronts as well.

But the effects of the larger trend on the sport are innumerable and growing. So trying to find one-time symptom-by-symptom fixes for each manifestation is an ultimately hopeless task. The nature of this sweeping issue of the balance between business and sport requires a more overarching approach in response, and an ongoing source and mechanism of nurturing the game for the future.

The goals of this overarching address of the issue must be twofold: to restrain the weight the business side has over the sport side, and to beef up the sport side in counterbalance. And to do this and steward the game on an ongoing basis, hockey needs permanent groups charged with these tasks.

First of all, you can't stop business, but clearly the business of hockey can be regulated by a group charged with appraising, monitoring, and engineering the effects it has on the sport. (Think of this as not shrinking the size of the hockey business, but handling it so that less of its weight falls on the scale that is against hockey's sport-needs.) Such a group would also foster the particular values of the sport, and of sports in general, to strengthen the identity and integrity of the sport as a counterweight to business interests. But what group is going to do these things? As far as having permanent standing and major influence, the NHL and the NHL Players' Association are the powers that be in the field, but they consist of specific vested business interests within the field: in the NHL's case, it's thirty franchises; in the NHLPA's case, it's seven hundred or so player-members. Their respective Board and Executive Committee and respective executive officers are responsible for serving their constituents' business interests. So to ask them to be responsible for preserving the sport, potentially against those business interests in certain cases, would be a conflict of interest, and it would be unreasonable to impose that expectation on them.

Recently, at the end of the lockout, the NHL and NHLPA created a Competition Committee consisting of a few representatives from each group to advise on the issue of the NHL's on-ice game. This is certainly a very positive step over what many saw as a void in this area before, and it has already provided guidance for the sport through the implementation of some beneficial rule changes for 2005–06. But the fact remains that this committee, and even the NHL and NHLPA that they represent, consist of only a tiny fraction of the millions of people throughout the world whose lives are touched by the sport of hockey as participants or fans or in other capacities. But meanwhile, as the sport's pinnacle, the example set by professional leagues and players for the conduct of the sport inescapably exerts a profound if not overwhelming influence on the character of the sport at every other level, and the experiences of those involved in it. From this point of view, these bodies represent interests that are both conflicted and too narrow to serve in the capacity needed as fully dedicated custodians of the game.

Also importantly, these groups represent interests that are "short-term" invested: the career of the average NHL player or coach is very short – and even the longest ones are much shorter than in most fields in society; managers, executives, and owners' tenures are often not much longer, and sometimes shorter. Even for these people – typically, of all their time involved with the sport, only during one fraction of it are they represented. So the result is, long-term interests of the sport and those involved in it can be shortchanged by a preponderance of concern for short-term interests of the sport, and of those involved in it during their brief time as "current" pros. This may work for business (or may not, even though it is often practiced), but it surely is unsuitable for a sport that is a public treasure, handed down from previous generations, and our duty to preserve intact for future ones. So which group can be counted on to consistently look after hockey in the interests of the sport itself? Of the whole of the game, and all those it touches – and over the long-term? The answer is none. It seems to me this is a major deficit that needs to change.

One of the sports that has been most successful at protecting its sport side and at the same time is also one of the most financially successful and fastest-growing sports is golf. Golf has powerful governing bodies explicitly dedicated to the preservation, regulation, and values of the sport itself. The USGA in the United States and the Royal & Ancient in Britain (as well as smaller ones like the RCGA in Canada) inhabit a top level that arches over tours, tournaments, clubs, and players and oversees the game, governing the way it is conducted from amateur levels up to and including professional tours. In hockey, national associations like Hockey Canada and USA Hockey are exclusively responsible for amateur hockey and international tournaments, so they don't apply to the NHL or other professional leagues. And these associations don't have much influence on the professional hockey leagues either. In fact, only recently was Hockey Canada formed from a number of smaller organizations and at present, the influence seems much stronger in the other direction – from the NHL on Hockey Canada. There is simply no comparison between these associations in hockey and the power and influence of the golf bodies.

In addition, significantly, in 1968, professional golf recognized the divergent interests and mandates of the premier professional tour, and the larger needs of all of golf's professionals, patrons, industry, and game. So the PGA split into the PGA Tour (the circuit played by top tournament pros) and the PGA of America, a group dedicated to the more widespread needs of professional golf, and all the people involved in the field of golf, in both senses of that term. In hockey, this has not happened: both groups remain rolled into one, in the body of the NHL. And the NHL looks after its own interests, equivalent to the PGA Tour, while there is nothing equivalent to the PGA of America in hockey. There is the International Ice Hockey Federation, but it is just a federation of the national associations, with no say in the conduct of hockey in the NHL, and again it is more influenced by than it is influential upon the NHL.

The result is, in golf there are two levels of governing bodies (versus zero in hockey) that arch over the tour and protect the larger interests of the sport of golf – and they have been very successful at doing this. What sport has a better record of preserving the spirit of the game, the character and values of the game, of maintaining the rules and their intents, and honour and sportsmanship than golf? And golf does it on a huge scale – currently it's played by more than 50 million North Americans and growing extremely fast, versus approximately 1.2 million in hockey and growth that has been much slower (at least among males). It is further ironic in that, for all of golf's aristocratic roots and traditions, these associations are very democratic and effective in preserving the interests of the "masses" vis-à-vis the game from being overrun by business concerns, or elite interests, or letting the sport "deteriorate"; whereas in hockey, a game with working-class backyard roots, business influences have swept in with little resistance and distorted the sport in a myriad of ways in short order.

Again, if we look at big-league European soccer, the professional leagues are subordinate to the national associations, which are subordinate to the European (UEFA) and world (FIFA) governing bodies, charged with preserving and promoting the interests of the sport of soccer that is the leagues' foundation. Things are far from perfect in the soccer world, but, again with a few exceptions, they have been able to do a good job of protecting the sport inside the business, of trying to fine-tune it, of preserving sportsmanship and limiting the corrupting influences of money from driving the sport itself into chaos. They are ahead of the North American major sport equivalents, including hockey. They are also actively involved in promoting their respective sports at grassroots levels across the span of their territory: growing participation, fostering sportsmanship and fun, teaching and ingraining a respect for the game and its rules and for others, and a culture of healthy participation and competition within the sport. Not surprisingly, soccer is by far the most widespread sport in the world. It's a proactive approach to safeguarding the sport by promoting, bolstering, strengthening the sport all the way up: creating, fostering, preserving the good, as opposed to just taking an extant sport-business and trying to regulate away the bad.

The hockey associations have engaged in campaigns of this kind, and have had some notable successes, such as the "fair play" campaign that cut down on violence and boosted participation in certain amateur leagues. But in terms of having an influence on the character of professional leagues, as well as in view of the potentially enormous countervailing influences those professional leagues will likely always have on those below, we need to have governing bodies reach over the professional sport, not around it. So that when these bodies are out in the field doing the legwork of pushing the sport side of the game, people will listen, and people will heed.

Hockey could have one group, or multiple groups as in golf (one for professionals, one for the sport itself), each of these national but in co-operation with one another, or international. These would inject the interests of the people, the long-term, and the sport itself into the management of professional sports, in balance and co-operation with the management of the business of them that is there now. But it is critical that these groups have real power through binding rules, certification, sanctioning, or other methods, as in golf and soccer. And they need to have a continual and ongoing mandate: an annual meeting with binding recommendations, constantly studying, undertaking initiatives, responding to submissions for guidance, and arbitration of grievances. Perhaps if hockey had had this, they would have built the bigger rinks when they still could. Perhaps they would have clamped down on the goalie equipment before it grew beyond all reasonable need and proportion. Perhaps they would have rooted violence out of the sport before we had to have the ugly incidents that we have had. With these bodies, we would be able to clean up distortions in the way the game is played, and deal with off-ice concerns like the use of performance-enhancing substances, equipment and facility regulation, the monitoring of financial activity to make sure it is not corrupting but serving the sport, and the handling of grievances arising out of alleged improprieties.

These won't take the money out of hockey and sports, and they don't need to, but they will channel its flow in ways that prevent or minimize it from distorting or damaging the sport. They will regulate the pressure of business on sport in ways that allow the business to grow financially while at the same time nurturing the sport within it (which is no fantasy, as golf has proven). In the long run, we profit more by tapping the sugar maple, not by chopping it down. When you remember the interdependency, you realize this approach is safeguarding not only the sport, but the business in the long-term, in turn.

In addition, again as in golf, hockey can benefit by grassroots organizations under the blanket of the governing bodies – but independent in constitution – that are engaged in campaigns and efforts with the involvement of local organizations, minor hockey, coaches, players, parents, sponsors, media, and everyone else involved to push the values that the sport stands for, address issues that need to be addressed, and fill needs and niches that arise in serving the interests of the sport. There are some things like this today – such as the Safe and Fun Hockey that Orr, Bossy, and women's player Cassie Campbell have championed, and the ThinkFirst injury prevention campaign. I believe they can have a real and powerful influence, fostering attitudes of fun, sportsmanship, fairness, healthy participation, and building a strong tradition of the sport and the way it should be conducted, beginning by working with kids. They can help change the entire culture of the game from the ground up to become one that supports the values of the sport, and that frowns upon the kind of things that damage it. This would go far in strengthening the advocacy of sports and the things it stands for, create a "Big Sport" so strongly needed to counterbalance the "Big Business" in the new game.

Together, the governing-body umbrellas and the grassroots efforts would work from the top down and the bottom up to push and pull hockey back into balance with business influences, now and forever. Hockey would be able to grow in healthy ways, sustainable ways, nurturing the duality that the sport is and must be to survive over the long term, and as something worth cherishing. It will ensure the future of sports in society, and the important things they offer us: fun, fairness, good-natured competition, physical expression, and personal development. We will still have these "superheroes" in our society, including hockey – a wonderful character in the sport world, and the pride and passion of so many.

Disillusionment (left), Disappointment (centre), and Frustration (right). Alienation and Empty seats. Anybody and Nobody . . . If a picture says a thousand words, this picture might say a lot about the troubles within the love affair between the sports business and the public. (*AP Photo/Chris O'Meara*)

CHAPTER 12

PROVIDING FOR THE PUBLIC IN SPORTS

FACT AND FAN-TASY

In addition to the duality between hockey as business and sport examined in the last chapter, there is another important and often-overlooked duality to hockey (and other major league sports): their nature as both private business and public good.

On the one hand, professional sports teams are businesses, by practical fact owned by private interests, and by their legal incorporation operated for private profit. Whether the owner is a single individual, a small group, or a large group, however the organization is legally constituted, they are owned by private interests. The only major pro sports team left that is called "public" is the Green Bay Packers (a non-profit group), but even they are not really owned by the public (e.g., the town of Green Bay, or the state of Wisconsin), the shares of ownership are merely kept *open* to the public, for whoever out there chooses to buy into the ownership group and is able to obtain shares. The hundreds of millions of dollars worth of direct costs needed to acquire and operate a major professional sports team (franchise acquisition rights, cost of build-ing facilities, salaries for players and all other employees, material resources of operation, financing costs, taxes, and others) are solely the responsibility of the owners to bear. The enormous associated financial risks are solely theirs as well – if the team loses tens of mil-lions of dollars, it comes out of nobody's pockets but these owners'. They do this in exchange for the legal right, which they want, to try to make money through operating profits or increases in the value of the professional team. It is their initiative (to bear these costs, take these risks in exchange for that opportunity) that has allowed these teams to arise and continue to exist in the places they do. All of the assets of a team belong solely to the owners, including the right to the franchise itself, its name, and the player contracts. And if the team turns a profit, this too goes solely to the owners.

They are also staking their business and personal reputation on the line, no differently than owning any other business. So the owners have major economic interests at stake, and more, in pro-fessional sports teams. These teams come together into groups that co-operate for the mutual benefit of their member teams, and the governance of the game. They form a "league" or "association" to co-ordinate staging games and exclude outside competition; the team owners come together into a board of governors to create rules for competition and look after common economic interests, and they hire a league-wide executive to govern the combined entity in the interests of all of the members. The leagues then are aggregations of private interests in each of the teams, and themselves a private business group on a "global" (continental, in the NHL's case) as opposed to local scale.

At the same time, as things that we watch, witness, and follow, the major professional sports are also a public good. They are a big part of our communal culture in several different ways.

Just as the last chapter described how participation in sports offers individuals a healthy institutionalization of competitive impulses, so here on a larger scale do the major professional sports teams offer whole cities a healthy form of rivalry. Each major league sports team bears the name of a city (or region), serves as that city's sole representative in that competition, and carries its "flag" into "battle" against other cities and their teams, vying for the sake of pride, prestige, and achievement. The importance of this function of sports is highlighted by the fact that earlier incarnations of professional sport as travelling shows (including circus acrobatics, as well as baseball's Cincinnati Red Stockings and basketball's Harlem Globetrotters, who despite having a city name actually were barnstorming tours) have faded or been replaced by the system we recognize today of permanent teams in each city, competing against one another. No doubt, the ability of major sports' teams to explicitly represent a city is a big reason why the "major team sports" occupy most of the top rungs on the list of sports' popularity.

Professional sports also have a huge civic function as one of the most popular and most important forms of public entertainment. The presence of mass entertainment in western civilization, and its conception as even part of the task of governance, goes back more than two thousand years to the Roman games and the Greek theatre. It is an ancient and accepted vital practice for there to be such mass entertainments. Further, in today's society, sports are one of our most significant fields for prizing excellence and artistry. What do we witness and judge together, as medieval cultures did with chivalric competitions, or renaissance cities did through fine arts and architecture? We judge, we esteem, we marvel together at athletic competition. As such, sport has become a central source for us of heroes, role models, and the values they stand for. No longer prophets or saints, or politicians or generals, or painters or writers, or mythological or comic-book characters, but athletes (along with actors and musicians) have become the superheroes of our society, the people our children admire and aspire to emulate and to be. "With every step you take during the day, you have to be a model citizen. . . . You have to watch over your shoulder all the time and be the person that people look up to," NHLer Steve Thomas said of what it's like to have that responsibility.

By a whole host of measures, it is evident just what an immense part of our contemporary public culture sports are: They bring thousands together in attendance. Millions more watch, listen, follow, and support. Sports garner news headlines daily, and parades for victorious teams. The wide span of people they bring together in following them is as rare in our society as the fanatical devotion they inspire in more than a few. Spectator sports are among the hugest and most unifying elements of our society's culture. The current president of the United States, George W. Bush, catapulted his fortunes as part-owner of the Texas Rangers baseball team before moving on to be governor of Texas, and then president of the country. And the term *major* sports roughly tells us which ones are important enough to be considered significant to the public good.

According to Harvard sports law professor Paul Weiler, a Canadian and a hockey fan, and author of the book *Leveling the Playing Field: How the Law can make Sports Better for Fans*, sports really are in a special class by themselves. Sports' importance to our culture is a big reason (beyond tax dollars on ticket sales and parking, and revenue accruing to the local economy through patronage of nearby businesses) why some places actually build arenas or make other contributions (sometimes enormous) from public tax money to attract or maintain teams. Major sports teams attract people to a community and bolster civic spirit.

Even outside our own culture, sports serve the public interest. This is evident, for example, through professional soccer's popularity and importance around the world, in very different and perhaps improbable places like Africa, East Asia, and the Middle East. And consider the role sport plays internationally as a unifying force for people to follow jointly (think of the Olympics), and a civilizing force for people to vest their competitive identifications in. It fulfills basic natural desires we have to root, to support, to escape, to be awed. That's why sports are one of humanity's most universal obsessions.

Once again, both the private nature and public character of major pro sports are present at the same time. They are both private business and public good. As such, they fit into a rare and special category of things like education, healthcare, evangelism, and public service, for which this is true. The special duality in major professional sports as private business and public good means there is again a critical relationship to tend to at their heart (just as with the other fields in this category), and mutual rights we need to find ways to satisfy.

PRO SPORTS' "BETTER HALF"

I like to think of it as a marriage where there is a "sacred covenant" exchanging rights and obligations, privileges and responsibilities between the business parties (the teams and league) and the public (as represented by the fans, the general populace, and their representatives – government) in the mutual interests of both. It arose in the following way: Originally there were just sports, including hockey, which people enjoyed playing: no spectators, no businesses, no paid players. Later, players started to travel around for competitions against others for the sake of pride, and spectators became interested in watching these competitions. So there started to be more organized competitions and exhibitions. Then to make the competitions more organized, the exhibitions more sustainable, and to encourage the development of the skills the class of professional players had to display to the public, a business grew up around these. As such, the sport came first, the public good second, and the business third and last – most derivative.

Because of the way it originated, the covenant and its basic terms are implicit; self-evident, if never written. It's also a self-evident matter of fairness and equitability among alternatively interested parties today. The deal was and is a "give and take" along the following lines: The owners of the league and teams are given the right to run a business of the sport and have the opportunity to make money, in exchange for incurring the expenses and financial risks associated with fielding the team. The public as a whole has a right of access to the sport as a big part of public culture in exchange for doing what is necessary to support the sport and team financially, whether it be through attendance, viewership, other purchases, corporate sponsorships and patronage, and in some cases arenas or tax breaks and other measures. A team gains a stable and consistent base of fans and support in exchange for bringing that city into the competition, representing it, doing its best at every level (ownership, management, players) to represent that city well in competition. Likewise on a global level, a league gains fans for promoting that sport. Those involved with the sport, especially the players, gain hero or celebrity status in society and all the special treatment and perks that go along with it, in exchange for serving as role models, ambassadors, heroes to the public, and embodying the values the public associates with those.

As far as competition, the leagues have usually been pretty quick to swallow competing leagues. For example, the National loops in baseball, football, and basketball all swallowed rival American loops; in hockey, the NHL incorporated the remnants of the WHA. At other times, the public has not supported multiple competing leagues, such as the failures of football's XFL and the CFL's foray into the United States. And the government allows the major sports leagues to function like monopolies in ways it may not allow in other businesses. This includes allowing the mergers above, allowing teams to sell broadcast rights as a single entity, letting major leagues limit their number of teams, permitting labour-side practices such as drafts and player movement restrictions, and other examples. In exchange for tolerating these practices, governments expect major leagues to commit themselves to giving the public what it wants – the very best players against the very best, the most entertaining product that sport makes possible.

And the government often foregoes potential antitrust resources and allows leagues to grant teams sole rights to the sport in their city or region. The unwritten expectations are that the team shall meet the needs of the public good there. This means providing adequate accessibility to the local population, including to a wide enough cross-section of the public. It means appropriate representation – a franchise competing to its utmost, reflecting and representing the values and spirit of its community. It means team owners and managers not owning or managing any other teams in the same league. In exchange for the (non-financial) support of the team, franchises are to reach out in the community. And ownership has the freedom of doing whatever it chooses on any matter that does not infringe upon the public rights or good. This is the deal between sports business and the public, unwritten up until now, but perhaps analogous in the field of sports to the "social contract" supposed by John Locke, and accepted as the foundation of our societies' government. This tradeoff is what allows major spectator sports to exist, and for the mutual "needs and interests" of private business and the public good via pro sports, to be satisfied.

NEGLECTING THE PUBLIC

At a certain time (or for a long time) to a great extent, this is how sports worked. Business was successful and growing. Back when sports reached the popularity and importance they have today, sports were obviously highly accessible. The accessibility to a wide span of the populace, unlike other more "haughty" or "high society" forms of entertainment like operas, or classical (e.g., Shakespearean) theatre, was indeed one of the reasons sports replaced those as the leading entertainments, and attained a popularity and following unprecedented by antecedents in recent prior culture. Meanwhile, athletes were (or at least seemed to be) for the most part good role models and heroes. And a loyal relationship developed between cities and their teams. I'm not trying to depict a Camelot that never existed, but until not that long ago, pro sports had a somewhat different meaning, symbolism, and character than they have today. One that resonated with people right through society as something pure, simple, innocent, and different from the rest of the world around them. And that was part of what attracted them, and allowed sports to become what they have.

But lately, seeking to capitalize on the immense popularity sports have gained and the business opportunities associated with that, sports started to become Big Business, and throwing their new weight around, they have sometimes knowingly, sometimes unwittingly strode over the invisible lines of "the deal." And the more they have, the more the original and proper terms of that deal have become overlooked and forgotten by the *de facto* mode of operation. This is just one example of more general trends in our society toward deregulation and unfettered capitalism, toward privatization and the disappearance of civil society, toward the weakening of government and the strengthening of business – which harbour more pervasive concerns. But what matters to sports is that in their march to the drums of business, the public has at times ended up being trampled underfoot. The same process that over the last fifteen years in hockey (and slightly more in some other sports like baseball) has threatened to distort the inner sport, has also infringed upon the public good. The public is the oft-forgotten group in pro sports – integral to the industry, but excluded from the decision-making regarding it, and nowhere more disenfranchised than during hockey's year-long lockout. The point of view of the public in sports is one that needs to be considered in the whole, and that is what will now here be explored.

If you refer to the contract on page 397, you can see some of the things that make up the suggested rights which the public are owed and obligations they owe, in the unwritten contract of major sports. The public is largely doing what is expected of it, but business looks to have neglected some of its commitments, and used the "leftover" clause to improperly encroach upon things supposed to be set out on the side of the public. This has shrunk the public good, and weakened the equitable relationship at the heart of spectator sports – which ultimately hurts business too.

This is happening across the board, in a number of sports, in a number of ways. From a financial point of view, clearly over the past number of years, the public has been meeting this most basic obligation as much and more than could possibly be expected: there have been thousands of fans at games (at least until recently, close to capacity at most events, or quite sizable numbers of people despite the growing expense), millions more watching on TV or listening on radio for which fees make their way indirectly from fans through advertisers and broadcasters to teams. Fans have bought small fortunes worth of apparel and other paraphernalia, and fed massive media coverage. At the same time, the corporate public is doing its part by paying big money to sponsor major sports. Federal governments give these outside businesses tax writeoffs to use sports to entertain clients, cutting their effective costs as much as in half, at the general public's expense. And local governments have actually directly handed out huge sums (billions, combined), to teams to entice them to come or get them to stay through tax breaks, free land, building arenas, covering debts, and numerous other sport-friendly initiatives. For example, the city of St. Paul, Minnesota, spent $130 million to build the new Xcel Energy Center, voted the best entertainment venue in North America, in order to lure a new NHL team to replace the departed North Stars. Broward County, Florida, sold $215 million in revenue bonds to finance a new arena that would keep the Florida Panthers from bolting the Sunshine State.

But meanwhile on the flip side, the wider public has been losing ground on its most fundamental right of all, the right of access. Ticket prices have gone up so high that the majority of fans can't afford to go to games. According to *Money Players*, NHL ticket prices rose 48 per cent since '94. *Team Marketing Report*, a business publishing and research firm in Chicago, says it cost $240 for a family of four to attend an NHL game in 2002. And in some places, where demand is especially strong, prices have been *significantly* higher. On top of that, in many places, fans have complained in recent years of being gouged on related expenses: parking, food at games, licensed apparel, "seat licences," "club seats" which have an annual membership fee, seat "maintenance fees," and an ever-growing amount of hooks like that. Also, since typically the majority of seats to be sold are seasons' tickets, this places them even more out of reach of the pockets of most fans, and means that the same people and their circle can go to all the games, all season long, and renew their tickets year after year, so that many cities have waiting lists in the tens of thousands.

Do waiting lists prove prices aren't too high for people to afford? No, because in a city of millions, of course there will be tens of thousands who can afford to go to games – that's just a few percent of the population – but at the same time, there are millions who can't. What waiting lists do prove is that selling so many seasons tickets means even among the proportionally few that can afford to go, many are being excluded. The rest typically can follow sports on TV (or on the radio or the newspaper). One nice thing is that cable specialty channels have made for more games televised in recent years, but on the other hand, specialty-channel packages to get games can be expensive for many fans, and in some places and sports, TV viewership is further restricted by pay-per-view, or local blackouts. However, without ever being able to attend events, other experiences *alone* hardly give a sense of everything sport is about, for the populace. Sport ceases to be a cultural good – which is part of their nature, and the way they came to prosper – and becomes *strictly* entertainment.

Sports know that too. That's why the industry-leading NFL, despite a lucrative TV deal, has a "sellout or blackout" policy, ensuring attendance is never neglected. And almost always it isn't. The lucky among the mostly corporate elite, the wealthy, and a few die-hard fans who devote a huge portion of their income to tickets get to attend and be part of the formerly "public" experience. Except on very rare occasions, the rest of the public have lost live access and the experience of this major part of public culture, which should not be a luxury privilege, but, along with participation at lower levels, a crucial part of identification with the sport, which once again is so central to its future.

Sometimes the lost access happens on a mass scale. Well-supported teams leave their city for another locale, to the dismay of hundreds of thousands or millions of abandoned supporters. Many remember the NFL's Colts literally fleeing Baltimore in the middle of the night for Indianapolis (as government action was being prepared to stop them). More recently, the Browns skipped town on the city of Cleveland (before the NFL awarded Cleveland a new expansion "Browns" team to replace them). The huge metropolis of Los Angeles has been without a football team for several years now, since losing both the Raiders and Rams, who went to Oakland and St. Louis respectively. Hockey has seen an exodus of professional teams from Canada to the United States, including the NHL's Winnipeg Jets and Quebec Nordiques. And Minnesota – nicknamed "the State of hockey" – watched its North Stars pack up and leave for Dallas, Texas. It took several years and tens of millions in taxpayer money for the Twin Cities to obtain the expansion Wild to replace them. Franchises move despite strong support and long traditions because they can get better business deals somewhere else – a more favourable stadium lease, a greater share of parking and concessions, or in the case of Canada's lost NHL teams, a stronger currency for their revenue dollars. Meanwhile, fans across the former city are left to digest the injustice of having done so much to support their team, and nevertheless seen it leave, depriving them of an important and meaningful part of their city's culture.

In some cases, the sports team didn't end up moving, but the franchise used the threat of moving to extract more financial concessions from the public (more season tickets or special fees) and from the government (money for stadiums, better lease terms, etc.). According to the book *Leveling the Playing Field*, the number of professional sports teams in recent years that *haven't* tried to extract better financial terms by such suggestions or actual moves is very few. In some other cases, more common in the hugely successful sport of football, perhaps, than in hockey at present, there are cities that want teams, that are almost certainly ready and able to support teams, but are excluded, as leagues limit their number of franchises. Less teams means greater shares of lucrative national TV revenues each. In all these cases, the fundamental right of access of the public to major league sports is being limited or denied on a mass scale. The fans have a legitimate role in professional sports as spectators, they are more than consumers, they are witnesses and participants in a cultural good, and by denying them access, their rights to that culture are extirpated. Further, the fans' role is necessary and essential: without fans, the business of pro sports could not exist. Thus, cutting out such wide swaths of them is not only a breach of good faith, but also an unsuitable and ultimately unsustainable trend for the business of sport.

Beyond supporting multimillion-dollar player salaries, the public also gives athletes and coaches superhero status, special treatment, and appreciation and accolades for their role in sports. Even in big cities where impersonality in public is so much the norm, they are the exception – greeted by strangers, offered words of encouragement, favours, friendship. The word *celebrity* is appropriate, because indeed pro athletes are "celebrated" wherever they go. But once again, on the other side, is the other end of the bargain being held up the way it used to be? Schools invite players and coaches to come and speak to their students, and kids listen to them, even though they don't always listen to their teachers. And in those situations, players and coaches almost always say exactly the right things. But what happens when kids not uncommonly see those same players and coaches on TV or in the news practising different values than those they preached: whether it be lack of sportsmanship, or egotism and arrogance, or violence on the ice or off the field, or drug abuse, or unaccountability? Some social theorists argue that the special treatment given sports celebrities is in increasingly many cases having a spoiling rather than a gratitude-inducing effect: that appreciation passed to entitlement and expectation, and predictably got worse in several ways from there.

In addition, the Big Business game has meant more player movement between teams, and less individual integration in the community compared to in eras past. Some franchises do a great deal at the organizational level. And there are still players who make great efforts – much of their own initiative, and for which they should be recognized and commended – getting involved with charities, and being a part of their community (Adam Graves in New York, and Tie Domi in Toronto, are two, for example, that have been commended for their work, among many others). But the perception is that some take their hefty paycheques and then disappear into SUVs, gated communities, and summer cottages far away from all of which they rarely stray. But even if it is without objection from their organizations, overall it is to the resentment of the populace. From the public point of view, in granting players special status, in return they expect role models, ambassadors of their city, leaders in their community. Failing to meet public hopes or expectations in this regard creates a situation where society is deprived of them – which is at the very least a disappointing response that presents society with real practical problems. And again, it's a situation that is not sustainable. Society ultimately must fill these voids, and will find other heroes, other role models, other leaders, costing the business of sport, when it does, the special status it currently enjoys.

There are also monopoly-like sides to major league sports. Two important ones can be broken down into things I call the "*monopo-league*" (which consists of a league that operates as a monopoly in a given sport) and the "*mono-polis*" (which consists of a team having a monopoly on that sport in a given city or region), as well as many other practices that support them (as we described). On behalf of the public, governments tolerate this, which is not normally allowed in business, because of the special status of major pro sports as public goods, and with the expectation that the sporting community will deliver on its end of the bargain in return, by continuing to provide the public with the positive things long identified with and prized in sports, things which allowed sports to gain the status they have. But once again, sports are changing and the other end of the deal is being neglected. Many of the things the public wants or expects are waning in the modern business-dominated game. For example, frequent player movement give cities difficulty identifying with their teams and players. Some cities (even big-market cities) have suffered through an undercompetitive team for decades, while other teams compete for championships year after year such as the New York Yankees and Los Angeles Lakers. Some cities may lack representation or sufficient representation to begin with (L.A. with no football team, for example), because of the rules operating in the field. Then there is the extreme case of a labour-management dispute shutdown, when there is no sport at all, and the public good from it during is annihilated.

The government's deferential, preferential treatment (on behalf of the public) toward the business of sport in allowing these special privileges is not being repaid with the expected recompense. If the businesses don't provide enough of what's expected and governments no longer consider them worthy of what are effectively antitrust exemptions or special treatment, or feel the public good is better served by taking those privileges away, what will happen to the sports business? Once again, this shows how the sports business must for its own sake do a better job of factoring the public interest into its calculations of its own self-interest.

There are no doubt owners of hockey teams or other sports teams that have knowingly and often made decisions that cost them millions of dollars, for the sake of trying to please their city's fans at the expense of their business sense. Some may think me wrong in suggesting that the public interest has been neglected out of business preoccupation. But looking at the deeper picture, it is evident this simply cannot be so. Would anyone suggest sports fans' support is deficient? That could only be in places where the game is great, prices are reasonable, and crowds are sparse. But no owner would locate a team in such a place; and if an area once did support a team and support fell, it would be a very unusual case that demographic changes in the region (nothing to do with the sport) would account for it. Ultimately, it is only in the internal divisions of the business – salaries negotiated between management and players, expenditure differences permitted between one team and another – that costs could drown the support of revenues that come from supportive fans. The fans have no say in any of that, and if anything the government's tolerance on behalf of the public of sports' monopolism should dramatically help keep those costs down.

The fact is, what those business losses show – even ones an owner may have spent trying to subsidize the public good – is that

sports' businesses have some times been pinched by the same transformation of their industry into Big Business that is what has
impinged upon the public.

The significance of this transformation and the trends it's
causing – many positive, but also many problematic – is so enormous
it's difficult to comprehend. But for the public, it has meant the
things that they are entitled to and prize in sports are diminishing,
even as they meet the "covenant's" obligations, and indeed pour
more and more into the troubled marriage to make it work. And
for business, while it may seem profitable on a case-by-case basis,
in the larger scheme it is unintentionally undermining its own foundation. Is this part of why rinks had begun to have more empty seats
of late, why TV ratings growth is slowing down in many sports?
Some of the main major sports are doing very well attendance-wise
at the moment, other smaller ones have enjoyed growth in recent
years; there are still widespread and tremendous positive public
feelings around and elicited by professional sports, are bound to be
for years to come. But at the same time, clearly a number of effects
that the transformation of the industry into Big Business has had
on the public, have cast some clouds over the industry, created a
popular sense of "this cannot continue forever." That disillusionment or malaise – untended to – is bound to at some point translate into more acute problems.

If those problems reached the point of divorce, leaving sports
businesses without the public's support, or without private ownership,
obviously it would jeopardize the interests of the whole *ensemble* of
groups within pro sports. Aside from some historical examples and
rare exceptions, like the Green Bay Packers, no other form of ownership has been widely tried in sports. Public ownership of sports
franchises may have theoretical attractiveness to some, but our society
is largely moving the opposite way, tending toward privatization. On
the other hand, neglecting the public interest risks the government
protection and public support so critical to major league sports. Thus
for everyone involved, care needs to be taken for the cracks in this
relationship to be repaired.

POWER TO THE PEOPLE

So how can be reasserted and protected the rights of the public under the covenant of pro sports?

Clearly, business (like anything else) cannot be expected to police itself in the public interest, since business' direct interests would override its concern for the public interest. And in the minds of owners and managers who are relatively short-term invested, short-term business concerns will most often take precedence over long-term concern for pro sports' relationship with the public. By any standard of reason, the public by some measure has to stand for itself. But as was the case with the sport in the last chapter, in fact the public has no dedicated representation within the business. For example, as salaries and ticket prices went up – things which affect not only business and labour, but also significantly the public – the former groups repeatedly fought over the spoils while fans had no voice to say "Stop! We're paying enough already." Likewise, they have had no seats on league boards to say "we don't want that owner buying our city's team and moving it elsewhere," or on franchises' to say "we don't want that poor role-model playing for our city, wearing our children's favourite uniform," or whatever as the case may be. From negotiating tables, collective bargaining, management et al. has the public been excluded – with no officials, no cadre of lawyers, no representative – even as a lockout in hockey took the fans' sport away, and new terms decided under which it would come back. Of course, no one would say these things affect a member of the public to anything near the level they do players or owners – but they do matter in important ways to a group that is involved in the business, and as more than just "customers."

As it were, some of those terms decided, as well as some rule changes put in for 2005–06 were fan-friendly, and should please the public that had clamoured for changes. And a new "attitude of gratitude" for the loyalty of fans is on display, which should also be positively received by fans. The NHL and its players deserve commendment for this. In taking these steps, the NHL said in its announcement that it had talked to fans (among others) and looked at poll results, before deciding its course of action. That kind of inclusive approach is good for fans, and can only help the business, who rely on them as customers. But at the same time, those positive changes cover only a small part of the issues covered in this chapter (including just one sport), and perhaps more importantly, is the fact that tending to the relationship between business and public is not a one-time thing but an ongoing need. Committees recently created to oversee different aspects of the hockey business lack public representation on them; and even if it was granted, one would have to expect that a business (sensibly) acting in its own interests, would ensure that the whole balance of decision-making power remained their own.

So what should be done? Some might argue "if they don't like it, let them take their money somewhere else," but major leagues are without competition in their sport, so there aren't true alternatives. And major sports are not just a commodity, but an important part of culture, so it is neither fair nor reasonable to tell fans "take it or leave it." And if there was a mass change in culture, that left professional sports in the cold, that's hardly the solution we want. However, it is a potential response if things were bad enough – and no doubt part of the motivation for hockey's league-sponsored fan-friendly changes coming off the shutdown. And wisely so. By habit, sometimes we assume that sports have always been there and always will, and forget that this age of sports is only about 100 years old, just a blip on the radar of history; and that even within that century, sports have only really been big-time since more than halfway through, with the end of the World Wars, the growth in disposable time and income, and the proliferation of TV. And we forget, too, that there have been other mass entertainments, preoccupations, and traditions, many of which had great followings for equal or longer periods, but eventually succumbed to internal problems and external changes: Roman games, opera for two hundred years, circuses and travelling shows in the 1800s–1900s all were huge and enduring "crazes" to name a few, that gradually faded or quickly fell.

In a sport, a single labour shutdown has the potential to cause fundamental shifts in meaning, role and habits in the public. Now how about recurrent labour disruptions, rising prices, bad behaviour, franchise-musical-chairs, and all the other things the public has at times witnessed in recent years across sports? Some analysts wonder whether a change in culture is already happening, slowly in the back of public minds, even as the dollars and hype around sports sometimes spike to new highs, and fans by and large still show up and tune in. Such a landmark change would be difficult to recover from. Many prevalent cultural traditions – not just mass entertainments, but even bigger things such as forms of government – have passed away and not come back (the only thing that has bounced back time and time again is organized religion). A change in culture at the expense of sports wouldn't just cost those in the business, but probably the public as well – because in the forms it flowered under, sports offered people so much, and in today's world, they have the potential to supply us with even more.

What we need is a solution that preserves sports, but makes room for support of the public's interests in them. As a general rule, there is little individuals can do; strength in numbers is a usual strategy. Could fans form an association, like there is of players and owners (and other labour, business, and consumer groups)? The owners have their league and board, and players have their association, which act to protect their respective interests in the industry. Why not a "national fan association"? Contrary to popular supposition, it is not illegal to have one. There is, actually, an NHLFA. They have a Website you can go to. The problem is, they have no legally binding power like a board or union, and no practical leverage through threat of mass-action like those others have. This is because if they tried to play hardball with the business in this way, business would be able to simply employ a strategy of divide and conquer to defeat it – using limited access (which ironically is already one of the public's problems in sports) to turn fan against fan in competition for those limited tickets available. Fans who think or know that in the absence of an association they can win the competition with other fans for those limited tickets (such as those who already hold renewable rights to seasons tickets, or wealthy fans who can afford high ticket prices they know others can't) will resist joining, and the sports franchise will be happy to choose them as its customers, eliminating any hopes the fan association would have of gaining leverage through a potential boycott. In addition, it would be difficult for the fan association to really be able to exert any kind of social pressure on fans to join and work together like a players' association can, because fans are such a large, unwieldy, and difficult to define group. So business can simply work around any likely incarnation of a fan association. For these reasons, a fan association is not the most realistic method of doing anything about the problem, of trying to enforce terms of the unwritten "deal."

Besides, what about the duties sports have to the larger community, the general public – beyond those at games; who would push for the support of those responsibilities of sports? If there are no effective associations for fans, there are certainly none for the greater public-at-large. A similar problem prevents it: the general public has no organization that could represent it in this way. If someone tried to form one, it would have no authority to act on the public behalf, only of its members. And therefore it would have no legal standing, or power of any kind, and is an unreasonable suggestion.

Someone else might argue "if the public wants a say, let them buy the teams," but this isn't the covenant, it's a change to the covenant, a huge and fundamental change to it. And the current trends in our society are toward more private ownership, not less. In addition, although it may be circular reasoning, the complaints the public already has about pro sports have weakened the prizing of it as a public good, and therefore the worthiness in their eyes of such an investment. That's why a few years ago the Canadian federal government took the aid-package it had offered Canadian NHL teams, and former Cabinet minister John Manley pulled it back off the table, after public criticism erupted over the plan. Several public-funds-for-stadiums proposals have been rejected by voters across the United States and across different sports of late, proving there is a wider issue.

The alternative recourse to mass action and outright control is use of the law. Business is typically the one that gets to simply take initiative and flex its muscles. Players fall back on labour law. But in the case of the public, in our society, there are few effective consumer protections, and for non-fans in the public, even fewer third party protection laws. But for major league sports, there is one important set of laws that do exist and could be used to support the public – and these are the "antitrust" laws against monopolism. Remember major league sports' *monopo-league*, *mono-polis*, and monopoly-like practices that may be used to support them. In most other industries, such results and some of these practices would not be permitted by government, or stand up to legal challenge. In fact, baseball was given an explicit special antitrust exemption more than eighty years ago by what is generally said now to be a rather dubious legal judgment of the U.S. Supreme Court. Other sports have tried to claim it since, and been specifically denied any; and even baseball's claims on the scope of the exemption have been significantly curtailed by recent laws and judgments. Nevertheless, all of the major league sports have often benefited from *de facto* special exemptions to protect them as overseers of sports that are supposed to contribute to the public good. There are wide powers available to governments to step in at their initiative or upon request, but largely they have not – perhaps because they continue to operate the way they did at a time when the marriage between business and public was younger and healthier. Perhaps politics interfere, or other preoccupations supersede. But now that the public interest has become neglected on several fronts, many would argue it's time to act: the "marriage" needs professional help.

Indeed, in the wider scheme, this is exactly the government's role: it is a group of organizations whose purpose and task is to serve and protect the public interest. Governments and their officials are not popular in this era, and often for good reason, as the complaints people have about them probably dwarf those of sports or any other field. But put aside your disgust with contemporary government long enough for me to say that government has many arms of different kinds, and among them are ones that can be effective, in people's eyes. For example, specific departments or agencies like the Canada Council for the Arts, or the CRTC, or the FAA, or the FBI – may be examples of government groups that enjoy better reputations for effective action to more people than Legislative Houses or Senate Chambers. Ultimately, there is simply no way around the fact that the government is the only group out there that can protect the public interest, and that is its job. Teams and players have their representatives furthering their interests in the industry. It's time the people's representatives – the government – enjoined these others to mind the public's fundamental interests in the industry as well.

In fact, they've done so in certain instances before. One example in Canada was Premier Ralph Klein in Alberta, who, tired of seeing the Alberta teams struggling against a weak Canadian dollar and bigger markets outside his province, stepped in and imposed a surcharge tax on players on visiting teams, to subsidize Alberta's teams. It was – in my opinion, overall an unfair thing to do, and certainly not at all what I'm advocating – but he did stand up and step in, to try to help the Alberta public in sports. In the U.S., in 1980, Congress considered a Sport Violence Act and called NHL President John Ziegler to testify. "Title IX" legislation was enacted on behalf of women in sports. And most recently the issue of steroids and substance abuse has been taken up through the Clean Sports Act and Professional Sports Integrity and Accountability Act.

There is no doubt that pro sports don't like these initiatives, which they consider to be "outside" interventions, and commissioners and union directors will say "we can look after ourselves." But to a degree, that kind of argument could be turned on commissioners and union directors themselves – after all they are "outside" representatives brought in to look after *their* respective constituents' interests in sports (the teams, and players respectively). Shouldn't the people – for whom sports are more than a product, and given that sports in many ways enjoy direct public patronage –

be entitled to a representative as well? To dismiss the potential role of the government is to dismiss the attempt to ever protect the public interest, in something that is not only a monopoly, but an important public good.

A "NEW DEAL" FOR THE PUBLIC IN SPORTS

There are several ways the government can now reassert the fundamental rights and interests of the public in pro sports, to represent their vital role in the process, and to help restore and improve the health of the covenant between the public and the business of sports.

One plan that a number of sports law theorists have suggested is splitting up each of the major leagues (NFL, NHL, NBA, and MLB) into two leagues, with no collaboration between them. Their rationale is that through open competition, would come a better deal for fans. I don't like this idea – and I don't think most people in the public would either. The reason is that sports isn't just a business with no competition, it's also a public good. By splitting the leagues, we lose the aspects of that related to sports as a common forum for collective identification and civic rivalry, and of aspiration to elite levels of skill and achievement. The proof is the history of mergers and failed attempts at competing leagues in sports. But legislatures intervening in a piecemeal issue-by-issue fashion has also proven to be an impossibly ineffective strategy in the face of overlapping, evolving, and rapidly spreading issues. Leagues and players' unions wouldn't think of having officials look after their interests in pro sports in this way, with part-time, narrow-focused, short-lived drips of action. They have permanent representatives with comprehensive mandates. The public interest would also be best served by that same approach.

Part of that could be by the establishment of a special legal class or sector of business for professional sports, reflecting their status as a major public good, a special industry. Such distinct categories already exist for certain other fields, each with their own specific regulations and enforcement, including charities, nonprofits, trust funds, the aviation industry, telecommunications, the arms industry, the food and drug industries, healthcare, heritage industries, and others. Various fields including these examples have specific regulations and governance either because they are relied upon as public service providers, or because they must or do exist in a monopolistic form, or because generally it is deemed necessary in order to protect important public interests. I submit that pro sports meets *all* of these qualifications.

As such an integral part of our culture and of local communities, pro sports certainly qualify as public service. We have already discussed how sports' major leagues are like monopolies in many ways. And pro sports' are vitally important through the values they transmit to us, both through being the highest level of sport (which the last chapter described was so critical to physical and mental health, character, and co-operative spirit among people), and through the athletes and others involved, who as we saw in this chapter, serve as our society's heroes and role models for children. We oversee food, chemicals, doctors, and pilots to safeguard people's bodies; we regulate radio stations and universities to safeguard what is received by minds. Pro sports' substantially impact the public on both counts – as a field closely connected with physical health and fitness, and as a transmitter of values and heroes to children and society.

A few other mass entertainments may to some degree fit this category too, and share important similarities with sports. But as Harvard's Weiler said, sports really are different even than other entertainment industries; they are truly in a class by themselves. Given that that is the case, it would make sense for the law to mirror that by creating a distinct class for pro sports, as they have for these other fields. The establishment of this class could include spelling out the terms of pro sports complex relationship with the public, through a loosely worded "covenant" along the lines of the previously unwritten principles outlined earlier. And in order to reap benefits and patronage conferred on sports by the public (including tax breaks, arenas, effective antitrust exemption, etc.) professional sports would have to accept the terms and principles of their new legal standing.

Agencies like the CRTC, or FDA or Environmental Protection Agency, or Health Canada – only for sports – could be set up to oversee this, as well as other initiatives toward the same goals, and all the details. There is already a department set up to oversee sports in Canada – Sport Canada – but governing the relationship between pro sports and the public is not part of their job description or *modus operandi*. In the United States, unlike most countries, there isn't even such a federal department or agency for sport *at all*. We might establish a "Federal Sports Authority" ("FSA") and an equivalent in Canada, to oversee pro sports as a special industry and field, and guide the important physical influence, moral example and collective identifications they have across society.

This means regulating conditions in the field pertaining to public access, potential relocation, franchise acquisition, professional conduct, competitive equity, and so on – and provide a first line of monitoring, arbitrating, and enforcing the specified terms. There would be transnational co-operation between the two national bodies. And together, they would serve the interests of the public in sports. Specifically, this means ensuring fair ticket prices and wide enough availability, regulating conditions under which teams can leave a city, or a city would have to be given an opportunity to gain a team; standards of competition and professional conduct cities could expect from representatives (perhaps with codes of ethics like other professionals have in medicine, law, government etc.); rules to prevent and mediate potential shutdowns, so that players and management can come to agreements without getting to the point of cancelling games or seasons.

The creation of this class and government sports department should not be seen as a negative thing for the sports business – and not just because it helps preserve the important relationship underlying sports. But as part of it, teams could be given on a federal level (rather than piecemeal at state, provincial or local levels, one city competing against another) tax breaks and other financial incentives, as well as awards and recognition, for the contributions they make toward the local economy, civic spirit, and general and specific areas of the public good. In addition, the government could, for example, acquire and redistribute a certain proportion of tickets, or subsidize ticket prices based on income to help sports continue to be personally accessible and appeal to the widest possible audience, while still allowing players and owners to maintain and grow their incomes. It wouldn't just be about regulation and punishments, but about assistance, co-operation with, and appreciation for sports. A special and protected status for a field that is capable of doing so much for the public good.

In the context of a repaired relationship with a new more affordable, accessible, consistently responsible incarnation of sports achieved through the above measures, I'm sure people won't mind a little government money flowing into sports teams. If the government is interceding on behalf of the public to help sports provide affordable access, strong values and overall a much better deal for fans financially and in all aspects, such subsidies are no longer a bad tax, but a great investment, on many different levels.

On the whole, the task is strengthening the position of the public good in the marriage of (pro) sports and society, and enforcing the covenant between them, to the mutual advantage of both public and business. This means the long-awaited, long-overdue involvement of the fan, and the public in the governance and conduct of sports. But this must take place through the government – who represent the whole of the people with their authority, and have the power legally and practically to uphold and enforce the public good, and public rights. And we need this intervention of government to create a shift in this relationship, a new class of business, a new era in sports. In the words of Franklin Roosevelt, and along the same lines of what he had in mind, but applied to sports, lately the people have been getting a raw deal, it's time for a New Deal.

The benefits of this New Deal are unquantifiable. People today can hardly imagine any more a situation where they have fair prices, good access, a level playing field for teams, loyalty, good role models, and all that sports were supposed to offer. It would be a tremendous favour for fans; it would be a tremendous boon to the public. And because of the fundamental reliance of pro sports on the public, and on the special relationship they have with the public, it would pay major and long-term dividends for the business of sport. Its finances would be buoyed by better fan satisfaction on a deep and enduring level, the recultivation and maintenance of a broader socioeconomic base of potential and actual customers (fans), and the business qualifying for tax breaks and government incentives as a recognized public service. From a sport point of view, it would help leagues focus on sports issues rather than trying to juggle all kinds of other hats including those of public-watchdog and player-policeman, and it would give franchises stability and prestige through official status and awards as mentioned. Generally, it would help assure, long-term, the primary place in society and culture that sports have gained and want to sustain. It would enhance the value and importance of sports to society, and thus the value that sports gain from society in return (including on a financial level). It would clear the clouds on the horizon, and assure a bright future for sports in society. That sounds like a good deal.

THE COVENANT BETWEEN MAJOR PROFESSIONAL SPORTS LEAGUES AND THE PUBLIC

In exchange for the rights and privileges herein setout WE THE PUBLIC UNDERTAKE AND PROMISE The Business of Sports that

We shall grant you, the league and team owners, the right to run a business of our sport..

We will make your exhibition of our sport a major part of public culture, which **we** will follow and support en masse.

We will do what is necessary to support the league financially, including attending our sport or viewing it on television, purchasing merchandise, sponsoring the corporation, and if need be, contributing a fair share to the cost of building new stadiums, or provide tax breaks or other financial assistance.

In each of the cities where a team is based, **we** will give you a stable and consistent fan base.

We will grant those involved with the exhibition of our sport (i.e. the players) hero and celebrity status, and the special treatment and advantages this status includes.

We will not support competing leagues, and our government shall allow your league some monopoly-like practices, including mergers with competition, combining to sell broadcast rights, limiting the number of teams, entry drafts, free agency restrictions and others.

Our government shall in certain cases forego antitrust resources and allow your team a *de facto* monopoly on the sport in our city or region.

We grant you the privilege of overseeing the management of the league and team in our sport.

"Leftover clause": **We** grant you the right to do as you please on any matter that does not infringe upon the letter or spirit of our rights and privileges described herein, or upon the larger public good.

In exchange for the rights and privileges herein setout, WE THE BUSINESS OF SPORTS UNDERTAKE AND PROMISE the Public that…

We, the league and team owners, shall incur the financial costs and risks of having a league and fielding teams in your sport.

We will guarantee you, the public, access to our exhibition of your sport and not take it away from you by moving teams or having temporary shutdowns unnecessarily.

We will keep access as widely available and affordable as possible.

We will promote your sport among the wider public as much as possible.

We will base teams in cities, giving each of those cities representation in the competition in your sport, and doing our best at every level (ownership, management, players) to represent that city in competition and in character.

We, and especially **we** the players, will serve as good role models and heroes to the public, and as ambassadors of the sport who embody the values you associate with and expect from your sport.

We, the league, commit to giving you what you want – the very best players and the very best competition along with the most entertaining exhibition that your sport makes possible.

We, the local team, shall fulfill the needs of the public good in your local region by providing sufficient accessibility and appropriate representation of the team competing, and have no conflicts of interest with other teams, and reflect and represent the values and spirit your community desires.

We will reach out in your local community and develop a real relationship with you.

EPILOGUE

The financial side of sports today is a big and ever-growing one. Guiding it in desired directions for business, sport, and all of the different groups within a game is a major and sweeping challenge. With the end of the lockout and the new CBA of 2005, substantial progress has been made in stabilizing hockey's financial footing, shrinking the influence of money over competition, and having players and management pulling in the same direction of trying to grow the game. But in several ways, there is still a long way to go.

In conjunction with a better game on the ice, the key to making a financial breakthrough on the revenue side is growing the ground-base of participation and familiarity with the game. This could be accomplished through a grassroots campaign co-ordinated by a network of old pros employed by the league as instructors-ambassadors in each region. Pushing college – a rite of passage for most youth – as the road to the pros, and an ideal time and place in which to capture new fans, would help hockey enjoy the growth that basketball and football have thereby seen. Adding more tournaments to the schedule to generate attention and excitement for the sport can also help. On a deeper level, we have to take steps to protect the sport within the business, and the public interest in professional sports, which we can do with the help of governing bodies and governments respectively. Ultimately, interconnected as all these things are, it is the best way of assuring the financial security and prosperity of the business of sports into the future.

Guiding the financial side of the sport in desired directions means greater revenues for business, greater salaries for players, and at less cost to individual fans. It means being able to do good business, preserve the integrity of sports that appeals to us, and provide a public service in the process.

POST-GAME

ADDRESS

TO YOU FROM FAILING HANDS, WE THROW THE TORCH. BE YOURS TO HOLD IT HIGH. It is in the hands of this generation of hockey fans to grasp the torch and raise our game. (*CP PHOTO/Paul Chiasson*)

CONCLUSION

Raising Our Game

THE FORK IN THE ROAD

"**I**f you see a fork in the road, take it." So baseball's Yogi Berra famously once said.

Well, for the sport of hockey today, there is a fork in the road.

Not long ago, there was talk that hockey was amidst the darkest chapter of its long and storied existence. Within the kingdom of sports, within the sphere of society, the consensus was hockey was a species endangered. "The professional aspect of the game is teetering on the precipice of total collapse," *The Hockey News*' Adam Proteau summarized in the March 15, 2005, issue of the self-proclaimed "industry bible," a month after hockey became the first major sport to sit out an entire season in a financial dispute. The premier league that is the beacon of the sport was shut down. An industry whose fortunes relied on fan goodwill, was pushing them away. There had been dissatisfaction with the play of the game, repulsion by acts of extreme violence, and concern about injuries. But if there was a silver lining to the dark clouds, it was the hope on the part of patriots of the game that crisis would push the game to be better.

With the end of the lockout, has indeed come new hope. A salary cap has given small-market teams and their fans a more level playing field to compete on. A battery of rule changes have been announced and adopted with the goal of making the on-ice game more exciting again, for fans, players, coaches and teams. The game's two marquee players of all-time are back – Wayne Gretzky as coach in Phoenix and director of Canada's Olympic team, and Mario Lemieux on the ice as captain of Pittsburgh after missing most of the two preceding seasons with injuries. Two young stars joined them – consecutive number-one picks Sidney Crosby and Alexander Ovechkin – bringing more future hope and promise to the game. Off the ice, there seems a new appreciation for the game itself by those both inside and outside, who are passionate about it and had missed it. And a new gratitude toward fans from those inside the game for supporting it, and by fans for the new commitment to improving it.

But at the same time, the process has a long way to go. Some of the alterations made have the potential to ultimately be bold positive changes for the game, but need to be sustained, refined, or expanded: "I do think that a lot of these things will take time to develop," Brendan Shanahan said. "Certainly some of the changes will be immediate . . . but realistically there will be a time period." Said Stephen Walkom, "We're not kidding anybody. This isn't over by any means." There are also a considerable number of more changes needed to the on-ice game to build on and improve on those made, not only for the sake of the excitement in the game, but the way competition is conducted, and health and safety. Off the ice, I expect a strong return from the lockout, but maintaining and expanding the game's base of fans will be an ongoing challenge. So will trying to finesse the push to grow revenues alongside the need to keep the game affordable and accessible to the widest number of fans. And in more ways than through marketing acumen or newly evolving revenue streams. Managing relationships between management and players, between the professional level and those involved in the sport at other levels, and between the business and the public, will be continuous challenges. There is positive momentum, but there is some distance yet to travel.

A brilliant future for the sport is possible. Hockey in its essence has unparalleled raw attributes of appeal, and resources of several kinds to make for the most exhilarating, satisfying, and health-promoting sport out there. And indeed, at times in the past, it has. And it has been something that has elicited in people special feelings of uncommon depth in public life. It has those "unteachables" that it takes to be an incredibly popular and meaningful game to North Americans, and worldwide. Transformations taking place in the outside world (the prominence of sports and entertainment, a digital age, globalization) can in numerous ways help the game capitalize on key internal changes. The sky is the limit if hockey can find its way to realizing the incredible potential it has.

But even as all that is within reach, danger is not far away either. As even the most senior league executives have said, fallout from the lockout must be expected to be felt for some time to come. And at a minimum, it will in TV deals, the depth of fans' support through any potential adverse events, and future player relations. There is growing competition from other forms of entertainment, new sports and activities, and perhaps ultimately even other professional (European) hockey leagues. Affordability, both as participants and fans, to a wide enough span of the populace is a challenge. As society evolves, continued on-ice violence threatens unparalleled potential damage to the game. The values being exhibited within the sport, and transmitted by the sport are also of concern: "Anyone who think we don't have problems, get your head out of the sand. Because we do" Bobby Orr said. For all these reasons, the game can't just be better than it's been, it has to be better than ever, as great as it can. If the supposed threat of immediate extinction was a false alarm, progressive marginalization of the sport – "extreme" as Ken Dryden said or "irrelevant" as Orr said – remains a possibility the game must act to avoid.

There is indeed a fork in the road, or on the ice. The nature and meaning of hockey, its near-term and long-term future, are at stake, for all the people involved in it: players, coaches, managers, employees of related businesses, fans of all ages, and others. What sort of activity will it be? What sort of following will it have? What prosperity shall it enjoy? What meaning will it hold? What shall sports themselves mean?

These are all important questions, fundamental questions, that time and actions will tell. One can only hope that in the afterglow of a newly signed CBA and the game's return after a long absence, that these questions are not lost sight of. Likewise, that the importance of longer-term, larger-picture issues are not misjudged out of preoccupation with marketing campaigns or the press position of the moment. The excitement level in the game, the way competition is conducted (how games are decided, players' freedom to play, the way the game is officiated), and health and safety (from violence, injuries, and other aspects of the lifestyle) are all important issues that affect everyone involved. And the complex financial side – including desires to grow the business, managing relations between different groups, and with the inner sport itself – are important as well. They are all specifiable, analyzable, understandable issues.

In dealing with them, what the game needs is unprecedented openness and co-operation, and unbending commitment to action to address them, from those involved. There are other options – we have free choices, but not freedom from the consequences of those choices. An attitude of gratitude, support for reform, ideas and initiatives, are a positive and necessary beginning, but should not be the end. One thing that has become clear of late, is that people in hockey have high expectations, so while dismissive or shallow-focused approaches lead straight down, players, owners, management, media, and fans have all shown that they have the patience to endure short-term pain for ultimately greater gain. Meanwhile, only a game so great it is compelling will seize and capture the attention of potential new participants or fans.

At this moment, troubles lay behind, but challenges remain ahead. There are clearly diverging destinies available, as the game charts its course for the future. The path of deterioration in our world is well-worn. For the sake of hockey's players, coaches, owners, fans, children, the general public – for everyone touched by the game – I hope that as Yogi Berra said, we will take the fork in the road. That years hence, as poet Robert Frost wrote, we will be able to say "two roads diverged in a yellow wood, and (we) took the one less traveled by, and that has made all the difference."

RAISING OUR GAME

Searching for the deep understanding that would lead to the right solutions, trying to find them, and explain how they would work, has been the subject of this book, as well as the long journey and some-times difficult personal experiences that led to it.

Among them, the most critical, centrally-important, and far-ranging solution that we must take, in my estimation, also happens to be the simplest to understand and the most straightforward to implement, and that is changing to four skaters aside. Four-on-four is the most thorough solution to the problem there has been in recent years of the boring style of play. In one fell swoop, simply removing one player aside from the ice kills the suffocating squeeze that choked out excitement, opening up the game to unobscured speed, skill, and creativity and uninterrupted action. This in turn reanoints the intended elements of the game as the crucial experience of team play and individual play, and eliminates distortions related to the squeeze. Again in turn, the effect of this in cleaning up the play of the game makes the officials jobs much easier, and in opening up the game makes the magnitude of inevitable officiating mistakes much smaller – helping to diffuse the sometime explosive reactions.

Four-on-four is likely itself the most significant measure avail-able to reduce injuries, including the concussion epidemic, by making for far fewer collisions, and more time to prepare for them. To some degree, it can also help deter violence, by making for a game where penalties are easier to see, and where it is harder and less helpful to resort to any kind of goon tactics. The key to the current financial mess is growing revenues – and an incredibly, *compellingly* exciting game is the most pivotal way to make a breakthrough in attracting fans. All of this in something which is faithful to the integrity of the game – not just in my opinion, but also by those expressed by some of its most learned historians (Ken Dryden) and most fierce defenders (Don Cherry). Four and four leaves all the rules as well as the essence of the game intact, and in effect corrects for the growth of players and speeds on a rink size that didn't change, returning the space ratio and type of play produced to how hockey once was in eras of glory.

I am not so naive to think that four-on-four is a panacea: it does not substantially solve the problem of violence, and it cannot fulfill the need for nurturing the relationships between sport, business and society. But it does profoundly address many long and difficult issues in the game. And in that sense, seems almost providential. The novelty of it is something that will take time to accept, but aside from that, I see little substance to any concerns: The number of players on the ice, and other basic rules, have changed before – several times. The perception of what's "novel" fades with time, just as the idea of five-on-five did when hockey first changed to it, just as notions of a three-point line in basketball, and a two-point conversion in football did in those sports more recently.

Record books have dealt with changes in the number of games, in the official rules, in the on-ice play of the game many times before; if we want to use asterisks, we can. But ultimately, I believe four-on-four is inevitable. And there is great benefit to embracing it as soon as possible. It is the most powerful, the most painless, and the most practicable solution to a series of on-and-off-ice problems that have arisen out of an overcrowded ice surface.

Another major foundation of raising our game is a "No Discretion" policy with regards to calling penalties. The history of avoiding in hockey this policy embraced by most other sports was a history of greater difficulty, frustration, and other complications. For years, a clear, simple, and consistent standard has been desired – and by an increasing number of players and coaches, as the difficulties inherent in hockey's "judgment method" compounded with other changes in the game. Now, finally and thankfully – at least with regards to interference, this has been recognized and is being changed by the NHL. A change in the "culture" of the way the game is officiated is underway. And ultimately, we need that to extend to other kinds of fouls – everything illegal (everything other than a clean hit). What the ref sees, the ref should call – with no leeway, no exceptions, no expectation to consider a multitude of factors in a sport where lots is happening and decisions must be made in split-seconds. No Discretion, just like in other sports. With the help of four-on-four, No Discretion could stamp out the obstruction-harassment that restrains excitement, teams' skill, and players' ability – and allow excitement, enjoyment, and fun freer rein within the game. A No Discretion policy would also help officials not have to be on the hot seat all the time, and allow them to be mechanisms of the rules, rather than judges in the spotlight, trying to make thousands of judgments each being judged by thousands of partisans on each side.

In addition, No Discretion is one of the critical steps needed to counter violence. The knowledge that infractions occurring will be called without question or exception (as long as they are seen by any official, or on video replay) will decrease both the opportunity and the impulsion toward violence. And if fouls are being called, there is less reason for violence to escalate, and more to lose than to gain by a strategy of dirty play – so the motivation for violence will also decrease. This means the advantage to teams of continually offending will dry up, so that dirty players and teams who would commit a high proportion of violence would have to clean up their act to be successful and stay in the game. Eliminating the violence will also eliminate a lot of injuries, while decreasing the sheer number of infractions will cut down on the wear and tear that weakens players and makes them susceptible to injuries by other means. Calling things by the rules, and having the officiating seem more consistent with the rulebook and consistent from game to game, will increase fans' satisfaction and enjoyment of the sport, which should help boost the financial fortunes of the game, and the relationships between sport and business, business and public.

In conjunction with "No Discretion," the other half of the enforcement equation needed to curb violence and injuries is "Zero Tolerance," a policy of severe repercussions for violent infractions, including several automatic punishments. Violent fouls would be considered in a separate category from obstructive fouls, and they would be penalized differently (just as there are flagrant fouls in basketball, and cards in soccer for violent fouls). Harsher penalties for worse degrees of violent fouls, as well as much longer suspensions, combined with league tracking and automatic stepped penalties for repeat offences, will help to rid violence from the game. There will always be potential motives for violence, that we can't change. But we can make the price of such misconduct too steep for anyone to afford, and apply these penalties consistently and automatically, so that there will never be any doubt about the repercussions, or any leniency to hope for in deciding to go ahead with a violent act. The tracking and penalties would apply not only to individuals but to teams (like the team foul in basketball, and having to play a man down in soccer) so that violence cannot and will not be directed from above or employed by teams as a tactic ever again.

Of course, nobody likes harsh penalties, but that's exactly why they will work. Players will quickly stop committing violent infractions, to avoid those penalties, and stay in the game. Coaches will ensure their teams do, across the board. And on both counts, the game will do much to shed itself of the scourge of violence. That would be a landmark accomplishment in a game that has so often penalized itself by weak enforcement.

Another important step we must take is the development of smarter, better equipment. When inevitable collisions occur, softer-surfaced equipment will be much more forgiving on opposing players, so we don't bang each other up with each of our own rock-hard "protections." Sleeker equipment could protect players well, while reminding them that they are human and vulnerable, eliminating the false sense of security that encourages reckless play that takes such a toll on all players. Freer equipment would allow players to move better to avoid collisions, and move more freely in general, to avoid injury, and allow the body's natural defence mechanisms to move in such a way as to minimize potential damage. By having less players injured, we will keep more players playing (which saves teams' money), and more of the best players playing (which keeps fans buying tickets), providing financial dividends for the industry.

Being able to move better will also allow players to play better – perhaps similarly to how the light armour of the Mongols allowed them to fight better than the European knights in all their heavy and constrictive armour. This will make the game more fun to play and more exciting to watch. Likewise, smaller goalie equipment will open up more room for snipers, and rekindle the art of scoring, and make the game more fun and fair for participants, and more interesting for spectators. Smaller, more fitted player equipment might also improve fans ability to relate to the players as people, and better capture the movement and emotion of the sport.

Concerted education initiatives on a number of fronts, and at all levels of the game from young children just starting out in the game, to the pros can also help in several ways: Initiatives to defeat the negative mentalities that contribute to violence and unsportsmanlike play; efforts to educate players, team personnel and others involved about common and serious injuries, how to deal with them, and how to avoid them; grassroots programs to strengthen the sport in the balance of business versus sport, as in golf, so that when competitive, financial, media and other pressures mount, the sport has the strength to hold its own and find a direction that is beneficial to both. That way, we preserve it the way it is meant to be played, preserve the spirit it should be played with, the integrity of the game we all love.

Ultimately, for these types of undertakings to be as successful as we need them to be, we can't just leave amateur associations and advocacy groups to do it on their own, or do it on a piecemeal basis – we need the support and leadership of the pros, and especially the NHL – with a concerted and comprehensive plan, and a continuing program. They are not superfluous labours, or even just charity work – they are a crucial investment in the health and future of the game, the industry of the game, and their preservation in forms we desire.

Now that a new CBA has been signed, my hope is that a legitimate partnership is formed between the league and its players for the mutual benefit of both parties. And that a new attitude develops whereby both sides attempt to work together and find win-win situations rather than retreating into fractious conflict that hurts both sides, as well as third parties. Clearly the game cannot afford another lockout in 2009, and creative thinking will have to be employed to navigate future CBAs and any other contentious issue bound to arise, in ways satisfactory to all sides.

Linking players compensation to the growth of the business through a kind of "equity" in operating revenues, as has been done, is a great way to contribute to that kind of co-operative focus, while preserving the health of the business and the player jobs that depend on it. Greater revenue sharing between the various teams, as has begun, shows a willingness on the owners' part to work together, and is another way to keep the business healthy, keep every team afloat, and preserve player jobs. Allowing a greater component of performance or success-bonuses into future CBAs, and utilizing them in greater proportion in individual player contracts – is another sensible method (and one widely practiced in other areas of business) we can use in the future to foster the health of the business, ensure compensation is in line with returns, make life easier for managers, and keep the interests of all congruent. The forging of a new atmosphere of trust and co-operation between the sides is critical for the game to be able to compete in a future of increasing competition from diverse alternatives, each in possession of their own sophisticated and efficient management.

But the financial issues of the game can't just be boiled down to the need for a handshake with the players, even one on more owner-favourable terms, and disregarding the price paid to coerce it. As in all businesses, management will need to continually be effective as new circumstances, challenges and competition arise. One thing that could help everyone in the industry is raising the draft age until a player is imminently turning pro, and cutting the number of rounds down drastically, so that teams are drafting players not prospects, and signed picks are sound investments not expensive gambles. Financially, the focus at this point, more than anything is finding ways to grow revenues league-wide, sport-wide. Central to this must be freeing up the on-ice assets of the game, and cleaning up on-ice detriments – pushing for the *best hockey possible*. All the marketing in the world won't make a sport that in reality is middling popular, and no amount of criticism can stop an incredible sport's popularity from soaring.

The next most important step to grow revenues and promote the prosperity of the business is a real, comprehensive and widespread program for growing participation and involvement in the game at grassroots levels. A new strategy focusing on promoting college hockey (especially in the United States) in every school possible, as the primary road to the pros, is an important vehicle for introducing and captivating people with the sport in an inspiring setting tailor-made for the job, as the rise of football and basketball have shown. It is the key to making the long-sought and much needed widespread breakthrough with the American public. Canadian universities should be part of this initiative as well, helping reinvigorate the sport's fan base for the future even in traditional heartlands. Major junior hockey, under that scenario, could then serve as a precursor to the college level, much as prep school hockey currently does in the United States. And there could be summer junior leagues, like in basketball.

Another important strategy for growing the game is to form a network of former professional players across the continent, employed by the NHL and working with corporate sponsors and local community groups to plant and nurture the seeds of the game at the grassroots level. Together, they can do things like work for the building of arenas, teach the game, support local programs, and generally improve familiarity, access (including available ice and affordable equipment), participation, and development in the sport in each community. This is essential for the game to grow to greater popularity over the long-term.

Adding tournaments to the schedule, each with their own mystique similar to golf and tennis with their four majors, would lift the profile of the sport in a crowded entertainment market, and allow it to capitalize on the media attention garnered by such special events, and by dramatic sudden-death playdown tournaments like the NCAA basketball tournament. These tournaments would again provide a big boost in helping the game grow its following, while rewarding loyal fans with additional excitement, and giving teams more opportunities to capture fans with a sports "moment," and more grounds on which to sell success. All this, while at the same time, having these tournaments spaced throughout the year would increase fan interest through the whole regular season, as teams would always have something to play for – trying to qualify for the upcoming tournament, and give fans something to look forward to, something to potentially celebrate.

But the financial issues of today are only part of an ever branching tree of business influence extending its reach into every aspect of the sport, and sports' meaning and relationship to society. I believe we need to empower an overarching governing body for the sport of hockey itself (as have admirably served golf, and soccer throughout the world, for example) whose jurisdiction includes the professional leagues, and whose mandate is to protect and foster the sport, and preserve the balance between sport and business that allows both to survive and thrive. The business side has its boards, associations, and executives, and the sport should have specific representation as well, ensuring that as business grows and times change, the sport we grew up with and love doesn't get lost in the shuffle and suffer in the process. A Big Sport, in counterweight with Big Business, would supervise rules of conduct for it, the values it stands for, arbitrate grievances, and promote the sport to the public.

Steps are also needed to make room for the public cause in pro sports, and support their fundamental role in the covenant relationship of major spectator sports within our culture. This could include legislating a new special protected class of business for sports (like there are for public services, and cultural or strategic goods), and turning the "unwritten contract" between pro sports and the public into a written one. A governmental agency (like those we have for healthcare, or law enforcement, or the environment, for example) could help govern the relationship between sports and the public: preserving sufficient public access, keeping ticket prices and associated costs under control, regulating the use of public money, helping prevent and mediate labour disruptions, and establishing codes of conduct for leagues and athletes to ensure sports convey good values and purvey good role-models to the public into the future.

By spelling out and centrally doling out the public assistance that sports teams would in return be entitled to – in the form of tax breaks, stadiums, free rent, etc. – there would be uniform rules created across the board so that teams are no longer left with such uneven terms versus the competition, and cities don't have to deal with threats of their team moving. The government agencies would also provide other benefits, awards and recognition to sports leagues, teams and individuals, reflecting their acknowledged nature as a cultural good and their contributions to public service. Protecting the duality between sport and business, and nurturing the relationship between business and public, rather than abandoning them to random forces and short-term interests is essential to preserving the future prosperity of pro hockey and of other professional sports. And ultimately, this flows down to sports at all levels – so important and valuable to us for so many reasons.

Together, hopefully the steps in this book, in conjunction with those that have already been announced and are in the process of being implemented, should go a long way to addressing the most fundamentally important issues facing the game of hockey, and helping it to climb higher. The chains the game has suffered in in recent years cause us to underestimate just what kind of amazing creature the game is when free. At its heart, at its height – hockey was and can be a game of incomparable speed, agility, skilfulnesss, creativity, force, action and excitement. By unleashing the brilliantly pure essence of the game, we can recapture golden ages, replete with the likes of new Lafleurs, and of new teams and eras like that of Gretzky's Oilers. And put the awe back in hockey. Further, the game could move toward realizing the enormous potential it has in every important objective department. With its suitability to what we otherwise know of North American entertainment tastes, with the established roots hockey has around the world, with the critical mass of following it retained through even the darkest hours – is clearly evident a game that can conquer the world of sports and entertainment. The effects of achieving that would be great for all involved: the players would love playing; coaches and managers would appreciate the purity of the competition; the business would enjoy unprecedented prosperity, the reception by the fans would be tremendous; parents would encourage kids' aspiration to pursue a great game; and the media would run out of ink in praise.

These solutions are specific and practicable, but like most things in life, they are not set in stone, in that as time goes by, situations change, new issues evolve, and appropriate responses do as well. But for me, they represent a core of what is needed for raising our game, nurturing it for the future, and helping it attain its enormous potential, for the sake of all those involved in it.

WHY IT MATTERS SO MUCH

For a whole variety of reasons, that's a worthy goal. Not just to the many people like me who've spent a life in the game, who love and are devoted to it. Not just to those whose livelihoods are associated with it. But to the thousands of kids playing it, aspiring of it; to the millions playing at other levels, and watching who call themselves fans. To a country, whom it has given such fond and important memories as Paul Henderson's goal in '72, Mario Lemieux's in '87, the double-gold triumph of Salt Lake City 2002; and for whom it represents so much more than a game – so many things, wrapped up so integrally in the national cultural identity: a measuring stick of achievement, a source of heroes, a vehicle of healthy international rivalry, and much much more. And not just to Canada either, but to the other places to whom it has given great memories like the United States with its greatest sporting moment, the Miracle on Ice, and passionate players and fans from Russia, Sweden, Finland, the Czech Republic and several other countries around the world.

And also for more sweeping and objective reasons. In its essence, hockey is such an encompassing and perfect test of athletic prowess, such a fulfilling activity, a game of incredible excitement, energy, and room for creative expression. It is a game that can be played by people of such different talents, a game with such wide and varied grounds of appeal; a sport that has been and can be enjoyed by people of all levels, and at all ages. Such a wonderful and amazing sport – the greatest sport in the world by far – hockey is a sport truly special and without peer. At the same time, hockey's quest is representative of that of all sports in their struggle to chart the course of their future in society.

With an increasing number of competing alternative activities and entertainments, and with some of the fundamental meanings of sports jeopardized by internal and external changes in a new age, what will become of them in our culture's future? Now, and in the future, we need what sports are meant to offer us more than ever: An island of healthy preoccupation for young people in a sea of unhealthy alternatives. And lessons in character and spirit that are increasingly lacking in the gap left between formal education and the declining family unit. A source of physical exercise in the midst of an age of medically-declared "epidemic obesity," and reconnection with our physical selves in a way of life increasingly mechanized, sedated, and separated from nature. A positive form of competition that brings people together, and allows them to compete in constructive rather than destructive ways. A source of heroes in an age that admits of few, and of excitement, hope and aspiration for young generations searching for somewhere to vest them in. In hockey's quest to raise its game are at stake all these things embodied in sports and offered to society.

OUR QUESTION TO ANSWER

Through some of the pain the game has gone through lately, a new initiative for change in the best interests of the game has begun. With a new CBA signed and the NHL back in business, steps have indeed been taken, led by executive Colin Campbell and player Brendan Shanahan, and supported by an unprecedented number of others within and outside the game. The program they have begun is not only an important one in the history of the game, but an exciting one.

From a personal standpoint, I have also faced hard experiences to do with the game, experiences which forced the attention, discussions with others, exploration of facts, and long consideration that produced whatever truth is contained within this book. Like them, only without a personal stake in the game any more to have to risk as they did, I strove to do what I could for the hopeful betterment of the game as a whole. And so came this book, whose goal was contributing to the purification and raising of our game. Unlike them, I am not in position to take the final step – the most arduous and difficult, but also most fulfilling step – of putting plans into practice and seeing results.

For that, the ideas here need their support, and they themselves need the support of those interested in and dedicated to the game. Right now, there is a golden opportunity to raise our game. And there is a way. Not everyone will agree with what I have proposed, or even what steps the others have already taken. But hopefully those who disagree will recognize that it serves nothing to ignore issues, and remember it is easy to criticize but hard to improve, easy to suggest but hard to understand – and bring forth their own answers and reasons, so that together we can continue the process of advancing our game.

Beyond this, like a hockey team, the future of our game rests in the hands of we who are devoted to it. As inscribed on the Montreal Canadiens wall, quoting from "In Flanders Fields" . . . "to you from failing hands we throw the torch, be yours to hold it high." With this sacred duty, preceding generations entrusted their great game, our great game, to us. But it is to our children's generation that we – players, coaches, management, league executives, owners, and fans – are bound most, to resist individual interests or those of the moment, and someday be able to look them in the eye and pass on the torch, held high.

My hope was that this book would have a positive influence on that goal – supporting the positive work of some of the recent changes that have been made, aiding the people making them as they try to sustain them, and ultimately expanding upon them in ways beneficial to the game. In so doing, it has hoped to make what was mysterious to some clear, what was assumed by others open to question, what was equivocation by still others decision. But ultimately its purpose remains unfulfilled if it remains *only* an intellectual exercise, an interesting diversion, or even a convincing argument, whose life ends merely by adding to the debate in cold arenas and warm coffeehouses, or gathering dust on lonely bookshelves or in the back of minds, and never makes it into the field and onto the ice. Conviction is a beginning, an invitation to help serve and shape the changes that are the future of the game – in pivotal ways by those in positions of influence within the game, in prodding and supportive ways by others so committed.

Raising our game is more than will and words, it's action. In my view, life is too short for short-term thinking, too hard to make things harder by dwelling in problems that can be overcome, delaying what can be done. It is too fragile and transient to be led by self-interest, and too mysterious not to wonder and not to care. Sports are important to our world, and this sport is truly special among them. And so I end these words by echoing a call: Let's raise our game, and make it ours to hold it high.